Programming Business Applications in FORTRAN IV

Programming Business Applications
in FORTRAN IV

Phillip T. May *Washington University*

Houghton Mifflin Company
Boston
Atlanta
Dallas
Geneva, Illinois
Hopewell, New Jersey
Palo Alto
London

Printed in the United States of America.

Library of Congress Catalog Card Number: 72-7634

ISBN: 0-395-14047-1

Preface

This textbook provides an introduction to computer programming in the FORTRAN IV language. The book features the use of the FORTRAN language in the business environment and has these objectives:

1. to develop an ability to program the computer with particular emphasis on analyzing business problems
2. to provide an ordered approach to the development of the skills necessary to use the language
3. to allow the book to be used as a course supplement or to be used in a course devoted to a more thorough study of programming
4. to provide the user with continuous feedback during the learning process
5. to provide reference material for use after the initial learning process

Currently there is a large quantity of programming material in the FORTRAN language. The vast majority of this material is oriented to mathematics, engineering, or the sciences. FORTRAN is, however, widely used in business and economics education. Many applications in business are very suitable to the advantages of FORTRAN, especially analytical applications such as statistics, accounting, production, quantitative analysis, marketing management, and managerial economics.

The learning period required for developing initial programs is much shorter for FORTRAN than for many other languages, and the simple structure of the FORTRAN language facilitates the rapid learning of a usable skill. In curricula where "systems" courses are offered, a second language is usually learned. If FORTRAN is the first language pursued, the second language (e.g., COBOL or PL/I) is learned more rapidly in spite of its more structured requirements.

Most FORTRAN textbooks present a description of nearly all features of each language element when it is first encountered. This technique deluges the learner with more material than he can possibly use immediately (and sometimes more than he will ever use), and it often reinforces original suspicions that the language of computers is too complicated to learn. The step-by-step approach used in this book promotes the acquisition of basic language skills before moving to more involved refinements. Many language elements are presented several times but, with each encounter, are developed to a higher level of complexity.

Using the step-by-step approach, the instructor can tailor the material to his specific needs. He can use the full text in a one-semester programming course. For quarter or special short course offerings, or for use as supplemental material, selected language elements may be assigned, without assigning complete chapters. The remaining material may then be covered in another course or left for learning at the student's own pace.

After learning a programming language, it is impossible to recall all the details of the language. It is frustrating to have to reread the text each time a question arises. Therefore, Appendix D provides a reference guide with a brief statement of each language element and appropriate text page references for a more detailed review.

Unfortunately, learning a programming language cannot be accomplished by reading alone. For thorough assimilation, the material must be applied. This text provides three review levels. First, throughout the text, the student can test his depth of understanding through exercises that follow the sections covering an important portion of the language. Suggested solutions to the exercises appear in Appendix B. Second, each chapter concludes with questions to stimulate review of the entire chapter. Third, Appendix C provides a series of problems that may be flowcharted and prepared for computer processing. These problems range from simple to complex, and a number of the problems are interrelated. This permits assignment of a continuous problem with increasing complexity over several chapters.

This book can be used at all college levels. No mathematical background is required. The business examples used are equally appropriate at the junior college, four-year undergraduate, technical college, or graduate school levels. I have used this material at the graduate and undergraduate levels and in short courses with equally good results.

Success in learning a computer language improves when students understand something about the computer processing environment. In addition, they need a well defined method for problem analysis and the development of program solutions. Chapter 2 presents enough detail about the computer so that students can understand why specific FORTRAN language characteristics are necessary. Chapters 3 and 4 present an orderly method for developing a problem solution. This explanation of problem solution design serves the student well until he has acquired some confidence in the use of FORTRAN. At that time he may begin developing variations of his own.

A unique feature of this textbook is the discussion in Appendix A of the language elements related to magnetic tape and disk as well as an introduction to the basic features of job control languages. The material is written to be used with all manufacturers' computing equipment. Moreover, in the explanation of compilation, the distinction between manufacturer-supplied compilers and the WATFIV compiler is made and illustrated.

No book is completed without the combined efforts of many people. While I am unable to cite the contributions of each individual, I would like to thank Professors William A. Manning of Portland State University, Frank Holden of City College of San Francisco, and John Hurd of Eastern Michigan University for their valuable suggestions. Any shortcomings in the text can be assessed only against me and my inability to heed their suggestions.

I also wish to thank the members of the editorial, art, and production staffs at Houghton Mifflin Company for their assistance and suggestions.

I am deeply grateful to Dean Karl Hill who made financial and computing resources available to allow development of this material. His support has always been complete and continuous.

The International Business Machines Corporation was generous in granting permission to abstract portions of their FORTRAN language descriptions that appear in Appendix D.

Of course, one is never able to develop classroom materials without the support, scrutiny, suggestions, and stimulus of his students. To them I owe a deep vote of gratitude.

I especially wish to thank Mrs. A. W. Scheetz whose patience and skill in typing many drafts of the manuscript made completion of the book a reality.

I dedicate this book to my wife, Joan, and my sons, Gardner and Douglas. Their understanding, interest, and support during the development of the manuscript made the task worthwhile.

Phillip T. May

Contents

Programming Business Applications in FORTRAN IV

1
Introduction

How often have you heard that a computer is just a big, dumb, fast adding machine that has to be told everything? It is true that a computer does perform simple arithmetic, like an adding machine, but a computer can also store program instructions, receive and transmit data, as well as perform logical operations. We can combine these operations to perform a wide variety of tasks, such as inventory management, instant airline reservations, and complicated mathematical calculations.

It is more appropriate to regard a computer as a "precocious child" who needs careful instruction and will remember each direction given. The instructions that must be given to a computer are the key requirement which the user must develop if benefits are to be gained from using the computer.

In this book we will explore the FORTRAN IV programming language to develop your ability to direct a computer's actions. However, before we begin the discussion of programming, we should ask several questions about computers.

Why Learn About Computers?

The computer is the latest development in a long line of mechanical and electronic aids used in accumulating and processing information. This tool has had a tremendous impact in its short history and has altered most concepts of information processing. The stored program computer was developed in the late 1940s, but it was not until the mid-1950s that the first commercially available computer appeared on the market. Moreover, not until 1959 was the first business-oriented computer introduced. This computer was the IBM 1401 Data Processing System.

In the practice of management today, whether in a business or a non-business organization, managers who have the most appropriate and timely information make the most effective decisions. This condition is true regardless of whether the organization is large or small. A widely held misconception associates computers with only large organizations and assumes that computers are either too expensive or too complicated for small organizations. Today size is no criterion for computer use. Small users can have the same advantages of computerized power as large users; they may either purchase the necessary time from service bureaus or buy smaller computer models better suited to their needs.

Organizations seeking the advantages of computer processing generally have either an inability to handle the *volume* of data they generate or an inability to *analyze* data quickly enough to make it available for management's use. The problems of volume and/or analysis can plague organizations of any size. The misconception, cited above, grew out of the historical conditions which accompanied the growth of computer usage. The high acquisition costs of early computers made them economically feasible for only large organizations (primarily businesses and departments of the government). In addition, the complexity of developing applications was so great that only large organizations possessed the resources necessary for the development of computerized systems.

Computer systems have developed through several major stages which are referred to as "generations" in the computing field. Each generation brought vast improvements in two facets of computing. First, improvements in the machinery (hardware) have made computing operations more versatile and have enabled operations to take place with increasing speed. Second, the flexibility with which computers could be used has increased as the administrative systems (software) for controlling computers have evolved.

The technological improvement in both the hardware and software of computers has resulted in an ever-broadening base of computer users. Several factors have made this possible. The increased computational powers of the computer have been accompanied by a significant reduction in the cost per computation, and techniques are now available to allow more than one organization to use the same computer. These primary factors have brought computing capabilities down to a level which permits smaller and smaller organizations to employ computers economically.

Although large organizations undoubtedly spend the greatest amount for computing power, the computer is a tool which is important to all organizations and a tool which will become more important in the future. It is imperative, then, that all managers possess an understanding of the computer, its uses, and its limitations.

Why Learn About Programming?

The computer is an intricate and carefully coordinated *system* composed of devices which perform the following functions:

1. channel data into the system for processing (input)
2. manipulate input data (processing)
3. issue instructions to the system (control)
4. take the manipulated data and either:
   a. hold the results (storage), or
   b. report the results (output)

The diagram shown in Figure 1.1 depicts the basic components of a computer system. Note that, while all of the elements compose the entire *system*, technically, only the central processing unit is the *computer*. The devices which perform the functions of input, storage, and output are referred to as *peripheral* equipment. Of course, the implication is that they are peripheral or external to the central processing unit.

Figure 1.1   Basic Elements of a Computer System

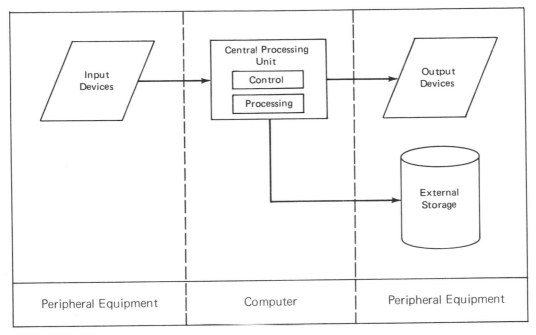

A computer system with its intricate number of elements must be kept under careful control so that it will function at its highest level of efficiency. To control the computer, the user must have a technique for communicating his instructions to the computer, and this, of course, is the function which programming provides. Programming, therefore, is a language or instruction technique. All languages exist to convey meaning between a sender and a receiver. In the practice of computer programming, the computer serves as one sender/receiver, and the programmer is the other sender/receiver. Programming languages permit a user to convey instructions to the computer and permit the computer to interpret the instructions correctly before taking action. Specific combinations of letters and symbols in programming languages have specific meanings which are relied on by both the programmer and the computer. This feature of a language is referred to as *syntax*. Learning programming is largely a matter of becoming familiar with the syntax of the language being used.

Programming enables the user to convert the speed and computing power of the computer to his use and, in the process, to control the computer system so that the actions of the system are directed toward accomplishing his processing requirements. Programming also provides a technique for learning how computers operate and for learning to apply a logical approach to problem solutions. When the programmer uses the computer, it becomes imperative that he develop a rigorous and logical approach to each problem solution. This by-product of the programming process is undoubtedly one of the most important contributions to the effective use of this tool.

Why Learn the FORTRAN IV Language?

A computer usually can be programmed in several languages. Therefore, the user must choose a language every time he wishes to program the computer. A variety of computer languages has developed in response to the special requirements of differing problems. Data being processed may be in alphabetic or numeric form, and processing requirements may range from handling voluminous data with small amounts of manipulation to requirements calling for small amounts of data but intensive manipulation. Generally, each computer programming language has been tailored to handle specific problem characteristics.

FORTRAN is a language which has basic characteristics associated with mathematics. Derivation of this association results from the original development of the language which began in the mid-1950s. The language was designed for the user with problems which are primarily of a mathematical nature. This language provides for the design of programs which need rapid calculations and efficient handling of numeric data. The facility for dealing with alphabetic data is also available but does possess some rather cumbersome traits.

The FORTRAN language is widely used and is available with virtually all manufacturers' computer systems and is therefore a universal language. FORTRAN has gone through several versions and the current versions are referred to as FORTRAN IV. In addition to being a widely used language, FORTRAN is a language which may be learned with relative ease, because its requirements are less structured than most other languages.

When you prepare instructions written in the FORTRAN language, you will be capable of utilizing a computer system ranging from small to large-scale. The primary differences related to the sizes of computer systems involve the central processor's memory capacity and speed, and/or the types and number of pieces of peripheral equipment which can be used. Figure 1.2 shows the hardware components of a large-scale computer system.

Figure 1.2   Hardware Components of IBM 370/165 Computer System

Questions

1. What are the characteristics of business data that make the use of a computer advantageous?
2. What are the functions performed by a computer system?
3. What is meant by the term peripheral equipment?
4. What is a programming language's syntax?
5. Why is FORTRAN described as a "universal" programming language? What advantages might be related to this characteristic?

2
Computer Systems Concepts

The Computer Systems Environment

Every computer system exists within some larger environment. The computer interacts with its environment by receiving input data, processing the data, and returning the computed output to its environment. The diagram in Figure 2.1 illustrates the relationship between the computer and the business environment.

A business data processing system is composed of several processing activities, operating in a coordinated manner, to assist in achieving some organizational goals. These processing activities relate to business functions such as the production of products, accounting, engineering and product design, personnel, financing, and marketing operations. Each function has its own processing subsystem. Therefore, a business system is composed of a network of subsystems. The computer is only one of these subsystems, although an extremely important one.

The illustration in Figure 2.1 depicts the internal business environment as a group of functional activities, each activity responsible for a specific task. A computer system is utilized most appropriately when it provides the firm with the ability to integrate information from all of the functional subsystems. Such an integrated computer system allows for business data collected in any of the functional subsystems to be made available for use in all other subsystems. The computer system should be viewed as a tool or processing aid existing to service the functional areas of the firm.

If we expand our view of a firm to include its external environment, we see that the firm is a subsystem within a larger environment, the firm's industry. This industry environment is, in turn, a subsystem of the national economy. As we move up from one system level to another, we find progressively more comprehensive systems. These interrelationships illustrate the concept of the "general systems theory" which attempts to establish the hierarchy of general relationships among areas of increasing complexity.

A business firm desires a well developed computer system that senses and captures data which is generated externally and which is relevant to the firm's operation. The external environments are as important to successful operation of the firm as the internal factors. Recognition that the computer subsystem is a facilitating device for the firm gives a proper perspective. Too often the computer system is viewed as controlling the firm rather than as an analytical and processing aid.

Figure 2.1   A Business Firm's Systems Environment

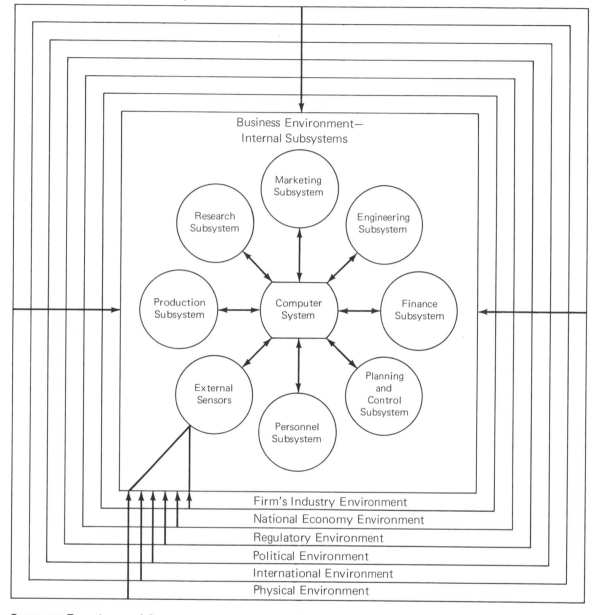

Computer Functions and Components

The preparation of a FORTRAN program requires at least an elementary knowledge of computer functions and components. Conceptually, the components are *input, central processor, storage,* and *output.* (See Figure 1.1.) Obviously, an operating computer system has specific physical units which perform each component's functions. (See Figure 1.2.)

The list in Table 2.1 shows the components of a computer system and suggests some of the physical units which perform each component's functions.

Note that there is a wide variety of physical units which may perform the conceptual functions of input and output. Also note that external storage devices can

Table 2.1   Computer System Components and Functions

Input ————————→	Central Processor ————————→	Output
Readers	**Internal Components**	**Report Devices**
punch card	arithmetic	line printer
punched paper tape	logic	visual display
optical scanner (OCR)	control	(CRT)
magnetic ink (MICR)	internal memory	console typewriter
mark sense		teletype typewriter
External Storage		**External Storage**
magnetic tape		magnetic tape
magnetic disk		magnetic disk
magnetic drum		magnetic drum
magnetic card		magnetic card
(data cell)		(data cell)
Other		punch card
console typewriter		punched paper tape
teletype typewriter		
light pen (cathode		
ray tube CRT)		
cash registers		

be used for both input and output. That is, output from the processing of one program may be recorded on a storage medium which is used as the data input to another program processed at a later time.

Data Handling Concepts

It is also important to understand what is involved in the handling of data and how this is related to a computerized processing system. In the sequence of business data processing, an event occurs which generates the data to be processed. An event of this type might be the sale of merchandise, performance of a repair service, signing a contract, etc. The significant factor in economic events of this type is that normally some record of the event is prepared to prevent the important facts from being lost. The usual technique for capturing the important elements of an event is to write them down immediately after the event occurs. Consider, for example, the merchant's use of sales slips to record sales, the repairman's issuance of a bill for his services, and the contractual agreement signed when making application for a credit card. In each of these cases the written document contains the important data necessary for current analysis and/or retrieval.

The handling of data related to a recorded event follows a path similar to that shown in Table 2.2. An example of a merchandise sale illustrates the recording and handling of data along this path.

The processing of data, from its capture to its report, is a matter of reducing the data to a form (code) which permits easy manipulation (processing). Accountants have used this basic concept of data handling for several centuries in the accounting process, though it was implemented without electronic aids. Thus, these concepts

Table 2.2 Steps in Handling Business Data

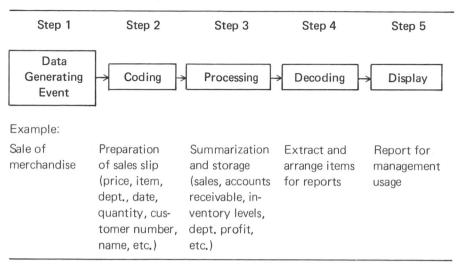

Step 1	Step 2	Step 3	Step 4	Step 5
Data Generating Event	Coding	Processing	Decoding	Display

Example:

Sale of merchandise	Preparation of sales slip (price, item, dept., date, quantity, customer number, name, etc.)	Summarization and storage (sales, accounts receivable, inventory levels, dept. profit, etc.)	Extract and arrange items for reports	Report for management usage

of data handling are not new, and when we relate them to the conceptual functions of the computer, we see that the computer fits perfectly into the data handling process.

Figure 2.2 The Business Data Handling Process Using a Computer System

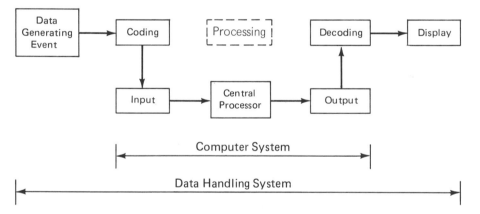

The relationship between the data handling process and computer system illustrated above tends to become more obscure as the development of computer systems becomes more complex. The desirability of quickly capturing the facts of an event has resulted in the expenditure of substantial efforts to push the input component of computer systems out closer and closer to the data generating event. Accomplishment of this objective does not alter the conceptual fact that an event must occur before it can be recorded, but it may substantially alter the techniques for recording the event. One of the most striking examples of early data capture involves the airlines. Prior to the implementation of current reservation systems, seats were sold at a variety of locations. The airlines summarized total seat reservations on a periodic basis and often found that the reservations sold exceeded the seats available to fill them. Processing these reservations usually involved significant time delays so that an airline did not have a valid picture of the seat inventories available.

The current reservation systems have pushed the computer processing system out to the data generating event. At the time of a reservation request, the request is directly entered into the processing system through an input console. The request is matched with the appropriate flight record and the computer immediately evaluates the availability of space to accommodate the request. The computer immediately confirms or rejects the reservation. In this fashion, the airlines can maintain accurate inventories of available seats and provide reliable service to their customers. The point to observe in this case is the fact that the computer processing system is designed to capture the relevant data as it occurs and display the computed output within a matter of a few seconds. In *on-line* systems of this type, the input is directly coded and transmitted to the computer for processing. Output has the same direct transmission characteristics and results in a message returned to the point which activated the input with no significant time delay. In such systems, the computer and the entire data handling process appear to have no lines of demarcation.

The majority of existing computer and data handling systems, however, are not of the on-line variety described above. These systems are generally referred to as *batch processing* systems. While the desirability of data capture close to the occurence of an event is still important, in these systems the computer processing is not immediate. Data items are accumulated and later processed in groups or batches. Normally these systems have readily identifiable steps. Data capture is usually in some written form. The coding step frequently requires the preparation of the data in a machine readable form. The ubiquitous punch card attests to this step in many systems. Input to the computer may be achieved by directly reading the punch cards or, in some systems, the cards are transferred to magnetic tape and then the tape is used as input to the computer. The computer processes the data, under the directions of a program, and either stores the results or decodes and displays the results. It appears that the batch processing technique more clearly identifies the steps in data handling but this appearance is related only to the timing and amount of human intervention which differentiates the on-line from the batch (or off-line) systems.

The term "machine readable" was used in the previous description of data handling and computer processing systems. This term reflects the important fact that data which is recorded in a form understandable to human beings is not in a form which is equally understandable to data processing equipment. Coding, in the process of data handling, involves the conversion of data to a form which is "readable" or "sensible" to the machines which will do the processing. Normally, input to a computer system is converted to some binary form. Binary coding simply means that any data element is represented by one of two states or conditions. Most computer related equipment is designed to use this binary characteristic of data representation. For instance, a punch card reader searches to see whether or not a punched hole exists, a magnetic tape or disk either possesses magnetized spots or fails to have such magnetized areas, and the internal memory of the central processor is constructed of a vast number of magnetic cores which are capable of reflecting the binary states of magnetism or non-magnetism.

The Central Processing Unit

Data which is machine sensible is essential to successful manipulations within the central processor. A basic understanding of the central processor's internal memory is a most important element in the ability to write sound FORTRAN programs. It is within the central processor's *internal memory* that (1) all input is initially stored, (2) the FORTRAN program resides, (3) all processing occurs, (4) output is initially stored, and (5) the system control instructions are located.

The diagram in Figure 2.3 illustrates the components of the central processor. The four key elements of the central processor are control, arithmetic, logic, and addressable memory. The control unit exercises control over both the central processor and the peripheral units used for input, output, and storage. The arithmetic unit performs all the steps in addition, subtraction, multiplication, division, and exponentiation. The logic unit makes value comparisons, and the addressable memory element allows the computer to temporarily store computed values. While all of the four functions take place within the central processor's internal memory, not all of the memory is accessible to the programmer. Only the addressable memory is available for the programmer's use.

Figure 2.3   Central Processor Components and Relation to Peripheral Devices

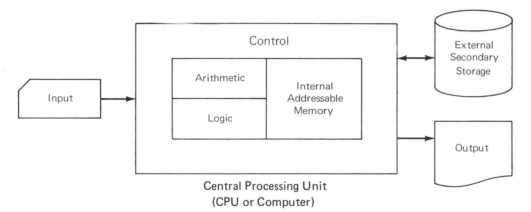

Addressable memory might be imagined as a series of home mailboxes on a city street. Every mailbox is identified by a *unique address* assigned to each house. Each mailbox provides space to hold its *contents* (letters, magazines, cards) which change from day-to-day. Note that the contents of a mailbox are separate from, and not the same as, its address.

Addressable computer memory locations, like mailboxes, have *addresses* which are used to identify each location. These addresses are completely separate from the alphabetic letters or numbers which are the *contents* of memory locations. A programmer uses the computer's internal addressable memory by making specific reference to the location addresses.

It is important to understand the relationship between the computer's memory and the execution of a computer program. The central processor's addressable memory is divided into two key areas: one holding the program and the other composed of free unreserved memory.

A computer program is a set of instructions which directs the computer's actions. When a program is to be used by the computer, the *entire set* of program instructions is *first* read into the processor's memory. The program is then stored. Program storage enables the computer to use the instructions repeatedly and relieves the programmer from writing the same instructions over and over. The free and unreserved memory is much like a "scratch pad" which an individual might use in the addition, division, comparison, or other manipulation of data.

Addressable memory locations have three important elements, two of which are of critical importance to the programmer. The three elements are (1) location number, (2) location name, and (3) location value. The diagram in Figure 2.4 illustrates these memory elements.

Figure 2.4   Illustration of Computer Addressable Memory

Memory Segment

(A)	(TOT)	(FOR)	(K1)	(NUM)	(LBS)	◄——— Location Name
000	001	002	003	004	005	◄——— Location Address
5.0	8.24	11.3	9	267	13	◄——— Location Contents

NUM ◄——— Symbolic Address
004 ◄——— Absolute Address
267 ◄——— Stored Data

Suppose we take one location from the above memory segment and examine its elements. Location number 004 contains the value 267 and has the assigned name of NUM. The manufacturer assigns 004 as an internal reference point. Every memory location has its own unique number or *absolute address*. Most manufacturers begin numbering memory at zero and sequentially number each location thereafter. Fortunately, the programmer does not have to remember the memory location numbers. Instead, the use of *symbolic addresses* makes the locations more meaningful. A symbolic address is a location name assigned by the programmer. He may assign any name to each memory location, and then the computer internally cross-references that name to its absolute address. When writing a program, the programmer chooses names which have a close relationship to the data that he is using. Suppose that, in the example illustrated above, the location NUM was to hold an employee number as part of a payroll program. The programmer assigns NUM as the symbolic name since it has a sensible relationship to "number" and is significantly more meaningful than 004, the absolute address. Furthermore, the programmer can refer, anywhere within his program, to the storage area holding the employee number simply by referring to NUM. The computer automatically looks up the cross-reference for NUM and moves to location 004. You should conclude from this discussion that the programmer needs to be concerned only with the assignment of symbolic address names and may ignore absolute address numbers.

Naming a memory location, however, should not be confused with the contents (value of the data) stored at that location. In the example, NUM is the programmer's name for the location, but the contents of the location is 267. When the program is processing employee 267's payroll data, this value will be stored in location NUM. Upon completion of this employee's payroll calculation, the program will begin processing the data for employee 268. Location NUM will then have the value 267 replaced by the current employee number of 268. The important point is that the *location name does not change, only the value of the contents changes.* This point is critical to an understanding of computer operations and the programming process. The diagrams in Figures 2.5 and 2.6 illustrate how a single program instruction will enter two different data values and store them in the same location, in this case, NUM.

Figure 2.5   First Program Instruction Execution

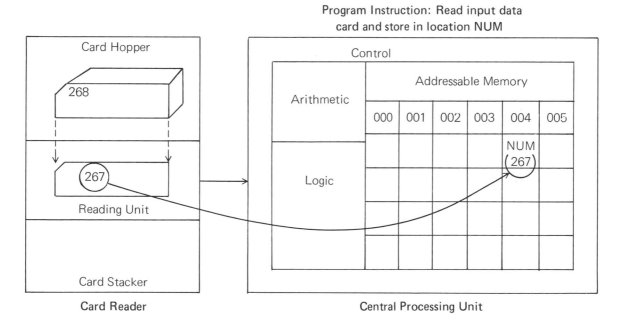

Another important feature of computer memory is that values which are stored are erased or destroyed when new values are placed in the same location. Note that, in the second execution of the read instruction, transfer of the new value 268 into location NUM destroyed the old value of 267. This characteristic of internal memory is called *destructive read-in.* While read-in is destructive, the opposite condition relates to extracting values from memory. For instance, if a programmer instructs the computer to take the value 268 and print it as output on a line printer, the 268 value will remain in location NUM *and also appear* as printed output. In effect, the computer copies the value 268. This property is called *non-destructive read-out.* A programmer must keep this characteristic of computer memory clearly in mind to avoid the inadvertent loss of values during processing. The diagram in Figure 2.7 illustrates the non-destructive character of reading from memory.

Figure 2.6 Second Program Instruction Execution

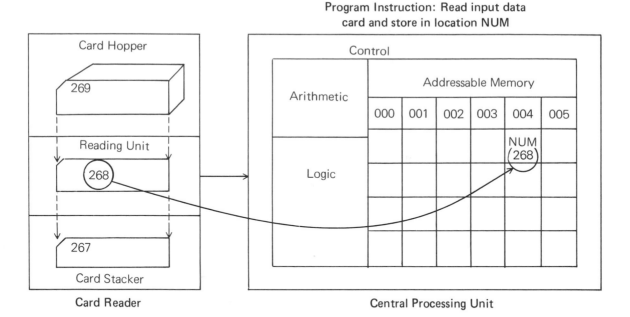

Program Instruction: Read input data
card and store in location NUM

Figure 2.7 Execution of an Output Instruction

Program Instruction: Retrieve and print
value stored at location NUM

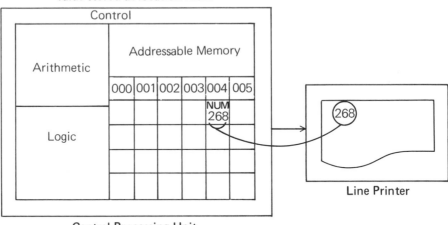

Any system, such as a computer system, which handles a large variety of tasks must operate in a carefully controlled manner. Two primary and interrelated techniques normally maintain control over a computer system. First, the system operates under the control of a series of instructions commonly referred to as an *operating system or monitor*. The purpose of this control technique is to administer the computer system so that the central processing unit (CPU) will process data as continuously as possible. The function of monitors or operating systems also extends to coordination of the computer system's peripheral input and output devices to provide the central processor with new data ready for manipulation or to take manipulated data and send it to the proper storage/output devices. This type of control is intended to minimize the idle time of the CPU and thereby economically meet the high cost and high speed demands of the computer.

The second type of computer system control is accomplished through the specific instructions given by the individual using the computer. This control is accomplished through a series of specific steps within the program. A *computer program* is a series of optional directions (called statements) selected by the programmer and arranged in the order which he feels will appropriately direct the computer to a problem solution.

The two types of control must be closely coordinated. The user, through his program, communicates to the operating system the directions which the computer should execute. The operating system, in turn, directs the physical units to read, write, process, store, retrieve, and so forth, in a sequence which completes the user's program in the most efficient manner possible.

The diagram in Figure 2.8 on page 16 summarizes the functions and components of a computer system. The functions of input, processing, storage, and output are depicted with a few examples of the components which might constitute a computer system. The block illustrating *input* shows that input may take a form as basic as reading punched cards or a form as intricate as the inflow of processed data from a remote computer which is connected through a wire or microwave system. The *processing* function is shown with its major elements of control and a central processing unit. Control is accomplished partially through the written program of the user and partially through the use of an operating system which coordinates the entire computer system. The interrelationship of the program and operating system is crucial to efficient processing of input data and to the operating system's control over the peripheral units.

The area illustrating *storage* demonstrates how the computer can recall previously processed data during current processing. The efficient retrieval of data from storage is best accomplished through the use of equipment which is designed to read rapidly and requires a minimum amount of physical handling. In this area, magnetic tape involves handling when tapes must be mounted, but reading is relatively fast. Magnetic disk illustrates a storage medium which requires very small amounts of handling and provides for extremely fast reading. The *output* function of the computer system may take a wide variety of forms. The processed data may be (1) displayed in picture form as on a cathode ray tube, (2) printed on a line printer, (3) saved in a magnetic form peripheral to the central processor, such as data written on a magnetic tape, (4) returned to storage devices which are on-line to the central processor, or (5) transmitted over a communications system to a remote computer. It is essential that programmers appreciate just where within the computer system the program becomes involved and how this program relates to the functioning of the remainder of the computer system.

Questions

1. What is a business data processing system?
2. What are the components of a computer system? Do you see any corres-

Figure 2.8   Computer System Functions and Components

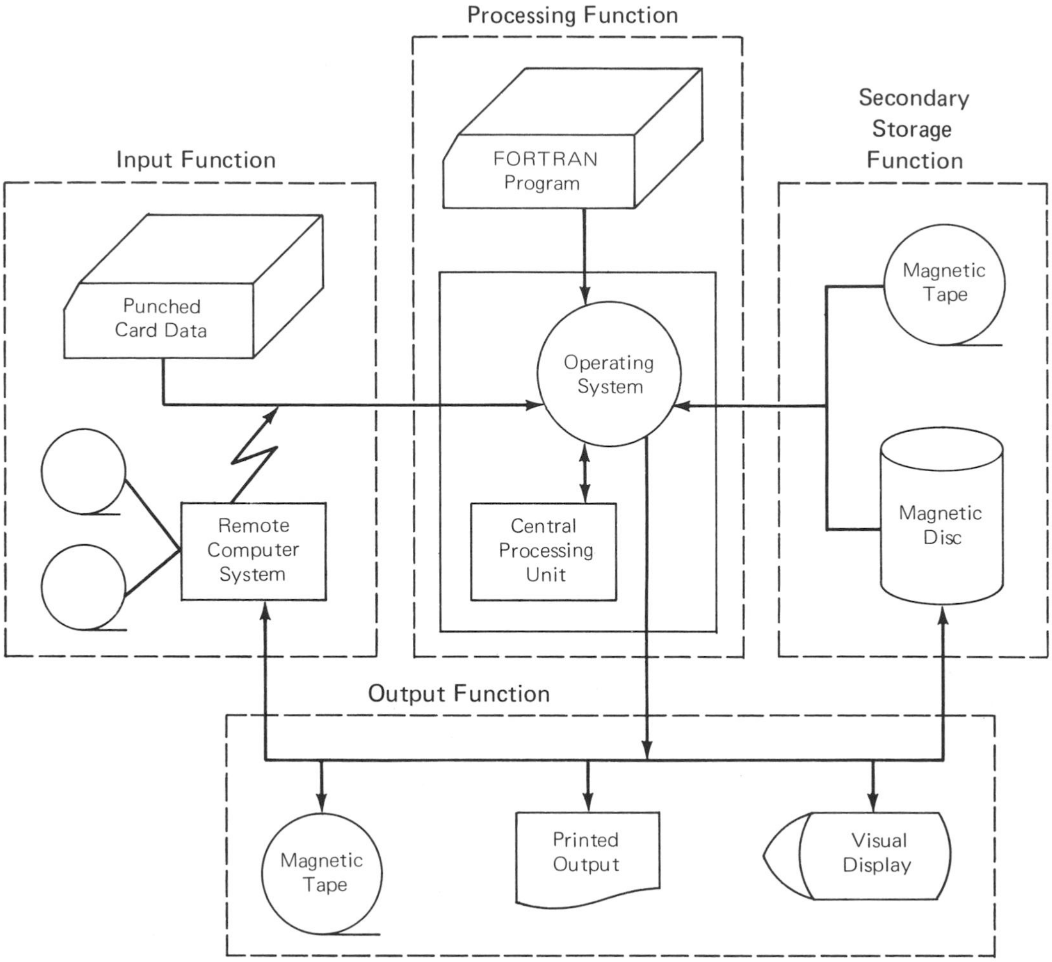

pondence between these components and the way in which your own thought process is executed?

3. Which type of physical unit, in a computer system, serves both an input and output function? How does this aid the computer system?
4. Describe the data handling process. Think of an example, with which you are familiar, that illustrates the use of this process.
5. How does the computer system fit into the data handling process?
6. Define the terms on-line and batch processing. How are they different?
7. What does the term "machine readable" have to do with the operation of a computer system?
8. What is the difference between addressable memory and secondary storage?
9. What are the differences among the memory components (1) symbolic address, (2) absolute address, and (3) contents?
10. Why is information read-in to computer memory destructive, while information read-out is non-destructive?

3
Designing Computer Programs

The development of a computer program requires eight basic steps: problem identification, problem flowcharting, program preparation and coding, punching of the source program, compilation, processing, debugging, and program completion. The steps occur in a specific order, although some steps may receive less formal treatment as a programmer becomes more expert. Carefully study the diagram in Figure 3.1, which illustrates these steps, before preparing a program.

Step 1—Problem Identification

Problem identification is more critical to the completion of a satisfactory program than any of the following seven steps. It is impossible to solve a problem using a computer without a *clear understanding and identification of that problem.* Inadequate recognition of a problem's key elements is the factor most often responsible for poor computer performance. This step is generally difficult and the programmer should invest a significant proportion of his time in problem identification. If he does not spend enough time at this stage, he may find that his well written program fails to solve the real problem, or perhaps solves the wrong problem. Depending on the complexity of the problem, the result of a careful analysis may be simply a listing of the factors with which the program must deal. Or it may be a formal written statement of the problem supported by a detailed description of all the considerations necessary to the solution of the problem.

Step 2—Problem Flowcharting

A computer is both fast and versatile, but it requires the meticulous specification of what actions it should take. For the user, there is seldom the opportunity to allow the computer to make an undirected decision. Therefore, the programmer must decide, prior to writing his program, exactly which steps the computer should take to solve the problem identified in Step 1. The formal specification of the computer's processing steps results in a diagram called a flowchart. As the term implies, this is a chart which *depicts the precise flow of the computed actions.* The flowchart shows the logic involved in the problem solution and therefore is a step-by-step sequence which the programmer will describe to the computer through the FORTRAN language instructions.

Figure 3.1   Problem Analysis, Design, and Compilation Process

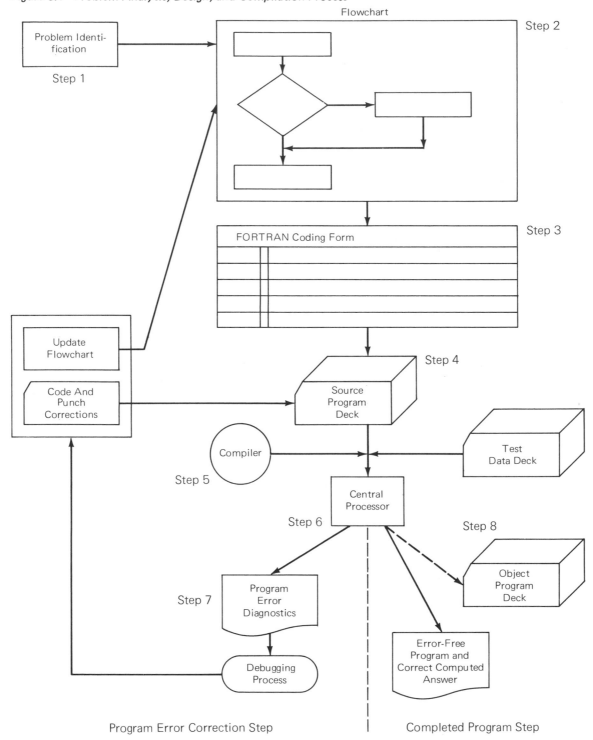

Program Error Correction Step   Completed Program Step

Step 3—Program Preparation and Coding

The preparation of a successful FORTRAN program is possible only after the programmer has identified the problem and has determined the logical flow necessary to its solution. The success of this third step depends upon the quality of the first two steps. The programmer prepares the FORTRAN program by *writing language instructions which follow the logic and sequence of the flowchart.* The language instructions are generally first written on a FORTRAN coding form. This form contains multiple lines with one line used for each FORTRAN instruction. A completed program may take several pages and is the flowchart converted into the FORTRAN language.

Step 4—Punching of the Source Program

The fourth step converts the program, written and coded in Step 3, to a form which the computer system can read. The most common medium for this conversion is the preparation of a deck of punched cards. This deck contains one card for each line coded on the FORTRAN coding form. Each card, therefore, contains one instruction to the computer. When the computer system reads each card, the pattern of punched holes enables the system to convert the FORTRAN instructions into the internal binary form used by the central processor. Because the program deck contains the instructions which will be used as the source of the computer's processing, this group of punched cards is called the *source program deck.*

Step 4 may require the preparation of a second deck of punched cards containing test data. Usually, the programmer will test the validity of his program by inserting data which should return answers already known to him. Through the processing of this *test deck,* the accuracy of the FORTRAN program can be determined prior to its use with the real problem data.

Step 5—Compilation

A computer is a versatile machine which can be programmed in a variety of languages. Each language has its own syntax so that the user must tell the computer exactly which language he is using. The operating system conveys this message to the computer. The FORTRAN program submitted by the programmer is then *converted from the FORTRAN code to the binary form* which can be manipulated by the computer. Step 5, the process of conversion, is called *compilation.*

Each computer system which uses the FORTRAN language is equipped with a FORTRAN compiler which automatically translates the source program. A compiler is a prewritten program, stored in the computer's memory, which is called each time a source program is entered into the computer. The compiler program scans each source program instruction and converts it to the binary form. When the process of compilation is complete, the FORTRAN program will be entirely in binary form and is called an *object program.* It is the object program which is actually executed by the computer when the problem data is processed.

Step 6—Processing

At this point, the program has been written, coded, and compiled. The programmer has also prepared test data for processing. The computer now attempts to *execute the program instructions* so that the test data will be read, manipulated, and a correct test answer computed. There are two possible results from the processing step:

(1) the program fails to complete successfully the processing and Step 7 is required, or (2) the program processes correctly and the test answer is correctly computed, as shown in Step 8.

Step 7—Debugging Process

If the program fails to complete the processing accurately, the programmer must make an effort to eliminate the "bugs" and correct the program. As a portion of the execution process, the computer will usually note the errors it encounters and will make an attempt to identify the source of each error. The computer then prints out error messages for the programmer. These messages are called *diagnostics* and refer to the instructions which were in error.

Numerous factors can cause errors, but errors most often occur in: (1) keypunching, (2) data format, (3) FORTRAN syntax, (4) sequential logic, and (5) execution.

Keypunching

Keypunching errors are similar to errors made while typing. Generally, they reflect inaccurate punching from the coding forms. They can easily be corrected by punching correct instructions in a new card. The correct card is then substituted for the incorrect card in the source program deck.

Data Format

Data format errors occur when the test data is punched in a form that disagrees with the form the program instructed the computer to expect. Two possible corrections are available. The programmer can either repunch the data to conform with the program directions or rewrite the program to conform with the data format as it exists.

FORTRAN Syntax

Syntax errors indicate that the programmer has written instructions in a form which does not correspond to the specifications of the FORTRAN language. The programmer can correct these errors by punching the correct language specifications on new cards and replacing the incorrect instructions.

Sequential Logic

Errors in sequential logic result from an inadequate examination of the necessary sequential flow in the preparation of the flowchart (Step 2). This type of error is generally serious and requires reexamination of the flowchart to find the erroneous logic, recoding the instructions to correct the logic, and punching the correct instructions.

Execution Errors

A computer's abilities do have limitations. For instance, a program which calls for a number to be divided by zero will result in an infinite answer. A computer is incapable of making this computation. Therefore, the computer is designed to indicate execution errors of this type. Rewriting and replacement of the erroneous instructions will correct these errors.

After completion of any corrections, the programmer should (1) restate the flow-chart to show the corrected program and (2) submit the source deck, with the test data, for reprocessing (return to Step 4).

Step 8—Program Completion

Once the programmer has completed the debugging process and the program is error free, the *output* from processing will be a *printed listing* which shows the *source program* and the *computed answer* derived from the test data. The source program deck will also be returned to the programmer so that he can reuse the program cards with the actual problem data to be processed.

Step 8 provides an option which may be useful when the program is very long or will be run on a regularly recurring basis. This option calls for punching the *object program* in a deck of cards. The purpose in electing this option is to avoid the compilation step (Step 5) in future processing. The object deck is punched in binary machine language code rather than the FORTRAN language code. With future use, it can be read directly into the computer's memory. The computer system will automatically punch the object deck when the programmer makes a request for this option.

An additional advantage gained in Step 8 is the *documentation* supplied by the printed listing of the source program. This listing is the only readable evidence of the completed program's instructions. It is the best reference for future review and/or alterations in the program. Development of the flowchart in Step 2 is another key element in documenting the completed program. These two documents, the flowchart and the program listing, should be sufficiently clear so that any user will understand the program's logic and instruction sequence.

Although the illustration and description above show the object program being punched into a new deck of cards, it is entirely possible and appropriate to have the object program written on magnetic tape or stored on magnetic disk. Subsequent processing will use either the tape or disk as input for reading the object program into the computer's memory. When programs are run on large data processing systems and the programs are very long, efficiency favors the use of the tape or disk for object program storage because of their substantially greater reading speed in comparison to the speed of the card reader.

Program Execution

When the program is complete, it is then appropriate to use the program, with the real problem data, for computation of the desired problem solution. This is the *execution process*. The diagram in Figure 3.2 illustrates this process.

The execution process may begin from either the source program or the object program. Recall that Step 8 in the design process could be completed either (1) by listing the correct program or (2) by punching an object program deck. The form in which the design process was completed determines which of the two execution options will be used.

Option 1 requires the recompilation of the source program each time it is run. If the design process did not result in punching an object deck, then the execution process will have to use the source program, recompile the program into the computer's internal code, and process the problem data.

Figure 3.2 Execution Process

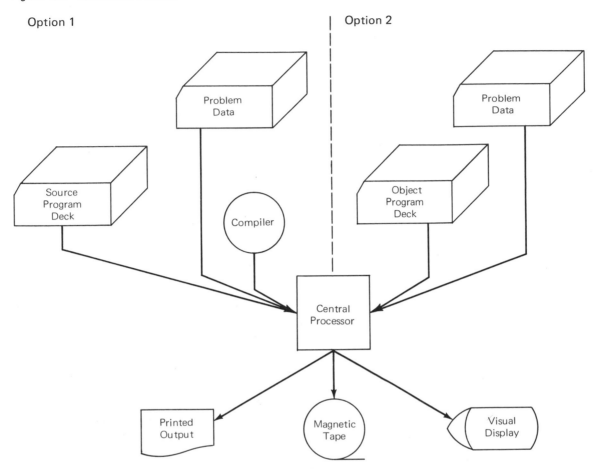

Option 2 eliminates the need for compiling the source program because it assumes that the program has been punched in object form as a result of Step 8 in the design process. Execution in this case requires entry to the computer of only the object deck and the problem data. Processing takes place immediately.

The computed answers to a problem may appear in one of several output forms. There are three general forms which are most frequently used. Printing output provides a "hard-copy" which is understandable to the user and results in a document which may be physically handled. Magnetic tape (disk, drum, and the like could have been shown here) results in storage of the computed answers in a form which is readable only by the computer system. This is one of the most efficient forms for use in future processing. Visual display of the computed answers on a cathode ray tube offers ease in reading for the user but gives no permanent record of the answers unless the system is also equipped to record the output on another device such as the printer or magnetic tape/disk.

Questions

1. Why is problem identification so critical to the success of a computer program? What makes problem identification so difficult?
2. What part does flowcharting play in the solution to a problem through the use of a computer? How important is the preparation of a flowchart?
3. Use only the diagram in Figure 3.1. What is the purpose of each step in this process?
4. Why is the compilation step critical to your use of a computer?
5. Which of the errors cited in Step 7, the debugging process, seems to be the most important? Why?
6. What is the difference between a source program and an object program? Why are there two programs created in the programming process?
7. What are the conditions which make saving an object program advantageous? Cite an example to support your reasoning.
8. If an error is corrected in the debugging process, what advantage is served by going to the effort necessary to correct the flowchart?
9. What is the difference between test data and problem data? Why do two types of data exist?
10. Do you think it is possible for a FORTRAN program to be compiled, show no diagnostic messages related to syntax errors, and still not be able to process test data? Why?

4
Approaching A Computer Problem

Problem Analysis and Solution

The key problem in learning programming is determining just where to start. The development of a successful program requires that we first identify the problem and then analyze its elements. The analysis of a problem revolves around three questions.

1. What is the desired result which the problem solution should provide?
2. What data elements are involved in reaching a solution?
3. What are the critical processing factors?

Normally the symptoms of a problem are the elements most readily observed. Unfortunately symptoms do not always reveal the basic problem. It is impossible to analyze accurately the situation surrounding the symptoms without first defining in some way the desired result. Diagnosis of the problem situation should reveal the data elements needed to solve the problem. It also should reveal some of the essential processing requirements.

After the programmer has defined and noted the information requirements, his next step is to consider the sequential or logical actions that need to be taken in manipulating the problem data. Careful design and specification of the steps in data handling provide the programmer with two major benefits. First, this process offers an opportunity for the programmer to review his logic in data handling. Obviously, the illogical manipulation of even proper data will result in an incorrect answer. Second, the product of an accurate processing design is a guide to the preparation of the FORTRAN language statements.

Summation Example

At the risk of oversimplifying the elements involved in problem solution, consider the following example. Suppose that an analysis of a problem situation indicates that the summation of three numbers should be made.

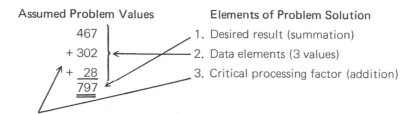

Assumed Problem Values   Elements of Problem Solution

```
    467 ⎫                    1. Desired result (summation)
  + 302 ⎬ ←                  2. Data elements (3 values)
  +  28 ⎭                    3. Critical processing factor (addition)
    797
```

The summation of three numbers is a task so simple that it appears unnecessary to observe the details as shown above. If instructions are to be given to a computer, however, even a simple process such as this must be analyzed in its most elementary parts. A computer system knows nothing about this arithmetic process until the specific instructions are given.

Review the three problem solution elements cited above. In this simple example, the specification of the desired result is quite easy. The important point to observe is that the term "desired result" does not mean the answer 797 but, rather, the outcome of the process—in this case the summation of values. Most people have difficulty in developing the ability to think of problem solutions in terms of a general result. If a successful computer program is to be prepared, the program's design should provide a generalized solution which is correct regardless of the specific values that are being processed. In the example, a successful program to accomplish summation should work equally well with any three values, not just the three values given in the example.

The second element in the problem solution is acquisition of the data values that we wish to use. In this example the values are 467, 302, and 28. Acquisition of the appropriate data for processing is often a difficult task but is highly important in deriving an accurate solution. Often, values are not readily available or must be acquired through preliminary processing of other data. The key to correct data acquisition is well developed problem identification and specification of the desired result.

The third element in problem solution is determination of the critical processing factors. The example involves only one critical processing factor: addition. This element is obviously important with respect to how the data will be manipulated. Most computer programs perform multiple manipulations of data and involve a wide range of processing factors. As the number of different manipulations increases, the programmer must consider the order of the manipulations as well as the processing factors themselves. Determination of the processing order is the factor which gives the development of program logic such importance.

Loss of Contract Bids Example

To illustrate the approach to problem solution a bit further, consider a problem with the following symptom. A manufacturer has lost several recent contracts because he failed to bid as low as his competitors.

Problem identification. An analysis of the situation indicates that the production process is apparently efficient, and, in the development of bids, material costs and overhead charges are properly calculated. However, the estimates for direct labor charges are based on an average cost of all manufacturing departments even though all products made do not go through every manufacturing department.

The problem relates to the manufacturer's incorrect labor estimates in bids submitted. This problem is caused by the fact that labor rates and the times involved in production vary substantially from department to department. Identification of the problem in this case reveals that the loss of contract bids was the symptom which indicated an underlying problem. A solution to the problem, therefore, requires processing the labor costs to arrive at accurate figures for the labor cost per unit in each department and, of course, their use in making contract bids.

Elements of Problem Solution.

1. *Desired results:*
   accurate figure of the labor cost per unit for products manufactured in each department
2. *Data elements:*
   payroll data related to direct labor for all manufacturing departments and units produced during the same periods covered by the payroll data
3. *Processing Factors:*
   separation of payroll data into departmental units,
   separation of production data into departmental units,
   calculation of the cost per unit for direct labor for each department

After calculating current costs per unit for direct labor, these costs may be entered in the bidding process. This example has been simplified to illustrate the approach to problem analysis and overlooks such additional refinements as varying pay rates within departments, lost time charges, and the like.

The order in which data elements are processed is frequently an important consideration, though not always critical. In this problem it is immaterial whether the payroll data or the unit production data is separated, by department, first. However, both of these steps in processing must be finished prior to the calculation of the cost per unit. The payroll and unit data both are prior and necessary elements entering into the cost per unit computation. Therefore, they both had to be calculated prior to calculating the direct labor cost per unit. It is essential, then, that the programmer plan not only *what data* to process but the *order* in which the data should be processed.

Exercise 1[1]

Read the situations given below and for each situation write a statement expressing:
a. the desired result
b. the data elements needed
c. the processing factors or steps to be taken (pay close attention to those situations where the *order* of the processing steps is important)
1. A department store would like to determine the average dollar size of its sales for one month.
2. A department store would like to determine the average dollar size of its sales for each month and for the year.
3. The business manager of University College wants to know:
   a. the average tuition paid per student
   b. the average tuition paid per credit hour taken

[1] Suggested answers to odd-numbered problems in the exercises will be found in Appendix B.

 c. the total tuition for the college

 d. the average number of credit hours per student

4. The supervisor of Haystack County is under attack by the citizens because of what they feel is an inequitable tax structure. What can the supervisor do to respond? The following income tax data is available.

Income Level	Taxes Paid (Group Total)	Number of Taxpayers
$ 0–2500	$ 50000	15
2501–5000	75000	35
5001–7500	500000	200
7501–10000	750000	400
10001–25000	800000	500
25001–50000	600000	100
50001–100000	400000	50
100001–250000	300000	20

Flowcharting

The preparation of a computer program that logically acquires, manipulates, and reports information requires the consideration of all possible processing requirements before writing the program instructions. Several techniques have been developed for assisting the programmer to design a computer program logically. The practice of flowcharting is the most common of these techniques. Basically, flowcharts are nothing more than pictures or graphical representations of the steps to be taken during execution of the computer's processing. A flowchart lists each processing step and connects these steps so that they will follow a logical order. The preparation of a flowchart results in a series of symbols with connecting lines drawn to indicate the flow of processing steps.

A flowchart may be drawn on either of two levels. The most general level flowchart is known as a *System Flowchart*. This flowchart depicts all the steps and devices necessary to input, process, and output all data elements of a major system. Examples of major systems include an accounting system, personnel system, or inventory control system. Each of these systems contains a series of subsystems.

The second, or detail, level of flowchart is known as a *Program Flowchart*. This flowchart specifies the minute steps which the computer must take to solve a single problem. Normally, a large number of Program Flowcharts will be developed in support of each System Flowchart.

The development of flowcharts will:

1. aid the analysis of program logic
2. simplify the task of coding FORTRAN instructions
3. provide documentation to accompany completed programs
4. assist in locating errors during initial executions of the program

A series of symbols depict the steps followed on a flowchart. The flowcharting symbols shown and explained in Figures 4.1 and 4.2 are standard in application. Each symbol contains an example of the type of notation that may be found in it.

Figure 4.1 Program Flowchart Symbols

Input/Output

Function: to indicate program input/output of information.

Processing

Function: to specify manipulation of data elements within a program.

Decision

Function: to represent the testing, or comparison, of data items with an indication of the next step to be executed.

Stop

Terminal

Function: to indicate the terminus of a program. A flat oval containing the word START indicates the beginning of the program. STOP indicates the logical end of the program.

Arrows

Function: to indicate the directional flow of the program steps.

     (off-page)

Connectors

Function: to reference the exit from, or entry to, another part of a flowchart. A circle gives reference to a connection on the same page. The off-page connector references a connection to be made on another page.

Preparation

Function: to indicate a program change or instruction modification.

Figure 4.2   System Flowchart Symbols

Punched Card

Function: to indicate the use of punch cards for input (reading)/output (punching).

Document

Function: to specify output displayed through the use of the line printer.

Magnetic Tape

Function: to indicate the use of magnetic tape for input/output/storage of information.

On-Line Storage

Function: to specify data storage for later input/output using magnetic drum or disk (random access).

Keying

Function: to indicate data preparation through the use of a key driven device as used with punching, verifying, or typing.

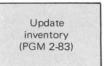

Processing

Function: to indicate the alteration of data through calculations, location change, or combination as a result of a computer program. Each rectangle represents one program.

Merge

Function: to specify the combination of two or more sets of items into one set.

Extract

Function: to indicate the removal of one or more items from a set.

Figure 4.2 Continued

Off-Line Storage

Function: to specify the retention of data not used currently in the system.

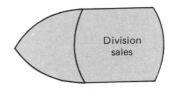

Display

Function: to indicate the use of a cathode ray tube (CRT) for the display of information. Frequently used with an information retrieval subsystem.

Communications Link

Function: to show transmission of information from a remote location to a central processor via a telecommunications link.

     (off-page)

Connectors

Function: (same use as with program flow-charting) to reference the exit from, or entry to, another part of a flow-chart. A circle gives reference to a connection on the same page. The off-page connector references a connection to be made on another page.

The symbols presented above have specific definitions for the professional programmer. It may seem appropriate to use some of these symbols interchangeably between system flowcharts and program flowcharts. This, in fact, is often the case in practice.

It will be easier to learn program flowcharting by using only a few of the symbols. This will eliminate a preoccupation with the selection of symbols and keep the emphasis on a problem's analysis and the design of a program's logical flow. You might use only the rectangle and diamond symbols in flowcharting until this art becomes easier to perform. An important flowcharting convention should be noted. The general flow of programs is drawn to move from *top to bottom* and from *left to right* on a page. The flowcharts illustrated in this material will use several symbols. Naturally, when a program is developed for formal use, a well developed flowchart becomes a necessity for complete documentation of the program.

Flowchart Logic

There are only two basic logical flows in any type of problem solving process. First, where the processing actions follow a sequential order, the flowchart indicates this order in *sequential logic* as illustrated below. This flowchart technique is used when the requirements of processing specify that step 1 precedes step 2.

Sequential Logic

Second, flowcharting may require the illustration of a processing requirement for *decision logic*. This type of logic arises when a point is reached in a program where further processing steps are taken as a result of testing some alternatives. Several different types of decision logic are formally recognized, but nearly all involve the comparison of some values. Based upon this comparison, one of several actions may be taken. For example, if a trucking firm was processing data to find the best way to ship heavy loads, the firm might have a decision point in a program to test the following condition: is the load to be shipped more or less than 30,000 pounds? Loads less than 30,000 pounds are shipped on trucks driven by our employees. Loads equal to or greater than 30,000 pounds are shipped through the railroad piggyback system.

Figure 4.3   Illustration of Decision Logic

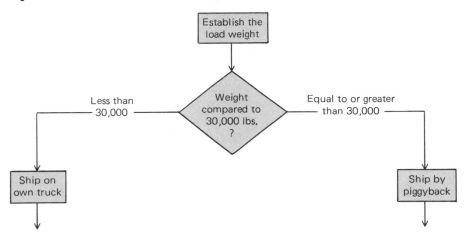

The flowchart in Figure 4.3 illustrates the program's decision process for this condition.

This flowchart illustrates a two-value comparison. The value of the load weight is being compared with the value 30,000 pounds. There were three possible outcomes from this comparison: less than, equal to, and greater than 30,000 pounds. Note how two outcomes directed the program flow to the same step. This was for the equal to and greater than 30,000 pounds results. Other two-value comparisons may lead to any one of three outcomes. The flowchart in Figure 4.4 illustrates this possibility.

Figure 4.4   Two-Value Comparison with Three Outcomes

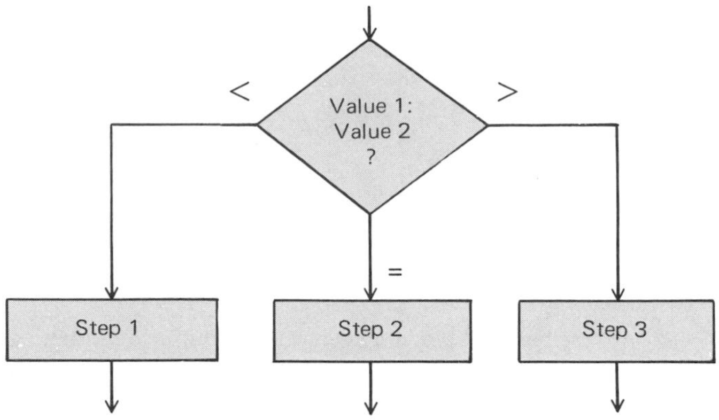

Note here that the symbols $<$, $=$, and $>$ have been used to represent the results of less than, equal to, and greater than, respectively. This convention is more compact than the written terms and might be preferred on that basis. (Also note that : means "compared to.")

One of the primary characteristics which places the computer in a class far above the adding machine is its ability to exercise some logical decision processes. While two-value comparisons are essentially the limit of the computer's logical process, it is entirely appropriate to link several comparisons and thereby achieve the effect of multiple decisions. For instance, if we modify the freight example, we could test the following conditions. Is the load to be shipped more or less than 30,000 pounds and are shipping distances more than 600 miles or less than 200 miles? The following sets of conditions require the actions indicated.

1. If weight is less than 30,000 pounds and mileage is less than or equal to 600 miles, use own trucks.
2. If weight is less than 30,000 pounds and mileage is greater than 600 miles, use piggyback.
3. If weight is equal to or greater than 30,000 pounds and mileage is less than or equal to 200 miles, use own trucks.
4. If weight is equal to or greater than 30,000 pounds and mileage is greater than 200 miles, use piggyback.

The conditions have been compounded so that not only is weight an important consideration but so are the two different mileage factors. The flowchart in Figure 4.5 illustrates this multiple value comparison.

The programmer must keep in mind one additional characteristic of computer systems. This characteristic involves the computer's *automatic sequential processing of instructions,* unless the computer is instructed to deviate from the sequence. The programmer can assume and count on the fact that the computer will execute instructions in the sequence in which they were written except when one of those instructions specifically says to jump out of sequence and begin processing at some other point in the program. The technique of changing the processing sequence is called *branching.* Frequently, a decision will cause branching to take place. The freight illustration in Figure 4.5 has several branches. One of two branches is

Figure 4.5 Flowchart Illustrating Multiple-Value Decision Logic

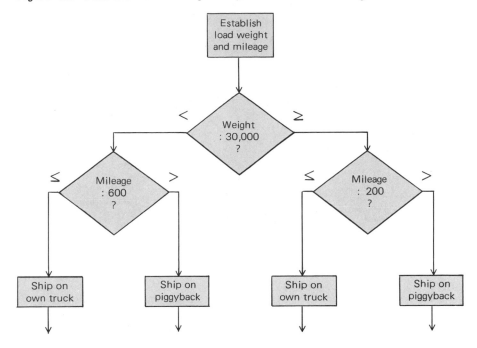

taken as a result of the test concerning weight, and branching is also the outcome of the mileage tests. Other types of branching, such as unconditional branches, looping, and the like are important to the development of computer programs and will be discussed in subsequent chapters.

The concept of flowcharting is designed to provide the programmer with a device for combining both sequential and decision logic to accomplish the design of a processing flow, which, after conversion to FORTRAN instructions, will direct the computer to execute the instructions correctly. Each flowchart must have a logical beginning, must illustrate the processing flow, and must proceed to an equally logical termination point.

Flowcharting Examples

The flowchart in Figure 4.6 applies to the summation problem discussed on page 25. That problem was in very simple form and involved only the use of sequential processing. The processing requirements of that problem called for (1) entering the values to be summed, (2) performing the summation, and (3) writing the result. The logical order of those steps is easy to see and there can be no optional order in which to take the steps. Because the computer takes instructions sequentially, the programmer can specify the three steps in order; he has no reason to consider any branching instructions.

We will use a flowchart for the contract example to illustrate the interrelationship of sequential and decision logic in program design. The analysis of the problem indicated that processing would require (1) reading certain payroll data, (2) separation of the payroll data by departments, (3) reading data on unit production, (4) separation of the production data by departments, (5) calculation of the labor

Figure 4.6 Flowchart for Summation of Three Values

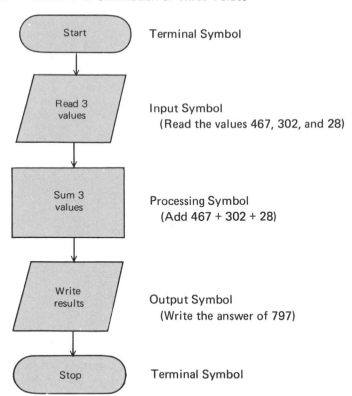

Start — Terminal Symbol

Read 3 values — Input Symbol (Read the values 467, 302, and 28)

Sum 3 values — Processing Symbol (Add 467 + 302 + 28)

Write results — Output Symbol (Write the answer of 797)

Stop — Terminal Symbol

cost per unit in each department, and (6) writing the results of the calculations. In the flowchart shown in Figure 4.7, two segments of sequential steps end with a decision that leads to a possible branch out of the sequential flow. If we assume that the payroll and production data is quite voluminous and cannot be contained in one punch card, we must test (a decision) to determine whether any additional data is to be read before moving to the next sequential step.

The successful completion of this program does not depend upon reading the payroll data first. The flowchart could have specified the reading of production data first. No matter which order is chosen, the data is read, separated by department, and stored. However, both the payroll and the production data must be read before any calculation can be made. The order chosen in this flowchart is purely arbitrary.

Throughout the remainder of this book, flowcharts will accompany problem illustrations to demonstrate the relationship between program logic and the FORTRAN code.

Exercise 2

Take each of the four situations in Exercise 1 and prepare a flowchart to match your analysis. Pay careful attention to the sequential and decision logic requirements of your analyses.

Figure 4.7   General Flowchart for Computation of Labor Unit Costs[1]

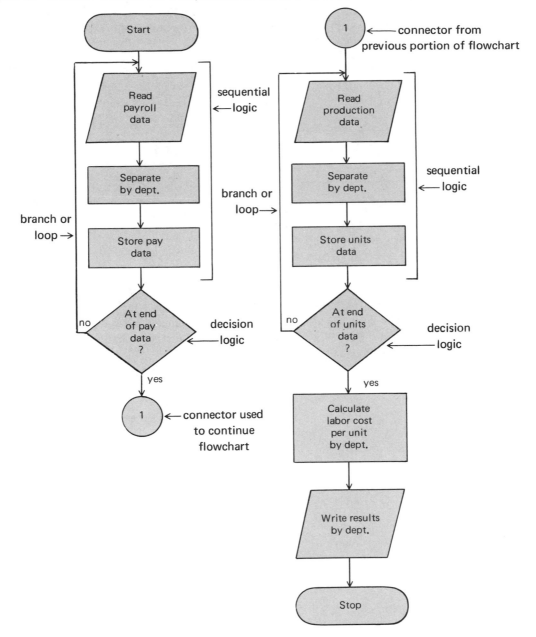

[1] Program flowcharts may vary in their level of detail. This flowchart could be described as a "macro" or general flowchart. It shows the major steps which the program must take. At the other extreme, a "micro" or detailed flowchart would show a symbol for each program instruction written.

Questions

1. What is the purpose behind identifying the elements of a problem as (1) desired results, (2) data elements, and (3) processing factors?

2. What is a flowchart? What value does it have in the programming process?
3. What is the difference between a System Flowchart and a Program Flowchart?
4. Identify each of the following flowchart symbols and explain the purpose for each symbol.

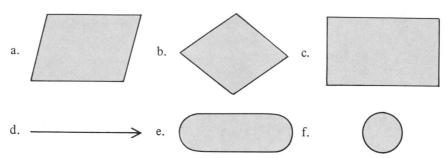

5. Define each of the following terms:
   a.   sequential logic
   b.   decision logic
6. Computers have been defined as "sequential machines." Based on your acquaintance with computer processing logic, what does this definition mean?
7. What does "branching" mean in computer processing?
8. Why do flowcharts flow from top-to-bottom and left-to-right on a page?
9. Study the following decision symbol. What flowcharting error does it illustrate? Explain.

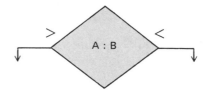

10. What is the difference between a "macro" flowchart and a "micro" flowchart?

5

The FORTRAN IV Language

Basic Program Elements and Input Statements

A computer program is a series of statements, selected and arranged by the programmer, which will direct the computer to a problem's solution. Construction of program statements must follow a rather rigid set of syntactical rules which are identified as a language. The language we will explore is known as FORTRAN IV. This name is a contraction of the words *FOR*mula *TRAN*slation, and IV is the number of the most recent version of the language.

Recall that the central processing unit brings in data from a peripheral device and then applies processing instructions to manipulate the data. If a system is to handle data accurately, a description of the data's form has to be given to the central processor. In addition, the device which holds the data must be identified for the computer. A similar, but reverse, procedure occurs when the processed data is ready to be displayed. Again, the central processor is given a description of exactly how the data should appear and which peripheral device is to be used for display. A FORTRAN program contains the instructions for handling these key aspects of data processing:

1. Input: description of data type, form, and quantity
2. Processing: steps required in manipulation
3. Output: description of data type, form, quantity, and captions or headings

A Program Illustration

The following illustration, using our summation example, gives an overview of these programming considerations. The flowchart, data card, and a program to accomplish processing are shown in Figure 5.1.

The program illustration contains several significant points which the programmer should clearly understand before he prepares a FORTRAN program. Note the interrelationship between the flowchart and the written FORTRAN program. The three key steps of reading data, performing the processing, and writing the computed result are easily traced in this example. Without knowing the specific requirements of the FORTRAN language, the words READ, SUM, and WRITE refer

Figure 5.1   Flowchart, Program, and Data Card for Three-Value Summation

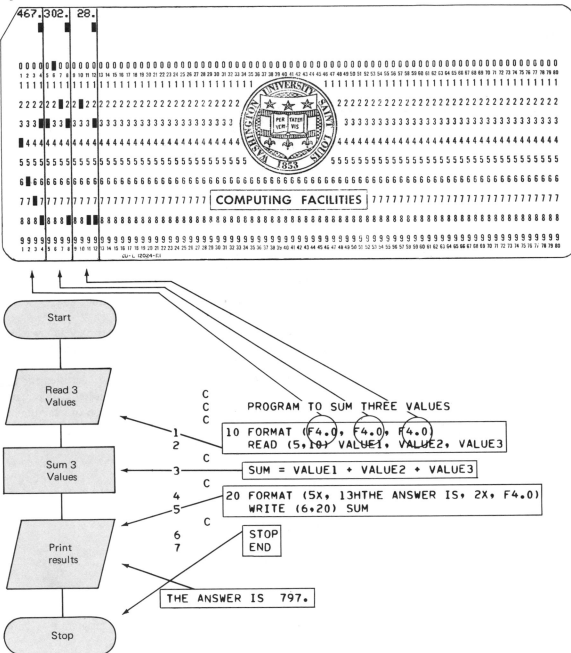

directly to the flowchart. The order of these instructions also corresponds to the order required to compute the correct answer.

This program was designed to call in data from the card reader. A punched card in the card reader holds the three numeric values. This card, as shown in Figure 5.1, has three values clearly printed at the top of the card. Because the computer cannot read the printing, the numeric values are punched in the appropriate columns of the card. For instance, the first value of 467. is punched in columns 1-4. The digit 4 is represented by the punched hole at the intersection of column 1 and row 4. The second digit is punched in column 2-row 6. The third digit and decimal point are similarly punched. Because these three numbers and decimal point belong to a specific value, columns 1-4 are defined as a *field*. Columns 5-8 are punched so that the second field represents the value 302., and columns 9-12 are a third field holding the value 28.

The READ instruction, on line 2 of the program, activates the card reader. Note that the numbers being read have assigned variable names: VALUE1, VALUE2, VALUE3. Line 1 of the program is called a FORMAT statement. This statement describes the form of the data being read.

In addition, note that the value 28 does not require three punched card columns, but it was punched so that the value is in a field whose size corresponds to that of the other two fields. The number 28 was punched in the extreme right side of the field. This punching technique is known as "right justifying." The data card has 80 columns. Although only 12 columns were used in this illustration, the card reader would still have to read a card with all 80 columns even though some columns were not used.

The processing specifications of this program are simply stated. Line 3 contains the only processing instruction in the program. This instruction shows that the addition of all three values will equal a total which the program calls SUM.

The instruction which causes the printer to display the computed result contains the words WRITE and SUM (see line 5 of the program). WRITE is the command word which causes printing to occur, while SUM is the storage location name, in computer memory, which holds the computed sum. Recall the discussion of data transfer from memory to a printed line (see page 14). This example demonstrates that output process. The answer stored in the computer's memory is 797 and, while printing only this value would have been possible, it is more meaningful to have some caption accompany the answer. In this instance, the words THE ANSWER IS are used as the caption. These words are not a part of the computed answer so the programmer has to provide them. Line 4 of the program shows how the caption is provided. Line 4 is an output FORMAT statement and within this statement the words THE ANSWER IS appear.

The words STOP and END must appear at the end of all FORTRAN programs. STOP indicates the *logical* end to a program while END specifies the program's *physical* end. These words also correspond to the conclusion of the flowchart.

This brief example shows that the preparation of a FORTRAN computer program follows the logic of a flowchart, specifies how values are read, directs the processing, and displays the result upon completion of processing. Now let us examine the individual elements of the FORTRAN language in more detail.

FORTRAN Data Modes

The FORTRAN language permits several possible forms of numeric data. These forms are called *data modes*. Most commonly, numeric data is handled as either *integer mode* quantities or *real mode* quantities. Any numeric quantity (positive or negative) can be converted from the integer to the real mode or vice versa.[1]

---

[1] Other modes, such as exponential, double-precision, and logical, are described in a later section.

An *integer mode* numeric quantity is a *whole number,* such as 5, 21, 30, −44, or +67. As a whole number, the quantity will carry *no fractional value.* In the FORTRAN language, an integer mode numeric quantity is written as a whole number and does *not* have a *decimal point.* For example, the numbers *5* and *5.0* and *5.* all carry an identical numeric value. In the FORTRAN language, however, only the number *5* would be considered an integer mode quantity.

A *real mode* numeric quantity is identified as a number capable of carrying a *fractional* or decimal *value.* The decimal value may run from zero to any larger figure. The *key* identifier of a real mode number in the FORTRAN language *is* the *decimal point.* Referring to the example above, the numbers *5* and *5.0* and *5.* all carry an identical numeric value. However, in FORTRAN, only the numbers *5.0* and *5.* are real mode quantities, because they are written with the use of decimal points. Of course, numbers such as 5.826, −5.904, and 3.2 are also real mode quantities. Therefore, any numeric quantity which carries a fractional value must be manipulated as a real mode number in FORTRAN.

The computer will handle numeric values of both modes in positive or negative form. Values may be entered with or without an accompanying sign. The sign convention followed in mathematics is adhered to in computer processing. When a number is preceded by a negative (minus) sign, the value is treated as negative during processing. Numbers preceded by a positive (plus) sign *or* preceded by *no sign* are processed as positive values.

To summarize, any numeric quantity *without* a decimal point is handled as an *integer* mode value while a numeric quantity *with* a decimal point is handled as a *real* mode value. A sign is optional for positive values but must accompany negative values.

Exercise 3

1. Circle any of the following numbers which *are not* in the real mode.
   a. 287   b. −5   c. 28.   d. +13.7   e. 137
   f. 42   g. −87.   h. 2   i. .14   j. +2.3
2. Convert any *circled* items in (1) above to the real mode.
3. Circle any of the following numbers which *are not* in the integer mode.
   a. −0.28   b. 3.7   c. 28.   d. +287   e. 48
   f. 72.0   g. 2   h. −33   i. 0.4   j. +15.6
4. Convert any *circled* items in (3) above to the integer mode. What impact will this conversion have on fractional values?

FORTRAN Data Names

The ability of a computer to store and manipulate numeric data must be accompanied by a system for identifying *exactly* where this numeric data is located in the computer's memory. The engineering characteristics of a computer preclude people from seeing what takes place internally, but these same engineering characteristics enable the programmer to control the numeric data *wherever* they are located. In the FORTRAN language, ability to control data location is accomplished by assigning a *name* to *each location* used (see page 12). The names used for locations may vary with each programmer and with each program. Fortunately, the computer will remember a specific memory location and the name attached to that location. This computer "housekeeping" ability provides the programmer with the opportunity to reuse the quantities stored at any location by merely citing the appropriate name. The computer will determine the cross-reference between the name and the actual location in its memory and then manipulate the data as directed by the programmer's statement.

An additional capability of the computer's "housekeeping" function relieves the programmer of some very tedious work. When the programmer uses a new name, he does not have to know its exact location in the computer's memory. The computer will automatically select an available position in its memory and associate the proper name with the location. Through the name-location, cross-reference system, the programmer has effective control over data, but has no practical need to know exactly where the data are physically located.

The specification of location names, known as *data names,* must confrom to the FORTRAN rules for data modes, and a *name must begin with an alphabetic character.* To differentiate between the real mode and the integer mode, the alphabet has been divided into the following segments:

Letters	Mode	Example
A through H	Real	A, BAT, DZ, HOW
I through N	Integer	KAR, K2R, MY, I
O through Z	Real	OOP, YAM, SPEC, U

Note how *only the first letter* in a data name denotes whether the name is associated with the real or integer mode. Three of the names shown in the examples were BAT, KAR, and YAM. The names *BAT* and *YAM* are in the real mode because the initial letters *B* and *Y* are from the groups of alphabetic letters designed for the *real mode.* Of course, *KAR* begins with the letter *K* and therefore is associated with the *integer mode.*

Suppose a programmer desired to store the value of Pi (π), or 3.1416, in the computer's memory for later use in his program. (Assume an accuracy of four decimal places.) This value is a real mode numeric quantity and the name Pi begins with the alphabetic character P, which is a real mode alphabetic character. It is now possible to construct a statement which will direct the computer to store the value of Pi at a location which will be referred to subsequently as PI. The programmer can write the statement as:

PI = 3.1416

When the computer reads this statement, it will find an available location in its memory and do two things: (1) attach the name PI to the location and (2) place the numeric value 3.1416 in that memory location. If the programmer subsequently refers to PI anywhere in his program, the computer would automatically move to the location known as PI and take the quantity 3.1416 for use in the manipulation specified by the programmer's statement.

If we assume that we have a computer with only three possible storage locations, and we write a statement for setting PI equal to 3.1416, the diagram in Figure 5.2 will show the process for entering the quantity in the computer's memory.

Figure 5.2   Loading a Statement in Computer Memory

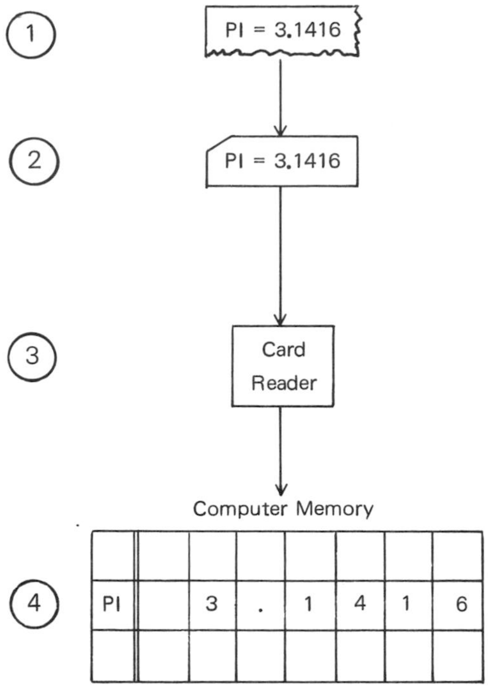

1. The programmer writes a statement setting the variable name PI equal to a value of 3.1416.
2. The statement, as written, is punched into a card which can be read by the card reader.
3. The punched card is read by a card reader and is converted to electronic pulses which are transmitted to computer memory.
4. The computer finds an available unused memory location (not necessarily the first location). It then stores the value and creates a proper name reference for the location.

To summarize, the FORTRAN language has two modes for handling data quantities: (1) the integer mode and (2) the real mode. Reference to data stored in the computer's memory is accomplished by giving each data location a reference name. The name must be related to the data by beginning with a proper alphabetic character which is either a real character (A-H or O-Z) or an integer character (I-N).

Exercise 4

1. Circle the following data names which are *not* in the integer mode.
   a. ITEK   f. WASH
   b. ABC   g. UNIV
   c. GOGO   h. BOOK
   d. MILK   i. C12
   e. P   j. ZIM
2. Circle the following data names which are *not* in the real mode.
   a. JAM   c. XRAY
   b. AQZR   d. LET

e. A14   h. BLG
f. J28   i. RAIL
g. KIM   j. NOW

3. Convert the following names from their existing mode into the opposite mode.
   a. A   f. C1F2
   b. IJK   g. HAM
   c. RACK   h. LOW
   d. Z37   i. S28R
   e. MEE   j. NUM

The programmer must observe a few specific rules when he writes data names. These rules are necessary so that the computer can expect a uniform construction for the names and therefore process programs more efficiently. The name attached to a particular memory location must:

1. contain *only* combinations of alphabetic and numeric characters[2]
2. *not* contain special characters (hyphens, asterisks, spaces, dashes, and the like)
3. *begin* with an alphabetic character.
4. have *no more than* six (6) characters in the name (all letters must be capitalized)[3]

When selecting a name the following suggestions might be kept in mind:

1. *Short names* are easiest to handle in writing programs.
2. Names which have *some meaning* related to your data make writing and future review of the program easier.
3. Avoid the possibility of using the same name more than once in a program; varying *any one* alphabetic or numeric character in a location name is sufficient to have the computer differentiate the names.

Relating the above rules and suggestions to the example of PI = 3.1416, observe that:

1. PI begins with an alphabetic character.
2. PI is less than 6 characters in length.
3. PI does not contain anything other than alphabetic or numeric characters.
4. PI is a short name.
5. PI has a meaningful relation to the data associated with it.
6. Only one location should be given the name PI.

Ordinarily, a name should be assigned so that it is in the same data mode as the numeric quantity associated with it. In the example of PI = 3.1416 this rule was followed. The *name* and the *numeric quantity* were *both real mode items.* A subsequent discussion will explain deviations from this suggestion.

The following examples illustrate valid and invalid variable data names:

Valid Names
a. SALES (real mode)
b. NUMBER (integer mode)

---

[2] Some processors permit the use of the dollar-sign ($) as an alphabetic character, but this character is probably best ignored in the learning process.

[3] Though 6 is the most common size, some processors permit the use of names with a different number of maximum characters (refer to the manufacturer's applicable manual).

c. POLICY (real mode)
d. AD1B2 (real mode)
e. KKK5 (integer mode)

Invalid Names
a. 24AK (must begin a variable data name with a letter)
b. COMPUTER (too long; only six characters allowed)
c. INTY −5 (only alphabetic and numeric characters allowed)
d. $PGM (OK if $ is allowed by the system)
e. CAL5/2 (only alphabetic and numeric characters allowed)

Exercise 5

1. Write a data name for each of the following items (disregard the data mode in this exercise).
    a. year (for example, could be written as YEAR, YR, etc.)
    b. depreciation
    c. sales
    d. inventory
    e. expense
    f. number
    g. equipment
    h. salaries
    i. life
    j. total

2. Identify the names written in (1) as being in the integer or real mode and then write another name for the same item but *in the opposite* mode.

	Mode	Name
a. YEAR	real	IYEAR
b.		
c.		
d.		
e.		
f.		
g.		
h.		
i.		
j.		

FORTRAN Constants and Variables

FORTRAN data is subdivided into two classifications called *constants* and *variables*. This particular division is based upon the use made of the numeric quantities included in the data. Both constants and variables can be written in either the integer or real modes.

A *constant* is a value which appears *within a FORTRAN statement* in numeric form. In the example PI = 3.1416, the numeric portion of the statement is a constant. If this value is not changed, that is, remains *constant,* throughout the processing of the entire program, then the numeric quantity is termed a constant and the data name PI could also be considered a constant.

Numeric constants may be either in the integer or real mode. The distinguishing factor between the modes is the presence or absence of a decimal point. The *presence* of a *decimal point* is required when the programmer intends to use a *real mode constant,* such as 1., −1.3468, or 200.5674. The *absence* of a *decimal point* is required with an *integer mode constant,* such as 1, 200, or 2874.

A *variable* is a *data name representing a memory location* which may contain a range of values. The value stored at a variable location will depend upon the processing of the computer program. Therefore, the data name is a symbolic representation of a location which will hold a value of unknown proportions at the time the programmer writes his program.

Suppose we want to write a program which would calculate the average time spent by five programmers in writing a series of computer programs. Our firm is interested in having this average for making future programming time estimates in the data processing department. The actual time spent by each programmer was:

Programmer #1: 7.5 hours
Programmer #2: 4.3 hours
Programmer #3: 10.8 hours
Programmer #4: 5.6 hours
Programmer #5: 1.3 hours

In processing this data, we should reserve at least one location in the computer's memory for holding the summation of the programmers' hours. We could use one of several names to represent this data location, and a logical one is *HRS.* HRS is a *variable data name*[4] *because* the exact numeric *quantity* which *this location* will hold *varies* from 0.0 (prior to processing) to a total of 29.5 (after adding all of the programmers' times). In this example, we chose the name HRS because it met all of the rules for the construction of a data name, and also because it had a meaningful relationship to the type of data found at this memory location.

For this example, the location designated by the programmer as HRS will serve a purpose much like that of an adding machine. As each programmer's hours are entered into the computer, the quantity at the location HRS will increase in the following way:

	Hours Added	Cumulative Value of HRS
1. Prior to processing	–0–	0.0
2. Process programmer #1 hours	7.5	7.5
3. Process programmer #2 hours	4.3	11.8
4. Process programmer #3 hours	10.8	22.6
5. Process programmer #4 hours	5.6	28.2
6. Process programmer #5 hours	1.3	29.5

Remember that a *constant* is a numeric value entered and stored in the computer's memory without an intent of having the computer change the numeric value. A real

[4] Variable data names are variously called "data names," "variable names," and "variables." In all cases, reference is to symbolic names assigned to memory locations.

mode constant is entered with a decimal point. An integer constant possesses no decimal point. The location of the constant is given a data name beginning with a letter corresponding to the same mode as the constant.

A *variable* is a FORTRAN data name used by the computer to store numeric quantities which will vary in size during the program's processing. The variable name may begin with a letter from either mode. However, the mode selected for the variable name will determine the mode of the numeric quantity stored at that location.

Exercise 6

1. Examine the following numeric constants and the related data name. How will the numeric value be stored in the computer's memory?

Constant	Stored As
a. ABC = 4.25	4.25
b. IJK = 50	_____
c. DEG = 37	_____
d. I2 = 16.7	_____
e. CAB = 15.8	_____

2. Circle the following variable names which are *not* in the integer mode.

a. BYE   f. B2
b. IBA   g. H4G
c. JAZ   h. KA2
d. ZAP   i. NOT
e. ABI   j. TON

3. Convert all of the names in (2) into the opposite mode.

a.   f.
b.   g.
c.   h.
d.   i.
e.   j.

We have discussed data modes, constants, and variable data names but none of these elements alone accomplish processing. Consequently, we must now examine the language characteristics which will enable us to answer the following questions:

1. How is data brought in to the central processor?
2. How does the computer complete its processing?
3. How does the processing system transfer information out for display?

The next several sections will deal with these questions.

The Punch Card

The punch card[5] is a medium used for entering both program instructions and data. An example of a standard punch card containing numeric, alphabetic, and special characters appears in Figure 5.3.

[5] Technically, a punch card is known as a Hollerith card. This card was designed in the 1880s by Herman Hollerith while working with the Census Bureau. The use of punch cards for tabulating the 1890 census proved the value of these cards. The tabulation was completed more quickly and at less cost than could have been possible using hand methods.

Figure 5.3 Standard Punch Card

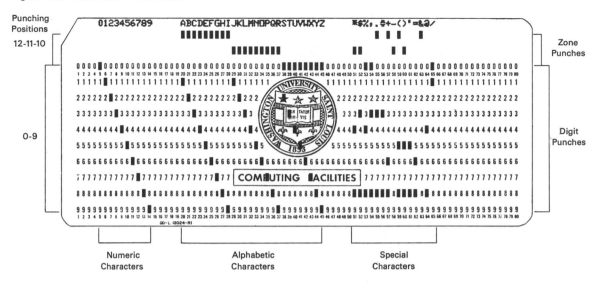

A punch card contains 80 columns, and each column can hold one numeric, alphabetic, or special character. The vertical height of each column contains a maximum of twelve punching positions, or rows. The ten positions 0-9 are printed in each column on the sample card in Figure 5.3 The eleventh and twelfth positions are located above the zero. The twelfth position is at the top edge of the card and is referred to as the + position. The eleventh position is located between the twelfth and tenth positions and is referred to as the − position. In addition, the position printed as zero is designated as the tenth position.

Observe that each column containing a character has the character printed at the top edge of the card. The 12-11-10 positions are referred to as *zone punches*. The positions 1-9 and 0 are called *digit punches*. The tenth position serves double duty as both a numeric zero and a zone punch.

Any column which contains a numeric value uses only one punch in the appropriate row, 0 through 9. However, columns holding either alphabetic or special characters use a combination of zone and numeric punches.

FORTRAN Input Statements

In order to process problem data, a program must first instruct the computer to read data into the computer's memory. The program must also give instructions to display the results upon completion of the program. These two tasks are accomplished through *Input and Output Statements*.

The directions for both input and output are very simple. The programmer uses only two *command words*. The command for entering data is READ, and the command for displaying data is WRITE.[6] The programmer, however, must give the computer clues about what the computer should READ or WRITE. He provides clues through *FORMAT* statements. These statements specify the exact form of the input or output and are called *specification statements*.

---

[6] The additional use of the commands PRINT and PUNCH are allowed by some processors.

Examples of READ and WRITE statements, with their accompanying FORMAT statements, are shown below.

READ Statement

    READ (5,22) DATA, CASH
22 FORMAT (F12.3, F8.2)

WRITE Statement

57 FORMAT (5X, 7HTOTAL =,F20.4)
    WRITE (6,57) SUM

A FORMAT specification statement must accompany *every* input (that is, READ) statement and *every* output (that is, WRITE) statement.[7]

Review of the example statements will show that FORMAT statements may precede or follow READ and WRITE statements. As a matter of fact, they may appear anywhere within a program preceding the END statement. As an arbitrary practice in this text, the FORMAT statements will generally be placed immediately prior to READ and WRITE statements.

Input: FORTRAN FORMAT Statements

When the input to a computer program is accomplished through the use of punched cards, the input FORMAT statement must describe the layout of the cards. A punch card contains a *maximum* of 80 columns that can be used for input data. Of course, fewer than 80 columns may be utilized but the FORMAT statement cannot describe input of more than 80 columns for any one card.

For an illustration of the construction of a FORMAT statement, refer to our earlier example dealing with averaging the programmers' time. The five times were 7.5, 4.3, 10.8, 5.6, and 1.3 hours. If we punched these hours into a card *without* any consideration for *uniformity* in format, a string of consecutive numbers would appear as shown in the diagram below.

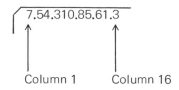

Column 1   Column 16

Each digit and each decimal point would use one column on the card, and therefore all the numbers occupy the first 16 columns of the card.

Uniformity in data format is a desirable objective in computer processing. Uniformity promotes accuracy in punching data and frequently permits efficiencies in writing FORMAT statements. In this example consideration of the numbers contained in the input suggests a way to achieve uniformity in their format. The largest single number is 10.8 and it takes four card columns. It happens that the other four numbers require only three card columns (7.5, 4.3, 5.6, 1.3), but we could specify that they too be placed in four column fields. It would only be necessary to place a zero prior to the most significant digit in a number and it would then fill four card columns without changing the value of the numeric quantity. For instance, 7.5

[7] Some processors do allow the use of unformatted READ and WRITE statements. See applicable manufacturers' manuals.

could be punched 07.5 and require four card columns. The number would retain the same numeric value as it had without the leading zero.

If each item of data is punched so that it fills a four-column field, the data card's FORMAT could be described as "five fields containing four columns in each field." This description is not suitable for programming so a shorthand method giving the same information has been developed. Keeping in mind that the data falls into either the real or integer mode (that is, possesses or lacks a decimal point), the *letter I* has been specified for use with input descriptions which contain *integer data.* In this example, the items of data contain decimal points and fractional values. Therefore they are not in the integer mode but in the real mode. The letter *F* has been designated for use in describing *real* input *data* and would be used in this case. We must also give the *field width* to the computer (that is, how many card columns does the input data fill). In this example, each field fills four card columns. We could describe the character of *each item* of input data *as F4.* The computer, however, will not know that we intended each input item to contain a place for a single decimal fraction unless we indicate this fact in our input format.

The method used for indicating this decimal information is to follow the field width (*F4*) with a *decimal point and a numeric value* indicating the number of places the data has to the right of the decimal point. In the example, the programmers' times are measured fractionally in tenths of an hour. This measure requires the use of no more than one decimal place. Therefore, we should alter our description to indicate this fact by specifying a single field as *F4.1.* The same field description applies to all of the five input fields as shown below.

07.5	04.3	10.8	05.6	01.3	Programmer times
F4.1	F4.1	F4.1	F4.1	F4.1	Field formats

The preparation of a FORMAT statement is now quite simple. Knowing (1) the mode and form of our input data and (2) that each field can be described with the code F4.1, we can transmit this information to the computer by using the word FORMAT and describing the number of fields that the computer should read. The field descriptions are enclosed in parentheses. The following FORMAT statement would be appropriate for our example.

FORMAT (F4.1, F4.1, F4.1, F4.1, F4.1)

Note the correspondence between the field formats shown in the data card above and the description of those fields in the FORMAT statement. It is possible to shorten FORMAT statements by showing the *number of consecutive identical fields* as an integer number placed in front of the F specification. This number is called a *repetition factor.* For example,

FORMAT (5F4.1)

This FORMAT statement is identical to the previous FORMAT in its ability to describe the character of the input fields. Input FORMAT statements have only one purpose: to specify the form of input data. They do not cause the computer system to take any action. The READ command initiates the action. Therefore, the FORMAT statement is a *non-executable* statement.

One additional point needs to be made about input FORMAT statements. Because these statements exist to provide the READ command with a description of the data being entered into the system, we must have some means of connecting each READ command with its appropriate FORMAT specification. This connection is made through the use of *statement reference numbers*. A reference number is placed so that it precedes the word FORMAT and is separated from it by at least one space. The programmer specifies all reference numbers. In nearly all systems, the reference numbers must be integers (that is, without decimal points) between 1 and 99999. The completed FORMAT for our example is:

50 FORMAT (5F4.1)

The number 50 is an arbitrary choice and could have been any other value between 1 and 99999. The use of reference numbers will become more meaningful after considering the elements of the READ statement.

The use of a FORMAT statement for *integer mode data* is nearly identical to its use for real mode data. The width of the field is indicated by a numeric value located after the *I* alphabetic character. The only significant difference from the FORMAT for real mode data is the absence of a specification for decimal places. If we assume the five fields of time data for the programmers had described only even hour intervals, the times and the FORMAT description would have been:

08	04	10	05	01	Times
I2	I2	I2	I2	I2	Formats

This FORMAT would be written as either:

50 FORMAT (I2,I2,I2,I2,I2)

or

50 FORMAT (5I2)

A single input card may contain *both* real and integer mode data. The I and F codes will both be utilized in the FORMAT statement.

To summarize, a FORMAT statement describes the exact layout of the input data. The following rules apply to the construction of FORMAT statements.

1. Place an identification number (*statement number*) to the left of the word FORMAT. The programmer selects this number, and it may range from 1 to 99999. Use any one statement number *only once* in a single program.
2. Place the word FORMAT after the statement number.
3. Place parentheses after the word FORMAT, and within the parentheses:
   a. describe the *mode* of the data input as either integer (I) or real (F)
   b. describe the *field width* of input data by placing a numeric value equal to the field width after the I or F
   c. follow the field width description of real mode data by inserting a decimal point and indicating the *number* of *decimal places* that will be included in the data
   d. separate each data field description with a comma
   e. indicate identical and repetitive field descriptions by placing a numeric value equal to the number of repetitions *before* the I or F mode indicator.

The following examples demonstrate the above rules.

1. Suppose an input card had the following information punched in the first 15 columns:

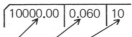

Assume that this was input data for a program which calculates the interest on a $10,000 note at 6% for 10 years.

The following FORMAT statement describes this data.

3 FORMAT   (F8.2, F5.3, I2)

The relationship between the data and the FORMAT statement is:

Values	10000.00	0.060	10
Format	F8.2	F5.3	I2

2. Suppose an input card had the following information punched in the first 23 columns:

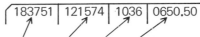

Assume that this input relates to the sale of product 183751 (cols. 1-6) on December 15, 1974 (cols. 7-12) made by salesman number 1036 (cols. 13-16) for a value of $650.50 (cols. 17-23).

The following FORMAT statement describes this data:

105 FORMAT (2I6, I4, F7.2)

The relationship between the data values and the FORMAT is:

Values	183751	121574	1036	0650.50
Format	2I6		I4	F7.2

Exercise 7

Prepare complete FORMAT statements in the most compact form possible for each of the punched card layouts shown below. The vertical lines are for field separation only and do not represent a card column. Assume that all cards will be punched beginning in column one. The use of Xs is to represent numeric values which would appear in the cards.

a. | XXX | XX | XXX.XX | XX. | X |

b. | XXX | XXX | XX.X | X.XX | XX. | .XX |

c. | X | X | X | X | X | .X | XXX |

d. | XXXXX.XX | XXXXX.XX |

e. | XX | XX. | XXX. | XXX.XX | X | X | X. |

f. | XX.X | X.X | X.X | X | X.X | X.X |

Input: FORTRAN READ Statements

READ statements, which FORMAT statements accompany, are very simply constructed. *READ statements cause* the computer system to take *action,* whereas the

FORMAT statements merely specify the form of input data. The READ statement is therefore referred to as an *executable* statement.

For our example dealing with the programmers, the following pair of statements will read in their times.

50 FORMAT (5F4.1)
    READ (5,50) PT1, PT2, PT3, PT4, PT5

Examination of the READ statement indicates that it is composed of several key elements as shown below.

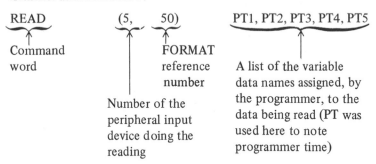

Command Word.   The word READ in a program initiates the input action.

Peripheral Device Number.   Many computer systems can read from several different input devices, including punch card and punched paper tape readers, magnetic tapes, and magnetic disks. It is essential that the system know from which device it should read the data. To facilitate identification of these devices a number is assigned to each unit. The numbers are assigned by each computer facility and may differ among facilities. A number which is often used to identify the card reader is the integer 5. This number is used in the example above and indicates that the computer system should READ from device 5, that is, the card reader. Device numbers for your system may be obtained from the computing facility personnel.

FORMAT Reference Number.   The FORMAT reference number provides the computer with a cross-reference to the FORMAT specification statement which describes the form of input data. This number, in conjunction with the input device number, gives the system the necessary information to read from the correct device and to accept the data in the precise form intended. In this case, 50 refers to the FORMAT statement describing the programmers' time data.

Variable List.   The list, which follows the parentheses, gives the programmer an opportunity to specify names the computer should attach to the data when it is in memory. The names must be in the same mode as that described in the FORMAT statement. The computer will assign the names to the data in the order listed. Each name must be unique; two memory locations may not have the same name. When the computer associates a variable name and the data read in, this is referred to as *defining the variable*. The names PT1, PT2, PT3, PT4, and PT5 were used in this example to name the five locations which would hold the five data values read.

The following illustration, using the programmers' time, summarizes the relationship between the FORMAT and READ statements, the device number and the card reader, the format description and the data, and the variable data names and the storage of data values in the computer's memory.

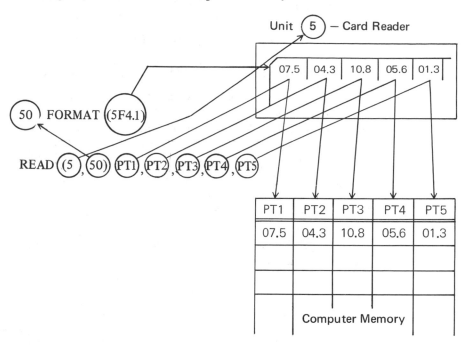

The READ statement activates an input device and is prepared in accordance with the following rules.

1. The word READ is the *initial* element in the instruction (although the command READ could be preceded by a statement number as will be explained in a later section).
2. Parentheses *must* follow the word READ and contain:
   a. an integer number identifying the input device to be used in reading.
   b. an integer number identifying the FORMAT statement which describes the input data form.
   c. a comma separating the device and FORMAT reference numbers.
3. A list of one or more variable data names follows the parentheses. The programmer selects the names in the list, and they must conform to the mode of the input data. Names are associated with data in sequential order so that name 1 is assigned to data value 1, name 2 to data value 2, and so forth.

The following examples illustrate the use of READ statements and are related to the data items described on page 51:

1. When reading data dealing with interest calculations on a note, assume that the following variable data names are used:

   PRIN used for the principal amount of the note
   RATE used for the interest rate on the note

LIFE used for the length of time covered by the note

The relationships among the data card, FORMAT, and READ statements are:

Input data
card

FORMAT
statement

READ
statement

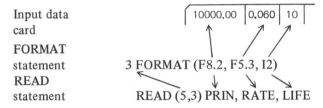

2. When reading the sales data shown on page 51, it is not as easy as in the previous example to find variable data names which are both meaningful and in the correct mode. This example illustrates how a programmer may have to make slight changes in names to match the data modes.

IPROD will be used for the product. PROD could not be used without a modification because the letter "P" would indicate a real mode item, while the data for the product number is in the integer mode. Adding an "I" to PROD changes the mode of the variable name to the integer mode. It is only the first letter which is important in setting a name's mode.

JDATE will be used for the date (any letter, I through N, may be used to set the integer mode).

MAN will be used for the salesman's number.

SALE will be used for the amount of the sale.

The data, FORMAT and READ relationships are:

Input data
card

FORMAT
statement

READ
statement

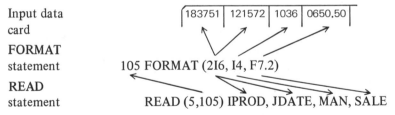

To summarize, reading data into the computer requires the use of two statements. The *FORMAT* statement describes the exact structure of the data entering the computer. The *READ* statement causes the computer to read the data, in accordance with the prescribed format, and to assign an identifying variable data name to each location where data will be stored. Now the computer can manipulate the data as the remainder of the program specifies.

Exercise 8

1. Turn back to Exercise 7. Using your FORMAT statements, prepare a READ statement to accompany each FORMAT statement. Use single alphabetic characters (A, B, C, etc.) in constructing your variable name lists. Be careful to keep the data modes in mind as you select your names. Also, remember that the same variable name can be used only once in each READ statement.

2. Suppose you want to write a program for recording data concerning the sales of machinery. Assume you have decided on the following data fields for each element of data about the machinery. One card will be prepared for each machine. (X = one card column and punching will begin in column 1.)

| XXXXX | XXXX | XXX.XX | XXX.XX | XX.XXX |

Suppose further that the fields will be used for the following information (and in this order):

a. Machine number

b. Code for machine type

c. The machine price (selling)

d. The machine cost

e. The markup rate on cost

Now write a FORMAT statement to describe this card, and then write a statement to read this card using your FORMAT statement.

Questions

1. What are the three basic steps in a FORTRAN program? What is the purpose of each step?

2. What is a field on a punch card?

3. Define each of the following terms:
   a. data mode
   b. data name
   c. constants
   d. variables

4. What is the importance of zone and numeric punch positions with regard to the characters in a punch card?

5. What is the overall purpose of FORTRAN input statements?

6. What is the specific function served by:
   a. FORMAT statements?
   b. READ statements?

7. Explain what the relationship is between the field width in a FORMAT statement specification and a field on a punch card.

8. What is a repetition factor?

9. What is the purpose of a variable list in a READ statement?

10. Explain the specific interrelationships among:
    a. memory location names,
    b. FORMAT statements,
    c. READ statements,
    d. memory location contents, and
    e. problem data cards

6
FORTRAN Processing

Basic FORTRAN Processing

Processing: FORTRAN Assignment Statements

A programmer must follow a specific form when he prepares statements which will enable him to exercise control over the actions of the computer. In FORTRAN, these statements are called *assignment statements* and follow a typical algebraic pattern. The pattern uses an *equal sign (=) as the focal point of a statement.* To illustrate how the equal sign is used in statement construction, we will study the processing requirements for calculating the average time consumed by the five computer programmers. We should prepare a flowchart of the process, first, to be sure of our computational requirements. The program will call upon the computer to read the five time values and compute the average of these values. Calculating the average requires (1) summation of the values and (2) a division of the sum by five. The average will then be displayed. A flowchart for this problem appears in Figure 6.1.

The first step in processing involves summation of the five time values. Recall that the READ statement, shown on page 52, has already placed the five values in memory and named them PT1, PT2, PT3, PT4, and PT5. We can sum the values by writing the following statement:

HRS = PT1 + PT2 + PT3 + PT4 + PT5

The computer would use an available memory location and add the values PT1, . . . , PT5 to the location. The identification tag HRS is placed on that location for future reference.

The equal sign is used as a divider. Therefore the statement really tells the computer to "Set (or assign) HRS equal to the sum of all the programmers' hours." *The computer requires a programmer to write assignment statements which tell it to place the result of any expression found on the right side of the equal sign in the location specified on the left side of the equal sign.*

A FORTRAN assignment statement is a very simple combination of constants and variables placed on the left and right of an equal sign. The rules of FORTRAN impose the following requirements for assignment statements:

1. A single variable data name is the only item which may appear on the *left* of the equal sign, that is, *no* constants may appear on the left of the equal sign.
2. An equal sign is the *only* symbol which may separate the data name on its left from the expression on its right.

Figure 6.1   Flowchart for Calculation of Average Programmer Time

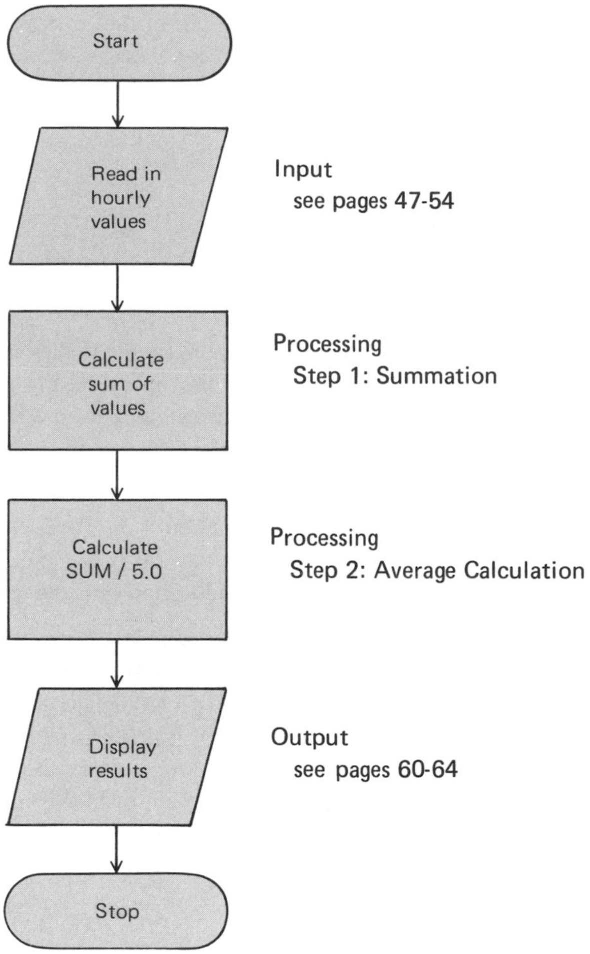

```
            ┌─────────────┐
           (    Start      )
            └─────────────┘
                  │
                  ▼
            ┌─────────────┐        Input
           / Read in      /        see pages 47-54
          /  hourly      /
         /   values     /
        └─────────────┘
                  │
                  ▼
        ┌─────────────┐            Processing
        │ Calculate   │            Step 1: Summation
        │ sum of      │
        │ values      │
        └─────────────┘
                  │
                  ▼
        ┌─────────────┐            Processing
        │ Calculate   │            Step 2: Average Calculation
        │ SUM / 5.0   │
        │             │
        └─────────────┘
                  │
                  ▼
          /─────────────/          Output
         / Display     /           see pages 60-64
        /  results    /
       └─────────────┘
                  │
                  ▼
            ┌─────────────┐
           (    Stop      )
            └─────────────┘
```

3. The following expressions may appear on the *right* side of the equal sign:
   a. a single constant in either mode,
   b. a single variable data name in either mode, or
   c. any combination of constants and variable data names, preferably all in the *same mode.*[1]

FORTRAN assignment statements appear in the following form:

Variable Data Name	=	Constant(s) and/or Variable Data Names
This is the location name which *stores* the *results* of the manipulation specified on the right side of the equal sign.		These constants and/or variable data names are combined or *manipulated,* and the results are sent to the storage location named on the left side of the equal sign.

[1] Combining constants and variable data names from opposite modes, in the same expression, will cause some processors to generate an error message due to this "mixed mode" condition. A good practice is to avoid mixed modes even with processors which will handle this condition.

FORTRAN uses a set of *symbols* or *operators* to combine the constants and variable data names to the right of the equal sign. These constants, variables, and symbols, appearing on the right of the equal sign, form an *expression*.

To summarize, a FORTRAN assignment statement has the following components:

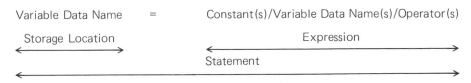

Variable Data Name   =   Constant(s)/Variable Data Name(s)/Operator(s)

Storage Location   Expression

Statement

Processing: FORTRAN Operators

When writing a FORTRAN assignment statement, the programmer can manipulate numeric data by placing the operators between the constants and variable data names in an expression. These symbols are called *arithmetic operators*.

+ a plus sign for addition
- a minus sign for subtraction
* an asterisk for multiplication
/ a slash for division
** two asterisks for exponentiation (raise to a power)

The only peculiar operators are those for multiplication and exponentiation. We typically associate an X with multiplication and a raised numeral, as in 24^2, with exponentiation. In the FORTRAN language, however, the operators for this type of data manipulation *must* be written as * and **, respectively.

The operators permit a programmer to combine several variable data names and/or constants in one expression. In the programmers' time example, we totalled the hours with the following statement:

FORTRAN statement: HRS = PT1 + PT2 + PT3 + PT4 + PT5
Arithmetic equivalent: (29.5 = 7.5 + 4.3 + 10.8 + 5.6 + 1.3)

This statement tells the computer to take the values found at locations PT1, PT2, PT3, PT4, and PT5 and, after adding them together, set HRS equal to the total.

Of course, we could accomplish the same thing through a set of statements. If the computer processed the following six separate statements, in the order shown, it would calculate a total identical to that of the previous single statement.

Statements	Arithmetic Action
1 HRS = 0.0	0.0 = 0.0
2 HRS = HRS + PT1	(7.5 = 0.0 + 7.5)
3 HRS = HRS + PT2	(11.8 = 7.5 + 4.3)
4 HRS = HRS + PT3	(22.6 = 11.8 + 10.8)
5 HRS = HRS + PT4	(28.2 = 22.6 + 5.6)
6 HRS = HRS + PT5	(29.5 = 28.2 + 1.3)

With this set of statements, the computer would take separately the value which is in HRS and add to it PT1, PT2, and so forth, and store the newly computed value in HRS. This is a much more cumbersome way to write the program, but it does accomplish the same objective as the single addition statement shown above.

Note that statement 1 is written as HRS = 0.0. This statement was necessary so that HRS would have some value when it was used in statement 2. Writing a statement, like statement 1, which sets a location equal to a constant is called *initializing*. This practice is important to the preparation of a program. Any variable data name which is used in an expression on the *right of the equal sign* must have a *prior value*. If a variable data name has no value when used in an expression, an error message is printed noting that the "variable is *undefined*." At this point, we have discussed two methods of initializing. One method uses the READ command with a list of variable data names. In this method, the variable data names are assigned values as they are read in. The second method of initializing is that shown above, where a FORTRAN assignment statement sets a variable data name to some value.

The arithmetic operators, other than plus (+), accomplish the tasks normally found in algebra. The following independent and hypothetical examples illustrate the use of these arithmetic operators.

1. Multiply H and G and set SUM equal to the result:

   SUM = H * G

2. Subtract 8.5 from A and set TOT equal to the result:

   TOT = A - 8.5

3. Divide ABC by XYZ and set K2R equal to the result:

   K2R = ABC / XYZ

4. Square (raise to the power of 2) R and set SQ equal to the result:[2]

   SQ = R ** 2

Exercise 9

1. Write a FORTRAN statement for each of the following:
   a. Set i equal to two
   b. Set g equal to twenty-seven
   c. Set y equal to thirty-two and one-half
   d. Set m equal to four hundred
   e. Give a the total value of s added to t
   f. Give j the result from x times 2.4
   g. Give k the result from dividing m by n
   h. Give h the result from deducting 3.264 from v
   i. Give A2 the result from squaring r, and subtracting a
   j. Give z the result from cubing L, adding LL, and subtracting LLL
2. What is the error (if any) in the following data names?

a. 12JAN	d. N	g. ITEM-1	j. AIR4
b. PROD	e. ITEM	h. BOOK-VALUE	k. P+M
c. PROD 34	f. ITEM*	i. NUMBER	l. VALUE

[2] The exponent (the number following the double asterisks) may be an integer number or integer variable name, and with many processors may also be any real number or variable name. Furthermore, real variables may be raised to integer powers (and to real powers with some processors) without violating the rules of "mixed mode." See the applicable manufacturer's manual.

Processing: Arithmetic Statements

Any FORTRAN statements which *use the arithmetic operators* for addition, subtraction, multiplication, division, or exponentiation are described as *arithmetic assignment statements*. Because FORTRAN is best suited to problems which require arithmetic calculations, these statements are of key importance.

On page 56 the first step in processing the programmer time values was shown as:

HRS = PT1 + PT2 + PT3 + PT4 + PT5

This statement was written to sum the five time values and to make the sum available for the second step in this program's processing. The second step requires an instruction which will calculate the average of the five times. The following statement will calculate that average.

AVE = HRS / 5.0

This statement follows the logical sequence of the program (see the flowchart on page 57) and directs the computer to divide the value stored at location HRS by 5.0. Execution of this statement will, of course, calculate the average time and this value will be stored at a new location having the variable data name AVE. We determined earlier that the five time values totalled 29.5 hours. Division of this total by 5.0 gives an average time of 5.9 hours.

In our example program, we now have read the problem data (programmers' times), summed the times, and computed the average time. The remaining program requirement is to display these results. The next section will discuss the applicable output statements.

FORTRAN Output Statements

Output: FORTRAN Format Statements

A computer can transmit the results of its internal manipulations in several forms. At the direction of the programmer, output may be printed, punched into cards, written on magnetic tape, displayed on a console typewriter, appear on a television screen (known as CRT for Cathode Ray Tube) or in several other forms. One of the most significant forms of output, of course, is computer directed printing on a line printer. To accomplish output printing, the programmer must include in his program both a FORMAT description and a command word, similar to that used for input data.

The rules for preparing FORMAT statements, discussed earlier, apply equally well to the FORMAT specifications for computer output. However, there are a few additional considerations with output.

When directing the computer to display output on a line printer, the programmer must instruct the computer about the exact presentation he desires, just as he had to instruct the computer about the exact form of the input data it would read. This means that the FORMAT statement will have to *describe the placement of each character* that will be printed on a line of output. Each printed line possesses a total of *121 or more character positions* beginning at the left edge of the output paper.

The character line width is an essential consideration when planning the placement of output data on a line, and care must be exercised as this width is actually reduced by one character. The first character space on a printed line is reserved for *carriage control* (discussed on page 131) and *the computer will not print anything in this first position*. In effect, then, the printed line can make use of a *maximum of 120 characters*.[3]

The description of an output line most frequently uses four types of specifications. The *I* specification is used for integer numeric data, the *F* specification for real numeric data, the *H* for written information, and the *X* to indicate spaces. The FORMAT description for a printed output line is different from the FORMAT for input only in that the programmer must now count and describe a line with 120 character spaces rather than a card with 80 columns. The use of I and F specifications is identical for input and output data.

The *H specification*[4] permits the programmer to print any characters which are *not the result of processing activity*. The *letter H identifies* a portion of the printed line as being in the *Hollerith code*.[5] This code is useful for writing headings, captions, and other messages *related* to computed output. The use of the H code requires two essential steps.

1. The programmer *must write out* the printed information in *exactly* the manner which he desires the computer to print it.
2. The programmer must *count* the *exact* number of *spaces* which the Hollerith message will take on the printed line. This count must be given to the computer so that it will be able to recognize the end of the message.

If we refer once again to the programmers' hours example, we would want to identify the figure representing the computed total hours with a caption stating this fact. An appropriate caption would be one which identifies the computed figure as "TOTAL PROGRAMMER PREPARATION TIME". The computer can print this caption if we use the H code. The description would be written as:

33HTOTAL PROGRAMMER PREPARATION TIME

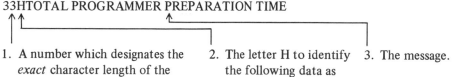

1. A number which designates the *exact* character length of the message. This count *must* *include spaces.*

2. The letter H to identify the following data as a Hollerith message.

3. The message.

Note that the first letter of the message must begin immediately after the letter H, unless the programmer desires a space in this character position. *The H code is one place where spaces become very important in the FORTRAN language.*

The programmer uses the *X specification* when he wishes to skip character spaces along a printed line. With this specification, the computer inserts blank characters in the printed output line. This method of spacing accomplishes the same thing as the allowance of spaces within a Hollerith coded message. However, use of the X specification has two advantages over the H code.

[3] Printer carriage widths vary with different computer systems. Virtually all printers will display a line of 120 characters, though 132 character widths are available on many systems. See the applicable manufacturers' manuals. We will use a 120 character line in this text.
[4] An alternative to the H code in FORTRAN IV is the quote mark ('). Discussion of this alternative appears on page 234.
[5] The Hollerith Code receives its name from Herman Hollerith (see footnote 5 in Chapter 5).

1. It can be used for spacing when no Hollerith coded messages are being used.
2. It provides a shorthand technique for specifying spaces. The H code requires leaving the actual number of blanks within the FORMAT statement.

The X code must be preceded by a numeric value equal to the number of spaces desired. Note that because the first space on any output line is reserved for carriage control instructions, an advisable practice is to begin a printed line 5 characters from the left edge of the paper. This spacing is accomplished by beginning the FORMAT statement with a 5X specification. Of course, any other arbitrary number of spaces could be used.

Suppose we wanted the output line for the programmers' time to appear as in Figure 6.2.

Figure 6.2 Printed Output Showing Total Time

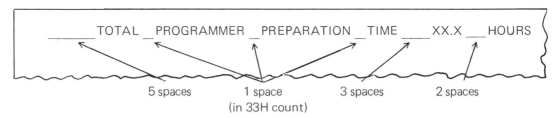

The complete FORMAT statement for this line would be:

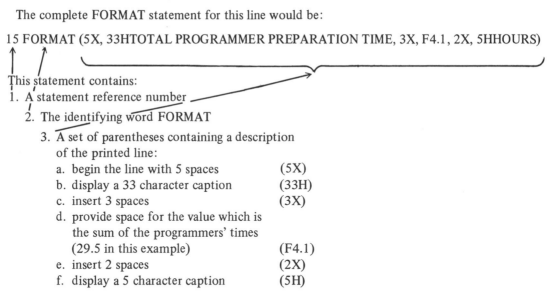

15 FORMAT (5X, 33HTOTAL PROGRAMMER PREPARATION TIME, 3X, F4.1, 2X, 5HHOURS)

This statement contains:
1. A statement reference number
2. The identifying word FORMAT
3. A set of parentheses containing a description of the printed line:
   a. begin the line with 5 spaces   (5X)
   b. display a 33 character caption   (33H)
   c. insert 3 spaces   (3X)
   d. provide space for the value which is the sum of the programmers' times (29.5 in this example) (F4.1)
   e. insert 2 spaces   (2X)
   f. display a 5 character caption   (5H)

An alternative FORMAT statement to print this line is shown below. This FORMAT statement includes the 5 spaces preceding the word TOTAL and the 3 spaces following the word TIME within the first Hollerith specification. In addition, the 2 spaces following the printed numeric value are included within the second Hollerith specification. Note the necessary change in the Hollerith counts. The first H code increased from 33H to 41H and spaces were inserted between the 41H code and the beginning of the word TOTAL. The second H code was increased from 5H to 7H to include the additional 2 spaces.

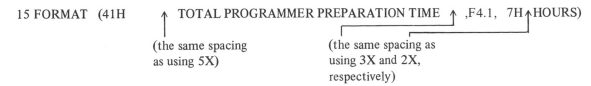

15 FORMAT   (41H   TOTAL PROGRAMMER PREPARATION TIME   ,F4.1, 7H HOURS)

(the same spacing   (the same spacing as
as using 5X)   using 3X and 2X,
                           respectively)

Our example program also calculated a second figure, the average processing time. Display of this figure requires a FORMAT description similar to that for the total processing time. Suppose we want the output line for the average time to look like the line shown in Figure 6.3.

Figure 6.3   Printed Output Showing Total and Average Time

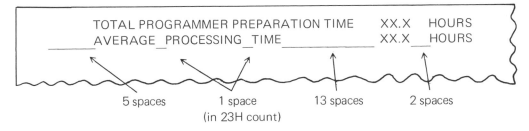

TOTAL PROGRAMMER PREPARATION TIME   XX.X   HOURS
AVERAGE PROCESSING TIME   XX.X   HOURS

5 spaces   1 space   13 spaces   2 spaces
                  (in 23H count)

The FORMAT statement for this second line would be:

20 FORMAT (5X,23HAVERAGE PROCESSING TIME, 13X, F4.1, 2X, 5HHOURS)

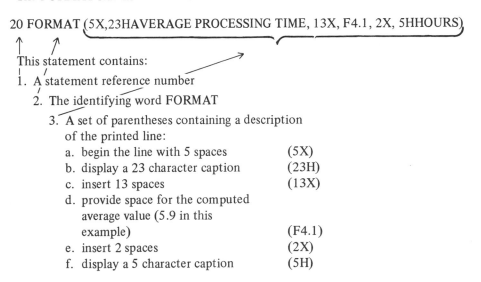

This statement contains:

1. A statement reference number
2. The identifying word FORMAT
3. A set of parentheses containing a description
   of the printed line:
   a. begin the line with 5 spaces   (5X)
   b. display a 23 character caption   (23H)
   c. insert 13 spaces   (13X)
   d. provide space for the computed
      average value (5.9 in this
      example)   (F4.1)
   e. insert 2 spaces   (2X)
   f. display a 5 character caption   (5H)

An alternative FORMAT statement that includes the spacing within the Hollerith codes would be similar to the FORMAT statement shown above.

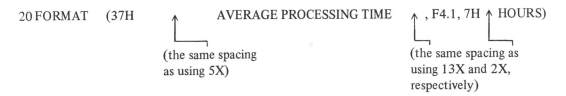

20 FORMAT   (37H   AVERAGE PROCESSING TIME   , F4.1, 7H HOURS)

(the same spacing   (the same spacing as
as using 5X)   using 13X and 2X,
                           respectively)

Output: FORTRAN Write Statements

The FORMAT statements we have discussed indicate the exact construction of the printed lines. The programmer activates the computer system to print lines by using the command word *WRITE*.

The command word WRITE must be followed by two integer numbers which specify an output device number and a FORMAT statement number. Following these reference numbers, the programmer must list any variable data name(s) which contain computed information that he wants to print. The computer will move to the memory location associated with each variable data name, retrieve the numeric quantity stored at that location, and insert it in the printed output line.

In our example of programmers' time, the sum of the five time quantities was located in a memory area specified as HRS. To print this value, the variable name would be inserted in the WRITE statement as follows:

WRITE (6,15) HRS

This statement instructs the computer to WRITE an output line on the line printer (identified by the integer 6)[6] in accordance with FORMAT statement 15. The computer will insert the numeric value, stored in location HRS, in the appropriate place on the printed line.

The output statements for our example appear below. The first statements would be:

15 FORMAT (5X,33HTOTAL PROGRAMMER PREPARATION TIME, 3X, F4.1, 2X, 5HHOURS)

WRITE (6,15) HRS

In this set of statements, the variable name *HRS* would be associated with the FORMAT statement element *F4.1. The value* stored at location HRS will be written in the four character spaces designated as F4.1.

A similar set of output statements are required to print the second line of output. These statements are:

20 FORMAT (5X,23HAVERAGE PROCESSING TIME, 13X, F4.1, 2X, 5HHOURS)

WRITE (6,20) AVE

Again, the FORMAT reference numbers are matched, and the value stored at location *AVE* is inserted in the area described as *F4.1* on the output line. The output function using the WRITE statement is clearly similar to the input function which uses the READ statement. In all cases, the FORMAT statement provides data specifications and the READ/WRITE statements cause execution.

To summarize, the printing of output on the line printer requires the use of two related statements. The FORMAT statement specifies the exact form of the output line and the WRITE statement activates the system to accomplish the printing. The FORMAT statement uses any combinations of I, F, H, and X specifications to describe a line. The WRITE statement must reference the output device and FORMAT statement and state any variable names associated with each I and F specification.

---

[6] Device numbers are likely to vary from installation to installation, as explained in connection with the READ statement. The integer 6 is a fairly common number used to specify the line printer and will be used in this text. Refer to the applicable installation manual.

Exercise 10

1. Prepare FORMAT and WRITE statements so that an output line would appear as follows:
   a. Begin 8 spaces from the left margin.
   b. Print CURRENT QUARTER.
   c. Allot 2 spaces.
   d. Provide two spaces for the integer numeric value corresponding to the current quarter.
   e. Allot 4 spaces.
   f. Print SALES VOLUME.
   g. Allot 2 spaces.
   h. Provide space for a real numeric value which might reach 8 digits with two of the digits being fractional values.

2. Prepare a FORMAT statement for each of the lines shown below. This exercise will require 5 separate FORMAT statements. Interpret the characters in each line as: b = blank spaces, X = numeric values, and . = decimal points or periods.
   a. bbbQUANTITYbbXXXXbbPRICEbb$bXX.XX
   b. bbbbbTHISbISbEXERCISEbNUMBERbXX
   c. bNEGATIVEbITEMSb=bbXXX
   d. bbbbCOSTbISbbXXX.XXbbbANDbRATESbAREbbXX.XXbbXX.XX
   e. bbERRORb-STATEMENTbXXXbISbTOObLARGE

3. Prepare WRITE statements for each of the FORMATs in (2) above. Select any variable names you desire.

4. Identify and correct the errors in the following independent statements.
   a. FORMAT 5X, F6.3, F7.2, F8.0
   b. FORMAT 5X, 6HSUMMATION, F4.0)
   c. WRITE (6,8), X, Y, Z
   d. WRITE (6,9) "PROGRAM ERROR"
   e. WRITE (6,6) ABLE FOX, I=2

Completing the Program

The completion of a FORTRAN program requires the use of two important statements. The *STOP* statement signals the *logical end* of the program. The *END* statement signals the *physical end* of the program. It is important to understand the difference between these statements.

The STOP Statement

A computer will process data until it reaches a logical conclusion to the program. Normally, the *logical end* to processing occurs when all applicable statements have been executed and the computed results have been displayed. A program may have more than one logical end. While most relatively modest programs will have only one logical conclusion, larger programs will usually contain multiple branches which may be taken throughout the program and which will, in turn, lead to one of several logical endings. A simple example of a program having more than one logical ending is a program designed so that it would logically end when (1) the correct processing of data had been completed, or (2) when an error in the data was encountered. While it would always be hoped that correct processing would be accomplished, a logical end to the program would have to be reached when an error condition was encountered.

All programs will have at least one logical end, and this ending is signalled by the STOP statement. When the computer encounters this statement, it will terminate execution. Omission of this statement will result in an error message because the computer will not be able to reach an identifiable termination point in its processing.

The STOP statement is written as the single word:

STOP

The END Statement

The END statement is placed at the *physical end* of the program and will always be the last statement in a program. Further, while a program may have multiple STOP statements, it has only one END statement. This statement tells the computer that there are no more cards in the source program deck and that compilation of this program is complete. The statement is not executed but merely specifies the physical end of the program deck.

The END statement is written as the single word:

END

The Comment Statement and The Comment Card

The FORTRAN language provides the *programmer* with an opportunity to insert his *own comments any place within the program.* It is always advisable to use a comment card to begin a program. This card may contain any information desired. However, the inclusion of the programmer's name, program name, and other appropriate identification is recommended. The computer does *not process* the comment card. The *information on the card is merely reproduced as it is written by the programmer.*

It is important to recognize that *comments* will *appear only within the listing of the FORTRAN program* returned after processing. The assumption that the comments will appear in the computed output is a common error. This is not the case! FORMAT statements are the means for adding comments, captions, headings, and the like to computed output.

The programmer constructs the comment statement by placing a *"C" in the first column* of a punch card. Beginning with column 2 (or any column after 1), any information may be punched in the card. The message should end with column 72, because the computer will not process columns 73 through 80. If one card does not provide enough space for the complete comment, a second, third, or more comment cards may be added. The only requirement is to begin the comment card with a "C" in column 1.

Summary: The Complete Programming Process

We have now covered the complete programming process. The FORTRAN language can perform considerably more complex manipulations than we have demonstrated, and they will be discussed in subsequent sections. The major steps in any program's development, however, remain the same. A good way to summarize the programming process is to review these steps.

Problem Identification and Analysis

Problem identification and analysis involve careful establishment of the processing goals. Recognition must be made of the real problem and not merely a symptom of the problem. This step also involves the analysis needed to design a program which will accomplish the desired data processing.

Flowcharting

The flowchart shown earlier is reproduced below in Figure 6.4 to illustrate this step in the programming process. Once the problem has been identified and analyzed, the flowchart becomes the vehicle for logically expressing the individual instruction steps which will be executed by the computer during processing.

Figure 6.4

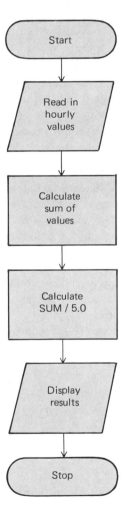

The development and use of flowcharting serve several important functions for the programmer. Of course, the major purpose is to aid in structuring the program steps. In this function, the flowchart enables the programmer to check his logic and make sure that the program will arrive at a logical ending. An important secondary use of the flowchart arises when an initial run of the program indicates that the program has not logically completed processing. By reviewing the flowchart, it is usually possible to discover the logical errors and it provides an opportunity for program redesign. When the program is complete and all errors have been eliminated, the flowchart becomes a valuable piece of program documentation. This documentation is critical to later review of the program when the instruction steps alone would not present an easily understood picture of the program.

Coding the Program

After completing the program flowchart, the programmer should make sure that he has analyzed the problem adequately and that the proposed processing solution has a logical flow from beginning to end. The next step is to write the program instructions. Because the written program will be punched into machine readable cards, a special coding sheet may be used to write the program. This sheet provides the proper guidelines for preparation of the program statements. A program written on a coding sheet for the programmers' times is shown in Figure 6.5. After the coding sheet is prepared, *each line will be punched into one punch card.* The resulting deck of cards will be read, along with the problem data cards, into the computer for processing.

The rules for using coding sheets are very simple. They are as follows:

1. Column 1: used for the letter "C" *only* when a comment card is being prepared.
2. Columns 1-5: used to register reference numbers such as those used with FOR-MAT statements. Reference numbers may appear anywhere in these 5 columns.
3. Column 6: used *only* when the information being written exceeds the available space of one line (that is, runs past column 72). Normally statements will easily fit one line and in this case column 6 remains *blank.* Continuation of the information from a previous card is permitted if a character, other than zero, is placed in column 6. The number of continuation lines permitted varies with computer systems, though a maximum of either 10 or 20 continuation lines is most common. (Refer to the applicable manufacturer's manual.)
4. Columns 7-72: used to write the FORTRAN statements.
5. Columns 73-80: ignored by the compiler and may be used for any non-program purpose, such as program name or sequence numbering, or they may be left blank.
6. Note that *blanks are ignored by the computer, except in the case of the H code in FORMAT statements,* and therefore instructions may be written without using any spacing. It is a good practice to use spaces, however, as rereading programs is usually necessary and spacing makes this task much more pleasant.

Punching the Program

The coding form prepared in the previous step is used as the guide in keypunching the FORTRAN program. The punching step involves conversion of each line on the coding form into an equivalent instruction line in punch card form. The punch card should contain the same characters as shown on the coding form, and the characters should be punched in the same columns indicated by the coding form.

In the example coded on the coding sheet in Figure 6.5, both the program and data were written. When these instructions and data are punched, a deck of cards

Figure 6.5   FORTRAN Coding Form

IBM   Form X28-7327-4
                                               Printed in U.S.A.

FORTRAN CODING FORM

Program	PGMER AVERAGE TIME	Punching Instructions		Page	of
		Graphic	Card Form #		Identification
Programmer	P. T. MAY	Date	Punch		73 80

C FOR COMMENT

FORTRAN STATEMENT

```
C *** SAMPLE PROGRAM - P.T. MAY ***
C
C CALCULATION OF PROGRAMMER AVERAGE PREPARATION TIME
C

   50 FORMAT (5F4.1)
   15 FORMAT (5X,33HTOTAL PROGRAMMER PREPARATION TIME,3X,F4.1,
      12X,5HHOURS)
   20 FORMAT (5X,23HAVERAGE PROCESSING TIME,13X,F4.1,2X,5HHOURS)

      READ (5,50) PT1,PT2,PT3,PT4,PT5
      HRS = PT1 + PT2 + PT3 + PT4 + PT5
      AVE = HRS/5.0
      WRITE (6,15) HRS
      WRITE (6,20) AVE

      STOP
      END

07.504.310.805.601.3
```

Note: For illustrative purposes, the data card used to enter the hourly data is shown as the last line on the coding form. This is not a requirement of FORTRAN, although the coding form is convenient for this use.

would be produced as shown in Figure 6.6. In order to actually run the program deck, several additional cards are also required. These additional cards are called control cards and transmit required data to the operating system. A brief discussion of these cards is given on page 72 but, to illustrate the makeup of a complete program deck, they are shown here as the cards with a $ in column 1.

Running the Program

The program and data deck prepared in the previous step are ready to be run on the computing system. Submission of the program deck will result in having the cards read, the FORTRAN instructions compiled, and a listing printed. The listing is shown in Program 6.1 and includes a line-by-line reproduction of the FORTRAN instructions as well as the computed problem solution.

Program 6.1 contains no error diagnostic messages. Program 6.2 has several errors introduced to illustrate the manner in which the error messages are printed. Note that the FORTRAN instructions are listed line-by-line and that error messages either follow the statement containing the error or are listed at the bottom of the

Figure 6.6 Punched Card Program Deck Punched from FORTRAN Coding Form

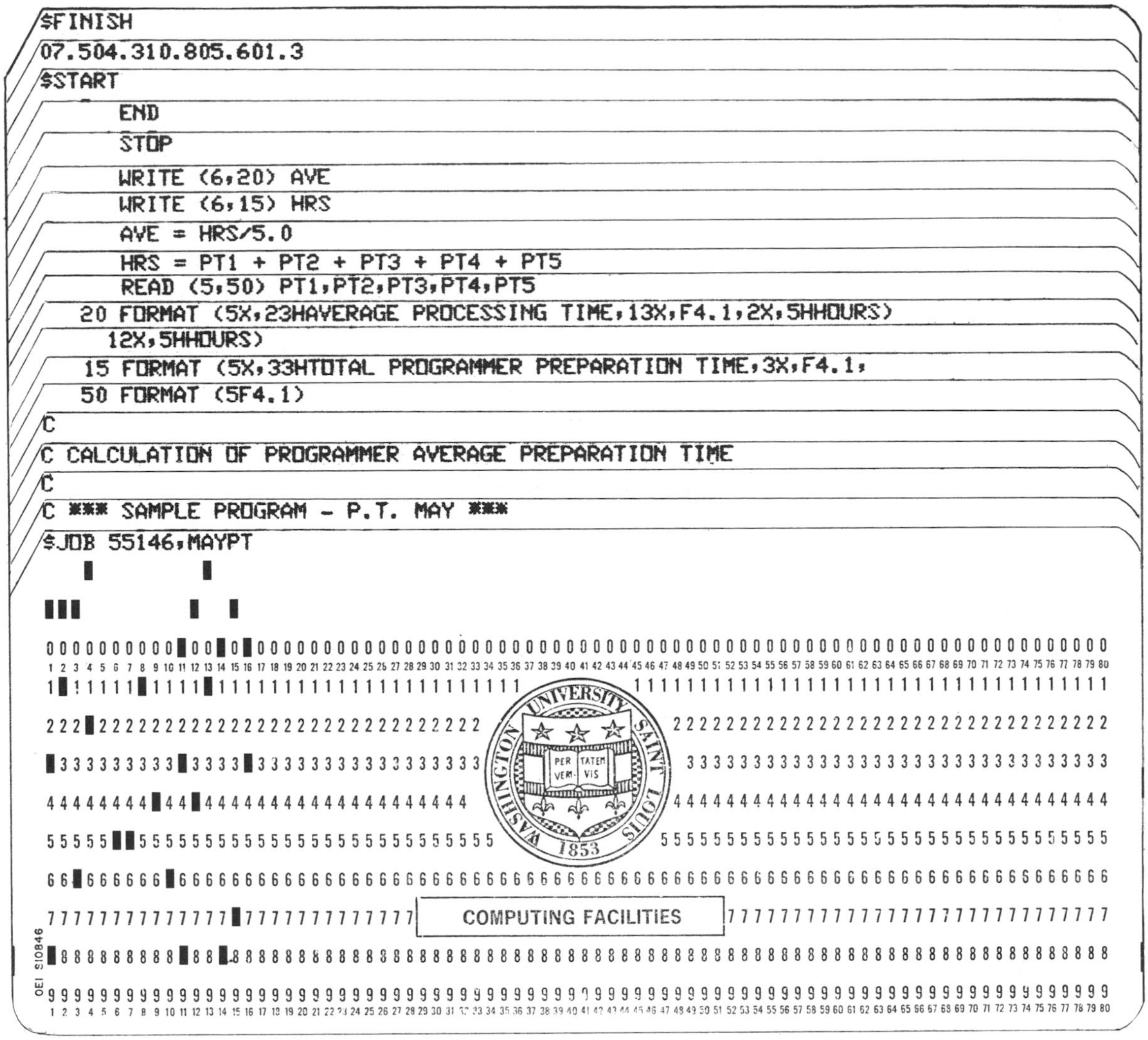
$FINISH
07.504.310.805.601.3
$START
END
STOP
WRITE (6,20) AVE
WRITE (6,15) HRS
AVE = HRS/5.0
HRS = PT1 + PT2 + PT3 + PT4 + PT5
READ (5,50) PT1,PT2,PT3,PT4,PT5
20 FORMAT (5X,23HAVERAGE PROCESSING TIME,13X,F4.1,2X,5HHOURS)
12X,5HHOURS)
15 FORMAT (5X,33HTOTAL PROGRAMMER PREPARATION TIME,3X,F4.1,
50 FORMAT (5F4.1)
C
C CALCULATION OF PROGRAMMER AVERAGE PREPARATION TIME
C
C *** SAMPLE PROGRAM - P.T. MAY ***
$JOB 55146,MAYPT
WASHINGTON UNIVERSITY SAINT LOUIS
PER VERITATEM VIS
1853
COMPUTING FACILITIES
OEI S10846

Note: This deck of program cards corresponds directly with the coding form shown in Figure 6.5. One card is punched for each line used on the coding form. No cards are included for blank lines. The order of the cards, from the beginning to the end of the deck, matches the order of the lines, from top to bottom, on the coding form.

program with a reference to the statement which caused the error. The compiler has automatically numbered the statements on the left-hand side of the program. These numbers are different from the statement reference numbers provided by the programmer.

Error diagnostics will vary somewhat among installations and compilers, but the essential nature of the messages does not change. They are an immeasurable aid to debugging a program and, while they frequently are frustrating to receive, the task of correcting errors would be nearly unmanageable without these messages.

The process of program preparation will remain essentially identical to that just described, regardless of the relative computational complexity. The remaining sec-

Program 6.1   Error-free Program

```
      $JOB  55146,MAYPT
      C
      C *** SAMPLE PROGRAM - P.T. MAY ***
      C
      C CALCULATION OF PROGRAMMER AVERAGE PREPARATION TIME
      C
 1        50 FORMAT (5F4.1)
 2        15 FORMAT (5X,33HTOTAL PROGRAMMER PREPARATION TIME,3X,F4.1,
             12X,5HHOURS)
 3        20 FORMAT (5X,23HAVERAGE PROCESSING TIME,13X,F4.1,2X,5HHOURS)
 4           READ (5,50) PT1,PT2,PT3,PT4,PT5
 5           HRS = PT1 + PT2 + PT3 + PT4 + PT5
 6           AVE = HRS/5.0
 7           WRITE (6,15) HRS
 8           WRITE (6,20) AVE
 9           STOP
10           END


      $START
TOTAL PROGRAMMER PREPARATION TIME    29.5   HOURS
AVERAGE PROCESSING TIME               5.9   HOURS
```

Program 6.2   Illustration of Program Error Messages

```
          $JOB  55146,MAYPT
          C
          C *** SAMPLE PROGRAM - P.T. MAY ***
          C
          C CALCULATION OF PROGRAMMER AVERAGE PREPARATION TIME
          C
 1            50 FORMAT (5F4.1)
 2            15 FORMAT (5X,33HTOTAL PROGRAMMER PREPARATION TIME,3X,F4.1,
                 12X,5HHOURS)
 3               FORMAT (5X,23HAVERAGE PROCESSING TIME,13X,F4.1,2X,5HHOURS)
**WARNING**      NO STATEMENT NUMBER ON FORMAT STATEMENT
 4               READ (5,50) PT1,PT2,PT3,PT4,PT5
 5               HRS = PT1 + PT2 + PT3 + PT4 + PT5
 6               AVE = HRS/5.0
 7               WRITE (6,15) HRS
 8               WRITE (6,20) AVE
 9               STOP
**WARNING**      MISSING END STATEMENT;END STATEMENT GENERATED
***ERROR***      MISSING FORMAT STATEMENT     20 USED IN LINE        8


          $START
```

tions of this text will explore the variety of features available in the FORTRAN language. The majority of these features either will add greater flexibility in designing programs or will provide an increase in computing power. One objective in programming is to transfer as much computing effort as possible to the processing system. To accomplish this, the preparation of a program should result in the most efficient use of processing time and memory space.

Basic Principles of Systems Control and Control Cards

This section will briefly cover the principles of systems control essential to the execution of a FORTRAN program. A more detailed explanation appears in Appendix A.

Systems Control

All computing systems require the programmer to specify certain information to the system, in addition to submitting his FORTRAN program. This information is used in controlling the computing system to assure that each job is accounted for properly, that the FORTRAN program is compiled, that correct input/output devices are ready for use, that adequate memory is available, and so forth.

The principles of control are quite similar among computing systems. However, the complexity of computing systems has resulted in the development of extensive control programs called *operating systems*. Each operating system has its own special requirements, but the following example, based on the IBM 360 Operating System, will demonstrate the basic systems control principles.

Control specifications are transmitted to an operating system via punch cards. The schematic drawing in Figure 6.7 illustrates the control cards necessary to run a FORTRAN program which has card input and printed output. In this system, all control cards are begun either with double slashes (//) or a slash-asterisk combination (/*).

The schematic drawing shows seven control cards, two of which are identical. An example of each type of card and its purpose is explained below.

Figure 6.7   Schematic Drawing Illustrating System Control Cards for a FORTRAN Program

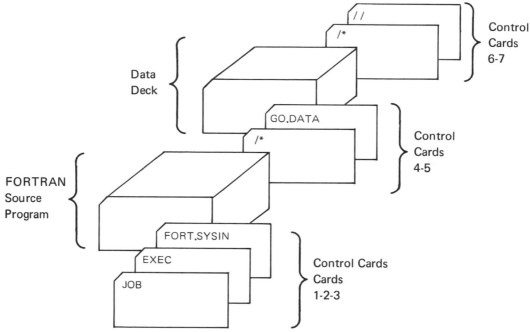

Control Card 1: JOB Card

//TESTPGM   JOB   (55940,SEVR),'MAY PT'

jobname   card   accounting   programmer's name
            type   information   (optional)

A JOB card identifies the program as a new job to the system, specifies the job name, conveys certain information to account for the job, and gives certain optional information, such as the programmer's name.

Control Card 2: EXEC Card

//   EXEC   FORTGGO

       card   procedure to be
       type   executed

The EXEC card indicates which system procedure the operating system is to execute. This control card's specifications trigger the execution of a program, in the operating system, which brings the "G" level compiler into memory (FORTG) and accomplishes compilation of the FORTRAN source program.

The GO portion of the procedure specification indicates to the operating system that, after compilation is complete, the system should begin processing the problem data cards (that is, GO!).

Control Card 3: FORT.SYSIN Card

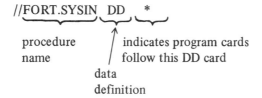

//FORT.SYSIN DD   *

procedure   indicates program cards
name   follow this DD card
            data
            definition

This card calls on the operating system to retrieve a procedure which is stored (that is, catalogued) in the system's memory. This procedure describes several system characteristics, such as record size, record form, and the like about the FORTRAN program which follows this card.

Control Card 4: Delimiter Card

/*

delimiter
symbol

The FORTRAN source program is called a data set. Each data set is defined in a DD card (FORT.SYSIN DD *) and must be followed by a delimiter card. This card indicates the end of the data set to the operating system. When the delimiter is sensed, control is returned to the operating system.

Control Card 5: GO.DATA Card

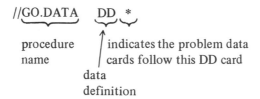

//GO.DATA   DD *

procedure   │ indicates the problem data
name   │ cards follow this DD card
        data
        definition

This card indicates that the data cards are to be read according to the specifications in the catalogued procedure GO.DATA. The purpose of this procedure is similar to the FORT SYSIN but applies to the problem data cards. They are now defined as a second data set.

Control Card 6: Delimiter Card

/*

delimiter
symbol

This delimiter card marks the end of the problem data cards for the operating system. The data cards are a second data set and must be followed by a delimiter card. Control is returned to the operating system.

Control Card 7: Null Card

//

null
symbol

This statement indicates the end of the entire job for the operating system. Control resides with the operating system, and, if another program follows this one, it will be processed.

WATFIV—A Simple System Control Alternative

The system control specifications discussed in the previous section have a simple alternative. This alternative makes use of a special compiler called WATFIV. The WATFIV compiler is extremely fast, produces excellent, clear diagnostic messages, and requires very simple control card specifications. This compiler was developed at the University of Waterloo (Canada) for the FORTRAN IV langauge. Hence the name WATFIV.

This compiler is especially appropriate for instructional work in learning FORTRAN and for any initial program development. However, for actual production computing, computing equipment manufacturers normally have compilers which provide more efficient object codes than WATFIV. The WATFIV compiler works under the direction of the operating system but is stored in the computer's main memory (core). This makes the use of the compiler extremely fast and reduces turnaround times to a minimum. The diagnostic messages are superior to most manufacturers' compilers. Therefore, debugging programs is aided considerably.

The WATFIV compiler has some limitations in that it does consume core, is often limited to card-to-printer input/output, and does not support a few of the FORTRAN IV features. On balance, however, it is a superior compiler for basic programming. The sample program shown on page 71 was executed using the WATFIV compiler. The number of required control cards is only three, as opposed to seven under the operating system. The following schematic drawing in Figure 6.8 illustrates the WATFIV control cards. Each card is explained following the illustration.

Figure 6.8   Schematic Drawing Illustrating WATFIV System Control Cards

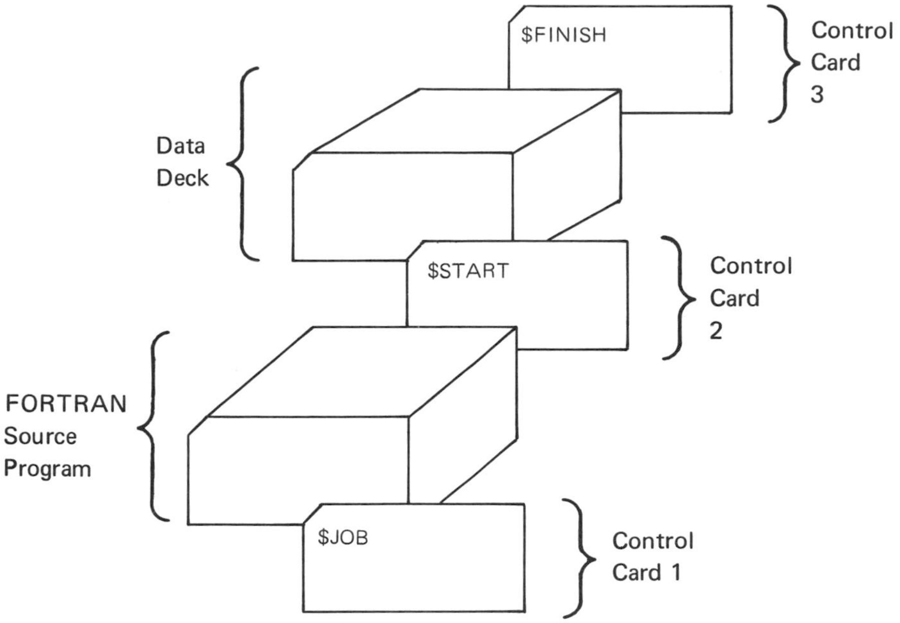

All control cards under WATFIV begin with a dollar sign ($). This sign is followed by either JOB, START, or FINISH. These are special control instructions to the operating system and trigger the use of the WATFIV compiler. Following compilation, the program is executed.

Card 1: JOB Card

$JOB   55146,MAYPT

accounting information
and other options

job and procedure indentifier to
indicate use of the WATFIV compiler

The purpose of this card is to identify the job to the system and to invoke use of the WATFIV compiler. The options available include a wide range of items in addition to those shown above.

Card 2: START Card

$START

identifies the beginning of the
execution step (that is, GO step) for
the program

The START card signals the operating system to begin execution of the object program. Any problem data cards used by the FORTRAN program follow this START card.

Card 3: FINISH Card

$FINISH

identifies completion
of the program

This card causes the operating system to terminate execution of the program. It serves a purpose similar to the delimiter and null statements discussed earlier.

Questions

1. What is the definition of an assignment statement?
2. What is the purpose of an equal sign (=) in an assignment statement?
3. What is the difference between an expression and a statement?
4. List the FORTRAN arithmetic operators and define the function of each.
5. What is an undefined variable data name? How can this condition be avoided?
6. What is the difference between input and output FORMAT statements?
7. What meaning does each of the following codes have in a FORMAT statement?
   a. I   b. H   c. X   d. F
8. What is the difference in purpose served by the STOP and END statements?
9. What is a comment card, and where will it be printed?
10. What use is made of the following columns on a coding form?
    a.   Columns 1-5
    b.   Column 6
    c.   Columns 7-72
    d.   Columns 73-80
11. Explain how the columns on a coding form relate to the columns on a punch card.
12. How many punch cards are prepared for each line on a coding form?
13. How is a line continued when it runs over column 72 on a coding form?
14. What are diagnostics? When do they appear?
15. Explain the function of control cards.

7
Complex Expressions and Non-sequential Control

The FORTRAN language provides for considerably more flexibility than indicated in Chapters 5 and 6. This chapter will begin to explore some of the FORTRAN features which provide the programmer with greater computing power and program flexibility.

FORTRAN Expressions

FORTRAN expressions do not have to be constructed as simply as the addition and division operations illustrated in Chapter 6, and, in fact, the complexity of many problem requirements could not be handled by such basic expressions. When you increase the complexity of program expressions, however, you must comply with several rules of statement construction.

An expression is any *combination* of *variable data names* and/or *constants* that are *connected* by FORTRAN operators and that appear on the *right side of the equal sign*. The FORTRAN language requires substantial care in the construction of a program's expressions. A computer processes an expression by executing the arithmetic operators in the following order:

1. exponentiation[1]
2. either multiplication or division in the order in which they are found when moving from left to right through the expression
3. either addition or subtraction in the order in which they are found when moving from left to right through the expression

The programmer can *modify* the order of processing *only* through the use of *parentheses*. The computer manipulates variable names and/or constants found within parentheses *prior* to processing the remainder of the expression. The variable names and constants within parentheses are also processed in the order given above, and, when a set of parentheses itself contains parentheses, the expression within the innermost set is processed first.

As an example of the use of parentheses and the order of processing, assume that the following variable names and values are stored in computer memory:

A = 3.   B = 2.   C = 10.

[1] Exponentiation occurs from *right to left* when consecutive operations are written (that is, X ** 3 ** 2 ** 5).

Compare the result from processing the following four statements with the single statement given below. Note that, when four statements are used, intermediate values are temporarily stored in SUM, TOT, and TOT2 so that these values will be available in later computations.

Statements	Explanation	
1 SUM = A * B	Multiply 3. × 2.	Answer of 6.0
2 TOT = C - 8.5	Subtract 10. - 8.5	Answer of 1.5
3 TOT2 = SUM / TOT	Divide 6. / 1.5	Answer of 4.0
4 SQ = TOT2 ** 2	Exponentiate 4.^{2}	Answer of 16.0

These four steps could be written as a single expression with the result stored in location SQ.

SQ = A * B / C - 8.5 ** 2

However, writing the statement in this form would *not* accomplish the desired result because of the processing rules followed by the computer. *Without modification,* the computer would execute the single statement as:

1.	square 8.5, then	Answer of 72.25
2.	multiply A and B, then	Answer of 6.0
3.	divide the result of step 2 by C, then	Answer of .6
4.	subtract step 1 from step 3	Answer of -71.65

This is clearly *not* what was intended!

Modification of the *expression with parentheses* will eliminate the errors inherent in writing a complex expression without parentheses. The computer will process all elements *within parentheses first* and then return to the processing order given above. To write the previous four statements as one, parentheses should be used as follows:

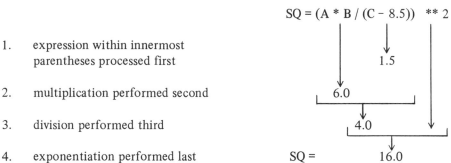

1. expression within innermost parentheses processed first

2. multiplication performed second

3. division performed third

4. exponentiation performed last

The following illustration shows the relationship between the set of four individual statements and the single statement. When the single statement is executed, any necessary intermediate values are automatically computed and temporarily stored by the computer.

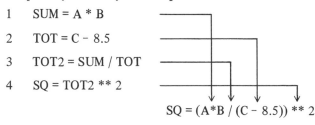

1   SUM = A * B

2   TOT = C - 8.5

3   TOT2 = SUM / TOT

4   SQ = TOT2 ** 2

SQ = (A*B / (C - 8.5)) ** 2

This example illustrates the order of processing when one set of parentheses is contained within another set(s) of parentheses (referred to as nesting). The computer processes the expression within the innermost parentheses first. Processing then continues with the next outer parentheses. Execution of succeeding outer parentheses continues until the outermost set of parentheses are processed.

When you have a statement containing a complex series of operations, it is a good practice to use many pairs of parentheses to ensure the proper processing of data. If unnecessary parentheses are used, they are ignored by the compiler when converting statements to object code.

The programmer must adhere to a few simple rules when constructing expressions in the FORTRAN language. These rules are:

1. *No two arithmetic operators* may be placed next to each other, for example, /*. (Exponentiation does not violate this rule. The compiler is designed to handle two asterisks as exponentiation.)

Invalid	Valid
N = J / − K	N = J / (−K)
A = X * − Y + B	A = X * (−Y) + B

2. All variable names and constants within an expression *must* be separated by an arithmetic operator. The implied multiplication of algebra is not allowed in FORTRAN.

Invalid	Valid
M = JN + K	M = J * N + K
B = CD	B = C * D
(assuming J, N, C, and D	
are different variable names)	

3. The variable names and constants used within an expression preferably should be of the *same mode*. Some computers will not process "mixed mode" expressions, and computers which will process mixed mode expressions must go through an inefficient conversion process changing all elements in the expression to the same mode before execution.

Invalid	Valid
J = A / N	J = IA / N
C = E * K	C = E * AK

4. No more than *one variable data name* may be placed to the *left* of an *equal sign*. That variable name, however, does not have to be in the same mode as the variables and constants appearing to the right of the equal sign. The mode of the variable name on the *left* of the equal sign determines the mode of the stored result.

Invalid	Valid
J / K = A	A = J / K (result stored in real mode)
A * B = K	K = A * B (result stored in integer mode)
G + H = Y + Z	(depends on purpose of computation)

5. *No numeric quantities* may be placed to the *left* of the *equal sign*. The purpose of a FORTRAN statement is to calculate or manipulate values as directed by the expression appearing on the right side of the equal sign and to place the resulting value at the location designated by the variable name written to the left of the equal sign.

Invalid	Valid
10. = X	X = 10
A + 5.3 = B	B = A + 5.3

6. *No spaces* are *required* within a written expression or statement. However, for the programmer's ease in reading, it is advisable to insert spaces throughout the statement. Both of the following statements are valid.

N = J + M ** 3 / (L – 4)
N=J+M**3/(L–4)

To summarize, the elements necessary for the construction of a written FORTRAN program instruction are:

1. a variable data name to the left of the equal sign
2. an equal sign
3. an expression to the right of the equal sign—and this expression may contain any of the following:
   a. a single variable data name, and/or
   b. a single constant, or
   c. any combination of variable names and constants provided that:
      (1) preferably they are all of the same data mode,
      (2) they are separated by any of the following symbols:

      + for addition
      – for subtraction,
      * for multiplication,
      / for division,
      ** for exponentiation, and

      (3) parentheses are used to modify the order of arithmetic operations.

Exercise 11

1. Write a separate FORTRAN arithmetic statement for each of the following algebraic equations.

a. $s = a + 2r^2$

b. $h = \dfrac{a}{b + 4s^2}$

c. $n = \dfrac{k^3}{a + b} + 2$

d. $b = b(b + cd) - (sc - wd)$

e. $y = .0015 \left(\dfrac{p + am}{p - am} \right)$

f. $c = -i + j$

g. $t = a + \left(\dfrac{bc}{d} \right) + m^2 - gh$

h. $i = \dfrac{c(a + b)}{d} + e^5 \left(\dfrac{a + b}{c} \right)$

2. Take each of the following sets of four FORTRAN statements and rewrite each set into a single statement.

a. 1 A = D+R   3 C = B**2
    2 B = A*E   4 TOT = C/G

b. 1   R = A/B   3   T = S**3
    2   S = R**2+Q*U   4   ANS = T+3.145−Z*(W/X)

Dangers in FORTRAN Arithmetic

The use of parentheses within an expression can be critical to the accomplishment of accurate processing. For instance, if we were to convert the following algebraic equation into a FORTRAN statement, we could easily write the statement incorrectly. Only through the use of parentheses can we instruct the computer to handle the variables in the correct order.

Algebraic Equation	Incorrect Statement	Correct Statement
$xyz = x - \left(\dfrac{y^2}{z}\right)^3$	XYZ = X − Y**2/Z**3	XYZ = X − (Y**2/Z)**3

Two other arithmetic errors, frequently encountered when learning FORTRAN, present a danger to all programmers unless they exercise care in constructing statements. The first danger relates to the mode change when moving across the equal sign, and the second danger involves the computer's handling of integer arithmetic.

Changing Modes and the Equal Sign

The computer will execute arithmetic statements in either the real or integer mode as indicated in the expression given to the right of the equal sign. A warning was given earlier to avoid the condition of "mixed modes" within any one expression. It is entirely appropriate, however, to change the mode of an expression's computed result by writing a variable name of the *opposite* mode on the left of the equal sign. This does not cause a mixed code condition. The processor will routinely store the computed value in the mode of the variable name appearing to the left of the equal sign. The following two examples are valid statements.

(1)   INT = AMT * RATE   (2)   VALUE = NUM * KOST

The danger in each of these cases is that the computed values will be stored without recognition of the possible loss of accuracy in their manipulation. Suppose that the values of AMT and RATE were $500.00 and .075 before execution of the first example. Multiplication of these two amounts results in a computed value of $37.50 (500.00 × .075). The value 37.50 (dollar signs are not carried internally by the computer) is in the real mode because the variables begin with A and R. Note, however, that the location INT, where storage is to take place, is an integer variable (begins with I). When the computer takes 37.50 and moves *across* the equal sign, to store this value at location INT, it will drop, or truncate, the fractional value .50, *without rounding,* and store 37 at location INT. Obviously, a danger in FORTRAN arithmetic is the loss of values when care is not taken to name storage locations in the correct mode.

A slightly different danger is encountered in the second example. Suppose that the values of NUM and KOST were supposed to be 100 and $27, respectively. Execution of the example containing these variables results in a computed amount of 2700 (100 × 27) represented internally as an integer number. Movement across the equal sign to store the computed amount at location VALUE would change the 2700 from the integer to the real mode. Hence, it would be stored as 2700. and be associated with a decimal point. In this second case, there was no loss of value but if it was intended that the computed value remain in the integer mode, this statement would violate that intention. You can avoid this type of danger only by keeping the FORTRAN modes on both sides of the equal sign in mind.

Truncation and Integer Arithmetic

There is a great danger that some values may be lost when the computer is instructed to *divide* values which are stored in the integer mode. These values are the fractional amounts which result from dividing numbers which are not even multiples of each other. This problem does not exist in the real mode because it is specifically designed to handle fractional values. In the integer mode, the execution of addition, subtraction, and multiplication presents no danger, but consider the following illustration of division:

I = 800
J = 9
K = I / J

Execution of these three statements would result in storage of the value 88 in location K. The division of 800 by 9 results in a remainder of .88888+, but when performed in the FORTRAN integer mode any fractional value is *immediately truncated without any rounding*. This characteristic of the integer mode requires extreme caution on the part of the programmer to avoid the unintentional loss of values.

Truncation will *not* be compensated for by changing the third statement, above, to A = I / J. This type of statement would result only in the storage of 88. (that is, it changes the computed value to the real mode), because truncation takes place *prior* to the storage of the result.

It is clear that the programmer must be alert to possible problems arising from these dangers, and he must carefully prepare program statements which will avoid them.

Exercise 12

1. Calculate the resulting values from each of the following independent arithmetic statements. Prior to calculating each result, assume that the statement variables have the following values:

A = 4.5   I = 4
B = 3.0   J = 3
C = 1.6   K = 1

a. L = I/J   L = _____   i. I = I*2   I = _____
b. M = J*K   M = _____   j. C = C+1.   C = _____
c. N = K-I   N = _____   k. K = J**3   K = _____
d. D = C*A   D = _____   l. H = A*B**3   H = _____
e. E = B/C   E = _____   m. Z = B/2.*A+C/A   Z = _____
f. H = C-A   H = _____   n. W = A**2/B**3   W = _____
g. A = I+5/J   A = _____   o. X = B+C-A**4   X = _____
h. M = A/B   M = _____   p. G = (J+K)**2/5   G = _____

2. Circle the following FORTRAN arithmetic statements which are invalid and state why they are invalid.
   a. IA = M2 + J
   b. A + 3.0 = B*C
   c. W = I+−D
   d. G = G+G
   e. 4 = I+K
   f. L = K**2/M**2 −L
   g. DOLLARS = BILLS+HALVS+QTRS+DIMES+NICKL+PENY
   h. W = W

Non-sequential Control

Sequential processing of FORTRAN statements results from a built-in characteristic of computers. This characteristic causes the processor to execute instructions in the same order in which they are written, unless a specific command is given to deviate from the sequence. The most frequent cause of a shift from sequential to non-sequential processing is in response to a comparison (that is, a decision). The ability to instruct a computer to compare values, and subsequently decide what action to take as a result of this comparison, provides the programmer with a powerful dimension of control. The following section will examine some programming control measures included in the FORTRAN language.

Arithmetic IF Statement

One control technique available to the programmer is exercised through the use of the arithmetic IF statement.[2] This statement directs the computer to *test a computed quantity against the value of zero*. The result of this test will be (1) negative (less than zero), or (2) equal to zero, or (3) positive (greater than zero). The key element in using this control statement is the ability to have the computer compare a quantity with the value zero. The result of this comparison will give the computer its clue for selecting the next FORTRAN statement to execute. Consider the following example. Suppose a company markets three different products and has a computer program which reads punched cards containing the product identification (punched as 1, 2, or 3 in column 1) and the number of units sold (columns 2-7). The program tests each card to determine the product number recorded in column one and then transfers to an appropriate statement to compute the sales value of the units sold.

The flowchart in Figure 7.1 and the program segment (Program 7.1) illustrate the use of an arithmetic IF statement to transfer control to the correct pricing statement.

After the computer has made the comparison, it is directed (controlled) to the next executable program step. This next step does not have to follow sequentially the program statement which directed the comparison. The programmer has the ability to instruct the computer to move to any one of three program statements. Of course, these three statements are related to the three possible results from the comparison. The program is thereby provided with a three pronged choice resulting from the comparison. Due to this characteristic, the IF statement is referred to as a

[2] FORTRAN supports another IF statement called the logical IF. This second IF statement returns a binary result (true or false) from its test. The logical IF is discussed in Chapter 10.

*Figure 7.1   Partial Flowchart Illustrating the Arithmetic
IF Statement*

Program 7.1

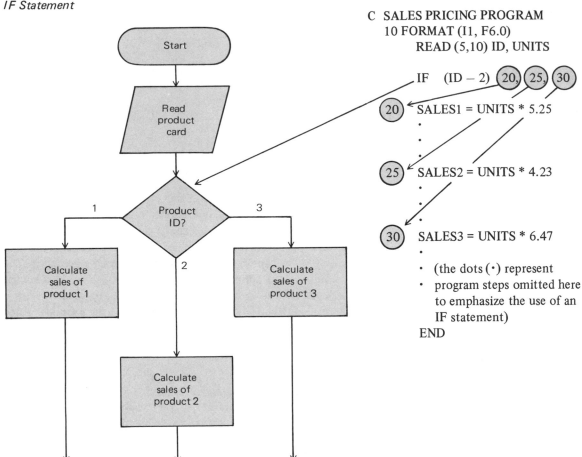

C   SALES PRICING PROGRAM
10 FORMAT (I1, F6.0)
    READ (5,10) ID, UNITS

IF   (ID − 2) 20, 25, 30

20   SALES1 = UNITS * 5.25
    .
    .
    .
25   SALES2 = UNITS * 4.23
    .
    .
    .
30   SALES3 = UNITS * 6.47

    • (the dots (·) represent
    • program steps omitted here
       to emphasize the use of an
       IF statement)
END

conditional branch. In Program 7.1, instruction 20 will be executed if there is a negative result, instruction 25 will be executed if the answer is zero, and instruction 30 will be executed if the comparison produces a positive answer (the statement numbers were arbitrarily chosen in this example).

The construction of an arithmetic IF statement is quite simple. The IF statement in the example was written as:

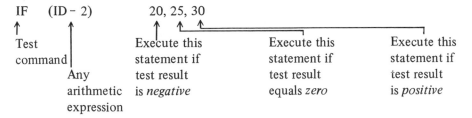

The IF statement contains only three basic elements: (1) the test command word *IF,* (2) any legal *arithmetic expression* (which may be a single variable name), and (3) *three integer numbers* which are the reference numbers of executable statements elsewhere in the program. When the computer encounters an IF statement, it executes the expression within parentheses and compares the result to zero. The example happened to use subtraction in the test expression. The expression could have been any other combination of constants and/or variable data names such as:

IF (TOTAL) 10,20,30   or   IF (NUM*K/4) 40,50,60

Table 7.1 explains how the comparison of ID and −2, in the example, results in a statement choice. The table also illustrates why the value of ID was compared to a value of −2. The use of −2 forced a result which, given the numbers that were read-in, had to be either negative, zero, or positive.

Table 7.1 Optional Branches from Execution of the Arithmetic IF in Figure 7.1

When ID has a value of:	And ID is compared to:	The computed value will be either:	The computed value compared to zero will indicate:	Therefore, the computer selects program statement:
1	−2	−1	−	20
2	−2	0	=	25
3	−2	1	+	30

The use of an IF statement is a powerful programming tool. This test enables the programmer to direct the program to a *maximum* of three statements. If it happens that the programmer desires the computer to select the same statement with two of the three conditions, he may repeat statement numbers. It is essential, however, to have three statement numbers follow the parentheses, even though two of the numbers may be identical. The two choice option using the arithmetic IF statement is illustrated in the following three examples.

IF (L − 10) 100,100,110
IF (VAL * TWO) 120,150,150
IF (ABC ** 2 − XYZ) 90,80,90

A Word of Caution. The first statement following an arithmetic IF statement must have a reference number or the computer will never be able to reach the statement. The number does not have to be one appearing in the IF statement although this is frequently the case.

Also, when an IF statement contains a long expression, too cumbersome to write within the parentheses, it may be more efficient to execute the expression in a statement prior to the IF statement and to set the result of the calculation equal to a single variable. Then, the single variable may be used in the IF statement. For example,

TOT = A * R / S ** 2 − W * W ** 2 − 3.4
IF (TOT) 75,76,77

The calculation of TOT could have been placed within the IF statement but was more efficiently handled in two separate statements.

To summarize, the IF statement achieves the following action:

1. The command word IF indicates to the computer that it must make a comparison.
2. The parentheses provide for specifying any FORTRAN arithmetic expression. The expression may take the following forms:
   a. A single variable data name placed within the parentheses. The computer will compare the value stored at this single named location to zero.
   b. Any properly written arithmetic expression placed within the parentheses. This means that addition, subtraction, multiplication, division and exponentiation, or any combinations of these, are permissible. The calculated result will be compared to zero. (Try not to mix modes in the arithmetic expression.)
3. The three numbers following the parentheses (separated by commas) designate any three FORTRAN statements to which the computer can transfer for subsequent processing. The selected statements are identified by their reference numbers.

Exercise 13

What are the errors (if any) in the following IF statements? Explain the errors and rewrite the statements in the correct form.

1. IF (A) 10,20   6. IF (D) 47,47,47
2. IF I * J) 22,22,23   7. IF (A ** 3 / B / (C – D) 50,51,50
3. IF (A * B / C) 30,30,31   8. IF (R – N 55, 56, 57,
4. IF (1 – A) 41,42,43   9. IF (I **) 60,62,64
5. IF (I – .9),44,45,46   10. IF (TOT – SUB * 1) 65,70,80

GO TO Statement

A second control statement allows the programmer to instruct the computer to move to any statement in the program *without qualification*. This statement does precisely what its name implies—it tells the computer to GO TO a specific statement. This type of transfer is referred to as *unconditional branching*. Preparation of this statement requires the use of the words GO TO followed by a single integer number which identifies the next statement that the computer will execute, such as GO TO 76.

For example, suppose that a program is designed to read a card, process the data, and then return to the READ statement to enter a new card. The computer should be unconditionally instructed to return to the READ statement after the processing steps are completed. The following illustration reproduces only the essential steps in this process:

```
   75 FORMAT (F12.5, I2, F6.1)
→ 76 READ (5,75) A,K,B
   ·
   · (additional processing steps)
   ·
   GO TO 76
   ·
   ·
   ·

   END
```

In this illustration, the dots (·) represent processing statements which are not essential to the explanation of the GO TO control statement. Note that after the completion of several processing steps, the *GO TO 76* statement will *unconditionally* return the computer to the READ statement. The use of the number 76 in the GO TO statement provides the necessary cross-reference to guide the computer to the next statement it will process.

For another example, refer to the SALES PRICING PROGRAM (Program 7.1). Suppose that, following each of the processing segments, we want the program to branch back to the READ statement. The program will need three GO TO statements to accomplish this branching as shown in the amended illustration in Figure 7.2 and Program 7.2. Three GO TO statements are necessary because the

Figure 7.2   Amended Flowchart Illustrating Arithmetic IF and GO TO Statements

Program 7.2

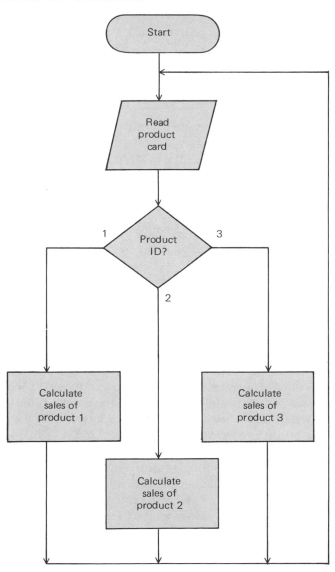

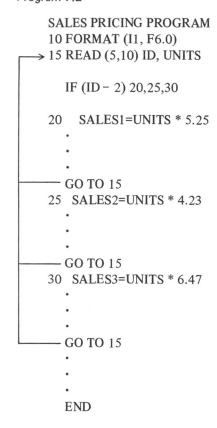

SALES PRICING PROGRAM
10 FORMAT (I1, F6.0)
15 READ (5,10) ID, UNITS

    IF (ID − 2) 20,25,30

20   SALES1=UNITS * 5.25
      .
      .
      .
— GO TO 15
25   SALES2=UNITS * 4.23
      .
      .
      .
— GO TO 15
30   SALES3=UNITS * 6.47
      .
      .
      .
— GO TO 15
      .
      .
      .
END

program has been written so that any one of three processing routes can be selected. Therefore, it is important to have a transfer statement at the end of each processing route so that the computer can return to the READ statement regardless of which segment it has processed.

Through the use of the GO TO statement, a computer has the ability to transfer to any statement within a program. The three GO TO statements used in the example above caused the program to transfer back to the READ statement repeatedly. This control technique allows the reading of multiple data cards. The data deck for this program is no longer limited to one card but may be of any size (limited by the memory capacity of the central processor) and can be envisioned as shown in Figure 7.3. ID is the variable name used for the first column (field) of data on each card, and UNITS is the variable name used for the second field of data. (See Program 7.2.)

Figure 7.3 Expanded Data Deck

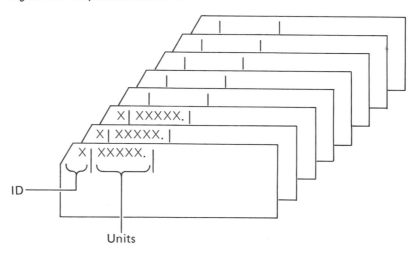

The Trailer Card

Business processing usually requires the handling of large quantities of data. The large volume presents a problem of how to indicate to the computer that the *final* piece of *input* data has been *read*. Sensing the end of a data deck is important in order to avoid an error condition. If the computer is directed repeatedly to read new data cards, it will eventually reach the end of the data deck. However, because the computer system reads only one card at a time, it can make no distinction between the first, second, third, fourth, or last data card. Even after reading the last card, the computer will attempt to read an additional card and, when none is available, will display an error message. Therefore, some technique is necessary to prevent the computer from attempting to read past the end of the data deck.

One procedure for determining the final input card would be to count the number of input items in advance and place this count in the computer's memory. The computer could then count the items as they were read and compare the count to the input total known in advance. When the two counts are equal, the computer would not be directed to read another card.

A counting procedure of this type presents several difficulties which make it undesirable. The primary disadvantage is related to the fact that, with vast quantities of data, counting in advance (and by hand) is tedious and time consuming. A simple method for detecting the completion of input reading is through the use of a *trailer card* (or sentinel card).

A trailer card is placed at the end of a data deck. This card contains a unique value which could not possibly be mistaken for an item of input data. The trailer card is read in the same manner as any other input data card; however, the program will contain a test immediately after each input card is read. This test will make use of the IF statement and, in essence, will ask the computer "whether the input card just read equals the value expected in the trailer card?". If the answer is no, the last card must not have been read and the input data should be processed. When the answer is yes, the trailer card must have been read and the computer should be directed to an appropriate statement other than the one used for reading input data.

In the SALES PRICING PROGRAM (Program 7.2), the FORMAT description for input data is FORMAT (I1, F6.0). Using this FORMAT specification, the trailer card could be punched with an item of data in the *first field* (that is, the I1) which could not possibly be interpreted as normal input. In this example, we will assume that it would be impossible for a product to have the number 9. Therefore, a card punched with a 9 in column 1 is placed at the end of the data deck. The data deck would now appear as shown in Figure 7.4. The trailer card may have the unique value punched in any field. This example uses a 9 punched in column 1 of the last card.

Figure 7.4   Expanded Data Deck with a Trailer Card

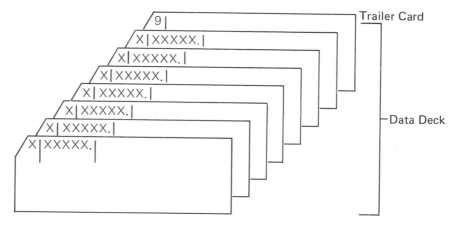

Insertion of the numeric value 9 in the trailer card will permit the programmer to prepare a test for this value. Using the IF statement, the test can be written as:

```
10  FORMAT (I1, F6.0)
15  READ (5,10) ID, UNITS
    IF (ID - 9) 16, 50, 50
```

The computer, when reading the trailer card, will store the value 9 in the location designated as ID (at the same time blanks[3] will be loaded into location UNITS).

---

[3] Technically, zeros are placed in location UNITS. In FORTRAN, any blank column on a data card is automatically converted to zero.

The IF statement instructs the computer to subtract 9 from the value located at ID. Of course, in this illustration, it will mean that 9 is deducted from 9 with a result of 0. When this condition occurs, the computer will select the middle statement number from the three numbers following the parentheses (that is, the first 50–IF (ID − 9) 16, 50, 50) and continue processing.

The test which we just demonstrated illustrates the use of an IF statement where only two choices exist. In this illustration the answer was either (1) the trailer card had been read, and therefore the computer should select statement 50 for subsequent processing, or (2) the trailer card had not been read, and therefore statement 16 should be processed. In this case it would have been impossible to have the test produce a positive numeric value. The trailer card contained a value of 9 and 9 was being deducted from this value. The *requirement* that *three numbers* follow the parentheses made the *use* of *two 50s* necessary. However, the second 50 was a dummy number and would never be used.

The use of a trailer card, and the test related to it, enables the programmer to read in any quantity of data. The only requirement is a trailer card, containing 9 in column 1, as the last item in the input data.

Combining the IF and GO TO Statements

With the IF and GO TO statements, the programmer can shift from the computer's inherent sequential processing order to a non-sequential processing order. This ability to control the computer provides the programmer with the technique of *looping*. Looping makes it possible to perform the same set of instructions repeatedly, and a substantial amount of programming effort will be saved. If programmers had to write all steps in a sequential order, they would have to write the same statements over and over, making programming a highly cumbersome, tedious, and inefficient task.

To illustrate the use of the IF and GO TO statements, as well as the trailer card, let us finish the SALES PRICING PROGRAM so that it will meet the following processing requirements:

1. Read six data cards (although with the trailer card it is not important to know that there will be six cards) plus a trailer card with a 9 punched in the first column. These cards will appear as follows:

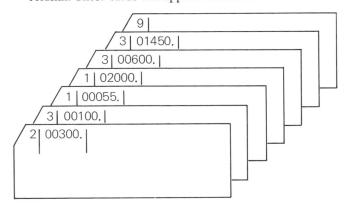

2. Perform the following steps for each product:
   a. compute the sales value of each transaction
   b. accumulate the total sales
   c. accumulate the total units sold
3. After sensing the trailer card, the program will:
   a. compute the total sales value of all transactions
   b. print the results of processing

A flowchart of the program appears in Figure 7.5, and the coded program instructions appear in Program 7.3.

Figure 7.5   Flowchart of the Sales Pricing Program

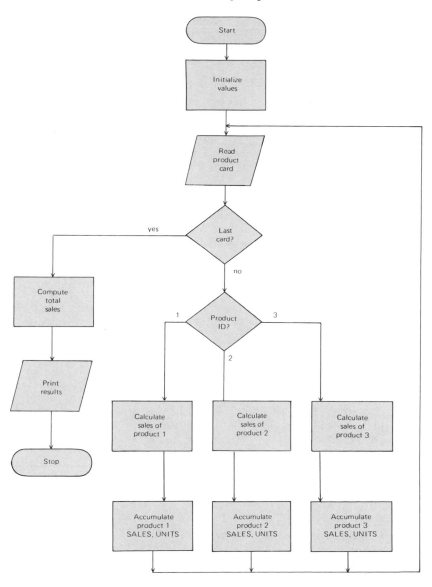

Program 7.3

```
      C
      C    *** SALES PRICING PROGRAM ***
      C
  1          TOTS1=0.0                                                   ─── Initialization
  2          TOTU1=0.0
  3          TOTS2=0.0
  4          TOTU2=0.0
  5          TOTS3=0.0
  6          TOTU3=0.0
      C
  7     10 FORMAT (I1, F6.0)                                            ─── Input Reading
  8     15 READ (5,10) ID, UNITS
      C
  9        IF (ID-9) 16,50,50                                          ─── Last Card Test
      C
 10     16 IF (ID-2) 20,25,30                                          ─── Product ID Test
      C
 11     20 SALES1=UNITS * 5.25                                             Calculate
 12        TOTS1=TOTS1 + SALES1                                        ─── SALES,UNITS
 13        TOTU1=TOTU1 + UNITS                                             Product A
 14        GO TO 15
      C
 15     25 SALES2=UNITS * 4.23                                             Calculate
 16        TOTS2=TOTS2 + SALES2                                        ─── SALES,UNITS
 17        TOTU2=TOTU2 + UNITS                                             Product B
 18        GO TO 15
      C
 19     30 SALES3=UNITS * 6.47                                             Calculate
 20        TOTS3=TOTS3 + SALES3                                        ─── SALES,UNITS
 21        TOTU3=TOTU3 + UNITS                                             Product C
 22        GO TO 15
      C
 23     50 SLSTOT=TOTS1 + TOTS2 + TOTS3 ◄──                            ─── Total All Products
      C
 24    100 FORMAT (5X,24HTOTAL SALES ALL PRODUCTS,2H $,F10.2)
 25        WRITE (6,100) SLSTOT
      C
 26    101 FORMAT (5X,23HPRODUCT A - TOTAL SALES,3H   $,F10.2,           Write
              112H  UNITS SOLD,2X,F10.2)                                  Results
 27        WRITE (6,101) TOTS1, TOTU1
      C
 28    102 FORMAT (5X,23HPRODUCT B - TOTAL SALES,3H   $,F10.2,
              112H  UNITS SOLD,2X,F10.2)
 29        WRITE (6,102) TOTS2, TOTU2
      C
 30    103 FORMAT (5X,23HPRODUCT C - TOTAL SALES,3H   $,F10.2,
              112H  UNITS SOLD,2X,F10.2)
 31        WRITE (6,103) TOTS3, TOTU3
      C
 32        STOP                                                          Program
 33        END                                                          Termination
      C
```

```
TOTAL SALES ALL PRODUCTS $   25968.25
PRODUCT A - TOTAL SALES  $   10788.75  UNITS SOLD    2055.00      Computed
PRODUCT B - TOTAL SALES  $    1269.00  UNITS SOLD     300.00      Output
PRODUCT C - TOTAL SALES  $   13910.50  UNITS SOLD    2150.00
```

With this program there are a few considerations which did not exist in previous, more simple illustrations. These considerations are:

1. The use of the IF statement to test for a last card and to identify product cards.
2. The use of the GO TO to loop back to the READ statement.
3. The ability to use ID and UNITS with each input card because their values are not needed after processing a card. This means that as each new data card is read, the values which were previously stored at the locations ID and UNITS will be erased and replaced with the values contained in the new data card.
4. The instruction form for summation of data. When summing, it may be necessary to accumulate a total by repeatedly adding a new value to an existing total. This requires writing the summation process as:

TOTS1 =TOTS1+SALES1

This statement says "The new total of sales for product A, located at TOTS1, equals the old total at TOTS1 plus the value of the current sales (that is, SALES1)." (Recall the need to initialize the first value as discussed on page 58-59). Previously, we have found totals by adding several variables directly as shown in statement 50 (SLSTOT=TOTS1+TOTS2+TOTS3).[4]

5. The expansion of the output FORMAT specification for printing the totals. Because of the increased amount of data being manipulated, there would be a high probability that the computed results would be quite large. Therefore, to provide sufficient size for a large output quantity, the code has been increased to F10.2. Ordinarily, the exact size of output quantities is unknown. The programmer must provide for an expanded output area which is big enough to accomodate the largest possible figure that will be displayed.
6. The use of a continuation code in column 6 of the second cards used in FORMATs 101, 102, and 103. When a single statement uses two cards, it is continued on the second card by inserting any non-zero character in column 6 of the *continuation card*. In this example, a 1 was used in column six of all continuation cards.

Exercise 14

Read the following program and answer the questions asked below.

```
C  YOU FIGURE THIS ONE
   20 FORMAT (5X, 10HTHIS IS IT,2X,I5)
      LARGE=0
    8 FORMAT (I5)
    9 READ (5,8) IT
      IF (IT −90000) 10,15,15
   10 IF (IT − LARGE) 9,9,11
   11 LARGE=IT
```

continued on page 94

---

[4] Note in Program 7.3 that the far left margin has numbers running consecutively from 1 to 33. These are line numbers assigned by the *compiler* during compilation. These numbers are always printed with the source program listing. The statement reference numbers written by the programmer appear with the program to the right of the compiler line numbers.

```
        GO TO 9
   15 WRITE (6,20) LARGE
        STOP
        END
```

1. What is this program designed to accomplish?
2. What is the largest number expected in the data that will be read?
3. Is this program going to use a trailer card? If so, how do you know? What will be punched in it?
4. What is the importance of the statement LARGE=0?
5. How will the output line appear?
6. How will the flowchart for this program appear?

Counting with the Computer

The use of a trailer card eliminates the cumbersome process of counting data by hand prior to processing. While counting data prior to processing is inefficient, it is not inefficient to instruct the computer to count the data as it is processed. This ability to count provides a handy tool for the programmer. It is frequently important to know the number of items processed. The count total might be used for informational purposes only, but it is also conceivable that the program will need to make use of the count in manipulating the data.

Instructing the computer to count is accomplished by the insertion of a simple summation statement in a program. The statement might take any of the following forms:

$$I = I + 1 \quad \text{or} \quad KOUNT = KOUNT + 1 \quad \text{or} \quad CT = CT + 2.0 \quad \text{or} \quad S = S - 1.0$$

The first arithmetic statement merely says "In the location specified as I, add the value 1 to whatever numeric quantity is now stored in I." If we were counting the number of cards read by the computer, we would insert this arithmetic statement immediately following the IF test for a trailer card. The essential elements of a program to do this are:

```
50 FORMAT (I4)
60 READ (5,50) KAR
   IF (KAR–9999) 10,11,11
10 J=J+1
     .
     .
     .
   GO TO 60
11 .
     .
     .
   END
```

This program reads one card at a time and the value in the first 4 columns is stored at location KAR. The trailer card has 9999 punched in it. The IF test determines whether the card read was the trailer card. If not, the program adds one to the counter J. If the trailer card is read, the program will skip counting that card and transfer to statement 11.

In the example of programmers' time in Chapter 6, the program was designed to read a card with five separate times punched into it (that is, FORMAT (5F4.1)). In averaging the total times, the average was computed by dividing the total hours by the constant 5.0. It would have been more efficient to have the computer count the number of separate data items read. This would have permitted use of the count in the averaging process. It would also allow the averaging to be accomplished regardless of the number of hourly times read, because the computer would continue to add to the count as long as new data cards were being read.

Counting the programmers' time presents an interesting illustration of a variation in the counting procedure. The input data cards *each* contain five programmers' time values. This would mean that counting the individual cards alone would not give a sufficient total for calculating an accurate average of all the times read. Assuming that every data card contains five values, it would be necessary to increase the counter by five each time a card was read. The counting statement would be:

COUNT = COUNT + 5.0

This statement will add five to the counter each time the statement is executed. Therefore, the counter will be set to 5, 10, 15, and so on, after each successive data card is read.

Assuming the total hourly data has been accumulated in location HRS, and COUNT contains the total individual hours read, the averaging statement would be written as:

AVE = HRS / COUNT   rather than AVE = HRS / 5.0.

COUNT was chosen arbitrarily as a name for the counter. Being a real mode name, it avoided a mixed mode condition when used in calculating the average. An integer counter, such as KOUNT, could have been used. The process of counting would have been more efficient because most computers manipulate integer values more efficiently than real mode values. This would result in writing the averaging statement as:

AVE = HRS / KOUNT

In this calculation, the processor would have to temporarily convert KOUNT to the real mode before executing the division. Mode conversion cannot be made by some computers, and it results in a mixed mode error condition. Computers which can make this conversion incur a processing penalty because of the inefficiency in conversion. Therefore, the programmer has a trade-off to consider. When a large amount of counting is required, with only a few divisions, an integer counter would seem most efficient. On the other hand, if frequent divisions are required, a real mode counter may be most efficient.

The Technique of Initialization

Earlier we discussed the concept of FORTRAN constants. The example we used to demonstrate the setting of a real mode constant was PI = 3.1416. The explanation indicated that when this statement is executed, the value 3.1416 will be stored at location PI. This value normally would not be changed during the processing cycle of the program. The statement which sets the value 3.1416 can be described as *initializing* the variable PI. The value placed at location PI is certainly the *initial value* stored in that memory area.

The technique of initialization has a much wider application than shown above. The technique, however, is basically one of setting values at a predetermined level and attaching a variable name to the location storing that value. The initialization of variables is made frequently at the beginning of programs. The first six statements in Program 7.3 illustrate this use of initialization.

Every variable used in an expression to the right of an equal sign must have some value (positive, negative, or zero) prior to its use. Initialization establishes this value and is said to define the variable. In many systems, an error condition arises when a variable within an expression has no prior value[5] and may generate an error message indicating that the "VARIABLE IS UNDEFINED." While initialization statements often appear at the beginning of a program, they may be used at any place a value needs to be set. The following program segments illustrate the importance of initialization when using the computer as a counter.

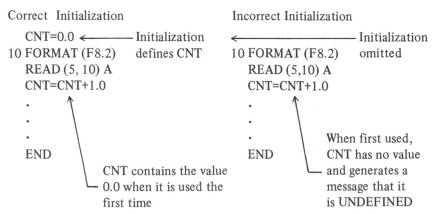

Correct Initialization

```
    CNT=0.0  ←————— Initialization
10 FORMAT (F8.2)      defines CNT
    READ (5, 10) A
    CNT=CNT+1.0
    .
    .
    .
    END
```
CNT contains the value 0.0 when it is used the first time

Incorrect Initialization

```
                 ←——————————— Initialization
10 FORMAT (F8.2)              omitted
    READ (5,10) A
    CNT=CNT+1.0
    .
    .
    .
    END
```
When first used, CNT has no value and generates a message that it is UNDEFINED

A variation in initialization occurs when a specific value is set, not by writing an arithmetic statement but, rather, by some other process, such as a calculation.

Suppose that we want to write a program to test input data against a limit. The limit is to be set by adding the first two input values. The limit size depends upon the input data and so could not be programmed in advance.

The following program demonstrates the initialization process under these conditions.

```
10 FORMAT (2I3)
    READ (5,10) M,N
    LIMIT = M + N
20 FORMAT (I3)
    READ (5,20) J
    IF (J – LIMIT) 30, 32, 34
    .
    .
    .
```

---

[5] Some systems will assume an undefined variable to be zero. However, this method is not precise and accuracy is assured only with initialization.

In this program, a data card is read according to FORMAT 10. The value of LIMIT is calculated and set prior to additional processing. LIMIT is initialized at this point and will be used with this initial value throughout the remainder of the program.

Exercise 15

1. Take the following five conditions and write two FORTRAN statements for each one to establish a counter (1) in the real mode and then (2) in the integer mode, which will:
   a. increase by 1 with each execution
   b. increase by 3 with each execution
   c. decrease by 2 with each execution
   d. double with each execution
   e. increase by 5.7 with each execution
2. Write FORTRAN statements which initialize:
   a. J at 0
   b. A at − 5
   c. KAB at 3
   d. BAT at 12
   e. DEL at −7.5

Questions

1. What are the elements which can be used in the construction of a FORTRAN expression?
2. What is the difference between a FORTRAN expression and a FORTRAN statement?
3. What is the hierarchy of processing applicable to FORTRAN expressions?
4. Explain, step-by-step, how the following FORTRAN statement would be executed:

$$ANS = (KAP + N) - JAC / (LT + (M * LO)) + NUM ** 2 ** 3$$

5. What does truncation mean? How does it relate to manipulation of numeric values in FORTRAN?
6. Explain the difference between sequential and non-sequential processing in a FORTRAN program.
7. What are the components of an arithmetic IF statement? What is the function of each component?
8. What is the difference between arithmetic IF and GO TO statements?
9. To what is each branch in an arithmetic IF related? What are the maximum number of branches which can be taken from one arithmetic IF? The minimum number of branches?
10. What is the function served by the use of a trailer card?
11. Under what circumstances would it be advantageous to use the computer to do counting?
12. What is the importance of initialization in programming? Why is it necessary?

8
Refining Data Manipulation

Data Arrays and Program Looping

FORTRAN Subscripting

Up to this point, we have had to locate and handle data by providing each storage location with a variable data name which was unique from all other location names. This is a relatively easy task when the number of locations is small. As the volume of data and storage locations increases, however, the selection of variable names becomes a more arduous task. For example, if we wanted to read and store data in five locations, the process for providing variable names has been the following:

Each storage location was named within the program, as shown below.

Memory Locations and Names

```
50 FORMAT (5I3)
   READ (5,50) K1, K2, K3, K4, K5
   .
   .
   .
   END
```

	K1
	K2
	K3
	K4
	K5

If we expand the number of input data items from 5 to 100, then the problem of specifying location names becomes cumbersome, to say nothing about the task of writing 100 unique names in the READ statement. Obviously, we need a more efficient shorthand method for specifying location names. A shorthand method for assigning location names does exist and is accomplished through the use of *subscripts*. A subscript in FORTRAN is essentially identical to subscripts used in mathematical notation. The manner of presentation varies from mathematical notation in only one respect: the FORTRAN subscript character is written in parentheses rather than being lowered. For instance, subscripts in mathematical notation would normally appear as A_4 or as A_i. In the FORTRAN language these same subscripts would appear as A(4) or as A(I). The essential difference is the use of parentheses and, when using symbolic subscripts, the use of capital letters rather than lowercase letters.

Subscripts are typically used when a program must accommodate an *array of data*. An array is nothing more than a list of data items. Frequently lists are composed of similar items, such as a list of inventory items. When an array of this type is used, the array is given a general name and the individual items in the array are identified through the use of subscripts. For instance, if we had 100 separate inventory figures, the list would be expressed algebraically as:

$$\text{Inty}_1, \text{Inty}_2 \ \text{Inty}_3, \ldots, \text{Inty}_{100}$$

In FORTRAN, these same array elements would be written as:

INTY(1), INTY(2), INTY(3), . . . , INTY(100)

The computer stores the data array so that it can associate the 100 locations in a linear fashion running from INTY(1) to INTY(100). The subscript attached to an array name merely designates a specific position within the list. An array is a reserved group of memory locations. Therefore, a *subscript* must be a *positive integer constant* (not zero) *or*, as will be shown shortly, a *positive integer variable name*.

It is possible to specify subscripts in a *symbolic* form. This form uses a variable name, which *must* be an *integer*, in the parentheses. Hence, Inty_i would be written in FORTRAN as INTY(I) and, if the computer program had specified I = 1, INTY(1) would refer to the first inventory item (that is, INTY(1)).

When specifying the items in a lengthy array, it is very convenient to use symbolic subscript notation. The programmer instructs the computer to keep track of the specific array items through the use of the computer's counting ability. The following example indicates how the computer can be programmed to read an array of data, apply subscript notation, and use its counting ability. Assume that five data values are to be read and these values are followed by a trailer card containing 999. A schematic of the array and a program segment to read and store values in the array are shown below.

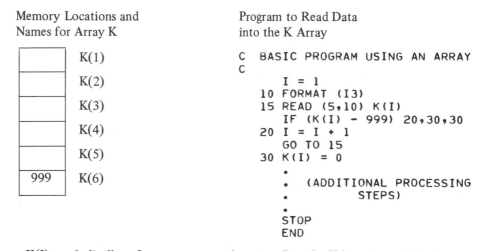

Memory Locations and
Names for Array K

	K(1)
	K(2)
	K(3)
	K(4)
	K(5)
999	K(6)

Program to Read Data
into the K Array

```
C  BASIC PROGRAM USING AN ARRAY
C
      I = 1
10 FORMAT (I3)
15 READ (5,10) K(I)
   IF (K(I) - 999) 20,30,30
20 I = I + 1
   GO TO 15
30 K(I) = 0
   .
   .    (ADDITIONAL PROCESSING
   .            STEPS)
   .
STOP
END
```

K(I) symbolically refers to any array location. Specific K locations will be determined by using the value of I. At the beginning of the program, the value of I is initialized at 1. When the READ statement is first executed, K(I) is equivalent to specifying K(1). The data being read would be stored in the first memory location of the K array. Next, a trailer card test is performed. A negative result sends the computer to statement 20 where I is increased to 2. Then the GO TO statement sends the computer back to READ. When the second data card is read, the computer again refers to K(I) which is now the same as referring to K(2). This process is repeated until the trailer card is read and identified. I will then equal 6. The trailer card is stored in location K(6). The IF test which identifies the trailer card transfers control to statement 30. This statement erases the trailer card value of 999 from K(6) (by inserting zeros in K(6)) since the value 999 is meaningless to any further processing.

The specific computer technique for associating an array location with a subscripted variable data name, such as K(I), is:

1. The variable data name is found in an instruction, for example, READ (5,10) K(I).
2. The computer looks up the subscript variable name I and secures the numeric value stored at that location.
3. The computer replaces the subscript I, in the READ instruction, with the numeric value of I.
4. The instruction is then executed as if it had originally been written with a specific integer number instead of the subscript. For example,

Location I	Instruction	Executed as
When I = 1	READ K(I)	READ K(1)
When I = 2	READ K(I)	READ K(2)
When I = 3	READ K(I)	READ K(3)
When I = 4	READ K(I)	READ K(4)
When I = 5	READ K(I)	READ K(5)
When I = 6	READ K(I)	READ K(6)

This example illustrates the programming flexibility which can be gained in handling data through the use of an array. The counter I is used to direct the computer to the appropriate array position. In summary, every time the variable name K(I) is encountered, the computer will (1) look-up the counter I (which is a variable data name itself), (2) insert the current value of I in the array name K(I), and (3) proceed to the specified K(I) location. This technique becomes more advantageous as the amount of data increases. This same set of instructions could be used with 500 or 5000 data values as well as the 5 values illustrated.

The DIMENSION Statement

The use of subscripted variables requires the programmer to give an additional specification to the computer. When *any* subscripted variable is used in a program, the computer must be told this fact at the *beginning* of the written program. The statement which gives this clue to the computer is called a *DIMENSION* statement. This statement does three things:

1. It identifies the *name* of the array.
2. It indicates the *size* of the array.
3. It establishes the *mode* of the array.

Indicating these items is very simple. The name of the array can be any variable name selected by the programmer. This name follows all of the previously specified rules for constructing a variable name. Note, however, that the parentheses and subscript following an array name *do not* count toward the six character limit of the array name.

Indicating the size of an array means specifying the *maximum* number of individual array locations which could be used to store values. It is permissible to specify an array size larger than actually used. The reverse is not true. The size specification tells the computer to reserve a specific number of storage locations in its memory.

Data may be stored in an array in either the real or integer mode. The mode of each array is set by the first letter in the array name. This characteristic is identical to the relationship between any variable data name and its mode.

In our subscripted array example (page 99), the program segment is incomplete because the K array does not have a DIMENSION statement to specify its name, size, and mode to the computer. The DIMENSION statement should be written as:

DIMENSION K(6)

This statement *must* be placed *first* in the program. In this example, the DIMEN-SION statement would be located just prior to the I = 1 initialization statement. The DIMENSION indicates that an array known as K will be used, that it will have a maximum of six storage locations, and that the data stored will be in the integer mode. The program segment would now appear as:

```
C   BASIC PROGRAM USING AN ARRAY
C   INCLUDING DIMENSION STATEMENT
C
    DIMENSION K(6)
    I = 1
10 FORMAT (I3)
15 READ (5,10) K(I)
    IF (K(I) - 999) 20,30,30
20 I = I + 1
    GO TO 15
30 K(I) = 0
    .
    .   (ADDITIONAL PROCESSING
    .          STEPS)
    .
    STOP
    END
```

If more than one array is used in a program, a single DIMENSION statement may specify the additional arrays. As an example, such a statement might be:

DIMENSION K(6), ABC(10), SALES(125)

It should also be noted that arrays do not have to be used only with input data. The values stored in an array could come from a series of computations within a program. The only requirements are that the array must be specified in a DIMEN-SION statement and that all uses of the array name must be accompanied by a subscript.

Reading data into an array has several desirable advantages. One key advantage is the immediate availability of all the stored input data for subsequent processing. Our previous programs, written without the use of arrays, made the handling of input data and its storage for later use difficult and cumbersome. A second desirable characteristic is the ability to refer to the array locations in symbolic notation while letting the computer determine the specific location numbers. In addition, the computer counts the items being read. When the input data has been read and stored, the subscript's value will equal a count of the items read. This count is then available for any further processing requirements.

Exercise 16

1. Assume the following arrays are used with the maximum number of data items indicated; write four DIMENSION statements to provide the proper amount of storage.

Array	Maximum Data
ABC	200
IBIC	15
R2	99
XYZ	12

2 Rewrite question 1 in a single DIMENSION statement. In what mode will each of the arrays be handled?

3. Use the name NOW for an array having a maximum of 20 storage locations and write the appropriate portions of a program which will:
   a. have a suitable DIMENSION statement
   b. READ in data cards having a FORMAT of I5
   c. test for the last card which will have the numeric value 99999 punched in the first 5 columns

FORTRAN DO Loops

In an earlier section we discussed the use of control statements to instruct the computer to repeat a specified operation several times. This technique is called looping and, so far, the use of a GO TO statement has been the primary element in closing the loop. An IF statement was used to provide a test and exit from the loop. The essential elements of a loop are shown below:

```
        DIMENSION K(6)
        I = 1
     10 FORMAT (I3)
  ┌─→15 READ (5,10) K(I)
  │     IF (K(I)−999)20,30,30
  │  20 I = I + 1
  └──── GO TO 15
     30 K(I) = 0
        .
        .
        .
        END
```

In this example, the loop is completed when the computer executes the *GO TO 15* instruction. Looping continues until the trailer card is identified by the IF test and control is transferred to instruction 30.

An alternative to GO TO and IF statements is the *DO statement.* This statement accomplishes exactly what the name implies: it commands the computer to automatically DO its looping a specified number of times (referred to as iterations). All procedural languages contain a command of this kind and writing this statement is most appropriate when the programmer must use processing statements repetitively. Rather than writing the same processing statements over and over, the programmer uses the DO statement to instruct the computer to execute a single set of statements several times.

The construction of DO statements is simple and logical. The following examples illustrate valid DO statements.

DO 10 KT = 1,20,1   DO 100 INT = 2,12

DO 18 I = 3,M,2   DO 60 L = J,N

DO 43 IJ = K,L,M   DO 50 J = 1,5,1

If we examine the last DO statement, we see that the statement has the following elements:

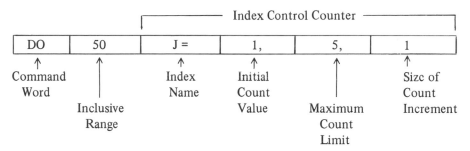

This statement instructs the computer to "Execute (DO) each program statement following the DO statement *through* (and including) instruction 50, five times, by initially setting the index J at a value of 1 and increasing (or incrementing) J by 1 each time the loop is completed." The computer will perform this set of statements five times, because the index control counter has the specifications J=1,5,1. The index must conform to the following requirements:

1. Index name: a non-subscripted integer variable name
2. Initial count value: a non-subscripted integer variable name *or* an integer constant that is positive but not zero
3. Maximum count limit: same description as initial count value
4. Size of count increment: same description as initial count value

The computer *automatically* returns to the DO statement when it has processed the instruction identified with the inclusive range number (50 in the preceding example). At this point, the computer will increment the value of the counter J and test it against the maximum value. If the counter *does not exceed* the maximum, the computer will again process the statements through the inclusive range number and make another test. When the counter finally exceeds the maximum count limit, the computer will transfer control to the first executable statement *immediately following* the instruction numbered as the inclusive range (the statement following 50 in this example).

Consider the following example. Suppose that the previous program, which read five values into the K array, had further requirements to add the values, print each value on a separate line, and then print the total of all values. We would augment the original program to read:

```
C   TWO TYPES OF LOOPING
C
        DIMENSION K(6)
        KTOT = 0
        I = 1
     10 FORMAT (I3)
     15 READ (5,10) K(I)
        IF (K(I)-999) 20,30,30
     20 I = I+1
        GO TO 15
     30 K(I) = 0
C
        DO 50 J=1,5,1
        KTOT = KTOT + K(J)
     18 FORMAT (5X,4HITEM,3X,I10)
        WRITE (6,18) K(J)
     50 CONTINUE
C
     19 FORMAT (5X,5HTOTAL,2X,I10)
        WRITE (6,19) KTOT
        .
        .
        .
        .
        .   (ADDITIONAL PROCESSING
        .          STEPS)
        .
        .
        .
        STOP
        END
```

This program now demonstrates two types of looping.

Loop 1.   The program reads five data values and stores them in the K array. The GO TO command forms this loop.

Loop 2.   The computer then selects the data items from the K array and adds them one-by-one to the location KTOT. After adding a value to KTOT, that value is printed on a single line with the alphabetic caption ITEM. The DO command forms this loop and the addition and printing activities will be repeated five times in accordance with the DO loop specifications. After completion of the DO loop, the computer will transfer to the first executable instruction following statement 50. This will be the WRITE statement.

Note several important aspects of the above example:

1. The DO loop processed through statement 50 and this statement was written 50 CONTINUE. The final statement within a DO loop may *not* be a control statement, such as IF, STOP, GO TO, and DO. The CONTINUE statement is not executed and avoids the possibility of ending the DO loop with a control statement. Note, however, a DO loop may end with any executable statement which is not a control statement.

2. The counter within the DO loop was specified as J. This same counter, being an integer, served double duty as the subscript for array K. The variable name used for a subscript is not important except that it *must* be a non-subscripted positive integer. Therefore, when J was equal to 1, writing the subscripted variable name *K(J)* is the *same* as K(1). The subscript directs the computer to the first data location in the K array. *It is the numeric value associated with the symbolic subscript which is important, not the particular variable name used as the subscript.*[1]

3. In writing the statement specifying the DO loop, DO 50 J = 1,5,1, the final 1 could have been omitted. The statement would then appear as: DO 50 J = 1,5. The computer will assume that the counter's increment is 1 when this number is omitted. When incrementing by any other value, such as 2, 3, or 4, the increment value must be given.

Flowcharting a DO Statement

The DO statement is sufficiently different from previous instructions to require an alteration in flowcharting symbols. A flowchart of the DO statement for our previous example appears in Figure 8.1.

Figure 8.1   Flowchart Segment Illustrating a DO Loop

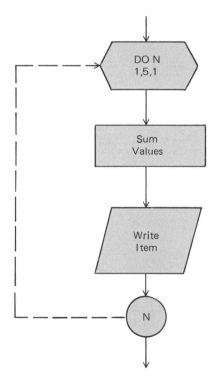

---

[1] While subscripts are frequently specified as single letters, such as A(K) or A(J), it should be recalled that a subscript is a variable name. Therefore, any integer variable name is an acceptable subscript and can be composed of more than a single letter. A(JOB), SALES(KOUNT), and J(JJ) are all legal subscripted variables.

The hexagon is used to indicate the use of a DO statement. Statement numbers are usually not known at the time of flowchart preparation. Therefore, we used the symbolic character N. This character is replaced by a number when the program has been written. The index values are inserted in either numeric or symbolic form (in the example, DO 50 J = 1,5,1). The action steps to be taken are flowcharted by using standard flowcharting symbols. The end of the DO loop is identified with the same symbolic reference used in the hexagon. A dashed line indicates the return path to the DO statement and its index. (In the example, N will be replaced with 50.)

The general concept of looping and the particular concept of DO loops may be summarized by reviewing the following elements contained in all loops:

1. initialization
2. incrementation
3. test
4. range or body

The illustrations below show these loop components and emphasize how the DO loop incorporates the first three elements in a single statement. The following program sums all the odd integer numbers from 1 to 100.

GO TO—IF Loop	DO Loop
KOUNT = 1 NUM = 0 → 5 NUM = NUM + KOUNT IF (KOUNT- 99) 15,25,25 15 KOUNT = KOUNT+2 — GO TO 5 25 · · · STOP END	NUM = 0 ┌──→ DO 15 KOUNT = 1,99,2 │ NUM = NUM + KOUNT └── 15 CONTINUE · · · STOP END

Initialization: in the
    KOUNT = 1 statement
 	
Incrementation: in the
    KOUNT = KOUNT +2
    statement
 	
Test: in the
    IF (KOUNT-99) 15,25,25
    statement
 	
Range: from statement 5
    through GO TO 5
	Initialization
	Incrementation } all in the DO
	Test statement
	
	Range: from the DO statement
	    through 15 CONTINUE

For an additional example of the DO statement's use, let us assume that a program dealing with retail customer accounts requires a segment which will compute each customer's receivable balance, including any finance service charge, at the end of a billing period. Assume that elsewhere in the program three arrays have been established to hold the beginning balances, payments, and purchases made during the month. Assume further that each array holds customer information stored in ascending order by customer account number. There are no more than 1000 customer accounts.

The arrays appear in Figure 8.2, a flowchart of the program segment appears in Figure 8.3, and the FORTRAN statements appear in Program 8.1.

Figure 8.2 Schematic of Customer Beginning Balance, Payments, and Purchases Arrays

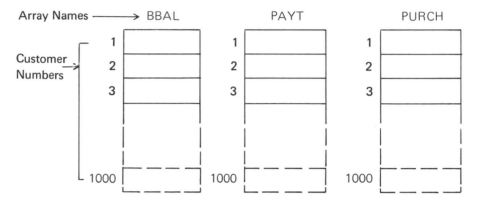

Program 8.1 Program Segment for Calculating Customers' Receivable Balance

```
C      MONTHLY CUSTOMER RECEIVABLE EXAMPLE
       DIMENSION BBAL(1000), PAYT(1000), PURCH(1000)
       •
       •
       •
       •
       DO 95 J=1,1000,1
       IF (BBAL(J)) 105,105,110
105    SC = 0.0
       GO TO 100
110    SC = BBAL(J) * .015
100    ENDBAL = BBAL(J) - PAYT(J) + PURCH(J) + SC
       IF (ENDBAL) 95,95,114
114    WRITE (6,115) BBAL(J), PAYT(J), PURCH(J), SC, ENDBAL
115    FORMAT (5X,11HOLD BALANCE,2X,F8.2,2X,8HPAYMENTS,2X,F8.2,2X,
      19HPURCHASES,2X,F8.2,2X,14HSERVICE CHARGE,2X,F8.2,2X,
      211HNEW BALANCE,2X,F8.2)
 95    CONTINUE
       •
       •
       •
       •
       •
       STOP
       END
```

Note the use of continuation numbers in column 6 of FORMAT 115.

Figure 8.3   Flowchart of Program Segment to Calculate New Account Balance

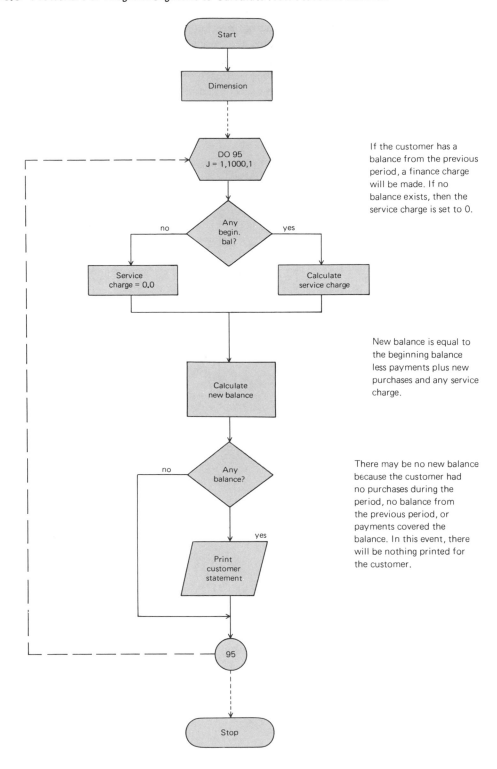

If the customer has a balance from the previous period, a finance charge will be made. If no balance exists, then the service charge is set to 0.

New balance is equal to the beginning balance less payments plus new purchases and any service charge.

There may be no new balance because the customer had no purchases during the period, no balance from the previous period, or payments covered the balance. In this event, there will be nothing printed for the customer.

A few rules must be observed when using DO loops.

1. The following rules of control must be observed in and around the DO loop:
   a. It is possible to transfer out of a DO loop *entirely* at any time. For example,

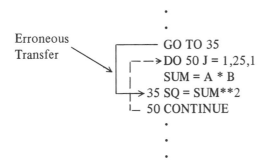

   .
   .
   .

   DO 18 L=1,4
   A = B+C(L)
   IF (A) 20,18,20 ⟵————————— If A is either greater than 0 or less than 0,
   18 CONTINUE   control is transferred out to statement 20.
   20 D=A**2
   .
   .
   .

   b. Control transfers may *not* be made *into* the *middle* of a DO loop. Entry must be made through the DO statement. For example,

   Erroneous
   Transfer ⟶

   .
   .
   .

   ————— GO TO 35
   ––⟶DO 50 J = 1,25,1
        SUM = A * B
   ⟶ 35 SQ = SUM**2
   ⊢— 50 CONTINUE
   .
   .
   .

   GO TO 35 transfers control into the DO loop which runs from the DO statement down through statement 50. All statements within the loop may be accessed only from outside the loop and through the DO statement.

   c. Control may *not* be transferred back to the DO statement *directly* but only through the statement at the bottom of the DO range. For example,

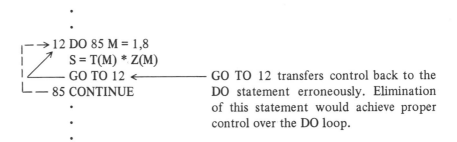

   .
   .
   .

   ⟶ 12 DO 85 M = 1,8
        S = T(M) * Z(M)
   ——— GO TO 12 ⟵————————— GO TO 12 transfers control back to the
   — 85 CONTINUE   DO statement erroneously. Elimination
                                        of this statement would achieve proper
   .   control over the DO loop.
   .
   .

2. It is *not* permissible to *redefine* the index counter within the DO loop. For example,

.
.
.

DO 27 J = 1,200,2
R = S**2+P
J = R ←————————————— The counter J cannot be set equal to R
27 CONTINUE   within the DO loop. If this value is impor-
.   tant to the program, an alternative state-
.   ment such as JJ=R can be used within the
.   DO loop to save the value.

3. When a DO loop is completed the maximum number of times, as indicated by the maximum count index, the program is said to have made a *normal exit* from the loop. After an exit of this type, the program should not make use of the DO loop's index because its value will be uncertain (referred to as undefined). When an exit is made from a loop *prior* to completing the maximum number of loops (an *abnormal exit*), the DO loop's index and value are available for use in further processing. For example,

Normal Exit   Abnormal Exit
.   .
.   .
.   .

DO 15 K = 1,3   DO 60 N = 1,8,2
  TOT = TOT + A*B   SUM = SUM + AMT
15 CONTINUE   IF (SUM– 37.5)60,60,75
.   60 CONTINUE
.   .
.   .
.   .

                                                      75 CAL = SUM + A(N)
                                                          .
                                                          .
                                                          .

When a normal exit is made from this loop, the value of K cannot be counted on as 3 or 4.

This loop has two possible exits:

a. A normal exit occurs when the loop has cycled 4 times (N=1,3,5,7), assuming that the IF test never has a positive result. After the normal exit, the value of N is not necessarily 7 or 8.

b. An abnormal exit occurs when the IF test shows that SUM exceeds 37.5. Under this condition, control transfers to statement 75. The value of N will be available for statement 75 and beyond.

When the values used in the index of a DO loop are known in advance, the use of numbers in writing the DO statement index is appropriate (as in the example J = 1,5,1). There are occasions, however, when one or more of the index values will not be known at the time the program is being written. The values used in the DO loop index may have to be developed by the computer as it processes the portion of the program *preceding* the DO loop statement. The program shown in Program 8.2 illustrates this point.

Assume a simple program which will read up to 100 employee payroll records, store the records in three arrays, compute individual, total, and average pay, and display the payroll. A trailer card containing 99999 will be used.

Program 8.2 Program Illustrating Symbolic DO Loop Index Parameter

```
         C       SIMPLE PAYROLL EXAMPLE
         C
                 DIMENSION NUM(100), HRS(100), RATE(100)
                 TOTPAY = 0
                 J = 1
              10 FORMAT (I5,F4.1,F5.2)
              15 READ (5,10) NUM(J), HRS(J), RATE(J)
                 IF (NUM(J) - 99999) 16,20,20
              16 J = J+1
                 GO TO 15
         C
              20 J = J-1
                 DO 30 K=1,J,1
                 PAY = HRS(K) * RATE(K)
                 TOTPAY = TOTPAY + PAY
              25 FORMAT (5X,8HEMPLOYEE,1X,I5,2X,3HPAY,2X,F10.2)
                 WRITE (6,25) NUM(K), PAY
              30 CONTINUE
         C
                 A = J
                 AVEPAY = TOTPAY / A
              35 FORMAT (5X,13HTOTAL PAYROLL,2X,F10.2,2X,
                 124HAVERAGE PAY PER EMPLOYEE,2X,F10.2)
                 WRITE (6,35) TOTPAY, AVEPAY
                 STOP
                 END
```

Input Section
READ
COUNT

Payroll Processing
COMPUTE
PRINT PAYROLL

Conclusion
COMPUTE AVERAGE
PRINT AVERAGE
STOP

Note the following points in this simple payroll program:

1. A DO loop is used to process the payroll, but it cannot be used to read input data. At the time data cards are being read, the total number of cards is unknown. Therefore, a GO TO statement is used to complete the reading loop. A DO statement would require a known value for the maximum count limit.

2. The number of data cards read were counted by the instruction:

   16 J = J + 1

   This count will be stored in variable location J and will be available for use as the maximum count limit in the subsequent DO loop.

3. Statement 20 shows the counter J being reduced by 1. This was necessary because J had been incremented to count the trailer card. This card contains no

valid payroll data. Therefore, the counter has been incremented by one past the count of actual payroll data. It is necessary, then, to reduce the counter J *prior* to its use as an indicator of the number of valid data cards read.

4. The counter J has been used in the DO statement to specify the maximum value, as follows:

DO 30 K = 1, J, 1

When the computer encounters this DO statement, it will look up the integer variable J and insert its *value* in the DO statement.

The above example illustrates a program which may be used with any number of employee records. Further, the number of employee records does not have to be known before the program is written. Generalizing a program in this manner increases the possible uses of the program. The counter will keep track of the number of payroll items read and insert this count into the DO statement. Of course, if the number of records were to exceed 100, the DIMENSION specification would have to be increased. For instance, if 199 items were anticipated, the DIMENSION statement would have to provide for 200 storage locations and would be rewritten as:

DIMENSION NUM(200), HRS(200), RATE(200)

The computer could then read as many as 199 payroll records (plus 1 for the trailer card), store them in the arrays, and provide a count of J = 199 for insertion into the DO instruction.

To complete our introduction to DO statements, we might consider what would happen when all index values are identical or when the maximum index value is less than the initial index value. Both of these conditions would be errors in writing DO statements but could happen inadvertently.

1. All index values identical. The following DO statement illustrates this condition.

DO 40 N = 1,1,1

Most computers test for an index's maximum value *after* completing a loop. Therefore, even with a set of identical index values, one cycle through the loop will be completed. After finishing this loop, the index is incremented to 2. This causes a normal exit from the loop because the index value exceeds the maximum count limit.

2. Maximum value less than initial index value. This condition would appear as:

DO 78 K = 5,4,1

Because computers test the index *after* completing a loop, one cycle is executed even though the maximum value exceeds the initial value before the loop is processed. A normal exit is made from the loop after one cycle.

Exercise 17

1. Write five DO loop statements each of which directs the computer to run through statement 75 under the following conditions:

	Index	Begins at:	Has a Maximum:	Increments By:
a.	I	1	4	1
b.	J2	7	12	3
c.	KI	3	N	2
d.	LMN	K	N	L
e.	IJK	1	29	5

2. How many times will the computer run through the loops in your DO statements in (1) above?

   a. _____   b. _____   c. _____   d. _____   e. _____

3. Identify the errors in each of the following DO statements.

   a. DO 10, K = 1,5,3
   b. DO 20 A = 2,4,6
   c. DO 30 J = 3,3,3
   d. DO 40 K = 1,J,+2
   e. DO 50I = A,B,(C – 3)

4. Using the partial program shown below, determine the number of loops which will be completed by the computer and, for each loop completed, indicate what the value of the K index will be as well as the numeric value stored at location MORE.

		Loop Number	Value of K	Value at Location MORE
•				
•				
•		_____	____	_____
MORE = 0		_____	____	_____
N = 20				
L = 15		_____	____	_____
DO15 K = 1,L,3				
MORE = MORE + N*(6+K)		_____	____	_____
15 CONTINUE				
•		_____	____	_____
•				
•		_____	____	_____
END				
		_____	____	_____

Expanding the READ and WRITE Statements—An Implied DO Loop

The READ statements presented in previous sections have required that input data be punched either (1) in just one card or (2) in several cards, providing that unique names were used for each field on each card. Similar restrictions have applied to the use of WRITE statements. Numerous other possibilities exist for reading input and for writing output data.

A convenient technique for repetitive reading and writing employs the concepts, discussed at the beginning of this chapter, which deal with arrays, subscripts, and a form of the DO loop. A basic alteration in instruction form is the inclusion of the DO-looping capability within READ and WRITE statements. For example,

8 FORMAT (10F5.2)
 READ (5,8) (AMT(J), J = 1,10,1)

The FORMAT and READ statements shown above indicate that ten values are punched in a single card (that is, FORMAT (10F5.2)) and that the computer is to read *across* the card. Ten values will be placed in an array called AMT. The READ statement includes an index written in a form identical to the index of a DO loop (that is, J = 1,10,1). This index controls the value of the subscript J which is associated with the array AMT. Automatic reading in this form uses the concept of the DO loop but does not explicitly employ the word DO. Therefore, we have an *implied* DO loop.

If we examine the implied loop portion of the READ statement, we see the following components:

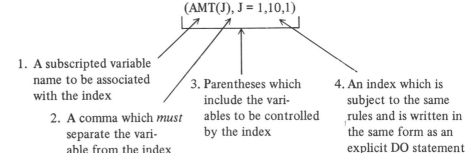

$$(AMT(J), J = 1,10,1)$$

1. A subscripted variable name to be associated with the index

2. A comma which *must* separate the variable from the index

3. Parentheses which include the variables to be controlled by the index

4. An index which is subject to the same rules and is written in the same form as an explicit DO statement

A WRITE statement with an implied DO loop is nearly identical to the statement used for reading. If the ten values read into the AMT array were to be printed *across* a single line of output, the following statements would accomplish this display.

9 FORMAT (5X, 10(F5.2,3X))
 WRITE (6,9) (AMT(K),K = 1,10,1)

It is important to recognize the differences between the explicit and implied DO statements. The illustration on page 115 explains these differences.

A wide variety of looping combinations can be constructed and only the programmer's ingenuity limits the number of combinations which can be used. It is desirable, however, to demonstrate several of the primary differences between the explicit and implied DO statements. The following examples provide some idea of the range of possibilities that exist for the use of these statements.

Explicit DO Statement	Implied DO Statement
DO 15 J = 1,3,1 15 READ (5,3) IRAY(J) This DO statement creates the loop by *specifically* listing the command word DO in a separate statement. The index (or counter) is incorporated within the DO statement. The READ statement provides the index cross-reference between the index J and the subscripted variable name IRAY(J). The DO statement uses *no commas* except to separate the initial, maximum, and incremental values of the index.	READ (5,3) (IRAY(J), J = 1,3,1) This statement creates a loop *without* specific use of the command word DO. The index is shown as a part of the command which causes execution, in this case READ. The READ statement includes *both* the index J and the subscripted variable name IRAY(J). The parentheses are necessary to denote the association of the index and the array name. The index J *must* be separated from the array name by a *comma* and parentheses *must* enclose the array name and loop index.

Example 1: Explicit DO Statement for Input

Assume the following data cards are to be stored in the IRAY array.

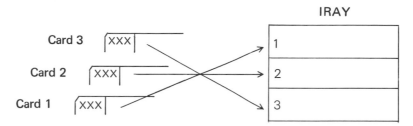

In this case, the program must be able to return repeatedly to the READ statement to fill the array before processing continues. The following program would accomplish the repeated reading (only the essential portions of the program are shown):

```
    DIMENSION IRAY(3)
    .
    .
    .
  5 FORMAT (I3)
    DO 10 J = 1,3,1
    READ (5,5) IRAY(J)
 10 CONTINUE
    .
    .
    .
    END
```

This program has provided for an array with three storage locations (IRAY(3)). The FORMAT describes the data form on each input card. The DO statement directs the computer to READ three times and, with each card read, to assign the punched value to the IRAY location equivalent to the current value of J. After finishing the loop three times, the computer would proceed to any additional processing steps.

During each cycle through the loop, the following relationships exist:

During loop	J will equal	Input data will be stored in
1	1	IRAY(1)
2	2	IRAY(2)
3	3	IRAY(3)

An *essential point* to recognize from the above illustration is that the program directed the computer to *execute repeatedly the READ statement*. This means that *with each execution of the command READ a new data card will be read*. In other words, the computer was directed to read three separate data cards.

Example 2: Implied DO Statement for Input

The use of an explicit DO loop in the above example caused the computer to read successive input cards and store only one value from each card. It would seem much more efficient to punch all three values consecutively *across* one input card. Assume that we had the previous values punched in one input card and desired to read the three values into the same array, named IRAY.

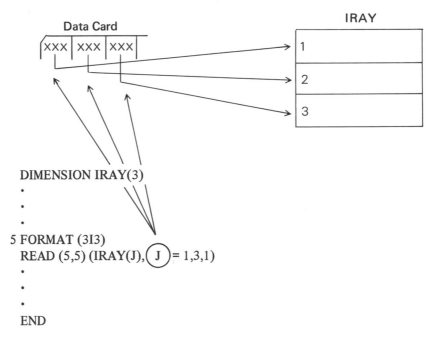

```
DIMENSION IRAY(3)
    .
    .
    .
5 FORMAT (3I3)
  READ (5,5) (IRAY(J), J = 1,3,1)
    .
    .
    .
  END
```

The program steps above enable the computer to READ *across* the data card and to fill the array, named IRAY. Note that to read *one* card required only *one* execution of the READ statement. To accomplish reading across the card, however, the programmer had to specify the number of items which the computer should read. An index similar to the DO statement index was used for this purpose. The DO looping function in this case is *implied* and the computer will insert the values of the index J as subscripts in IRAY(J).

Example 3: Implied DO Statement for Input

It is possible to use the implied DO loop to read consecutive cards. This action is taken when the FORMAT statement describes *fewer* fields than are called for by the index in the READ statement. This condition causes the computer to read *additional* cards until it has satisfied the requirements of the index. Assume the following:

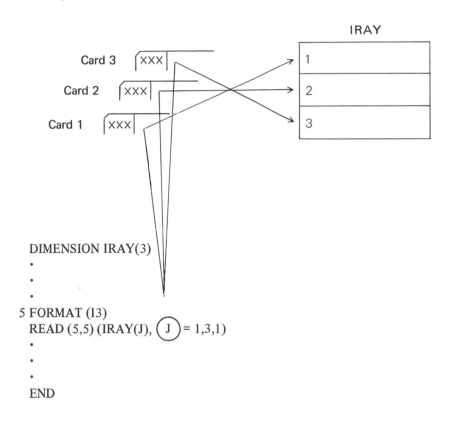

This program calls for 3 data values to be read. However, each card has only 1 value punched. To satisfy the index requirements of J = 1,3,1, the computer will *repeat* FORMAT (I3), reading a new card (called a new record) with each cycle of the implied loop. This illustration shows how an implied loop can be forced to execute the same actions as an explicit DO loop. (See Example 1.)

Example 4: Implied DO Statement for Input

More than one array may be filled with data punched in one card, and control over subscripts for both arrays may be exercised through a single index. Assume the following data card and READ statement (note that two arrays are controlled by a single index):

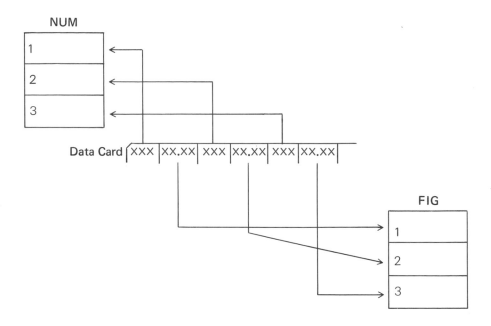

```
    DIMENSION NUM(3), FIG(3)
      ·
      ·
      ·
  5 FORMAT (3(I3,F5.2))
    READ (5,5) (NUM(I), FIG(I), I=1,3)
      ·
      ·
      ·
    END
```

The READ statement shown above, which includes an implied DO loop, is the equivalent of writing the instruction as follows:

READ (5,5) NUM(1), FIG(1), NUM(2), FIG(2), NUM(3), FIG(3)

Example 5: Implied DO Statement for Input

More than one set of implied DO loops may be included within a single READ statement. Each implied DO loop must be enclosed in parentheses and have an accompanying index to control its actions. The following data card and program illustrate this point. Note that two separate implied DO loops are used in a single READ statement.

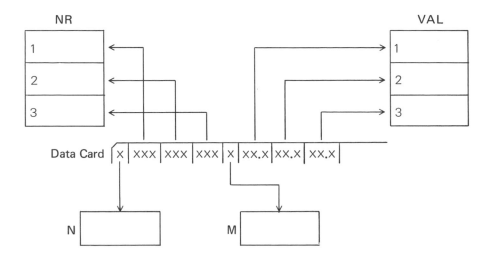

DIMENSION NR(3), VAL(3)
.
.
.
5 FORMAT (I1,3I3,I1,3F4.1)
  READ (5,5) N, (NR(K), K =1,3), M, (VAL(J), J=1,3)
.
.
.
END

The READ statement shown above is the equivalent of writing:

READ (5,5) N, NR(1), NR(2), NR(3), M, VAL(1), VAL(2), VAL(3)

Example 6: Implied DO Statement for Input

In order to generalize the applicability of a program, it may be convenient to first read a card which contains the maximum number of data cards that will be processed. In this case, the number would be inserted in the implied DO statement's index each time the program was used. Assume that 4 data cards will be read. This value will be punched in the first card and then used as a maximum count value in the loop index. The following example shows this process. Note that the value of N is taken from the first card and inserted as the maximum count value in the second READ statement.

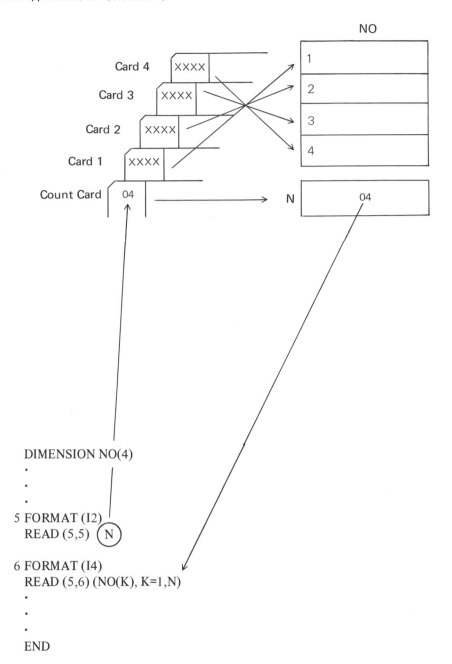

```
      DIMENSION NO(4)
      .
      .
      .
    5 FORMAT (I2)
      READ (5,5) (N)

    6 FORMAT (I4)
      READ (5,6) (NO(K), K=1,N)
      .
      .
      .
      END
```

Example 7: Implied DO Statement for Input

A variation of example 6 has the maximum index value punched as the first number in a card being read and then uses this maximum value in the implied loop as the remainder of the card is read. For example, assume the following data card and program.

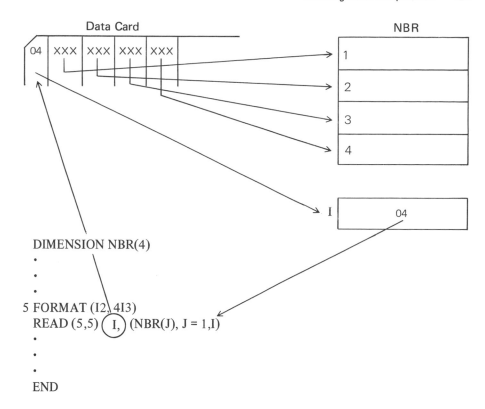

The value of I is read from the first two columns of the data card and is inserted as the maximum value of the index J when the implied loop is executed.

Example 8: Implied DO Statement for Input

As a last example in reading data, suppose that we have a program to read a series of data cards whose maximum size is unknown. Further assume that each data card has five values of the same format. A trailer card test is necessary after reading each card. The implied DO statement could be used to read the five values on any one card but, because the maximum value is not known in advance, the count parameters of the loop index must be expressed in a symbolic form. Each time a data card is read, the index parameters will have to be increased by 5 to enable the computer to place the next card's data values in the succeeding five array locations. The following program illustrates this process.

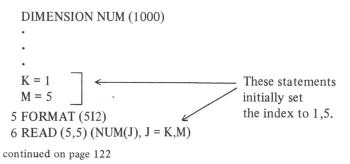

```
    DIMENSION NUM (1000)
        .
        .
        .
    K = 1                                  These statements
    M = 5                                  initially set
  5 FORMAT (5I2)                           the index to 1,5.
  6 READ (5,5) (NUM(J), J = K,M)
```

continued on page 122

IF (NUM(K) – 99) 10,15,15 ⟵――――― Trailer card test.

10 K = K+5 ⟵――――――――― These statements
   M = M+5   raise both index
   GO TO 6   values by 5.

15 ·
   ·
   ·

   END

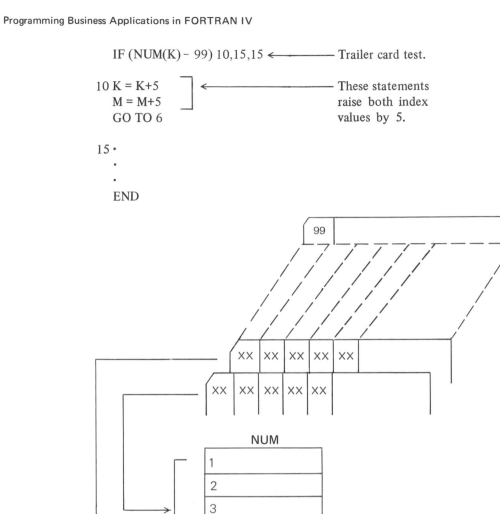

The example above illustrates how the values of the first five cards will be placed in NUM(1) ... NUM(5). Then the index parameters are raised to 6 and 10. The second card's values are therefore placed in NUM(6) ... NUM(10). The index parameters are then incremented to 11 and 15, and so on. This example uses the implied loop to read across each individual card, but provides for the reading of a variable number of total values.

The use of both explicit and implied DO loops for printing output is essentially identical to their application in reading. The command word WRITE is used for printed output and parentheses are inserted to enclose the variable names controlled by the loop index. In reading cards, a new record is equivalent to reading a new data card. In printing, each new line displayed on the printer is considered a new record. The *explicit DO statement* coupled with a WRITE command will *cause* the computer to print *separate and successive lines.* The *implied DO statement,* within a WRITE statement, will *cause* the printing of a *series of items on the same output line.* Because of the similarity between reading and writing, only two output examples will be given below.

Example 9: Explicit DO Statement for Output

If we reverse example 1 and assume that an array (called IRAY) has three values stored in it, then printing each of these values on a separate line could be accomplished by using the explicit DO statement. A program to show this process is given below.

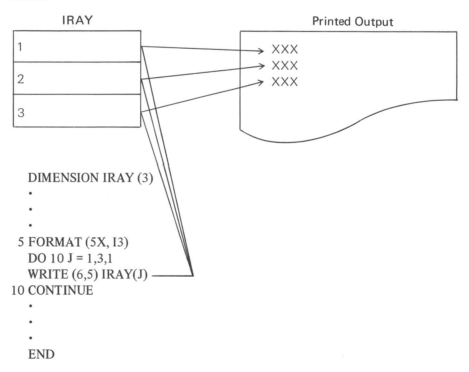

```
        DIMENSION IRAY (3)
        •
        •
        •
      5 FORMAT (5X, I3)
        DO 10 J = 1,3,1
        WRITE (6,5) IRAY(J)
     10 CONTINUE
        •
        •
        •
        END
```

This program selects each value in the IRAY array and prints the values on *successive* lines. The DO statement causes the computer to encounter the command word WRITE with each cycle through the loop.

Example 10: Implied DO Statement for Output

Now suppose that we want to print the three values stored in the array, IRAY, across a single printed line. An implied DO loop could be used just as it was for reading across a punch card. The following illustration shows how this printing is accomplished.

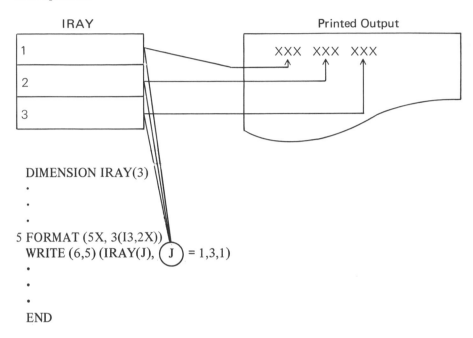

IRAY   Printed Output

1   XXX XXX XXX

2

3

DIMENSION IRAY(3)
.
.
.
5 FORMAT (5X, 3(I3,2X))
WRITE (6,5) (IRAY(J), J = 1,3,1)
.
.
.
END

This program selects the three values in the IRAY array and prints them *consecutively* on one line of output. The implied DO loop will cause the values to be printed *across* the output line.

We have illustrated the DO statement and implied DO statement with the use of subscripted variables. The combination of subscripts and DO statements provides the programmer with one of the most compact, yet powerful, capabilities for handling repetitive operations in the FORTRAN language. The use of the explicit DO statement is also permissible, and often desirable, with non-subscripted variables. This is, however, usually not the case with implied DO statements. Implied loops are essentially limited to the input and output tasks of a program and are normally used with subscripted variables.

Using the Implied DO Statement—A Word of Caution

The use of implied DO statements is nearly identical for both reading and writing. There is one significant difference, however, which should be observed when using this statement.

The following READ statement is invalid:

READ (5,40) (J, NR(K), K = I,J)

The error in this statement is the use of J *within* the parentheses. As written, the statement implies that with each cycle through the implied loop a new value of J will be read. This means that the statement is redefining the maximum value of the loop with each reading. This redefinition of an index is prohibited as we explained earlier.

The previous statement could be rewritten in the following valid form:

READ (5,40) J, (NR(K), K = I,J)

In this second statement, J is outside the limits of the implied loop's parentheses. Therefore it does not redefine the index.

The redefinition problem does not exist in constructing the WRITE statement. The following WRITE statement is *valid:*

WRITE (6,80) (J, NR(K), K= I,J)

Although this WRITE statement is identical to the invalid READ statement shown above, the difference deals with the fact that J is a constant stored value in the computer's memory and therefore does not redefine the index as it cycles through the implied DO loop.

Combining Explicit and Implied DO Statements

It is entirely possible and appropriate to *combine both* types of DO statements. For example, if a program required reading a group of input cards, the DO statement would accomplish the repeated reading. Each card in the group, however, could contain several items of similar data. An implied DO statement would accomplish reading across each card *prior* to completing the explicit DO loop. The combination of these two FORTRAN capabilities provides tremendous data handling power through the use of very few program statements.

Assume that a program segment requires reading 100 data cards and that each card contains 5 separate values. If these 5 values are temporarily stored in an array named DATA, the two looping statements could be used in the following manner:

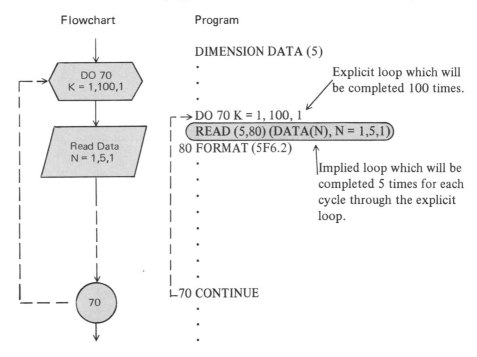

Flowchart

Program

DIMENSION DATA (5)

Explicit loop which will be completed 100 times.

DO 70 K = 1, 100, 1
READ (5,80) (DATA(N), N = 1,5,1)
80 FORMAT (5F6.2)

Implied loop which will be completed 5 times for each cycle through the explicit loop.

70 CONTINUE

The example, as outlined, would cause the computer to read 500 data items (100 loops times 5 data items per loop).

Exercise 18

1. Identify the errors in the following READ and WRITE statements:
   a. READ (5,6,(A,B,C(I),I=10,20,30)   d. WRITE (6,10), (A(K),K=M,N,10)
   b. READ (5,7,I,J,K,L(I),I=N,A)   e. WRITE (6,11) (ABC(J,J=1,10)
   c. READ (5,8) A,B, (IJK=1,6,3)   f. WRITE (6,21) IJ,K(M),M=I,IJ)

2. Write the FORMAT and READ statements for each of the following conditions. Item (c) will also require the use of a DO loop to accomplish reading.

a.

b.
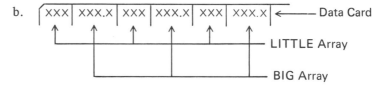

c.
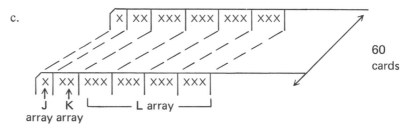

3. Write the FORMAT and WRITE statements for each of the following conditions. Item (b) will also require the use of a DO loop to accomplish writing.

a.
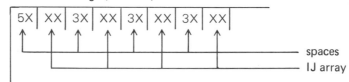

b.
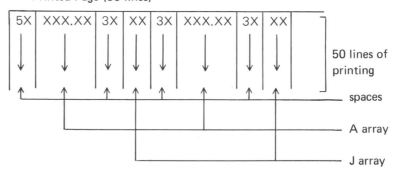

c.   Printed Page (one line)

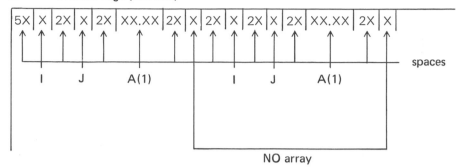

Questions

1. What is an array? What advantages can be gained through the use of arrays?
2. What function is served by subscripts?
3. Why are DIMENSION statements necessary when arrays are used in a program? What specifications are provided by the DIMENSION statement?
4. What are the differences between using DO statements versus GO TO and IF statements for looping?
5. What are the elements of a DO statement? What is the function of each element?
6. What is the purpose served by a CONTINUE statement? What type of error does it help avoid?
7. What is a normal exit from a DO loop? Explain.
8. What is an implied DO loop? When may an implied loop be used?
9. Why is the following statement invalid? Explain.

   READ (5,8) (N,DATA(J),J=5,N,2)

10. What are the elements of a loop? What function is served by each element?

9

Expansion of Input and Output Capabilities

Expansion of the FORMAT Statement

The FORMAT statements that we have used so far have been simple and uncomplicated. In certain circumstances, however, we may need more flexible, and therefore more complicated, FORMAT statements. There are several options available for handling complex FORMATs.

Input and Output: Repetition of Data Fields

At times we will want to repeat an identical description of several data fields. A parenthetical expression within the FORMAT will handle this problem. The following example demonstrates this shorthand usage and is referred to as "nesting." In the shorthand statement, the integer 2 in front of the interior parentheses is called a *group repeat.*

Simple Statement

50 FORMAT (I2, F4.2, I3, F4.2, I3, I7)

Shorthand Statement

50 FORMAT (I2, 2(F4.2, I3), I7)

Other data field repetitions are illustrated below. Almost any logical combination of data fields is permitted.

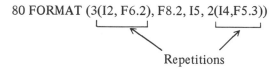

80 FORMAT (3(I2, F6.2), F8.2, I5, 2(I4,F5.3))

Repetitions

This is identical to writing the FORMAT specifications as:

80 FORMAT (I2,F6.2,I2,F6.2,I2,F6.2,F8.2,I5,I4,F5.3,I4,F5.3)

90 FORMAT (4(I5, 2(F8.2,I3),F6.3))[1]

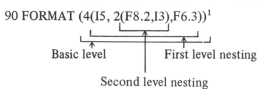

Basic level   First level nesting

Second level nesting

[1] Some processors allow only one level of field repetition nesting.

This is identical to writing the FORMAT specifications as:

90 FORMAT (I5,F8.2,I3,F8.2,I3,F6.3,I5,F8.2,I3,F8.2,I3,F6.3,
    I5,F8.2,I3,F8.2,I3,F6.3,I5,F8.2,I3,F8.2,I3,F6.3)

Of course, as formats become longer, or more repetitive, the shorthand method will become more useful and may be used with both READ and WRITE statements.

Input and Output: Several Records in One FORMAT Statement

Occasionally it might be advantageous to write only one FORMAT statement to specify the use of more than one input card or more than one line of output. The FORMAT elements to accomplish this task are shown below:

Multiple Records.

25 FORMAT (I4, F3.2/ F8.3, I4)   Two Records

The *slash* indicates termination of one record (that is, card or line) and the beginning of another record. A single READ or WRITE statement would handle both records. For instance,

WRITE(6,25)J,A,B,K   or   READ(5,25)J,A,B,K

Using the WRITE command, variables J and A would be printed on *one line* and variables B and K on *another line*. With the READ statement, variables J and A would be read from *one card* and variables B and K from *another card*.

Additional record descriptions may be included in a single FORMAT statement by using additional slashes to separate the record descriptions. The following examples illustrate multiple record FORMATs.

99 FORMAT (F5.2/I3,F2.0/F7.3)   Three records

54 FORMAT (I5/F6.3/F8.2/I6)   Four records

33 FORMAT (F9.2/I2,F2.0/I3/F10.3/I6)   Five records

Several Records with All Remaining Records Identical. An added modification permits one FORMAT statement to specify several different records and then to specify the remaining records as identical. An example is:

45 FORMAT (F8.4,I2/I4,I5/(F3.1,F8.7))

The first record will use *F8.4, I2;* the second record *I4, I5;* and *all successive* records *F3.1, F8.7*. When a FORMAT specification has been exhausted, the computer will repeat the FORMAT *beginning at the last left parenthesis* (that is, *F3.1, F8.7*).

Two other examples will illustrate this FORMAT modification.

44 FORMAT (I6,F7.3/(I3,I7))

Record 1—processed as I6,F7.3
All other records—processed as I3,I7

27 FORMAT (F5.4/(I5/F3.1))

Record 1—processed as F5.4
Records 2, 4, 6, etc.—processed as I5
Records 3, 5, 7, etc.—processed as F3.1

Skipping Records with the Slash. The use of successive slashes at the *beginning* or *end* of a FORMAT statement will generate additional records. Care must be exercised so that the use of multiple record FORMATs actually produces the desired results. The following FORMAT statement will result in the reading of input cards 1, 4, 7, 10, and so forth, or, if used for printing, will display data on lines 1, 4, 7, 10, etc.

70 FORMAT (F10.2,I3,F4.1//)

Some additional examples will illustrate a few other possibilities for skipping records.

83 FORMAT (//F8.3,F5.2/)

Skips records 1, 2, 4, 5, 6, 8, 9, 10, etc.
Processes records 3, 7, 11, etc.

22 FORMAT (/F5.3/I4)

Skips records 1, 4, 7, etc.
Processes records 2, 3, 5, 6, 8, 9, etc.

Skipping Records with the Slash—A Caution. Slashes at the *beginning* or *end* of a FORMAT statement will either cause the carriage to advance one line for each slash or skip one input card for each slash. The computer will skip *exactly* as many records as the number of slashes written. For instance,

60 FORMAT (///5X, I5)

With a WRITE statement, three blank lines will be advanced and printing will begin on a fourth line. With a READ statement, three cards will be skipped and reading will begin with the fourth card.

75 FORMAT (5X,I7,F10.2//)

With a WRITE statement, two blank lines will be advanced *after* printing one line. With a READ statement, two cards will be skipped *after* reading a card. (Be sure to have blank cards, two in this case, at the end of the input data deck so they may be skipped).

A slightly different and unusual line of reasoning applies to slashes appearing in the *middle* of a FORMAT specification. A *single slash* indicates the end of one record and advancement to the next line or card. *Two slashes* indicate the end of the first record, skipping of the second line or card, and then advancement to the third record. *Three slashes* result in skipping two records and so forth. Therefore, slashes in the middle of a FORMAT skip *one less* record than the number of slashes written. For example,

80 FORMAT (2X,I3,F8.2//5X,F5.2/)

With a WRITE statement, this FORMAT will result in the insertion of one blank line between the printed lines of output. With a READ statement, this FORMAT statement will result in reading every other card.

Two further examples will illustrate the use of slashes embedded within a FORMAT statement.

77 FORMAT (F6.4,I2///I5//F8.2)

Skips records 2, 3, 5, 8, 9, 11, etc.
Processes records 1, 4, 6, 7, 10, 12, etc.

36 FORMAT (F2.0,I4//I3///F6.2/)

Skips records 2, 4, 5, 7, 9, 11, 12, 14, etc.
Processes records 1, 3, 6, 8, 10, 13, etc.

Input: Skipping Columns

Occasions may arise where data to be processed already has been punched. If the programmer desires to use only a portion of the data, or if some card columns are blank, it is necessary to instruct the computer to skip certain input fields. Assume the following input format of prepunched data:

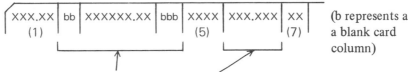

(b represents a a blank card column)

If the programmer desires to use only the first, fifth, and seventh fields, he will prepare the following input FORMAT:

60 FORMAT (F6.2,14X,I4,7X,I2)

The use of the X specification with input will instruct the computer to skip columns in the same manner as it guides the placement of blank characters on an output line.

The following four examples show data cards with accompanying FORMAT statements which illustrate the X code for skipping columns on input cards. (b = blank card columns.)

24 FORMAT (I2,3X,F3.0,2X,I1)
26 FORMAT (4(I2,2X))

28 FORMAT (I3,2X,F4.2//F3.1,2X,I4)

30 FORMAT (3(I2,2X),1X,2(I2,2X))

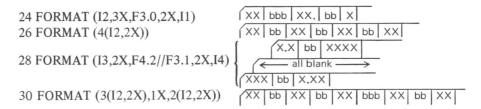

Output: Carriage Control

The line printer operates in a sequential manner similar to the sequential processing characteristic of the computer. This means that the programmer can rely on the computer to print output on successive lines. It is frequently desirable, however, to have output appear on other than successive lines. A technique for controlling the printer's carriage permits the use of spacing and insertion of blank lines. For instance, the following output

```
                    WEEKLY PAYROLL
        EMPLOYEE          GROSSPAYDEDUCTIONSNETPAY
        BILL SMITH        400.00120.50279.50
        JOHN GREEN        300.00100.00200.00
```

would be significantly more readable if it appeared as:

WEEKLY PAYROLL

EMPLOYEE	GROSS PAY	DEDUCT- IONS	NET PAY
BILL SMITH	$400.00	$120.50	$279.50
JOHN GREEN	300.00	100.00	200.00

The second presentation of payroll output is said to have been *edited* through the insertion of *spaces on each line* and through the insertion of *spaces* (that is, blank lines) *between lines*. The first spacing technique is generally accomplished by using the *X* specification in a FORMAT statement.

The second spacing technique (that is, inserting blank lines) is accomplished either by using slashes or through special instructions which control the printer's carriage. Output FORMAT statements may include the special carriage control instructions. The options for carriage control are exercised by assigning the appropriate control character to the *first* character position in the FORMAT statement.

In an earlier section, we stated that only 120 of the 121 character positions on a line printer are available for actual printing. The first character position is *always* used for carriage control and is *never* printed. If none of the special carriage control characters is written at the beginning of a FORMAT statement, the computer assumes that the carriage should be advanced to the *next* line before printing. To ensure the correct carriage advancement, the following special control characters should be used and a *1H* code *must* precede each special control character.

If you want to:		Use this character:	Example:
1.	Space up to the next line before printing your output line	blank	FORMAT (1H ,F12.2,I3)
2.	Insert one blank line before printing your output line	0 (zero)	FORMAT (1H0,F12.2,I3)
3.	Insert two blank lines before printing your output line	– (minus)	FORMAT (1H–,F23.2,I3)
4.	Restore the page (that is, space up to the top of a clean page) before printing your output line	1 (numeric one)	FORMAT (1H1,F12.2,I3)
5.	Suppress line spacing (that is, continue printing on the same line without advancing to the next line)	+ (plus)	FORMAT (1H+,F12.2,I3)

With these carriage control provisions at his disposal, a programmer may specify output to be printed in a very presentable form. However, it requires extreme care in planning the output. Centering, spacing, and the like for all output lines must be planned at the same time in order to assure FORMAT descriptions which will place the output in the line locations desired. The following example uses the payroll output shown on page 132 and demonstrates the correspondence between the page layout and the necessary FORMAT statements. Note that the first character is used for carriage control in each line FORMAT.

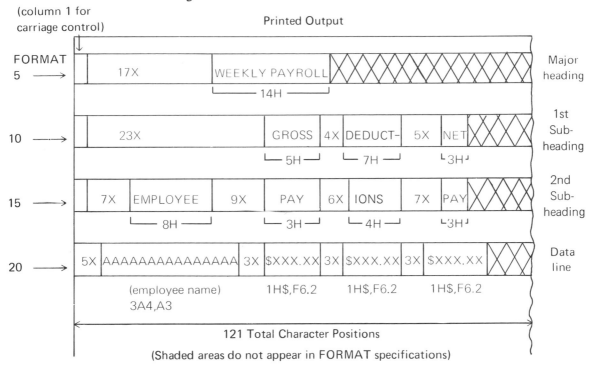

(column 1 for carriage control)

Printed Output

121 Total Character Positions

(Shaded areas do not appear in FORMAT specifications)

If the line FORMATs for the printed output are stated in separate FORMAT statements, they will appear as follows:

```
 5 FORMAT (1H1,17X, 14HWEEKLY PAYROLL)
10 FORMAT (1H-,23X,5HGROSS,4X,7HDEDUCT-,5X,3HNET)
15 FORMAT (1H , 7X, 8HEMPLOYEE,9X,3HPAY,6X,4HIONS,7X,3HPAY)
20 FORMAT (5X,3A4,A3, 3(3X,1H$,F6.2))
```

The first three FORMATs could have been written in a single FORMAT statement with continuation cards. That FORMAT would appear as:

```
5  FORMAT (1H1, 17X, 14HWEEKLY PAYROLL///
1 24X,5HGROSS,4X,7HDEDUCT-,5X,3HNET/
2 8X,8HEMPLOYEE,9X,3HPAY,6X,4HIONS,7X,3HPAY)
```

Printing Headings: The Concept of An "Empty" List

Now that we have discussed the preparation of FORMAT statements, it is important to consider how headings, which have no data values, are printed. The example above, which illustrates four separate FORMAT statements, uses three of the FORMAT statements for headings only. These three FORMAT statements would be printed with the following WRITE statements:

WRITE (6,5)
WRITE (6,10)
WRITE (6,15)

Each WRITE statement would cause a single line to be printed. Observe that *no* variable data name follows the WRITE command. Because of this absence of a variable name list, we refer to the statement as "empty" or as having an "empty" list. Of course, when printing a heading, this condition is appropriate as many headings are fixed in form and require no variable data.

Handling Alphabetic Characters as Data: The A Code Specification

Numeric data is handled quite efficiently by the FORTRAN language. Some of this efficiency is lost when the language is called upon to handle alphabetic or special character information. Nevertheless, it is very often essential for a program to include the manipulation of alphabetic/special characters. Storage of alphabetic/special characters varies with different computers but most machines hold from 2 to 10 characters in any one memory location. Of course, all processors will store at least 1 character in each memory location. The storage of alphabetic data with a structure of 1 character per location requires the establishment of an array when a group of characters is needed to form a word. For instance, a typical alphabetic data requirement is for the storage of employees' names. This would be an essential element for a payroll program.

If an input data card contains an employee name, as well as numeric data, provision must be made in the FORMAT specification for handling the alphabetic data. This is done through the use of the *A Code specification*. If it is assumed that the names of employees will fit within a 20 column field, the following data card and FORMAT statement illustrate their relationship.

In this example, each of the twenty possible alphabetic or special characters is identified by the 20A1 specification.

These 20 alphabetic/special characters will be stored in an array called NAME. Use of this array requires a DIMENSION statement such as:

DIMENSION   NAME(20)

The array listed in the DIMENSION statement appears below and may be subscripted in the same manner as all arrays.

NAME Array

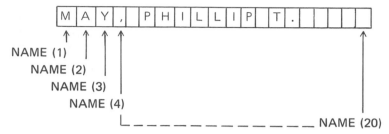

Assume that a firm's payroll calculations require reading a data card, calculating the straight-time, overtime, and total gross pay, and printing the results on a single line. Using the data card description shown above, the program would appear as:

```
    DIMENSION NAME (20)
  5 FORMAT (20A1, 2F4.1, F5.2)
    READ (5,5) (NAME (K),K=1,20), ST, OT, RATE
    STPAY = ST * RATE
    OTPAY = OT * RATE * 1.5
    TOPAY = STPAY + OTPAY
 10 FORMAT (1H0,9X,20A1,2(2X,F4.1),3(2X,1H$,F6.2))
    WRITE (6,10) (NAME (L),L=1,20),ST,OT,STPAY,OTPAY,TOPAY
    .
    .
    .
    END
```

This program will accomplish the following tasks:

1. Reserve 20 locations for storage of the NAME array.
2. Read a data card by loading the first 20 columns into the NAME array (blank columns will be stored as blanks), read the straight-time hours (40) and store them at ST, read the overtime-time hours (20) and store them at OT, and read the pay rate ($5.00) and store it at RATE.
3. Calculate the straight-time pay (40 × 5.00), overtime pay (20 × 5.00 × 1.5—that is, time and one-half for overtime), and total the gross pay.
4. Print the name, straight-time hours, overtime hours, the straight-time pay, overtime pay, and total gross pay on one line.

The line would appear as:

MAY, PHILLIP T.   40.00 20.0 $200.00 $150.00 $350.00

The example above illustrates the handling of alphabetic data; note the somewhat involved requirements for handling such data. The example illustrated the least efficient arrangement for processing alphabetic data. We assumed that only one alphabetic special character could be stored at each memory location. Handling alphabetic data in this manner is permissible with all computers, but most computers will store more than one alphabetic/special character at each memory location. The changes required to make use of this more efficient storage ability are simple. FORMAT statements should be altered to provide more compact storage and DIMENSION statements should specify smaller arrays.

For example, many computers store alphabetic/special data so that a maximum of 4 characters share the same memory location.[2] Our earlier example that stored employee names of up to 20 characters in length would now require only 5 storage locations. The positioning of 5 memory locations side-by-side would provide the 20 character storage needed for the longest employee name. With this alternative storage arrangement, the DIMENSION and FORMAT statements for the previous example would be changed to:

Previous Statements	Altered Statements
DIMENSION NAME (20)	DIMENSION NAME (5)
5 FORMAT (20A1, . . .)	5 FORMAT (5A4, . . .)

By writing the alternative storage specifications, the use of internal memory will be more efficient.

Use of the altered FORMAT statement 5A4 will cause storage of the array to appear as:

NAME Array

5 sets of A4 characters

The READ statement to accompany this altered FORMAT statement will now have the implied DO loop scaled down to 5 cycles as shown below:

READ (5,5) (NAME(K),K=1,5), ST,OT,RATE

The variable data name (array name) used to store the alphabetic characters in the previous example was NAME. This variable name would be associated with the integer mode if used with numeric values. Some processors allow only integer mode names (that is, names beginning with the letters I through N) to be used for A mode values. Other processors allow only real mode names (that is, names beginning with the letters A-H or O-Z), and some computers permit either integer or real names. Check the manufacturer's manual for the particular machine you are using.

Data in memory locations associated with the A mode may be *moved* to other memory locations but *numeric-type manipulation is not permitted.*[3] In addition, most processors require both the sending and receiving memory location names to be of the same mode. For example, suppose we wanted to move the NAME array in the previous illustration to another array named ID. We could use a DO loop to make this transfer, and the loop would appear as:

---

[2] This section refers to storing *alphabetic* characters. Technically, the A mode will handle either alphabetic *or* numeric data (termed alphameric). Processors vary as to the maximum number of alphameric characters which may be stored in one location. The numbers range from 2 to 16. See applicable manufacturer's manual.

[3] Comparisons of the size of one alphabetic or alphanumeric quantity with another can be made with the use of the logical IF statement. This statement is covered in Chapter 10.

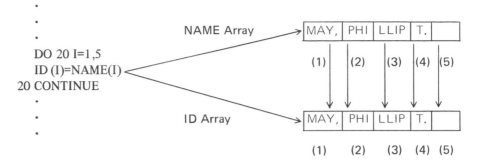

Of course, it is possible to use only a portion of these arrays. For instance, if we wished to print only the last name and the first name in the example above, the following FORMAT and WRITE statements would be appropriate:

10 FORMAT (5X, 3A4)   Only the first three elements in
    WRITE (6,10) (NAME (K),K=1,3)   the array would be printed.

To determine the maximum in storage efficiency, the maximum number of alphameric characters that will be handled as data should be divided by the maximum number of characters which the computer will hold in any one storage location. The result of this calculation will be the size specification for the DIMENSION statement and the corresponding FORMAT specification. Using the previous example, we find:

Maximum characters in one data field	Maximum characters in one memory location	DIMENSION size
20 /	4 =	5

Resulting FORMAT (5A4, . . .)

This FORMAT tells the computer to handle 5 sets of alphameric characters, four at a time (that is, 4 columns in one field).

Naturally, a situation could arise where the division shown above would not come out evenly. In this case, one additional storage location would be added to the DIMENSION to handle the overflow. For instance, suppose that we decided that we would need 23 characters for the maximum length of employee names. The division would then be:

23 / 4 = 5 3/4 storage locations required

Allocation of one additional storage location would accommodate the 3 excess characters. Therefore, the DIMENSION and FORMAT would be:

DIMENSION NAME (6)   FORMAT (6A4, . . .)
                  or FORMAT (5A4,A3, . . .)

The first FORMAT specifies 24 columns from each data card. The second FORMAT specifies 23 columns from each data card.

Using the H Specification for Alphameric Input

There is an additional method for handling alphameric input data. This method has limited usefulness and is more cumbersome than the use of the A specification discussed in the previous section. The use of a Hollerith, or H, specification may be employed in a FORMAT statement in the following manner:

FORMAT (20H   ,F8.2,2F10.2)

This FORMAT statement, using the H specification, provides for 20 characters of input but leaves the Hollerith specification blank. This procedure permits the computer to fill the 20 blank spaces with whatever data appears in the first 20 columns of the data card being read. The most cumbersome features of this method of data handling are (1) the requirement to leave a large number of blank spaces within the FORMAT and (2) the need to use the same FORMAT statement to write out the alphameric characters within the H code. This reuse of the FORMAT is necessary because the READ statement, used with the input data, is not capable of assigning a variable name to the H specification. Therefore, there is no way to store the alphameric data for use with another FORMAT statement. This condition means that the characters read in can be used only for printed output and only in the same form in which they were read. This use of the H code may be useful for reading in temporary items, such as a date which is used on a report heading. The date will change with each issuance of the report and can be punched into an initial data card. The program may then display the date immediately after the computer reads it.

For example, suppose an inventory report for the Jones Company had the following heading:

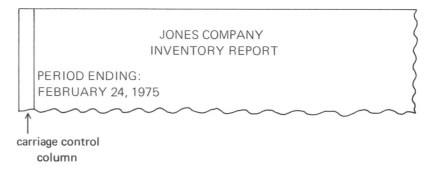

carriage control
column

The statements necessary to print this heading could be composed of one FORMAT statement to print the constant heading information and a set of READ and WRITE statements to input and display the date. The program, data card, and printed output are shown below.

Program Illustrating Input/Output Using the H Code

```
 5 FORMAT (1H1, 41X, 13HJONES COMPANY/
   141X,16HINVENTORY REPORT/1X, 14HPERIOD ENDING:)
   WRITE (6,5)
10 FORMAT (1X, 17H                        )
   READ (5,10)
   WRITE (6,10)
   .
   .
   .
```

The relationships among the date card, program segment to read the date card, and printed date are:

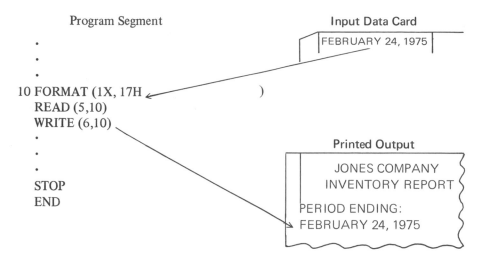

Program Segment

```
        .
        .
        .
10 FORMAT (1X, 17H                    )
   READ (5,10)
   WRITE (6,10)
        .
        .
        .
   STOP
   END
```

Input Data Card

FEBRUARY 24, 1975

Printed Output

JONES COMPANY
INVENTORY REPORT

PERIOD ENDING:
FEBRUARY 24, 1975

As an additional illustration, we can modify the payroll example to read the employee name by using the H code. The program (which has been modified to calculate only straight time pay), data cards, and output appear below.

```
5 FORMAT (1X,20H                        ,2F10.2)
  READ(5,5)HRS,RATE
  GROSS = RATE*HRS
  WRITE(6,5)HRS, GROSS
        .
        .
        .
  END
```

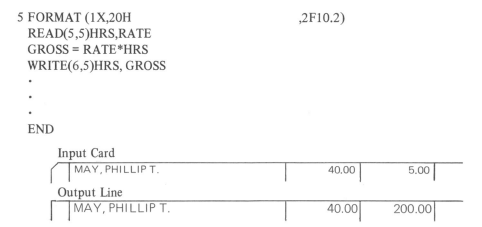

Input Card

| MAY, PHILLIP T. | 40.00 | 5.00 |

Output Line

| MAY, PHILLIP T. | 40.00 | 200.00 |

Note that the alphameric characters read under control of the H code will be reprinted as output *only* when the *same* FORMAT is used for input and output.

Exercise 19

1. Assume an input card with the following fields:

| XXX | X.XX | X.XX | XX | X | XXX.X | X | X |

  a. Write an input FORMAT statement for the above card in as compact form as possible.

  b. Write an input FORMAT statement which will be used to read *only* field 1. Write a READ statement to accompany the FORMAT statement (use your own variable name).

    c. Write input FORMAT and READ statements which apply to fields 1, 3, 5, 7, and 8 (use your own variable names).

2. Write *one* output FORMAT statement for each item below using the following specifications: I2,F8.2,F6.3,I5,F2.0.

    a. Begin output in the sixth space with remaining specifications as shown above.

    b. Begin output in the tenth space with the remaining specifications as shown above and with 2 spaces between each specification.

    c. Begin at the top of a new output page, place I2 and F8.2 on one line with 2 spaces between; F6.2 on a second line and indented 6 spaces from the left margin; and I5 and F2.0 on a third line separated by 3 spaces and indented 4 spaces from the left margin.

3. Prepare output FORMAT and WRITE statements to print the following heading at the top of a new page. Have two blank lines between the first and second heading lines and one blank line between the second and third heading lines (b = blank character position).

25b	WASHINGTONbbCOMPANY	26b
23b	MONTHLYbbSALESbbSUMMARY	24b

10b	DISTRICTbA	5b	DISTRICTbB	5b	DISTRICTbC	5b	DISTRICTbD	5b

Handling Numeric Values

All computers have limits on the size of numerical values which may be processed. In covering the FORTRAN language up to this point, we have used rather small numeric values and thereby avoided any difficulties due to numeric size limitations. It is important to recognize this limitation and, furthermore, to recognize that the *internal* representation of numbers may be different from the *external* representation with which we are accustomed.

Integer Values

We have treated integers as numbers which lacked decimal points. We have assumed that the computer would handle integer numbers differently than real numbers. Our only requirement has been to use the letter I in FORMAT statements or to begin variable names with the letters I through N when integer values were to be manipulated. The specific internal representation of integer numbers depends on the type of computer being used; however, the maximum range of values for integer numbers in all systems is relatively small. This is especially true if integer value ranges are compared with the ranges of real numeric values.

For computers which store values in a binary-coded-decimal form,[4] the maximum range for integer values is normally 4 or 5 digits which run from −9999 to +9999 or −99999 to +99999.

On the other hand, computers which store values in a binary form hold integer values which range from $\pm(2^{11}-1)$ for rather small processors (approximately 4 decimal digits) to $\pm(2^{47}-1)$ for large processors (approximately 14 decimal digits).

Obviously, it will be important for you to check the manufacturer's manual for the processor that you use to determine the maximum integer size permitted.

[4] Binary-Coded-Decimal (BCD) values are stored with each decimal digit in a separate location, although each is converted to a binary notation. Binary computers store entire numbers as one unit in a binary form.

Integer Conversion of Numeric Values

Several factors are very important to the successful processing of integer values. These factors primarily concern the external form of integers, because the computer will automatically convert values to their proper internal form. The programmer, then, is responsible for the accurate description of the input and output handling of these values.

Input. In earlier examples, we have seen that integers could be read with input FORMAT statements describing fields of varying sizes. For this discussion, assume an input data card with seven identical I6 fields. The card appears as:

| 123456 | bbb890 | 468bbb | –bb782 | +46321 | bbbbb0 | bbbb–0 |

FORMAT (7I6)

The seven fields are repeated below with an explanation of how the computer would store the value punched in each field. The lower case "b" represents blanks in the punch card.

Field	Punched Value	Internally Stored as:
1	123456	+123456
2	bbb890	+890
3	468bbb	+468000
4	–bb782	–782
5	+46321	+46321
6	bbbbb0	+0
7	bbbb–0	–0

Several important points should be noted:

1. Zeros are a critical factor in the reading of integer values. Any column within a field which is left blank is converted to a numeric value of zero. This factor causes significant differences depending upon the size and position of a value within a field.
   Note fields 2 and 3. Field 2 has blanks which *precede* the numeric value. These numbers are not significant to the integer value. Field 3, on the other hand, has blanks which *follow* the significant digits 468 and so are added to these digits with the resulting storage of the value 468000!
2. A value's sign takes one column when punched in an input data card. The use of a plus sign is optional, because a number which does not carry the plus sign is assumed to be positive. This is not true of negative values. The minus sign must accompany negative numbers.
   Note fields 1 and 5. Field 1 does not carry any sign and, furthermore, has used all six columns for data values. In storing this number, however, the computer will automatically assume that it is positive. Field 5, conversely, has the plus sign punched. This sign uses up one column in the field and was not necessary for the data's storage as a positive value.

3. A numeric value does not need to fill the specified field width (as illustrated in fields 2, 4, 6, and 7) but, unless they are right-justified, zeros may be added to any trailing blank columns.
4. While the signs used with most numbers are punched immediately preceding the number, the sign may appear any place within the field to the left of the number. Field 4 illustrates this point. The minus sign occupies the first column in the field and, though the sign is followed by two blanks, when the value is stored the sign will also be stored.

Output. Printing integer values is accomplished through the use of a FORMAT specification and WRITE command. The problems with printing are somewhat less severe than with reading. Assume that several lines of output are to be printed under the control of FORMAT (5X, I6). The following illustration shows the handling of several values when moved from storage to the output line.

Internally Stored Value	FORMAT (5X, I6)		
+246890	246890		
+3812	3812		
−28	−28		
−802457	******		
6231784	******		
	5X	I6	

The illustration above shows examples of the following rules for integer output values:

1. All values printed are right-justified in the output field.
2. A sign appears only with negative values and is printed immediately preceding the value.
3. Unused character positions are left blank and are not filled with zeros.
4. A special problem arises when a value is too large for the output specification in the FORMAT statement. The last two items illustrate this point. The first of these numbers has six digits but the need to print a minus sign causes the total number of character positions to exceed the I6 specification in the FORMAT statement. The second number has seven digits and automatically exceeds the FORMAT specification.

   Asterisks (*) have been used in the example to indicate values which exceed their related FORMAT specification. Different computers use varying methods for indicating this condition. Refer to the applicable manufacturer's manual to find the error notation method used.

Real Values

Real numeric values in FORTRAN include all numbers which contain a decimal point and therefore offer the possibility of carrying fractional values. Several types of real values may be represented in the FORTRAN language although we have considered only one up to this point. A very important factor to understand about real values is that the computer does not store real values as we write them externally but converts the *fractional* portion of a real number to an exponential form. This technique allows the computer to store values which have ranges substantially wider than would be allowed by the fixed number of digits permitted in any one storage location. This factor marks the most significant difference between integer and real numbers.

An exponent is a term used to describe a scale factor for any number. The scale factor varies with the type of computers. A computer which manipulates values in a decimal form has an exponent which raises values to powers of 10. A binary processor uses a scale factor which raises values to powers of 2. This process for handling real values is important to understand, although the conversions necessary for manipulation of values are automatically handled by the computer.

A real number, in computer memory, is composed of three elements:

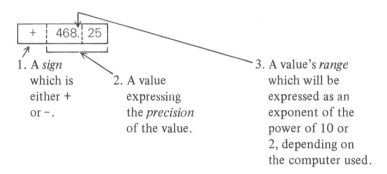

1. A *sign* which is either + or -.

2. A value expressing the *precision* of the value.

3. A value's *range* which will be expressed as an exponent of the power of 10 or 2, depending on the computer used.

A word of explanation is necessary about the three elements listed above. First, the *sign* is handled in the same fashion as explained for integer numbers. All values which are positive may be represented externally either with or without the plus sign. In either case, the values will be stored as positive. Values which are negative must have the minus sign if they are to be stored as negative quantities.

Second, the *precision* of a number refers to the number of *digits* which the computer will store for any one value. Different computers permit varying numbers of digits though these normally range between 7 and 12. Any computer could handle the value +468.25, shown above, because it is precise to five digits. Suppose we change this value slightly. Assume that a computer has a precision limit of seven digits and the value that we wish to store is -468.25679. This value contains eight digits but would be stored to a precision of only seven digits as +468.2567. Note that the least significant digit is dropped *without rounding.*

Third, the *range* of a number is determined by the maximum and minimum limits to which the computer will permit exponents to be expressed. Once again, ranges vary with different computers. Refer to the manufacturer's manual to find the specific range for your particular machine. To provide some perspective on range limits, note that some computers will handle exponents for decimal values with a range as narrow as ±38. Other processors will handle a range as wide as ±616. This means that the narrowest range would provide a decimal exponent of base 10 as large as 10^{+38} or as small as 10^{-38} and machines which handle the widest range would process an exponent of base 10 as large as 10^{+616} or as small as 10^{-616}.

The use of the exponential form is essentially a technique for moving a number's decimal point either to the left or right. For instance, the example above used the number 468.25 written in the common decimal notation. This same decimal value could have been written in several other ways which make use of the exponential form and which enable the decimal point to be moved without changing the value of the number. The illustration below shows several alternative ways to express this number.

$$.46825 \ (10)^{+3} \quad \text{means } .46825 \times 1000 = 468.25$$
$$4.6825 \ (10)^{+2} \quad \text{means } 4.6825 \times \ \ 100 = 468.25$$
$$46.825 \ (10)^{+1} \quad \text{means } 46.825 \times \ \ \ \ 10 = 468.25$$
$$468.25 \ (10)^{0} \quad \text{means } 468.25 \times \ \ \ \ \ \ 0 = 468.25$$
$$4682.5 \ (10)^{-1} \quad \text{means } 4682.5 \times \ \ \ \ \ .1 = 468.25$$
$$46825. \ (10)^{-2} \quad \text{means } 46825. \times \ \ \ .01 = 468.25$$

It should be obvious from the illustration that the decimal point can be shifted with no change in the value of a number when an exponent (ten to some power) accompanies the value. This example used a value of small enough size so that the precision of the number was easily handled by any computer. If we consider handling a value such as 7,000,000,000 with a computer having a precision of only seven digits, it becomes indispensable to have a notation which uses the exponential. This number could be written as $.7 \ (10)^{+10}$ and be handled by the computer as follows:

$$.7 \ (10)^{+10} = 7 \ 0 \ 0 \ 0 \ 0 \ 0 \ 0 \ 0 \ 0 \ 0$$

The .7 falls easily within the precision limitation of seven digits and the computer will automatically move the decimal point in handling the value so that it is properly treated as 7 billion. This illustration shows how important an exponential form is for handling large real values.

The following sections will explore ways to represent real values in their external form. Conversion to an internal exponential form is handled automatically by the processor.

Conversion of Real Values Using the F Code

So far, we have used the F code in FORMAT statements to correspond with the use of real numeric values. This code employed no *explicit* use of an exponent but required the preparation of numbers with both decimal points and fractional components. The size of these numbers, written without an exponent, is limited by the computer used. Therefore, no method exists with F code real values to read or write values having more digits than allowed by the precision of the processor. To overcome this limitation, another code exists which does use an explicit exponential notation. This code is known as the E code, and it will be discussed in a later section.

Input. We explained briefly the use of the F code for input in Chapter 5. In previous examples, FORMAT codes and punched data have been closely matched with respect to field size, and decimal points have been punched in all real input values. Punching decimal points is not a requirement for reading real values, however, and omission of the decimal point has some very strong advantages related to the ease of punching data. Because the decimal point is unnecessary for reading input data, it is recommended that data be punched with numeric values only and that the FORMAT code be used to indicate where the decimal point should be located. Recall that in a code such as F5.2, the F indicated that the input value was in the real mode, the 5 indicated that the value would occupy a total of five punch card columns, and the .2 indicated that the decimal point was to be located two places to the left of the right-most column in the field. A value could be punched in four card columns and thereby save one column (that is, the column which was previously used for the decimal point). The FORMAT code would then be changed to F4.2 in order to match the input data, as illustrated in the diagram below.

The data card illustrates the punching of real values both with and without decimal points. The data card's FORMAT statement is shown below the card. Note how the omission of decimal points in the second and fourth values is accompanied by a change in the F coding, but results in the storage of values identical to the first and third values. The conversion from punched card form to the internal storage form is shown in the table below the card.

| 78.36 | 7836 | 4081. | 4081 |

FORMAT (F5.2, F4.2, F5.0, F4.0)

Punched Value	FORMAT Code	Internally Stored as:
78.36	F5.2	78.36
7836	F4.2	78.36
4081.	F5.0	4081.
4081	F4.0	4081.

Input coding for real data has a great deal of flexibility but may result in numerous problems if not clearly understood. The following discussion will cover the major factors which may be encountered in reading real data values and should be carefully studied.

Assume that a data card contains nine values, all of which occupy six column data fields with the intention of having each number stored with three decimal places, unless otherwise indicated. The FORMAT for this card would read: FORMAT (9F6.3). A lowercase b has been used in the diagram below to indicate blank columns on the card.

Card ⟶ | 12.345 | b1.234 | bbb12. | 12.3bb | b12.3b | 123bbb | bbb123 | +12.3b | bb-b12 |

Field ⟶   (1)   (2)   (3)   (4)   (5)   (6)   (7)   (8)   (9)

The table below shows the conversion of these punched values to their internal form and is followed by an explanation of several considerations in handling real input values.

Field Number	Punched Value	Internally Stored as:
(1)	12.345	12.345
(2)	b1.234	1.234
(3)	bbb12.	12.
(4)	12.3bb	12.300
(5)	b12.3b	12.30
(6)	123bbb	123.000
(7)	bbb123	.123
(8)	+12.3b	+12.30
(9)	bb-b12	-.012

1. A value does not need to occupy the total field width. This is true of all but the first field shown above.
2. When a value does not occupy the total field width, all blanks are converted to zeros. When blanks precede the value, their insertion is normally not significant and the value does not change (see Fields 2, 3, 5 and 7).

   Field 9 is an exception because meeting the three decimal place requirement of F6.3 causes the computer to insert a zero in the space preceding the digits 12.

   When blanks follow the value and are converted to zeros, these zeros are counted in making the decimal placement (see Field 6).
3. Punching decimal points is optional. When the decimal point is not punched, the computer will use the F code specification to place the point (see Fields 6, 7, and 9). When the decimal point is punched and results in a fractional value different from the FORMAT code, *the punched decimal point overrides the FORMAT code*. This is true in Fields 3, 5, and 8.
4. A sign is optional with positive numbers but is required with negative numbers. The sign may appear anywhere prior to the punched numeric value (see Fields 8 and 9).

One very important consideration involves the conflict between a computer's limitation on the precision of numbers and the size of values which are to be read. If an input value exceeds the precision limits of a processor, the processor will drop (truncate) the least significant digits, without rounding, to bring the value within the precision limits. For instance, if a processor with a seven digit precision limitation was being used and a data value had nine digits, the two least significant digits in the value would be dropped when the value was read. Compare the data card and stored values below:

(two least significant digits)

Output. Printing real values presents few problems but nevertheless must receive careful consideration so that values will be printed where intended. The conversion process is nearly the reverse of that used for input of real values. In this case, stored values will be displayed by a WRITE statement using the control specified by its related FORMAT statement. The following table shows some of the most important points in handling output values.

Line	Internally Stored Values	Specification	Printed Output b = blanks
(1)	12.34	F5.2	12.34
(2)	12.34	F6.2	b12.34
(3)	12.34	F7.2	bb12.34
(4)	12345.67	F7.1	12345.7
(5)	12345.67	F7.0	b12346.
(6)	000.00	F5.2	b0.0b
(7)	-834.62	F8.2	b-834.62

The following rules apply to the output shown above.

1. A decimal point is counted as one character on an output value. Line (1) illustrates this item. Four digits are printed but the FORMAT statement specifies a field 5 characters wide (F5.2).
2. A value does not have to fill the entire field specified in the FORMAT. Lines (2) and (3) illustrate how the same stored value would be printed with increasingly larger F field width descriptions. All values are printed at the extreme right end (that is, right-justified) of the data field. When a value is smaller than the FORMAT specification, blanks are inserted to the left of the value.
3. When the stored value is larger than the FORMAT specification, the computer will round up to the least significant digit and print the rounded value. Lines (4) and (5) show this procedure. The value on Line (4) was reduced by one digit when it moved from storage to the printed line. Because the digit to be dropped was 7, and therefore larger than 5, the remaining least significant digit was raised by 1. This caused the 6 to be raised to 7 before printing.

   Line (5) called for printing a value with no decimal places. This caused rounding over the decimal point to the least significant digit and raised the stored 5 to 6 before printing.
4. If the value stored is zero, a zero will be printed (see Line (6)).
5. All positive values are printed without a sign. Negative values will have the sign preceding the most significant digit as shown on Line (7).

Printing real values also provides an easy method for inserting additional spaces on a printed line. This was shown on Lines (2) and (3) when the FORMAT code was expanded though the value to be printed remained constant. Needless to say, to avoid trouble, it is normally a sound practice to provide more width in an output FORMAT specification than is needed. When a FORMAT statement fails to provide enough space to display the significant digits in a value, an error condition will be indicated. The following table illustrates this situation.

For successful printing of real values, all systems require FORMAT specifications which are wide enough to display the following four items:

1. A minus sign for negative values.
2. All of the significant digits, in memory, which will appear to the left of (that is, precede) the decimal point.
3. The decimal point.
4. All of the digits, in memory, which will appear to the right of (that is, follow) the decimal point, as specified by the F code.

Stored Value	FORMAT	Output Error Condition
−78.3	F4.1	−¦78.3
F5.1 minimum specification required to display all elements of the value		insufficient space to print the minus sign
456.7890	F3.1	45¦6.8
F7.3 minimum specification required to display all elements of the value		insufficient space to print the two most significant digits

Note how the two examples above lacked provision for the required space. Skimpy FORMAT codes can easily spell trouble.

Exercise 20

1. Take each of the following punched values, with the indicated FORMAT specifications, and show how the values would be stored in the computer's memory after reading (b = blank card columns):

	Punched Value	FORMAT	Stored Value
a.	1234	I4	_____
b.	−b56b	I5	_____
c.	+b7	I3	_____
d.	bb−b89bb	I8	_____
e.	bbb	I3	_____

2. Take each of the following stored values, with the indicated FORMAT specifications, and show how the values would be displayed on a printed line (use b to indicate blank characters where appropriate):

	Stored Value	FORMAT	Printed Value
a.	+1234	I4	_____
b.	+56	I5	_____
c.	−789	I3	_____
d.	−90	I6	_____
e.	+2468	I5	_____

3. Take each of the following punched values, with the indicated FORMAT specifications, and show how the values would be stored in the computer's memory after reading (b = blank card columns):

	Punched Value	FORMAT	Stored Value
a.	123.4	F5.1	_____
b.	567.bb	F6.3	_____
c.	−89246	F6.2	_____
d.	b−035bb	F7.3	_____
e.	bb78.4b1	F8.2	_____

4. Take each of the following stored values, with the indicated FORMAT specifications, and show how the values would be displayed on a printed line (use b to indicate blank characters where appropriate):

	Stored Value	FORMAT	Printed Value
a.	−12.46	F6.2	_____
b.	+28.903	F10.6	_____
c.	+234.	F3.0	_____
d.	−35.786	F7.2	_____
e.	+321.	F8.2	_____

Conversion of Real Values Using the E Code

The previous section discussed the handling of real numeric values when they are written without the use of an exponential notation (that is, written in the F code). These values were limited in length by the processor's inherent precision limits. This limitation is especially crucial when large values are to be manipulated. An optional code is provided to handle large real values (although *all* real values could be handled in this code). This code uses the alphabetic character "E" to distinguish it from F code real values. The letter E stands for "times the power of 10" and is used to *explicitly* state values in their exponential form. The letter E is used to raise a value to a power of 10 regardless of whether a computer uses decimal or binary internal coding.

The rules for E code use are nearly identical to those which apply to the F code. The precision limits which indicated the number of significant digits for the F code also apply to the E code. As an example of the E code, suppose that a program was to process data pertaining to the Gross National Product (GNP). This program would have to deal with values which were in the billions of dollars. For example, the 1969 GNP was $931,400,000,000. This value has more digits than is permitted by the precision limitations of most computers. This same billion dollar figure can be handled through the use of a reduced number of significant digits coupled with the exponential notation of the E code:

1. *931400000000* is the same as $931.4(10)^9$ in exponential notation
2. $931.4(10)^9$ is shown in the E code as *931.4E09*

If this GNP value was entered in a program as a *constant*, it would be written as:

931.4E09

The letter E is included to indicate that the value is in the exponential form. An instruction statement which uses the GNP figure as a constant might appear as:

GNP = 931.4E09

Three key elements make up an E code value. Examination of the GNP value will indicate these elements.

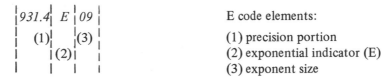

E code elements:

(1) precision portion
(2) exponential indicator (E)
(3) exponent size

Precision Portion (Mantissa). The precision portion of an E code value is subject to the same processor limitations as any other real value. If, for example, a processor which has a limitation of seven digits is being used, then the precision portion of the E code value may not exceed this limit without loss of some values. The precision portion *may* be preceded by a sign if the value is positive and *must* be preceded by a sign if the value is negative. Blanks within the precision portion are treated in the same fashion as the handling of blanks with the F code. All blanks are converted to zeros upon storage. A decimal point is optional. When a decimal point is omitted, it is *assumed* to follow the right-most digit in the precision portion.

Exponential Indicator. Every E code value *must* contain the letter E following the precision portion of the value. This letter merely indicates that the precision portion will be raised (multiplied) by some power of 10.

Exponent Size. The *integer number* which follows the letter E indicates the size of the power of ten to which the precision portion will be raised. This number may be positive, negative, or zero and is normally no larger than two digits (though a few systems may raise 10 to the ±616 power). If the exponent is negative, it must have an accompanying sign.

The following three values illustrate the optional treatment of E code values:

560.3E09	no signs, all elements assumed positive
$-12.35E05$	negative precision portion, positive exponent
$+$ 813E$-$05	positive precision portion, no decimal point, negative exponent

The E code is a shorthand method for expressing numbers. The equivalent decimal value of the three numbers shown above would be derived by multiplying the precision portion of the values by 10 raised to the exponential quantity stated. This conversion is illustrated below:

E Code Value		Equivalent Decimal Value
560.3E09	$= 560.3(10)^9$	$= 560,300,000,000.$
$-12.35E05$	$=-12.35(10)^5$	$= -1,235,000.$
$+813E-05$	$= 813.(10)^{-5}$	$= .00813$

It should be apparent from this explanation that the use of the E code is a method for moving the decimal point, in the precision portion of a value, either to the right or left of its original position. The precision portion of an E code value will either have the decimal point explicitly punched or, when it is omitted, the computer will assume that it appears to the right of the right-most digit in the precision portion. Consequently, multiplying the precision value by a positive exponent moves the decimal point to the right. Conversely, multiplying the precision value by a negative exponent moves the decimal point to the left.

The following table illustrates the movement of a number's decimal point by changing the size of the exponent used. Suppose we want the computer to handle a decimal value of -12.34. This value may be written in a variety of forms, using the E code, and yet retain the same equivalent value.

E Code		Meaning of Exponential Multiplication			Equivalent Decimal Value	
−.01234E03	=	−.01234(10)^3	= −.01234 X 1000	=	−12.34	positive
−.1234E02	=	−.1234(10)^2	= −.1234 X 100	=	−12.34	ex-
−1.234E01	=	−1.234(10)^1	= −1.234 X 10	=	−12.34	ponent
−12.34E00	=	−12.34(10)^0	= −12.34 X 0	=	−12.34	zero exponent
−123.4E−01	=	−123.4(10)$^{-1}$	= −123.4 X .1	=	−12.34	negative
−1234E−02	=	−1234(10)$^{-2}$	= −1234 X .01	=	−12.34	ex-
−12340E−03	=	−12340(10)$^{-3}$	≐ −12340 X .001	=	−12.34	ponent

Input. We have just shown the expression of numeric constants using the E code. These real constants possess the letter E within the value to indicate use of an exponent. This fact tends to become confusing when a value is handled as input and, therefore, must be described in a FORMAT statement. The source of confusion lies with the use of the letter E both within the FORMAT statement and within the value itself. Consider the following example where an exponential value of 246.846E05 is punched in the first 10 columns of a card. An E code FORMAT specification is needed to describe this value and is shown immediately below the input card.

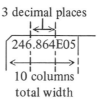

3 decimal places

246.864E05

10 columns
total width

FORMAT (E10.3)

Note how both the value and the FORMAT specification contain the letter E. Each case, however, serves a different purpose: the E within the value indicates the exponent power of 10 while the use of E within the FORMAT specification serves only to specify that the value is expressed in exponential notation.

The E code construction within a FORMAT statement used for input values is rather simple. The integer digit(s) following the letter E specifies the *total* width of the field. This width includes all columns whether used for signs, digits in the precision portion of the value, the letter E, digits in the exponent, or decimal point. In our example, all elements in the punched value took a total of 10 columns and therefore the code began E10. The number of decimal places which are assumed *within the precision portion* is specified by the use of a decimal point and a value indicating the number of places. Referring to our example again, we see that three decimal places were punched in the value, and that the FORMAT specification indicated this with the .3 notation. It is clear then that the E10.3 specification describes the E code value 246.864E05.

Punched values in the E code generally occupy a large number of columns and call for wide field specifications. The omission of a decimal point in punched input requires the computer to refer to the FORMAT code and provide the proper decimal point placement when storing the value. When a decimal point is punched in the input value, and the punched placement does not agree with the FORMAT code, the punched decimal overrides the code specification just as it does for the F code. Blanks (which are converted to zeros) and signs (which may appear anywhere preceding a value) are handled in the same manner as signs in the F code. The following illustration shows the storage of several different E code values.

	Card Columns 1–9 Punched* Values	FORMAT	Stored Values**		Decimal Equivalence
(1)	$-8.921E03$	E9.2	$-8.921(10)^3$	=	$-8921.$
(2)	$+49412E02$	E9.4	$+4.9412(10)^2$	=	494.12
(3)	$-32248E-8$	E9.3	$-32.248(10)^{-8}$	=	$-.00000032248$
(4)	$57834bE1b$	E9.5	$+5.78340(10)^{10}$	=	$57834000000.$
(5)	$-bb.246E8$	E9.1	$-.246(10)^8$	=	$-24600000.$

*b = blank card columns.
**The stored values in a binary computer may not be identical to the digits read. Items 2, 3, and 4 in the example will have the following approximations: (2) 494.119873046875, (3) -0.000000322479991154978, and (4) 57833996287.99999.

Note the following factors in handling the punched values:

Line 1: the punched decimal point overrode the E9.2 code.
Lines 2 and 3: the E9.4 and E9.3 codes provided the assumed decimal point placements.
Line 4: blanks which *follow* the integer digits are counted as part of the values when converted to zeros. In this case, both the precision portion and the exponent were raised beyond the intended values.
Line 5: blanks preceding a value do not change the size of the value and the sign may appear anywhere in the field preceding the value.

Output. The use of the exponential form for output values presents only one key consideration: you must *provide sufficient room* for the display of all significant digits. The E form of output *requires more than seven character positions*. Every E code output value has a fixed use for seven positions. The first three positions are reserved for a sign, the digit zero, and a decimal point. The other four reserved positions are used for the letter E, a sign for the exponent, and two character positions for holding the exponent.

All printed E code values begin with *b0.* when the value is positive. The plus sign for a positive value is not printed and the character position preceding the zero is left blank. When a value is negative, the E code value will begin with *-0.* and display the minus sign. The significant digits in the stored value will follow the decimal point and as many places as called for by the specification in the E code FORMAT will be printed. Of course, if the FORMAT specification calls for displaying more digits than the internal storage precision limits of the computer, the excess print positions will be filled with zeros.

The use of an E code within an output FORMAT statement serves to establish the total character width of the printed field, as was true for the F code. In addition, the values printed will be right-justified in the printed field. The following illustration shows the conversion of stored values to printed values with varying E codes.

Line	Stored Values	FORMAT	Printed Values*
(1)	$+1.23456(10)^0$	E15.6	bbb0.123456E+01**
(2)	$-246.89(10)^4$	E16.9	-0.246890000E+07
(3)	$+1.745(10)^{-2}$	E11.4	b0.1745E$-$01
(4)	$-3567.42183(10)^0$	E14.7	-0.3567422E+04
(5)	$+8.1623(10)^{25}$	E10.3	b0.816E+26
(6)	$-.123456789(10)^6$	E20.13	-0.1234567890000E+06

*b = blank character positions.
**Some processors leave a blank after the letter E when the exponent is positive. A negative exponent will always have a minus sign.

The examples shown above illustrate how the E code specifies the output characteristics of the printed value. In the FORMAT specification, the letter E indicates the exponential form. The digits following the letter E, and preceding the decimal point, indicate the total width of the printed field (and include the seven reserved character positions). Finally, the digits following the decimal point specify the number of significant digits which will follow the printed decimal point.

Note the following points about the examples shown above:

Line 1: to meet the total character width of 15, blanks had to be inserted preceding the printed value.

Line 2: to meet the 9 decimal places, zeros had to be inserted after the significant digits and the exponent had to be increased to indicate the proper placement of the decimal point.

Line 3: to meet the 4 decimal places, the exponent had to be decreased to indicate the proper placement of the decimal point.

Line 4: more significant digits existed than were called for in the FORMAT specification. The excess digits were dropped *after* rounding up to the least significant digit.

Line 5: more significant digits existed than were called for in the FORMAT. The excess digits were dropped without rounding because of the small value of the dropped digits.

Line 6: more decimal places were specified than significant digits were available to fill them. Zeros were inserted to fill the value to its overall width.

Errors are generated in a manner similar to the F code when fields, specified in output FORMAT specifications, are too narrow for the stored values. The most common error encountered is specification of an E code for less than seven character positions. This causes the computer to generate an error condition indicating the skimpy field specification. Obviously, the best rule is to add 7 positions to the number of output digits desired.

Mixing E and F Code Values

All real mode numbers can possess fractional values. Both E code and F code numbers are in the real mode and may, therefore, be mixed in arithmetic assignment statements. Technically, all real mode numbers are stored in identical form *internally,* and the E or F code is important only for *external* purposes (that is, in FORMAT specifications for describing input or output).

The following three statements illustrate the mixing of E and F code values:

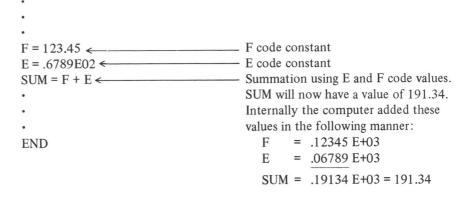

$$\begin{aligned}
&\cdot\\
&\cdot\\
&\cdot\\
F = 123.45 &\longleftarrow \text{—— F code constant}\\
E = .6789E02 &\longleftarrow \text{—— E code constant}\\
SUM = F + E &\longleftarrow \text{—— Summation using E and F code values.}\\
&\qquad\quad \text{SUM will now have a value of 191.34.}\\
&\qquad\quad \text{Internally the computer added these}\\
&\qquad\quad \text{values in the following manner:}\\
\end{aligned}$$

END

$$\begin{aligned}
F &= .12345\ E+03\\
E &= .06789\ E+03\\
\hline
SUM &= .19134\ E+03 = 191.34
\end{aligned}$$

Exercise 21

1. Use the data card shown below and indicate how the E code FORMAT should be written for each of the five values. Also write the equivalent decimal value of each E code data value shown on the data card (b indicates blank columns).

543809E04	–bb312.5E–3	b+12.34E+5	.7284317E1b	1E–b2
(1)	(2)	(3)	(4)	(5)

Value	FORMAT	Equivalent Decimal Value
(1)	_____	_____
(2)	_____	_____
(3)	_____	_____
(4)	_____	_____
(5)	_____	_____

2. Use the following stored values and the specified FORMATs to determine how the values would be printed as output. Indicate exactly which column would have each printed character. Use the lowercase b to indicate blank character positions where applicable.

Value	Stored Value	FORMAT	Printed Value
(1)	$543.809(10)^3$	E15.5	
(2)	$-312.5(10)^5$	E15.6	
(3)	$12.34(10)^{-3}$	E15.7	
(4)	$.7284317(10)^6$	E15.8	
(5)	$-1.0(10)^{-2}$	E15.9	

Questions

1. What is a group repeat? Explain and illustrate.
2. What does a slash mean in a FORMAT statement if it appears:
   a. at the beginning of the statement?

   b.   at the end of the statement?

   c.   in the middle of the statement?

3. What key difference is related to slashes appearing in the middle of a FORMAT statement as opposed to slashes at the beginning or end of the statement?

4. What is carriage control? When is it used?

5. How are carriage control specifications incorporated in a program? Illustrate.

6. What is an "empty" list? When is it used?

7. When is the A code used? What difficulty is associated with the A code?

8. How is the H code used for input? How does the H code differ from the A code?

9. When the computer reads a punch card field, what is the significant difference between blank columns to the right of an integer number versus blank columns to the right of a decimal point in a real number?

10. Where must a sign (+ or −) appear in a punch card field?

11. Where are values placed in a printed output field?

12. What are the three elements in a real number? What is the function of each element?

13. When does the computer automatically insert zeros in a printed output field?

14. What is meant by a "punched decimal point overrides the FORMAT code?"

15. What happens when the computer reads and stores a punched number which exceeds the computer's precision limit?

16. What is the primary difference between E code and F code values?

17. What are the elements of an E code value? What is the function of each element?

18. Why must an E code output value be described in a FORMAT specification of more than seven character positions?

19. When output values are printed, what does "rounding up to the least significant digit" mean?

20. Why is it possible for E and F code values to be mixed in an arithmetic assignment statement?

10
Non-sequential Control—
Additional Branching Statements

We introduced the concepts of non-sequential processing in Chapter 7. The arithmetic IF statement illustrates conditional branching while the simple GO TO statement directs the computer to transfer control without testing any conditions. Each of these statements uses the computer's logic capability. Several other commands are available for decision making and we will cover them in this chapter.

The LOGICAL IF Statement

The *logical IF* statement is another test statement which uses the command word IF. The logical IF is a conditional branching statement much like the arithmetic IF. The important difference is that the result from using the logical IF is a binary, or two choice, result. The logical IF tests a condition and determines whether it is *true* or *false*. Thus, the maximum number of possible branches resulting from use of this test is two. Recall that the arithmetic IF compared the results of an expression with zero and had three possible answers (less than zero, equal to zero, or greater than zero).

The syntax of the logical IF varies from the arithmetic IF, although the appearance is similar and may cause difficulty unless studied carefully. To illustrate the logical IF, recall the condition which exists in a program using a trailer card for indicating the end of an input data deck. Testing for the trailer card value is a binary test. The program will test each input data card to see whether it contains the trailer card value. The answer from this test has to be either true (yes) or false (no). Only these two results are possible. This type of test is characteristic of many other binary logical tests in computing.

Suppose that the trailer card used in a program contains the value 999. A logical IF statement to test for this card might be:

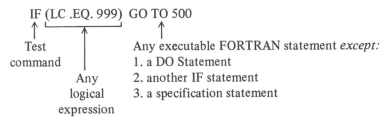

IF (LC .EQ. 999) GO TO 500

Test command

Any logical expression

Any executable FORTRAN statement *except:*
1. a DO Statement
2. another IF statement
3. a specification statement

The logical IF statement shown above contains three basic elements: (1) the test command word *IF*, (2) parentheses which contain the *logical expression* being tested, and (3) a *statement* which will be executed if the answer to the test is *true*. If the result of the test is *false,* the computer will automatically move to the first executable statement following the logical IF statement and process it.

As an example of the logical IF statement, assume that a program reads an inventory card, prices the inventory, and then continues with other processing steps. A trailer card will be inserted at the end of the data deck. This card will contain a value of 999. The data deck and program instructions appear below.

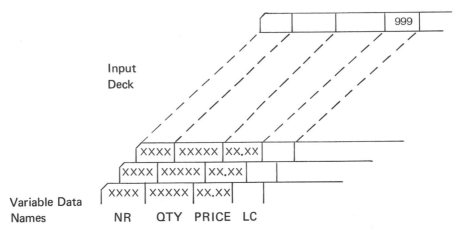

Variable Data Names   NR   QTY   PRICE   LC

In this data deck, the first four columns contain the inventory identification number. The next five columns hold the inventory quantity, and the next five columns contain the price. Columns 15-17 are used to indicate the trailer card value. These columns will be blank on all cards, except the trailer card, and will be read as zeros on all valid inventory cards.

C   INVENTORY PRICING PROGRAM

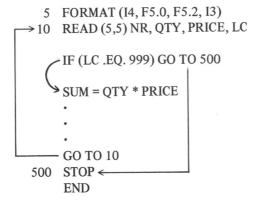

```
    5   FORMAT (I4, F5.0, F5.2, I3)
   10   READ (5,5) NR, QTY, PRICE, LC

        IF (LC .EQ. 999) GO TO 500

        SUM = QTY * PRICE
          .
          .
          .
        GO TO 10
  500   STOP
        END
```

The program reads each data card and then executes the logical IF statement to test for the trailer card value.

On all valid inventory cards, the value of LC (the variable name assigned to the trailer card field) will be zero. Therefore, the result of the IF test will be false (LC does not equal 999). The computer will branch to the SUM statement (false branch). When LC does equal 999, the computer will branch to instruction 500 (true branch).

In many cases, when a program is compiled, the logical IF statement will result in better object code than would the arithmetic IF statement. Thus, the use of the logical IF statement will add efficiency to the program when it is executed.

Relational Operators

The logical expression within parentheses may take on several different forms. In the example given above, the expression tested the equality of a variable named LC with the numeric constant 999. A new type of language specification was used in that expression. The expression for equality was written as .EQ. Of course, it could easily be inferred that .EQ. stood for "equal to." This specification *related* the variable LC to the numeric value 999. The symbol .EQ. is therefore known as a *relational operator*.

There are several other relational operators and the full list appears below.

Symbol	Meaning
.EQ.	Equal to ($=$)
.NE.	Not Equal to ($\neq$)
.LT.	Less Than ($<$)
.LE.	Less Than or Equal to ($\leqslant$)
.GT.	Greater Than ($>$)
.GE.	Greater Than or Equal to ($\geqslant$)

All relational operators are preceded and followed immediately by a period. Furthermore, the items being related preferably should be of the same mode. This, of course, avoids the possibility of mixed mode conditions that we discussed in chapter 7.

We can now expand the concept of a logical expression. The logical IF will test any of the conditions expressed by the relational operators shown above. The relational test may be made between constants, variables, arithmetic expressions, or any combination of these. The structure of a relational test is simply that one constant, variable name, or arithmetic expression appears to the left of a relational operator and a second constant, variable name, or expression appears to the right of the operator.

Examples of several valid logical IF statements are:

```
IF (A .LE. Z)  A = B + C
IF (J .GT. K) TEMP = R**N
IF (OLD .NE. 65.0) AGE = YEARS – 21.0
IF (SIX .LT. FIVE)  STOP
IF (NUM + ID .EQ. KT / M) GO TO 50
IF (LIX – 2 /  (KAR – N**2) .GE. MAX * (MIN * MAX)) COM = 3.0
```

Note that only one relational operator is used in each of the logical IF statements. In addition, all of the examples show a relation between arithmetic conditions. Avoid mixing modes if possible; however, many processors will accept mixed mode expressions and will convert all elements to the most complicated mode represented in the expression.

Logical Operators

In addition to the relational operators, three *logical operators* may also be used. These operators are:

Symbol	Meaning
.OR.	or (either-or, that is, inclusive)
.AND.	and (at the same time)
.NOT.	not (negates)

These operators must be preceded and followed by periods and they broaden the possibility for expanding the complexity of the logical IF statement. The expanded statements are referred to as *complex or compound conditional* statements.

In constructing logical expressions, a basic rule is that neither relational operators nor logical operators may be written in sequence. One exception pertains to the logical operator .NOT. It may appear immediately to the right of either .OR. or .AND.

The addition of logical operators to the construction of logical IF statements permits more than one logical expression to be tested. The following three examples illustrate how logical operators may be included within the logical IF statement.

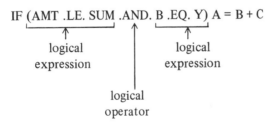

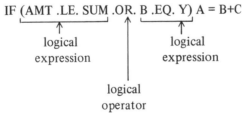

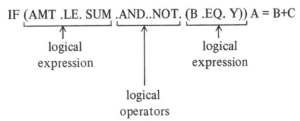

Note how a logical expression now appears before and after each logical operator. The logical expressions make use of relational operators and are, in turn, separated by logical operators. Use of the logical operator .NOT. requires that the logical expression to its right be enclosed within parentheses.

Three more examples which use logical operators are given below. Each example provides an explanation of how the computer will evaluate a complex conditional IF statement.

IF (A5 .GE. B4 .OR. CC .LT. GG) GO TO 600

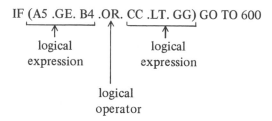

Evaluation: if *either* A5⩾B4 *or* CC<GG, *or* if *both are true*, execute GO TO 600. If both logical expressions are false, execute the statement immediately following the logical IF.

IF (A5 .GE. B4 .AND. CC .LT. GG) GO TO 300

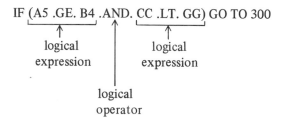

Evaluation: if *both* A5⩾B4 and CC<GG are *true,* execute GO TO 300. If either (or both) logical expression is false, execute the statement immediately following the logical IF.

IF (A5 .GE. B4 .AND..NOT.(CC .LT. GG)) GO TO 800

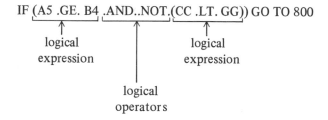

Evaluation: if *both* A5⩾B4 and CC⩾GG are *true,* execute GO TO 800. Note how the .NOT. effectively changes the expression (CC .LT. GG) to (CC .GE. GG). If either (or both) logical expression is false, execute the statement immediately following the logical IF.

Extremely complex conditionals can be constructed using combinations of relational and logical operators. However, this complexity may result in a loss of computing efficiency. The computer will compile the complex statement as a series of simple conditionals and will evaluate the entire conditional statement if it contains a .NOT. or a mixture of .OR. and .AND. operators.

In summary, the following example shows the interrelated components of the logical IF statement.

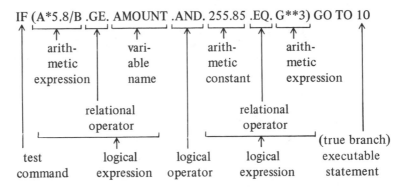

It is now necessary to amend the order in which processing takes place when logical IF statements are used. The normal hierarchy of operations was explained in Chapter 7. The following table indicates the order in which operations will be performed within the logical IF statement:

Executable Operation	Hierarchy
exponentiation	1st
multiplication and division	2nd
addition and subtraction	3rd
relational operators	4th
logical operators	
.NOT.	5th
.AND.	6th
.OR.	7th

Of course, modification of the above order may be accomplished with the use of parentheses. Operations within the innermost set of parentheses are completed first with execution moving toward the outermost parentheses. Within any set of parentheses, however, the order listed above is followed.

To illustrate the use of logical IF statements, assume that an airline uses a program for calculating the point at which each aircraft is to be taken out of service for an overhaul of its engines. The airline uses the number of hours the aircraft engines have been running and the total air miles flown as criteria for determining maintenance. For simplicity, assume that the airline will take an aircraft from service if it has either run its engines for 5,000 hours or flown 150,000 miles since the last major maintenance was completed. A daily log of each aircraft's activity is keypunched and processed with a summary card of the cumulative activity since the last overhaul. This requires the program to read a summary card and store the cumulative totals. Then the current day's activity card is read and the figures for the day are added to the summary data. Tests are made on the updated data to identify aircraft which should be scheduled for engine overhaul. If an aircraft is not to be taken from service, a new summary card will be punched for use with the activity data for the next day.

The input data cards for our problem appear below. The flowchart appears in Figure 10.1, and the program appears in Program 10.1. The total distance flown is the cumulative distance from a summary card plus the day's distance on an activity card. In addition, the engine hours are cumulative from a summary card plus the day's time on an activity card.

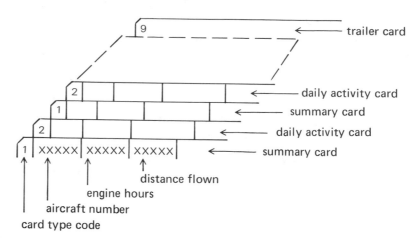

trailer card
daily activity card
summary card
daily activity card
summary card

distance flown
engine hours
aircraft number
card type code

Program 10.1

```
C  AIRCRAFT MAINTENANCE PROGRAM

        TOTDIS = 0.0
        TOTHRS = 0.0
   4    FORMAT (I1,I5,F5.0,F6.0)
   5    READ (5,4) ID,NUM,HRS,DIST
        IF (ID.EQ.9) GO TO 40
        IF (ID.EQ.2) GO TO 20        ◄──────────  Logical IF—identifies input
  10    TOTHRS = HRS                               cards as either summary or
        TOTDIS = DIST                              detail cards
        GO TO 5
  20    TOTHRS = TOTHRS + HRS
        TOTDIS = TOTDIS + DIST
        IF (TOTHRS.GE.5000.0) GO TO 30   ]◄─────  Logical IF statements—test for
        IF (TOTDIS.GE.150000.0) GO TO 30 ]         either of the conditions which
        IHRS = TOTDIS                              require engine overhaul
        IDIS = TOTDIS
        WRITE (7,25) NUM,IHRS,IDIS ]
  25    FORMAT (1H1,2I5,I6)        ]◄──────────  Statements to punch new
        GO TO 5                                    summary cards with values
  30    WRITE (6,35) NUM                           punched in the integer mode
  35    FORMAT (8HAIRCRAFT,I5,1HREQUIRES OVERHAUL)
        GO TO 5
  40    STOP
        END
```

Printed Output

```
AIRCRAFT 99999 REQUIRES OVERHAUL
AIRCRAFT 12345 REQUIRES OVERHAUL
```

Punched Output

```
167890  1020  52000
```

Figure 10.1

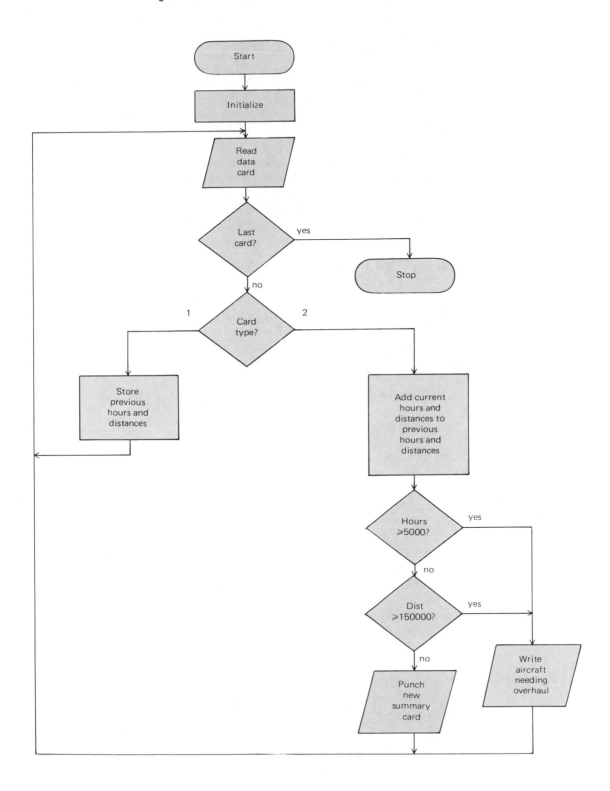

Note the following about the program:

1. The first logical IF statement tests for the trailer card. When a 9 is punched in column one, control will be transferred to statement 40 (that is, STOP).
2. The second logical IF statement tests for a 2 in column one of each input card. When a 2 is punched in this column, the program identifies a card as a detail card. The "true" branch is taken and transfer is made to statement 20.
   When a 2 is not found in column one, a 1 must have been punched and a summary card is indicated. This causes the "false" branch to be taken. The statement following the logical IF is executed (that is, statement number 10).
3. When the computer punches values into a new summary card, the cumulative hours and distances are punched in the integer mode to avoid the punching of decimal points. The conversion of values from the real to integer mode results in summary cards having values properly placed for reading when the program is rerun with new detail cards.
4. The two logical IF statements could have been written in a single statement as follows:

IF (TOTHRS .GE. 5000.0 .OR. TOTDIS .GE. 150000.0) GO TO 30

Exercise 22

1. Read each of the logical IF statements written below. For each incorrect statement, identify the error(s) and write a corrected IF statement on the line to the right.

   a. IF X.GE.Y GO TO 15 _____

   b. IF (A .LE. Z) A = B*C _____

   c. IF (N.LT..OR..EQ.K) STOP _____

   d. IN (A+5.0.AND.B/2.EQ.C) GO TO 50 _____

   e. IF (L.NE.M.AND..NOT.J+2.EQ.K) ,CONTINUE _____

2. Write a logical IF statement to meet each of the conditions expressed below.

   a. If CAR exceeds SMALL, set MAX to NUM cubed.
   b. If AMT equals SUM or is smaller than SUM squared, set AMT to zero.
   c. If NUM does not equal KTOT and simultaneously K is not greater than L or if M2 minus 5 is not less than N, stop.
   d. If TOP plus A is divided by B and is less than 6 or is greater than 12, go to statement 808.
   e. If TOTAL multiplied by TOTAL3 and at the same time DD plus EE are not greater than BUNCH, 3 should be stored at location N.

The FORTRAN Computed GO TO Statement

The unconditional transfer command, called the GO TO statement, directs the computer to transfer control immediately to a specific statement for execution. A modified form of this statement is also available. This form asks the computer to test a variable name and, depending upon the value of the variable, tells the computer to transfer control to one of several statements. This conditional control statement is written in the following form:

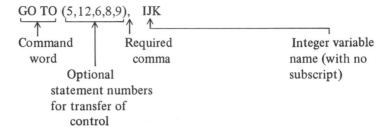

GO TO, of course, is the command word causing the computer to transfer control. The numbers within parentheses are *program statement numbers*. IJK is an integer variable name which must contain a positive value greater than zero. When the computed GO TO statement is executed, the integer variable's value specifies the next statement to which control is transferred. The following list shows the relationship between statement numbers and integer variable values in the example statement above.

If IJK has a value of:	Transfer to statement number:
1	5
2	12
3	6
4	8
5	9

The statement numbers shown above are only for purposes of illustration and the variable name IJK was chosen for the same purpose. *Any integer variable name* may be used and the statement numbers refer to *executable instructions* elsewhere in the program. The statement numbers need not be in any specific numerical sequence and may be repeated within the parentheses. Values of the integer variable begin at 1 and are assigned in a one-for-one order to the statement numbers appearing within the parentheses.

Often, when first encountered, the computed GO TO seems complex. The essential point is not to confuse the purpose of the numbers within the parentheses. *The numbers within parentheses are statement reference numbers* and *not* numeric values stored at locations within computer memory. Suppose that a computed GO TO statement is written as:

GO TO (8,3,3,7,12,13,15,15,20),ID

The computer will *test* the memory location having the integer variable name *ID* (hence, we will refer to it as a test variable) to determine the *numeric value stored* at that location. *Then,* depending upon the size of that numeric value, it will *select* the appropriate *statement reference number* from within the parentheses. Transfer of control is then made to that statement. The computer will always transfer control to the first listed statement number when the test variable (ID in this example) is equal to 1, it will transfer to the second statement number when the test variable equals 2, and so on. In the above example, the test variable and statement number interrelationships would be:

When the value stored at ID is equal to:

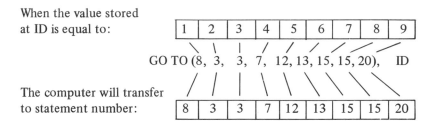

The computer will transfer to statement number:

Note that statement numbers may be repeated within the parentheses. In the above example, the statement numbers 3 and 15 were repeated. This means that when the test variable ID is either 2 or 3 the computer will transfer to statement 3 and, likewise, when ID is either 7 or 8 the computer will transfer to statement 15.

Be careful to distinguish between the integer test variable's value and the statement numbers in parentheses. In the example, only once were the ID value and a statement number identical. This occurred with the number 3 and it was included only for purposes of illustration. There is no requirement that any of the integer test variable's values and statement numbers agree.

Two cautions should be observed when using the computed GO TO. First, the integer test variable name may not be an array element. Second, if the test variable's value is less than one or greater than the number of statements in parentheses, the statement following the computed GO TO will be executed.

To illustrate the computed GO TO, suppose an insurance company is interested in accumulating data on the size of their insurance commitments by risk class of the insured. Assume that the desired information is (1) number of policies by risk class and (2) the total dollar value of insurance written for each risk class. Assume, further, that there are four risk classes for this type of insurance. The risk classes are coded 1 through 4. All data necessary is punched into cards and appears below. Assume the following card column assignments:

column 1:	Trailer value
column 2:	Policy number (ignored in this program)
columns 5-10:	Policy value (in even dollars)
column 11:	Risk class
columns 12-80:	Other data (ignored in this program)

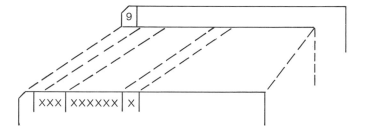

A flowchart and program segment to process the insurance data are shown in Figure 10.2 and Program 10.2.

Figure 10.2

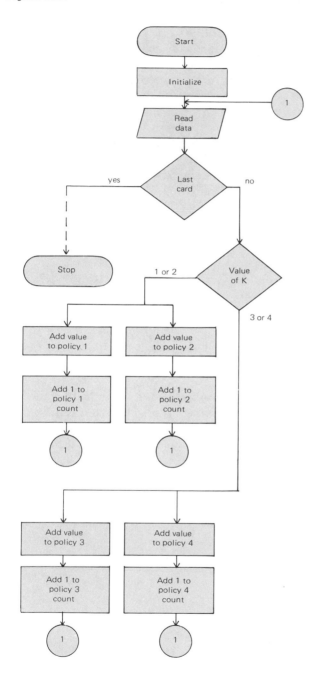

Program 10.2

```
C  INSURANCE PROGRAM
C  USE OF THE COMPUTED GO TO

      POL1 = 0.0
      POL2 = 0.0
      POL3 = 0.0
      POL4 = 0.0
      NR1 = 0
      NR2 = 0
      NR3 = 0
      NR4 = 0
15 FORMAT (I1, 3X, F6.0, I1)
18 READ (5,15) LC, VALUE, KLASS

      IF (LC.EQ.9) GO TO 50

      GO TO (20,25,30,35), KLASS

20 POL1 = POL1 + VALUE
   NR1 = NR1 + 1
   GO TO 18

25 POL2 = POL2 + VALUE
   NR2 = NR2 + 1
   GO TO 18

30 POL3 = POL3 + VALUE
   NR3 = NR3 + 1
   GO TO 18

35 POL4 = POL4 + VALUE
   NR4 = NR4 + 1
   GO TO 18

50 ·
   ·
   ·
   STOP
   END
```

Note how the value of the insurance risk class (variable name KLASS) was read from an input data card and then used in the computed GO TO test variable name. The computer transfers control to statement numbers 20, 25, 30, or 35 when the value of KLASS is 1, 2, 3, or 4, respectively.

The computed GO TO statement accomplishes decision tasks which could be completed with an IF statement, or series of IF statements. When a series of four or more tests is necessary in handling data, the computed GO TO might be a time-saving alternative to using several IF statements. The limitation which an IF statement possesses, of course, is that it may select from only a maximum of three alternative options with each test. The computed GO TO, on the other hand, may have more than three alternatives listed within the parentheses.

As a comparative example of the difference between the arithmetic IF and computed GO TO statements, assume that it is necessary to prepare a program to process sales data for a company which has six sales districts. Data will be read from punch cards and the first column of each card identifies the sales district. Assume the sales districts are numbered from 1 to 6. The program should first identify the sales district and then transfer to the specific statements which will process that district's data. To simplify the example, assume that the input card would appear as:

District   Sales
   ID   amount

The two program segments on page 169 illustrate how one computed GO TO statement would accomplish the same task as three IF statements, and, in addition, provide a more efficient object code.

The following disadvantages should be recognized when using the computed GO TO. One is the need for consecutive numbering of the integer test variable name beginning at 1. A second disadvantage relates to computing efficiency when the computed GO TO is used where three or fewer branches are needed. For a three branch test, the arithmetic IF provides a more efficient object code than does the computed GO TO. For a two branch test, the logical IF gives a more efficient code than either the arithmetic IF or the computed GO TO statements.

Exercise 23

1. Read the following program and then answer the question by filling in the blanks on the right on page 170.

```
C    COMPUTED GO TO
     ONE = 5.0
     TWO = 10.0
     TREE = 15.0
     FOR = 0.0
     FIVE = 0.0
     SIX = 0.0
     J = 0
50   J = J + 1
```

continued on page 170

Program 10.3

Value of ID	Computed GO TO	IF Statements	Value of ID

```
C Comment Card                    C Comment Card
        •                                 •
        •                                 •
        •                                 •
   10   FORMAT (I1,F9.2)            10   FORMAT (I1,F9.2)
   12   READ (5,10) ID, SALES       12   READ (5,10) ID, SALES
        •                                 •
        •                                 •
        •                                 •
        GO TO (51,52,53,54,55,56),ID      IF (ID-2)51,52,53
   51   •                           51   •
        •                                 •
        GO TO 12                          GO TO 12
   52   •                           52   •
        •                                 •
        •                                 •
        GO TO 12                          GO TO 12
   53   •                           53   IF (ID-4)54,55,56
        •                           54   •
        GO TO 12                          •
   54   •                                 GO TO 12
        •                           55   •
        •                                 •
        GO TO 12                          •
   55   •                                 GO TO 12
        •                           56   IF (ID-6)57,58,58
        •                           57   •
        GO TO 12                          •
   56   •                                 •
        •                                 GO TO 12
        GO TO 12                     58   •
        •                                 •
        •                                 •
        •                                 •
        STOP                              GO TO 12
        END                               •
                                          •
                                          •
                                          STOP
                                          END
```

Value of ID (Computed GO TO): (ID=1) 51, (ID=2) 52, (ID=3) 53, (ID=4) 54, (ID=5) 55, (ID=6) 56

Value of ID (IF Statements): (ID=1) 51, (ID=2) 52, (ID>2) (ID=3) 53/54, (ID=4) 55, (ID>4) (ID=5) 56/57, (ID=6) 58

```
        GO TO (60,70,80), J
80      FOR = TREE + ONE
        GO TO 100
70      FIVE = TREE – TWO
        GO TO 50
60      SIX = TREE + TWO * ONE
        GO TO 50
100     STOP
        END
```

What will the value of each variable be each time the computed GO TO is executed?

	J	ONE	TWO	TREE	FOR	FIVE	SIX
1st time	___	___	___	___	___	___	___
2nd time	___	___	___	___	___	___	___
3rd time	___	___	___	___	___	___	___

2. Identify the errors in the following computed GO TO statements and write a corrected statement on the line to the right.
   a. GOTO (J,L,M,N), INDEX   _____
   b. GO TO 2,20,18,1,6, ID   _____
   c. GO TO (5,8,7,3) ID+5   _____
   d. GO TO (16,3,3,3,4), K   _____
   e. GO TO (5,5,5,5) KAT   _____

3. Here is an exercise to check your understanding and implementation of the computed GO TO statement. Read the verbal descriptions and then write an appropriate computed GO TO statement for each description. Use KEY for the test variable name.
   a. Transfer to statement 2 when the test variable has a value of 1,3,5,7; otherwise transfer to statements 4,9,8,8 when the index is 2,4,6,8.
   b. Transfer to statement 5 each time the test variable doubles otherwise the statement numbers should be the same as the values of the test variable. The last statement number in parentheses should relate to the test variable value of 8.
   c. Transfer to statement 7 on each even value of the test variable. For the odd values of the test variable, the statement numbers should begin at 1 and double with each number used. The last statement number in parentheses should relate to the test variable value of 10.

The END= Specification within the READ Statement

A considerable amount of discussion has been devoted to the use of trailer cards for sensing the end of an input data deck (referred to as an end-of-file condition). The techniques developed for sensing the trailer card used either arithmetic IF statements or logical IF statements. An alternative exists for performing this end-of-file test and is somewhat more convenient than the techniques previously suggested.

The inclusion of an END= specification within a READ statement[1] indicates the

---

[1] This language element is not available on all processors. Consult the applicable manufacturer's manual prior to its use.

statement to which the program should branch when an end-of-file condition is sensed by the processor. This specification appears as follows:

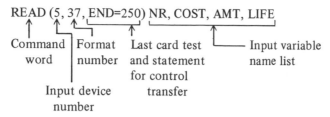

READ (5, 37, END=250) NR, COST, AMT, LIFE

Command word | Format number | Last card test and statement for control transfer | Input variable name list

Input device number

This statement directs the processor to transfer control to statement number 250 when the end-of-file condition is sensed. When a READ command is used repeatedly, the READ statement will eventually exhaust the data cards available to be read. When the computer reads the end-of-file record (a /* card as explained in Chapter 6), the end-of-file condition will be recognized. It is at this time that control will be transferred to statement 250 (or whatever statement number has been specified by the programmer).

Note that *execution of the END= option* occurs only when the processor *reads an end-of-file record.* It does not execute the END= option when the last valid data card is read.

As an example of the END= clause, the following program segment will illustrate a simple inventory pricing process. Assume that the input data deck will contain cards which have an inventory number, quantity on hand, and unit price punched. A data card will be read, the quantity and price multiplied, and, after further processing, control will be returned to the READ statement.

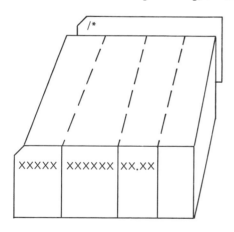

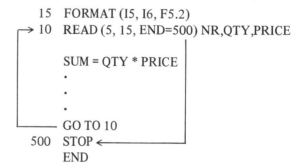

```
C  INVENTORY PRICING PROGRAM
C  USE OF THE END= CLAUSE

   15   FORMAT (I5, I6, F5.2)
   10   READ (5, 15, END=500) NR,QTY,PRICE

        SUM = QTY * PRICE
        .
        .
        .
        GO TO 10
  500   STOP
        END
```

Observe that, in this program, no trailer card was used at the end of the input data deck, and, of course, there was no trailer card test following the READ statement. After reading a valid data card, the processor transfers to the SUM statement and sequentially processes statements until it is directed to return to the READ statement. This return occurs when the GO TO 10 statement is executed.

After reading and processing the last valid data card, the GO TO 10 statement will send the processor back to READ. However, only the /* card remains to be read. Therefore, the END= statement will cause the processor to transfer to statement 500. This statement is a STOP command and processing terminates.

The *END=* clause is *optional* in constructing READ statements and is a very advantageous addition to the FORTRAN language. A very real possibility exists for programs to contain several sub-groups of data cards within a total data deck. When input data is organized in this form, it is optional whether a trailer card or an end-of-file record (/*) is used at the end of each group of data cards.

An illustration of a trailer card test and END= clause combination is shown in the following program. Assume that a firm is processing marketing research data collected in two different market areas. The data will be read in blocks, by market area. The input cards are coded with either a 1 or a 2 in the first column for market area identification. A trailer card containing a 9 in column 1 will be used to separate market area 1 data from market area 2 data.

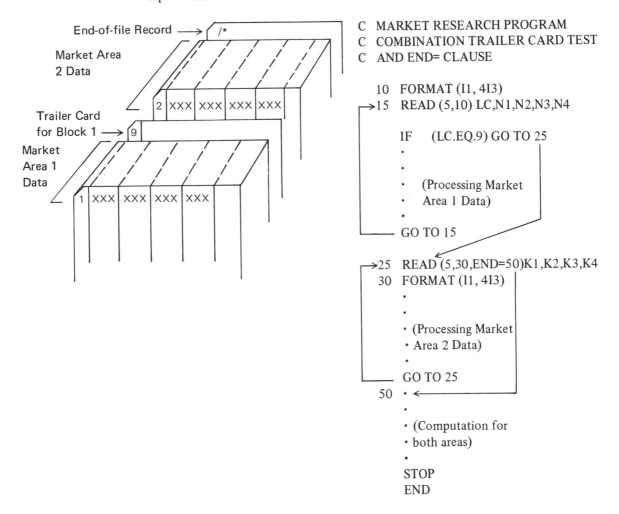

```
C  MARKET RESEARCH PROGRAM
C  COMBINATION TRAILER CARD TEST
C  AND END= CLAUSE

10  FORMAT (I1, 4I3)
15  READ (5,10) LC,N1,N2,N3,N4

    IF   (LC.EQ.9) GO TO 25
    .
    .
    .  (Processing Market
    .   Area 1 Data)
    .
    GO TO 15

25  READ (5,30,END=50)K1,K2,K3,K4
30  FORMAT (I1, 4I3)
    .
    .
    . (Processing Market
    . Area 2 Data)
    .
    GO TO 25
50  .
    .
    . (Computation for
    . both areas)
    .
    STOP
    END
```

Note the difference between the two READ statements. 15 READ is followed immediately by the trailer card test. This test will determine the separation between the blocks of data. The separation is sensed when the card with 9 in column 1 is read. 25 READ contains the END= clause to sense the end-of-file record for this program.

The ERR= Specification within the READ Statement

A second optional specification may be included within a READ statement and is constructed in a form much like the END= clause. This parameter is the ERR= clause[2] and appears as:

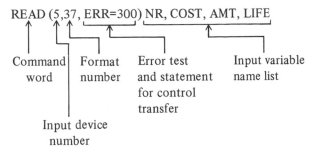

READ (5,37, ERR=300) NR, COST, AMT, LIFE

Command word

Format number

Error test and statement for control transfer

Input variable name list

Input device number

The ERR= specification provides the program with an option for handling errors which occur during the input or output transfer of data. This clause sends control to the statement number listed after ERR= when an error occurs during data transfer. Without this option, all processing will terminate.

It is important to understand the type of errors which will cause execution of this option. The errors must occur during the process of reading or writing and relate to data which is not acceptable to the input or output device. One example would be an attempt to read alphabetic or special characters in a field defined with an I or F code specification. Another example, calling for execution of the ERR= option, is the attempt to read data from a magnetic tape which contains some imperfection, such as a defective magnetic coating or a heavy layer of dirt. The tape device would not accept the data and when this error condition is sensed, the computer system will direct the tape handler to attempt rereading the data. If this is unsuccessful, transfer is made to the statement number specified in the ERR= option.

This language element's key advantage is the ability to continue processing a program even though an input error has been sensed. This, of course, assumes that the type of error will not be disastrous to the accuracy of the computed results.

In spite of its advantage, there is a possible drawback to the use of the ERR= specification. Many users of computing equipment will be involved with systems of some complexity. These complex systems often contain special job scheduling, or spooling, capabilities which accumulate and store multiple programs on an external storage medium while awaiting processing.

When the system is ready to process a program, it will read the program from the external storage medium, *not from a card reader*. For instance, although the programmer may have submitted a program card deck, if the external storage medium is magnetic disk, at the time of execution his program will be made available to the central processor from the disk storage. This makes use of the ERR= option very difficult. Inclusion of the ERR= option within a READ statement will not work where input is assumed to be from a card reader, but the system is really reading from a disk unit. Therefore, on complex systems, the ERR= option may be ignored by the system if not used properly.

---

[2] This language element is not available on all processors. Consult the applicable manufacturer's manual prior to its use.

The ASSIGN Statement and Assigned GO TO Conditional Branch

Another conditional branching statement, using the GO TO command, is available in the FORTRAN language. This statement is the assigned GO TO. However, it is not available in all versions of FORTRAN and is less flexible than the computed GO TO. Many programmers avoid the assigned GO TO statement because of these drawbacks. A redeeming feature of this statement, however, is the fact that it is the fastest of the conditional branches. Therefore, if its use can appropriately be made, processing efficiency may be gained.

The *assigned GO TO* really *requires* the use of *two statements*. One statement assigns a statement number prior to branching and appropriately is designated by the word *ASSIGN*. The second statement makes the branching decision and uses the command words *GO TO*. As a matter of fact, the appearance of this GO TO statement is very similar to that of the computed GO TO. The following illustration shows ASSIGN and GO TO statements as they would appear within the sequence of a program's instructions.

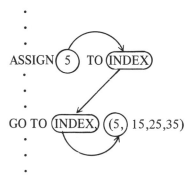

The ASSIGN statement assigns a number to an integer variable which will, in turn, be used in the GO TO statement. The *number assigned to the integer variable must be one of the statement numbers appearing within the parentheses in the GO TO statement.* The arrows in the above illustration show the relationship between the ASSIGN and GO TO statements.

The elements of the ASSIGN and GO TO statements are shown below.

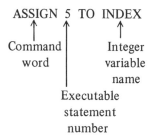

The following requirements apply to the ASSIGN statement:

1. The word ASSIGN must be used to make the assignment of a statement number for subsequent use in the GO TO statement.
2. The assigned executable statement number must appear within the program and must be one of the numbers listed within the parentheses of the GO TO statement. The statement number must be an integer.

3. The variable name used in the ASSIGN statement must be an integer variable name. This variable may not be used for any other purpose in the program.
4. A statement number assignment must be made prior to the execution of a GO TO statement.

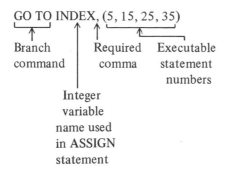

GO TO INDEX, (5, 15, 25, 35)

Branch command

Required comma

Executable statement numbers

Integer variable name used in ASSIGN statement

The following requirements apply to the GO TO statement:

1. The integer variable name must have been used in a previous ASSIGN statement.
2. The numbers within parentheses must be statement numbers appearing within the program. *No specific order is required for these numbers,* as was true with the computed GO TO statement. There is no value associated with the order of the statement numbers and they may appear in any order, regardless of the order in which they may be used for branching.

To illustrate the ASSIGN and assigned GO TO statements, assume that a firm has a program designed to compute the freight expenses for its shipments. Merchandise is shipped by rail in either the firm's own trucks via the rail piggyback system or in boxcars. Boxcar shipments may use a full boxcar or may be made in less than carload lots. Each of these shipping methods carries a different shipping charge. Shipping charges are determined by multiplying weight, distance, and the applicable freight rate. The input cards for this program appear as:

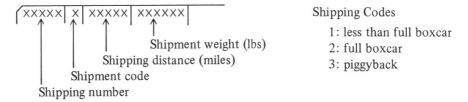

Shipping Codes

1: less than full boxcar
2: full boxcar
3: piggyback

Shipment weight (lbs)
Shipping distance (miles)
Shipment code
Shipping number

A flowchart and program appear in Figure 10.3 and Program 10.5, respectively.

Program 10.5

```
C  FREIGHT CALCULATION PROGRAM
C
       TOTFRT = 0.0
    4  FORMAT (I5,I1,F5.0,F6.0)
    5  READ (5,4,END=400) IDNUM,KODE,DIST,WEIGHT
       IF (KODE-2) 10,20,30
```

continued on page 177

Figure 10.3

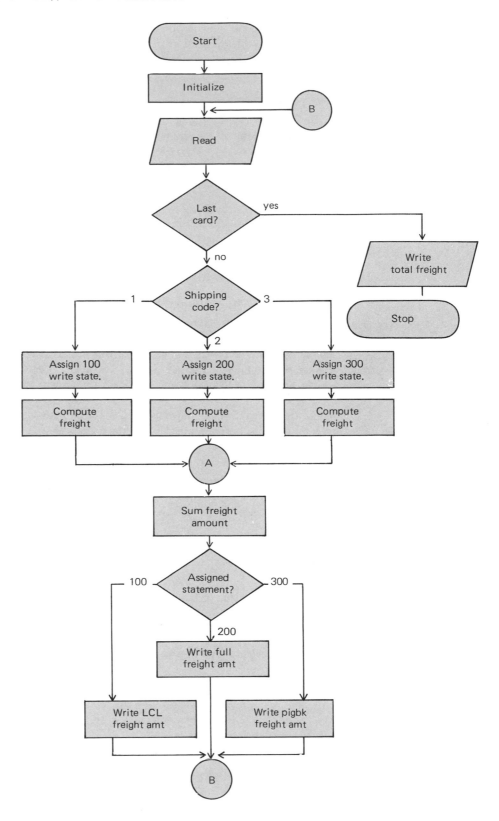

```
 10    ASSIGN 100 TO LIST ←
       FRT = WEIGHT * DIST * .000675        ⎡ ASSIGN statements used indicate
       GO TO 90                             ⎢ the WRITE command associated with
 20    ASSIGN 200 TO LIST ←                 ⎣ each shipping method
       FRT = WEIGHT * DIST * .000225
       GO TO 90
 30    ASSIGN 300 TO LIST ←
       FRT = WEIGHT * DIST * .00005         ⎡ GO TO command which
 90    TOTFRT = TOTFRT + FRT                ⎢ uses the ASSIGNed
       GO TO LIST, (100,200,300) ←          ⎣ statement numbers
 95    FORMAT (5X,8HSHIPMENT,I5,20H LESS THAN CARLOAD -,
     1 17H FREIGHT COST = $,F10.2)
100    WRITE (6,95) IDNUM,FRT
       GO TO 5
195    FORMAT (5X,8HSHIPMENT,I5,15H FULL CARLOAD -,
     1 17H FREIGHT COST = $,F10.2)
200    WRITE (6,195) IDNUM,FRT
       GO TO 5
295    FORMAT (5X,8HSHIPMENT,I5,12H PIGGYBACK -,
     1 17H FREIGHT COST = $,F10.2)
300    WRITE (6,295) IDNUM,FRT
       GO TO 5
395    FORMAT (//5X,25HTOTAL FREIGHT CHARGES = $,F10.2)
400    WRITE (6,395) TOTFRT
       STOP
       END
```

Computed Output

```
SHIPMENT 12345 PIGGYBACK - FREIGHT COST = $       5.00
SHIPMENT 23456 FULL CARLOAD - FREIGHT COST = $      22.50
SHIPMENT 34567 LESS THAN CARLOAD - FREIGHT COST = $      67.50


TOTAL FREIGHT CHARGES = $      95.00
```

Branching Through the Use of System Switches

A final group of decision techniques is available to the programmer through either external switches located on the central processor's console or internal system switches (routines) which may be accessed through FORTRAN statements. These control techniques are somewhat specialized and are probably best omitted until you possess a reasonable facility with the FORTRAN language. In addition, these testing techniques are the least standardized elements in the language. Consult the manufacturer's manual for the specific form required before you use these tests.

External Switches

The external switches are located on the console of the central processor. The switches are normally referred to as *sense switches*. Their use provides the programmer with the option of specifying external tests which are made while the computer executes a program. The sense switches may be set by the computer operator to either an "on" or an "off" position. The position of any sense switch may then be tested by the program. Normally, a program will test the positioning of a switch and either continue processing, because it was properly set, or print a message to the operator with instructions for altering the switches and/or any other operations that should be performed.

The most common forms for testing sense switches are through IF tests or CALL statements. Each of these forms is explained below.

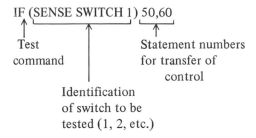

The first number following the parentheses applies to the "on" condition and the second number to the "off" condition.

An alternative technique for testing these switches calls a system routine to do the testing. The form appears as:

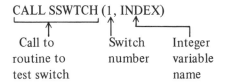

The integer variable name will be set to 1 if the switch was found "on" and to 2 if the switch was "off." The integer variable may then be tested for its value by an IF or computed GO TO statement.

A program segment to illustrate the use of a sense switch test is shown below:

```
       .
       .
       .
    CALL SSWTCH (2, ID)
    GO TO (15, 45), ID
15  LINE = A + B*Y
       .
       .
       .
45  TOTAL = A + B + C
       .
       .
       .
```

The CALL statement causes the sense switch number 2 to be tested for its condition. If it is "on," ID will be set to 1. If it is "off," ID will be set to 2. The computed GO TO then tests ID for its value. If the value is 1, statement 15 is executed. If ID has a value of 2, statement 45 is executed.

Internal Switches

A second major group of tests applies to *program switches*. These switches are entirely internal to the processing system. They may not be physically accessed as are the sense switches on the computer console.

This group of switches covers a wide group of condition tests. The two most useful switches relate to conditions (1) of overflow or underflow (that is, when the processor computes a numerical result greater than or less than the numerical range which it can store) and (2) when attempts to divide a value by zero are made (this test is known as a divide check). Construction of the instructions to test these switches is very similar to the instructions for sense switch tests. Examples are shown below.

Overflow/Underflow (Form 1).

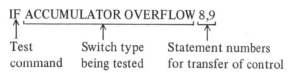

IF ACCUMULATOR OVERFLOW 8,9

Test command   Switch type being tested   Statement numbers for transfer of control

An overflow condition causes transfer to statement 8, underflow to 9. If neither overflow or underflow exists, the statement following the IF test will be processed next.

Overflow/Underflow (Form 2).

CALL OVERFL (INDEX)
GO TO (8,9), INDEX

The CALL statement activates a routine to test for the overflow/underflow conditions. Index is then set with a value reflecting the condition. A computed GO TO will then test the integer variable and branch accordingly.

Some systems set values at 1 for overflow, 2 for no overflow, and 3 for underflow. In these systems the above test would be:

CALL OVERFL (INDEX)
GO TO (8,9,10), INDEX

Divide Check (Form 1).

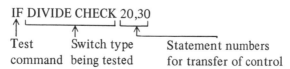

IF DIVIDE CHECK 20,30

Test command   Switch type being tested   Statement numbers for transfer of control

If an attempt to divide by zero has been made, the switch will be "on" and control transfers to statement 20; if "off," control transfer to 30.

Divide Check (Form 2).

CALL DVCHK(INDEX)
GO TO (20, 30), INDEX

The CALL statement calls a routine to test for division by zero. INDEX is then set to 1 or 2 to reflect the result of the test. 1 indicates the division was attempted ("on") and 2 indicates no attempt ("off"). A computed GO TO will then test the integer variable and branch accordingly.

Exercise 24

1. Refer to the market research program shown on page 172. Assume that the variable names N1, N2, N3, and N4 are to be used for both market area 1 and market area 2 data. Indicate how you would rewrite the program to accomplish this change. (Hint, if in trouble: the program needs only a single READ statement.)

2. a. Read the following statements and identify the errors in each. Rewrite the statements, in correct form, on the lines to the right.
   1. ASSGN 17 to A _____
   2. ASSGIN L TO R _____
   3. ASSGN J5 TO MAX _____
   4. ASSIGN 22, TO KK _____
   5. ASSIGN 10 TO G _____

   b. Assume that the following statements appear within a program:

   ASSIGN 25 TO K
   ASSIGN 34 TO K
   ASSIGN 27 TO K

   Based on the ASSIGN statements, identify the errors in the following GO TO statements. Rewrite the statements, in correct form, on the lines to the right.
   1. GO TO (25,34,27), K _____
   2. GO TO (34,27,25) K _____
   3. GO TO K (25,100,27,34) _____
   4. GO TO K, (34,27,25) _____
   5. GO TO K, (25,27,34) _____

3. Read the following program segment and indicate the values of variable locations A, KT, and MAC at its completion.

```
10 A = 21.0
40 A = A-6.0
30 ASSIGN 23 TO KT
35 IF (A/3.0.GE.3.9) GO TO 28
80 GO TO KT, (23,16,37)
28 ASSIGN 37 TO MAC          A _____
45 GO TO 16
15 ASSIGN 40 TO MAC          KT _____
90 GO TO 20
16 A = (A+3.0)/2.0           MAC _____
50 GO TO 15
20 GO TO MAC, (40,37)
23 CONTINUE
37 STOP
```

4. a. Write a test for SENSE SWITCH 1 using the CALL command and a related computed GO TO statement. Use the integer index ITEST when testing the switch. Transfer to statements 10 and 20 depending on the results of the test.

   b. Identify the errors in the following statements and rewrite them correctly on the lines to the right.

   1. CALL OVERFLOW, ID   _____

      GO TO ID, (50,60)   _____

   2. CALL DVCHEK (40,50), ID   _____

      IF (DVCHEK–ID) 40,50,50   _____

Questions

1. What function is served by a logical IF statement? Explain how the logical IF varies from the arithmetic IF statement.

2. What are relational operators? What do they relate? Be specific.

3. What are logical operators? How do they differ from relational operators?

4. What significance is related to the change in the hierarchy of operations when relational and logical operators are added to a statement? Give an example to illustrate your answer.

5. How could you rewrite the two logical IF statements in the Aircraft Maintenance Program (page 162) so that the same conditions are tested but different operators are used?

6. Compare the computed GO TO statement and the assigned GO TO statement. How are these statements alike? Different?

7. Under what circumstances does the computed GO TO offer an advantage over the arithmetic IF statement? When does it fail to offer an advantage?

8. What is an end-of-file condition? How is it indicated? What FORTRAN specification makes use of this condition?

9. What is assigned by the ASSIGN statement? Explain.

10. What is the difference between external system switches and internal system switches? Explain.

11
Additional Refinements in Data Manipulation

In FORTRAN, regardless of the command words or statement construction given, only two basic types of data manipulation are possible: sequential and non-sequential processing. Sequential execution of instructions results from the computer's inherent design characteristics. In this case, the computer processes statement after statement in the same order in which they are written. Non-sequential processing results from the use of branching commands, such as IF statements and GO TO statements.

The FORTRAN language possesses a number of additional factors which may add flexibility to the manipulation of data. We will discuss these factors in the following sections.

Manipulation of Subscripts

Subscripts are most frequently written as either an integer variable name or integer numeric constant within a set of parentheses. For instance, TOT(J) or TOT(2). All FORTRAN systems also accept some manipulation of subscripts within the parentheses. These alterations may involve addition, subtraction, and multiplication. The following combinations are permissible:

Combinations of Subscript Elements	Examples
variable	TOT(J)
constant	TOT(2)
variable + constant	TOT(J + 3)
variable − constant	TOT(J − 5)
constant * variable	TOT(3 * K)
constant * variable + constant	TOT(4 * L + 3)
constant * variable − constant	TOT(5 * N − 5)

Note the order in which variables and the constants appear. In addition, most systems specify that no subscript may itself be subscripted. An example of this illegal construction is TOT(J(I)). Should this circumstance arise, setting a variable name equal to the value of J(I) will then permit its use as a subscript for TOT. For example, the two statements

K = J(I)
A = TOT(K)

have the same meaning as *TOT(J(I))*.

A number of the more recent FORTRAN systems will also allow division (/) and exponentiation (**) within subscripts. In addition, the order in which constants and variables appear is not limited to the combinations shown above. The following examples illustrate the use of division and exponentiation within subscripts.

TOT(N / 6)
TOT(K ** 4)
TOT(K - 8 * L / 3)
TOT(M / 3 - J ** 3 + L)

Furthermore, the prohibition against subscripts being themselves subscripted is relaxed in some of the newer systems. In any event, subscripts, whether simple or complex, should always be positive integer values and never zero or negative. Check the appropriate manuals for the computer you are using before preparing complex subscripts.

Let us examine a simple example of the use of subscript manipulation. Assume that a firm sells its products to both wholesalers and retailers. Data on sales to these two types of outlets have been read and stored in an array identified by the variable name UNITS. The firm has 50 separate marketing areas but has stored the input data by wholesale and retail classifications within each marketing area. This required an array with 100 elements. The wholesale and retail unit sales for any one marketing area are stored in adjacent array locations. Therefore, marketing area 1 sales are stored in UNITS(1) and UNITS(2), area 2 in UNITS(3) and UNITS(4), and so on. Assume that one step in the program will be to add the two sales figures for each marketing area and store them in a new array identified as SUM. The UNITS and SUM arrays are shown below in schematic form.

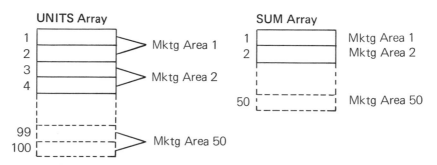

The flowchart segment in Figure 11.1 (page 184) and partial program in Program 11.1 will accomplish the addition.

We can make the following observations about the program:

1. The DO loop will be cycled only 50 times. The increment specified is 2, and it causes the index N to move from 1 to 3, 5, 7, . . . , 99.
2. Each time through the loop, two sets of locations are added together. This is accomplished by use of the subscript manipulation.
3. A separate subscript variable (K) had to be used for the SUM array because that subscript was increasing only half as rapidly as the N index (used as a subscript for the UNITS array).
4. The table following the flowchart summarizes the values associated with each loop cycle:

Figure 11.1 Partial Flowchart Illustrating Subscript Manipulation

Program 11.1 Program Segment Illustrating Subscript Manipulation

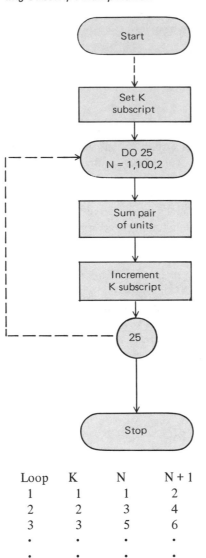

```
C  MARKETING AREA
C  SALES SUMMATION PROGRAM
   DIMENSION UNITS(100)
      .
      .
      .
   K = 1
   DO 25 N = 1,100,2
   SUM(K) = UNITS(N) + UNITS(N + 1)
   K = K + 1
25 CONTINUE
      .
      .
      .
   STOP
   END
```

Note how the use of a subscript alteration, UNITS(N+1), caused the value of location UNITS(N) to be added to the next sequential location, N + 1.

Loop	K	N	N + 1
1	1	1	2
2	2	3	4
3	3	5	6
.	.	.	.
.	.	.	.
.	.	.	.
49	49	97	98
50	50	99	100

Alternative Exponent Modes

In previous explanations of exponentiation, we have used only integers for the exponent, for example, A = B ** 2 or K = J ** 2. The storage locations A and K will hold the values from squaring B and J, respectively. When a real mode value is exponentiated (such as location B), the mode of the intermediate result is *not changed*, even though the exponent is an integer number (such as 2). However, it is permissible to exponentiate integer mode values with real mode exponents. In this case, the mode of the intermediate result *is changed* to the real mode.

Table 11.1 shows the possible combinations of values and exponents with their resulting modes.

Table 11.1   Combinations of Real and Integer Numeric Exponents

Mode of Numeric Value	Mode of Exponent	Mode of Result	Example
Integer	Integer	Integer	K ** 3
Integer	Real	Real	K ** 4.5
Real	Integer	Real	A ** 6
Real	Real	Real	A ** 2.7

When the processor encounters a statement such as B = A ** 2, an evaluation is made of the expression to the right of the equal sign. For this example, assume A = 2.5. The value stored at location A will be multiplied by itself. This multiplication, of course, results in the squaring of 2.5. The value of this manipulation is 6.25 and is temporarily stored in a register while the computer prepares to transfer it to location B. As shown in Table 11.2, the value 6.25, while temporarily stored, is called an *intermediate result*. The programmer does not have access to the intermediate result.

The mode of the intermediate result will be an *integer only* if the value being exponentiated and the exponent are *both* in the integer mode. When *either* the value being exponentiated *or* the exponent is in the real mode, the exponentiation will be done in the *real* mode.

In the statement B = A ** 2, the intermediate result of 6.25 will be transferred to location B and will be stored as 6.25 with no change in mode. For another example, assume that location J = 3. In the statement N = J ** 2.5, the intermediate result will be in the real mode, because the exponent is in the real mode. The processor will first convert the value of J from 3 to 3.0 and then raise it to the power of 2.5. The result is 15.59. The final step will be to move the intermediate result to the storage location identified as variable N. When this transfer step is made, the computer will convert the value from the real to the integer mode. This results in the truncation of the intermediate value, and N will be assigned a value of 15.

Table 11.2 summarizes the eight possible combinations from exponentiating integer and real values to integer or real powers.

It is also possible to exponentiate a value which is itself exponentiated. Parentheses should be used to give preference to one of the exponentiation actions, if needed. For instance, the following statement is exponentiated from *right to left:*

SUM = TOT ** 2 ** 3

If we alter the statement through the use of parentheses, this computation will be exponentiated from *left to right:*

SUM = (TOT ** 2) ** 3

The intention of the computation will determine which of the options should be used.

Table 11.2 Examples of Real and Integer Exponents Raised to Real or Integer Powers

F = 6.2 A = 2.5 K = 4 J = 3 (X = intermediate value)		
Statement	Intermediate Result	Final Result
B = A ** 2	X = 6.25	B = 6.25
N = A ** 2	X = 6.25	N = 6
B = K ** 2	X = 16	B = 16.0
N = K ** 2	X = 16	N = 16
B = J ** 2.5	X = 15.59	B = 15.59
N = J ** 2.5	X = 15.59	N = 15
B = F ** 3.7	X = 854.77	B = 854.77
N = F ** 3.7	X = 854.77	N = 854

All of the examples of exponentiation that we have presented so far have used numeric constants for the exponent. For instance, to write SUM squared, we have written the exponentiation as SUM ** 2. Numeric constants are not necessary in every case. A variable name may be used for an exponent, and the computer will insert the value, stored in the variable named location, as the exponent. Therefore, if location name K holds a value of 2, we may write SUM squared as SUM ** K and achieve the same result as SUM ** 2.

FORTRAN permits us to exponentiate with variable names in the same combinations of real and integer modes as it allows for numeric exponents. Table 11.3 summarizes these combinations.

Table 11.3 Combinations of Real and Integer Symbolic Exponents

Mode of Numeric Value	Mode of Exponent	Mode of Result	Example
Integer	Integer	Integer	K**J
Integer	Real	Real	K**A
Real	Integer	Real	A**K
Real	Real	Real	A**B

Expressions may also be used as exponents, just as they are used for any other type of arithmetic manipulation. Parentheses become necessary, however, so that the expression will be evaluated prior to the exponentiation. Consider the following example:

MAX = NR ** K / 2

This statement will be evaluated by the computer as NR ** K; then the result will be divided by 2. The order, of course, is due to the rules of processing which place exponentiation ahead of division.

If the statement is changed to

MAX = NR ** (K / 2)

the division will be completed prior to exponentiation because the parentheses alter the order of processing. It should be apparent from the example above how important the use of parentheses is in using an arithmetic expression for an exponent.

Some final comments, with regard to exponentiation, deal with the construction of exponents for maximum efficiency. First, even though the FORTRAN language allows the use of any combinations of real and integer values and exponents, most systems are capable of executing a statement containing an integer exponent much more quickly than they can for a statement with real exponents. Integer exponentiation usually involves successive multiplication of the values being raised to the exponent power. Real mode exponentiation, on the other hand, requires the computer to call and execute a separate internal routine which uses a power series calculation. This process is normally more time consuming than the integer exponentiation and should be avoided, if possible.

A second comment pertains to the preparation of statements using small powers of exponentiation, such as squaring and cubing. While it is correct to write $M = K ** 2$, a more efficient construction of this statement would be $M = K * K$. The computer can usually execute the multiplication of one value by itself more rapidly than it can execute the internal set-up for exponentiation. The same type of efficiency is gained by writing the statement $A = C ** 3$ as $A = C * C * C$.

Exercise 25

1. The manipulation of subscripts refers to the ability to do a limited amount of calculating within a variable name's subscript. Assume that two storage locations contain the following values:

   $N = 4$ $K = 3$

   Using the values shown for N and K, compute the subscript value which the computer will use for each of the items given below:
   a. TOTAL(N / 2) will be subscripted as TOTAL( )
   b. TOTAL(5 * K + 2) will be subscripted as TOTAL( )
   c. TOTAL(N ** 2 / 8 + K) will be subscripted as TOTAL( )
   d. TOTAL(K − 3 + N) will be subscripted as TOTAL( )
   e. TOTAL(K − 2 * N) will be subscripted as TOTAL( )

2. When exponentiation takes place, the mode of the values being exponentiated may be in either the real or integer form, depending upon the construction of the exponent. For each of the following items, determine what the intermediate and final results of exponentiation will be. Assume the following values for the variables used:

   $A = 3.4$ $B = 1.2$ $J = 2$ $K = 7$ (X = intermediate value)

Statement	Intermediate Result	Final Result
a. $R = A ** J$	X = _____	R = _____
b. $N = (K ** J) ** 2$	X = _____	N = _____
c. $E = J ** K$	X = _____	E = _____
d. $M = B ** (2 ** J)$	X = _____	M = _____
e. $C = K ** B$	X = _____	C = _____

3. Refer to the sales summation program in Program 11.1. The variable SUM used K as a subscript. Each time the program passed through the DO loop, the value of K was incremented by one. Study this process and determine a computational algorithm which could be used within the subscript of SUM to automatically

calculate the proper subscript value. This computation will be completed with each loop and replace the use of K as the subscript.

Nested Program Loops

The basic purpose of the FORTRAN DO loop is to provide repetitive processing of a set of program statements. Obviously, simple DO loops provide a tremendous increase in computing power. Our previous discussion of DO loops may have implied that only a single DO loop was permitted for use with a group of executable statements. This is not the case, and the use of loops within loops, or nested loops, is both permissible and desirable wherever appropriate. With each new level of loops, the degree of computing power is increased substantially. However, the complexity introduced by the *nesting* of DO loops means that the programmer must be very careful to avoid looping through incorrect sets of statements.

This section will describe some of the precautions that must be exercised when DO loops are nested in a program.

Basic Considerations

A DO loop begins with the DO statement and includes all subsequent instructions through the executable statement containing the statement number listed in the DO instruction. The following example presents a review of this concept.

```
┌ ─ ─ → DO 100 K = 1,5,1            ┐
│        MIN = 1.5 * LOW            │
│        KTOT = KAL + MIN / (K - 1) │
│        REAL = KTOT                │  range
│        AMOUNT = REAL * A          │
│        SUM = SUM + AMOUNT         │
│        LOW = LOW + (N / K)        │
└ ─ 100  CONTINUE                   ┘
```

Although this loop is used only as an illustration, it shows the basic characteristics of the DO loop command. The *range* of a loop includes the set of statements enclosed by the DO statement and the last statement carrying the range value. The last statement is called the *foot* of the loop.

We will review some of the basic rules for the use of DO loops because they apply to nested loops as critically as they do single loops.

1. A DO *loop must be entered through the DO statement.* Do not transfer into the range of a DO loop except through the DO statement.
2. *Transfer* may be made *out of a DO loop at any time* from within the loop (using statements such as GO TO, IF, and other decision commands).
3. The index used to control the DO loop *may not be redefined within the loop.* However, the control index may be used within the loop as long as its value is not changed. Changing its value would confuse the processor about which loop number it was executing.
4. Transfers among statements within a loop are permissible. However, *return to the DO statement may not be made directly.* Return to the DO statement must be made by transfer to the last statement (foot) in the loop.

5. The *last statement* in a DO loop must be a CONTINUE statement or an executable statement that is *not a transfer statement* (GO TO, IF, etc.). Obviously, if the last statement were a transfer, the computer would be confused about whether it should return to execute the loop again or transfer in accordance with the direction of the decision command.

Simple Nesting

A DO loop which includes one inner loop is the most simple level of nesting. The basic rules for this level of nesting also apply to all succeeding levels of more complex nesting. The following illustration shows the basic components for a simple nesting of DO loops.

```
--->  DO 100 K = 1,5,1
  |       A(K) = B + C
  |       CAR = SAL / (D - E)
  | -->  DO 50 N = 1,3,1
  | |       MAX = NO(N) / 6        inner      outer
  | |       LIT = NUM + L * 8      loop       loop
  | L- 50 CONTINUE                 range      range
  |       GET = GM(K) - A(K)
  |       TR5 = AMT * GM(K)
  |
 --- 100 CONTINUE
```

In this illustration, the two loops each have their own range of statements. The inner loop contains three statements ending with 50 CONTINUE. The outer loop contains two statements prior to the inner loop, three statements following it, and the inner loop itself. The outer loop ends with 100 CONTINUE. The outer loop will cycle a total of 5 times. The inner loop will cycle *3 times for each cycle of the outer loop;* thus, the inner loop will cycle a total of 15 times. This indicates the increase in computing power gained from nested loops.

Some of the additional rules that pertain specifically to nested loops are:

1. Transfer into the middle of an inner loop from an outer loop is *not* permitted. Access to the inner loop may be made only through its DO statement.
2. Transfer back into the middle of an outer loop from an inner loop is permitted. The inner loop is considered to be within the range of the outer loop and, therefore, this type of transfer to statements contained in the outer loop is permitted.
3. Transfer, or a jump, over the entire inner loop without executing any of its statements is permitted. After this jump, processing may continue within the outer loop.

The crucial point in the control of nested loops is an understanding of the concept that inner loops are contained within the range of outer loops. This, in turn, means that a great deal of care must be exercised to see that inner loops are treated as complete processing entities. Transfers into these interior loops must be respected, and entry may be made only through the DO statements. However, transfer out of the inner loop may be made to any point within the outer loop because execution will still be in the range of the outer loop.

The following illustrations present both a schematic drawing of several typical DO loop transfers and accompanying skeleton DO loops to provide statement examples of the looping. First, a number of valid loop transfers will be shown then, a group of invalid transfers will be demonstrated.

Valid Loop Transfers

1. Transfer out of the loop.

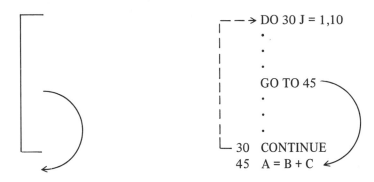

2. Transfer within the loop.

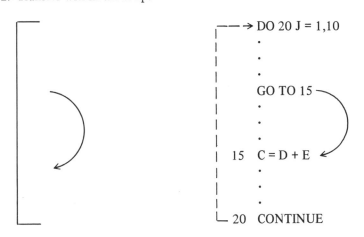

3. Transfer to the foot of the loop from within the loop.

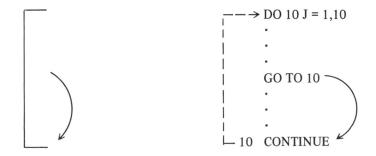

4. Transfer from a statement in an inner loop to a statement in the outer loop.

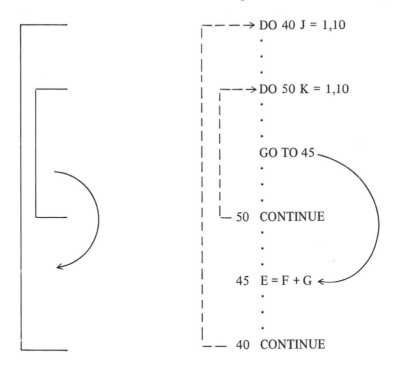

5. Transfer over complete inner loop with control maintained by the outer loop.

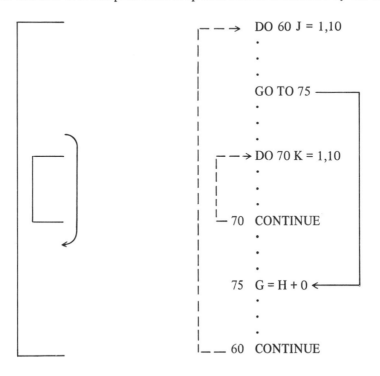

6. Transfer from innermost loop back up into outermost loop.

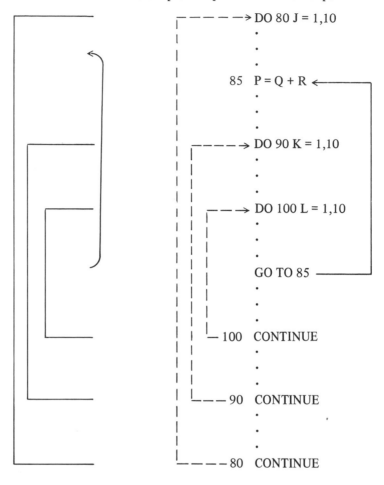

7. Transfer from first inner loop back up into outer loop.

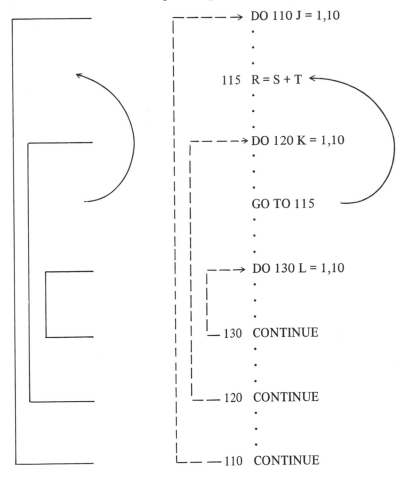

```
            DO 110 J = 1,10
              .
              .
              .
      115   R = S + T
              .
              .
            DO 120 K = 1,10
              .
              .
            GO TO 115
              .
              .
            DO 130 L = 1,10
              .
              .
      130   CONTINUE
              .
              .
      120   CONTINUE
              .
              .
      110   CONTINUE
```

8. Transfer over two interior loops.

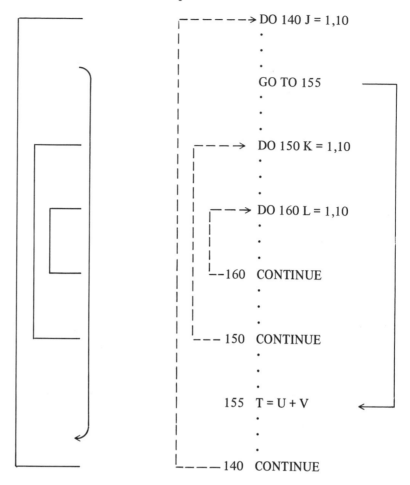

```
                              DO 140 J = 1,10
                                .
                                .
                                .
                              GO TO 155
                                .
                                .
                              DO 150 K = 1,10
                                .
                                .
                                .
                              DO 160 L = 1,10
                                .
                                .
                                .
                          160 CONTINUE
                                .
                                .
                                .
                          150 CONTINUE
                                .
                                .
                          155 T = U + V
                                .
                                .
                                .
                          140 CONTINUE
```

9. Transfer within one interior loop while transferring over another interior loop.

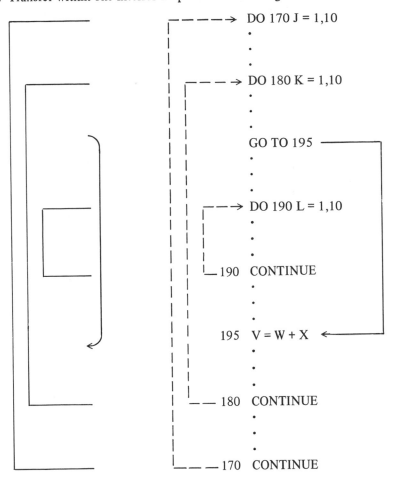

```
                    ┌ ─ ─ ─ → DO 170 J = 1,10
                    ┆                  •
                    ┆                  •
                    ┆                  •
                    ┆  ┌ ─ ─ → DO 180 K = 1,10
                    ┆  ┆               •
                    ┆  ┆               •
                    ┆  ┆               •
                    ┆  ┆            GO TO 195 ──────┐
                    ┆  ┆               •            │
                    ┆  ┆               •            │
                    ┆  ┆  ┌ ─ ─ → DO 190 L = 1,10   │
                    ┆  ┆  ┆            •            │
                    ┆  ┆  ┆            •            │
                    ┆  ┆  └─ 190  CONTINUE          │
                    ┆  ┆               •            │
                    ┆  ┆               •            │
                    ┆  ┆               •            │
                    ┆  ┆       195  V = W + X  ←─────┘
                    ┆  ┆               •
                    ┆  ┆               •
                    ┆  ┆               •
                    ┆  └─ ─ 180  CONTINUE
                    ┆                  •
                    ┆                  •
                    ┆                  •
                    └─ ─ ─ 170  CONTINUE
```

10. Two loops may use the same foot statement to end the loops.

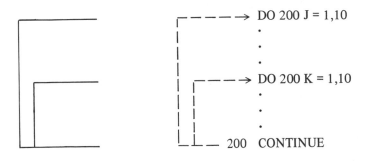

```
              ┌ ─ ─ ─ → DO 200 J = 1,10
              ┆               •
              ┆               •
              ┆               •
              ┆  ┌ ─ ─ → DO 200 K = 1,10
              ┆  ┆            •
              ┆  ┆            •
              ┆  ┆            •
              └─ └─ 200  CONTINUE
```

This last example requires a word of caution. The computer assumes that statement 200 is within the inner loop. Therefore, it is illegal to transfer to it with a GO TO or IF statement from the outer loop. Statement 200 may be reached only through execution of the inner loop.

Invalid Loop Transfers

1. Transfer into the range of a loop from preceding statements.

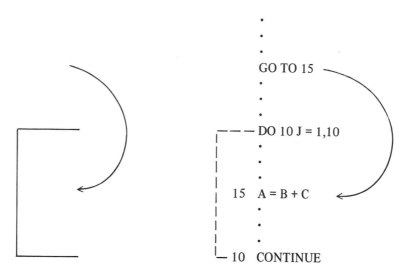

2. Transfer into the range of a loop from succeeding statements.

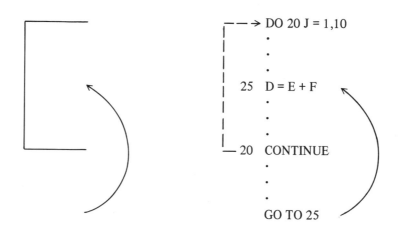

3. Transfer to the DO statement from within the loop.

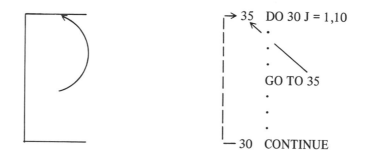

4. Transfer into the middle of an inner loop from an outer loop.

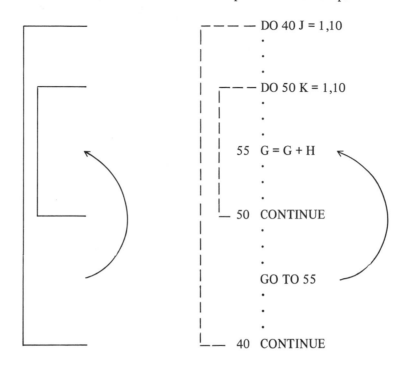

```
        ┌ ─ ─ ─   DO 40 J = 1,10
        │           ·
        │           ·
        │           ·
        │ ┌ ─ ─   DO 50 K = 1,10
        │ │         ·
        │ │         ·
        │ │         ·
        │ │   55  G = G + H
        │ │         ·
        │ │         ·
        │ └   50  CONTINUE
        │           ·
        │           ·
        │           ·
        │         GO TO 55
        │           ·
        │           ·
        │           ·
        └ ─   40  CONTINUE
```

5. Transfer into the middle of an inner loop from outside the outer loop.

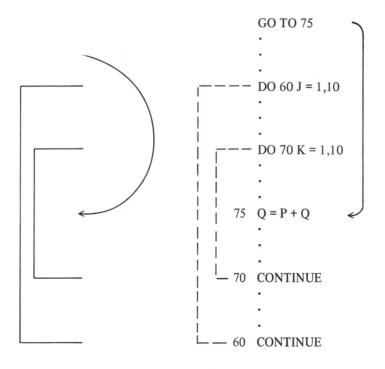

```
          GO TO 75
            ·
            ·
            ·
  ┌ ─ ─ ─   DO 60 J = 1,10
  │           ·
  │           ·
  │           ·
  │ ┌ ─ ─   DO 70 K = 1,10
  │ │         ·
  │ │         ·
  │ │   75  Q = P + Q
  │ │         ·
  │ │         ·
  │ └   70  CONTINUE
  │           ·
  │           ·
  │           ·
  └ ─   60  CONTINUE
```

6. Transfer to the foot of an inner loop from within an outer loop.

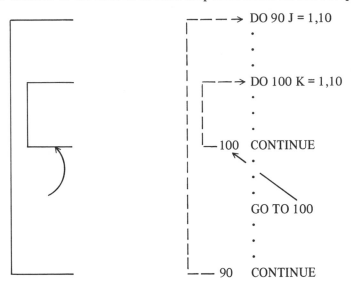

```
         ┌ ─ ─ ─ → DO 90 J = 1,10
         │              •
         │              •
         │              •
         │ ┌ ─ ─ → DO 100 K = 1,10
         │ │            •
         │ │            •
         │ │            •
         │ └ 100  CONTINUE
         │          ↖ •
         │            • \
         │            •   GO TO 100
         │              •
         │              •
         │              •
         │              •
         └ ─ 90   CONTINUE
```

7. Overlapping ranges for more than one loop.

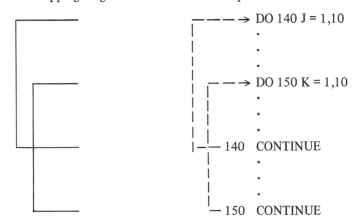

```
         ┌ ─ ─ ─ → DO 140 J = 1,10
         │              •
         │              •
         │              •
         │ ┌ ─ ─ → DO 150 K = 1,10
         │ │            •
         │ │            •
         │ │            •
         ├─┴ 140  CONTINUE
         │              •
         │              •
         │              •
         └ 150   CONTINUE
```

A complete program example for calculating moving averages will help to illustrate the use of nested DO loops. Moving averages are used extensively in business applications such as inventory control, business forecasting, and evaluations of accounts receivable. A moving average is simply the calculation of successive averages for a group of values. Each successive average includes the addition of a new value and the deletion of the oldest value from the previous group total. Suppose a firm wanted to determine the six-month moving average for a series of sales values. For simplicity, suppose the sales for a twelve-month period were:

January	$10,000	July	$ 70,000
February	$20,000	August	$ 80,000
March	$30,000	September	$ 90,000
April	$40,000	October	$100,000
May	$50,000	November	$110,000
June	$60,000	December	$120,000

With the data for twelve months, seven sets of six-month averages are possible. These inclusive months and the other pertinent figures are shown in Table 11.4. Naturally, the information on total sales and six-month averages would not be computed prior to using the program. The computer will do this! However, to follow what the program will do, it is beneficial to know these figures in advance.

Table 11.4   Six-month Moving Averages for Program 11.2

Average	Inclusive Months	Total Sales	Six-Month Average
1	January–June	$210,000	$35,000
2	February–July	$270,000	$45,000
3	March–August	$330,000	$55,000
4	April–September	$390,000	$65,000
5	May–October	$450,000	$75,000
6	June–November	$510,000	$85,000
7	July–December	$570,000	$95,000

In the above figures we see that each six-month average adds a new month's sales figure and drops the oldest month's sales. It should be clear that the process of calculating a moving average is a repetitive process, and a computer program to accomplish this task will make good use of the DO loop command. Actually, two sets of loops are required for this processing. An outer loop will control the seven cycles needed to compute the seven six-month averages. An inner loop will then accumulate the specific six-month sales figures for each cycle of the outer loop. Nesting these loops will accomplish the computations repeatedly until each of the seven averages has been calculated.

The following details pertain to the program:

1. Input data cards: two types of data cards will be used. The first card will contain the number of months of data to be used. The second, third, fourth, etc. cards will each contain up to 12 months of data.

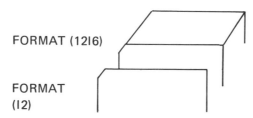

FORMAT (12I6)

FORMAT (I2)

2. Data storage: the basic sales data read will be stored in an array named MODATA. This array will be filled prior to the calculation of any moving averages.

MODATA

It may be useful to see how the maximum number of cycles was determined for the outer loop. This maximum number can be computed by use of the formula $(n - 6) + 1$ where n is the number of months of data read. Insertion of this formula within the program generalizes it so that data for any number of months may be used without changing any program statements. The initial data card read will specify the total number of months of data in the data deck. The flowchart and program are shown in Figure 11.2 and Program 11.2, respectively.

Figure 11.2 Flowchart for Program 11.2 to Calculate Six-month Moving Averages

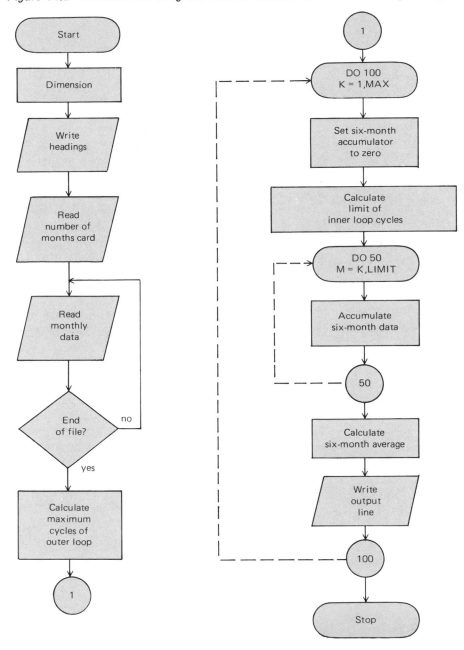

Program 11.2 Program to Calculate Six-month Moving Averages

```
      C
      C  6 MONTH MOVING AVERAGE PROGRAM
      C  ILLUSTRATES DO LOOP NESTING
      C
1         DIMENSION MODATA(120)
      C
2       2 FORMAT (1H1,14X,5HTOTAL,4X,8H6 MONTHS/
          16X,6HMONTHS,3X,5HVALUE,3X,10HMOVING AVE//)
3         WRITE (6,2)
      C
4       5 FORMAT (I2)
5         READ (5,5) MONTHS
      C
6      10 FORMAT (12I6)
7      12 READ (5,10,END=15)   (MODATA(N),N=1,12)
      C
8      15 MAX = (MONTHS-6)+1
      C
9         DO 100 K=1,MAX
10        MOTOTL = 0
11        LIMIT = K+5
12        DO 50 M=K,LIMIT
13        MOTOTL = MOTOTL + MODATA(M)
14     50 CONTINUE
15        MOAVE = MOTOTL/6
16     55 FORMAT (6X,I2,1H-,I2,2X,I7,4X,I7)
17        WRITE (6,55) K,LIMIT,MOTOTL,MOAVE
18    100 CONTINUE
      C
19        STOP
20        END
```

MONTHS	TOTAL VALUE	6 MONTHS MOVING AVE
1- 6	210000	35000
2- 7	270000	45000
3- 8	330000	55000
4- 9	390000	65000
5-10	450000	75000
6-11	510000	85000
7-12	570000	95000

Table 11.5 (page 202) shows the changes in the loop control values as the nested loops are executed. The assumption remains that there are 12 months of data requiring seven averages.

The PAUSE Statement

The FORTRAN language provides a command that allows a program's processing sequence to be stopped, but with an opportunity to resume execution. This command is written simply as:

PAUSE

Table 11.5

Loop	Loop Control Data Names			
Number	Outer Loop		Inner Loop	
	K	MAX	M*	LIMIT**
1	1	7	1	6
2	2	7	2	7
3	3	7	3	8
4	4	7	4	9
5	5	7	5	10
6	6	7	6	11
7	7	7	7	12

*M begins each new loop with the value of K from the outer loop.
**LIMIT is recomputed as K + 5 each time the inner loop is entered.

The PAUSE statement causes the processor to interrupt execution and, at the same time, display a message on the console of the central processing unit. The message will instruct the operator to perform some action. He may then cause the program to resume execution by inputting the appropriate start instructions through the console. Execution will begin with the program statement immediately following the PAUSE command.

This command has limitations in programs that use only the card input medium. Normally there is no reason to interrupt processing; however, the testing of sense switches could require program interruption (see Chapter 10). Programs that use magnetic tape or disk for input/output may require program interruptions with an instruction to the operator to mount a new tape or disk pack.

When the programmer wishes to display a message on the computer console, the PAUSE command is followed by the message which is enclosed within single quote marks. For example,

PAUSE 'MOUNT TAPE XR-00538 ON UNIT 9'

The significant difference between the PAUSE statement and the STOP statement is that the program may be restarted after execution of the PAUSE statement. The STOP statement brings the program to a logical conclusion and terminates all processing for the program.

Exercise 26

1. Review the following schematic drawings of a series of nested DO loops. Identify those loops which are incorrect and explain the errors which exist.

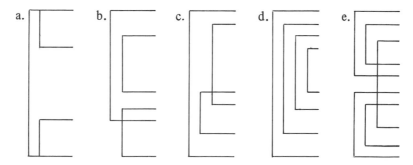

2. Review the following DO loop skeletons. Identify those which are incorrect and
explain why they are incorrect.

a.   DO 10
        ·
        ·
        ·
    DO 20
        ·
        ·
        ·
    DO 30
        ·
        ·
        ·
    DO 40
        ·
        ·
        ·
40 CONTINUE
        ·
        ·
        ·
30 CONTINUE
        ·
        ·
        ·
20 CONTINUE
        ·
        ·
        ·
10 CONTINUE

b.   15 DO 50
        ·
        ·
        ·
    GO TO 15
        ·
        ·
        ·
    DO 50
        ·
        ·
        ·
50 CONTINUE

c.   DO 80
        ·
        ·
        ·
    DO 90
        ·
        ·
        ·
90 CONTINUE
        ·
        ·
        ·
    DO 100
        ·
        ·
        ·
80 CONTINUE
        ·
        ·
        ·
100 CONTINUE

d.   DO 25
        ·
        ·
        ·
    DO 35
        ·
        ·
        ∘
    DO 45
        ·
        ·
        ·
35 CONTINUE
        ·
        ·
        ·
45 CONTINUE
        ·
        ·
        ·
25 CONTINUE

e.   DO 75   •
      •   DO 110
      •   •
      •   •
      DO 85   •
      •   DO 120
      •   •
      •   •
      DO 95   •
      •   95   CONTINUE
      •   •
      •   •
85   CONTINUE   •
      •   120   CONTINUE
      •   •
      •   •
75   CONTINUE   •
      •   110   CONTINUE
      •

3. If you wrote any of the following sets of statements, would they provide your program with a logical ending? Explain how each statement(s) will accomplish the logical ending for a program.

   a. PAUSE (STOP)   d. STOP
   b. PAUSE 'STOP'   PAUSE 'THIS PROGRAM IS FINISHED'
   c. PAUSE 'END'   END

                                e. PAUSE 'THE END'
                                   END
                                   STOP

DOUBLE PRECISION Specification

Precision in computing involves the number of significant digits needed to express the result of a computation. Every processor has a limitation on the number of digits which may be stored in one memory location. The engineering characteristics of each computer system set this limitation. For example, the number of real-mode digits which normally may be stored in one memory location of the IBM System 360 is seven. When values are used which involve more than seven significant digits, either precision will be lost or an alternative arrangement will have to be made to store additional digits.

The minimum storage limitation of a computer system is called *single precision*. The following three programs illustrate this point. Each program reads a data card with the digits 1 through 9 punched in columns 1-9, as shown below:

123456789

After reading a data card, each program immediately writes out the input values. TEST is the variable name assigned to the field containing the digits 1 through 9. The computer used in this example has a 7 digit limit.

Program 11.3
Input FORMAT (F7.0)

```
C
C   SINGLE PRECISION
C
    5 FORMAT (F7.0)
   10 FORMAT (20X,F10.0)
      READ (5,5) TEST
      WRITE (6,10) TEST
      STOP
      END
```

Program 11.4
Input FORMAT (F8.0)

```
C
C   SINGLE PRECISION
C
    5 FORMAT (F8.0)
   10 FORMAT (20X,F10.0)
      READ (5,5) TEST
      WRITE (6,10) TEST
      STOP
      END
```

Program 11.5
Input FORMAT (F9.0)

```
C
C   SINGLE PRECISION
C
    5 FORMAT (F9.0)
   10 FORMAT (20X,F10.0)
      READ (5,5) TEST
      WRITE (6,10) TEST
      STOP
      END
```

```
        1234567.                    12345670.                   123456700.
```

Each of the programs read an identical data card—a card containing nine digits. Program 11.3 read only 7 of the digits, Program 11.4 read 8 digits, and Program 11.5 read all 9 digits as specified in the input FORMAT statements. In Program 11.3 the WRITE statement displayed the 7 digits read. In contrast, Program 11.4 specified the reading of 8 digits, and the WRITE statement attempted to display the 8 digits. However, a 0 is the eighth digit printed. While an attempt to read 8 digits was made, the computer could not store the eighth digit (which would have been an 8) and inserted a 0 in the eight position when printing. This is the result of the 7 digit limitation in single precision.

Program 11.5 extends this example. The input FORMAT statement specifies that 9 digits should be read. This would include all of the digits 1 through 9. The output shows that only 7 significant digits were in memory and available for writing and two 0's were inserted to fill out the 9 digits.

Obviously, a problem will exist when the precision of a computed value should hold more than 7 digits. The FORTRAN language provides a method for specifying to the computer system that two memory locations should be connected and consequently double the number of significant digits used to store values. This realignment of memory is accomplished by use of the *DOUBLE PRECISION* specification.

DOUBLE PRECISION specifications in most computing systems actually more than double the storage size for significant digits. In the IBM 360 system, the number of significant digits stored for a real value with a double precision specification is 16. This size is more than double the single precision limit of 7 digits.[1]

The requirements for use of the DOUBLE PRECISION specification are very simple. It is only necessary to place an instruction at the *beginning* of a program as follows:

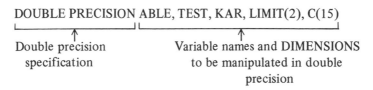

DOUBLE PRECISION ABLE, TEST, KAR, LIMIT(2), C(15)

Double precision
specification

Variable names and DIMENSIONS
to be manipulated in double
precision

---

[1] Precision limits on the majority of systems range from 7 to 11 significant digits in single precision to 14 to 25 significant digits in DOUBLE PRECISION.

The example statement shows that specifying a memory location as DOUBLE PRECISION is an uncomplicated process. However, several rules do pertain to DOUBLE PRECISION specifications, and they are:

1. The DOUBLE PRECISION statement must *precede all* other program statements. This allows the processor to arrange for the double storage locations prior to any use of the variables named.
2. The list of variables which follow the words DOUBLE PRECISION may be *single location names* or *array names*. In the example, the names ABLE, TEST, and KAR were single location names.

    However, if a DIMENSION statement followed the DOUBLE PRECISION statement and listed the name ABLE (20), then all 20 locations within the ABLE array would be handled in DOUBLE PRECISION.

    The example also shows the names LIMIT(2) and C(15). This specification DIMENSIONs the LIMIT array at two locations and the C array at fifteen locations. Of course, both arrays are handled in DOUBLE PRECISION.
3. All variables listed in the DOUBLE PRECISION statement are *automatically treated as real mode* variables. This pertains to variable names beginning with implied integer mode letters as well as those beginning with real mode letters. In the example, the variables KAR and LIMIT(2) begin with letters from the integer group (I-N) but will be treated in the real mode because of their use in a DOUBLE PRECISION statement.

The increased size of the significant digits stored in DOUBLE PRECISION will be illustrated with three additional programs. These programs each read a data card containing 18 digits in the first 18 columns, as shown below:

> 123456789012345678

The variable name TEST is used again to hold the value read. Note that the variable name TEST has been used in a DOUBLE PRECISION statement. This establishes the expanded memory location size for holding up to 16 significant digits.

Program 11.6	Program 11.7	Program 11.8
Input FORMAT (F16.0)	*Input FORMAT (F17.0)*	*Input FORMAT (F18.0)*

```
C                            C                            C
C   DOUBLE PRECISION          C   DOUBLE PRECISION          C   DOUBLE PRECISION
C                            C                            C
    DOUBLE PRECISION TEST        DOUBLE PRECISION TEST        DOUBLE PRECISION TEST
  5 FORMAT (F16.0)            5 FORMAT (F17.0)            5 FORMAT (F18.0)
 10 FORMAT (15X,F20.0)       10 FORMAT (15X,F20.0)       10 FORMAT (15X,F20.0)
    READ (5,5) TEST              READ (5,5) TEST              READ (5,5) TEST
    WRITE (6,10) TEST           WRITE (6,10) TEST           WRITE (6,10) TEST
    STOP                        STOP                        STOP
    END                         END                         END
```

```
    1234567890123456.         12345678901234560.         123456789012345600.
```

The effect of the increased precision can be seen in these programs. Program 11.6 read only the first 16 digits because of the F16.0 specification in 5 FORMAT. When the printer wrote the stored value, it produced a string of 16 digits. Program 11.7, on the other hand, read 17 digits in accordance with its FORMAT. When the stored digits were printed, only 16 significant digits were available, and a zero was inserted to fill the field. Program 11.8 read 18 digits but had 2 zeros inserted upon writing. These programs illustrate the size limitation of DOUBLE PRECISION storage. Certainly the increase from 7 digits in single precision to 16 digits in double precision is important. Still, double precision does have its own limitation at 16 significant digits. No automatic extension to triple precision, or beyond, is a part of the FORTRAN language.

The use of DOUBLE PRECISION offers several advantages in the preparation of a program. The first advantage is increased precision for handling large values, as demonstrated in the above programs. The second advantage relates to computers that complete their manipulations in the binary mode (as opposed to the BCD mode). In binary machines, the fractional portion of numbers is stored in the binary form. This will often result in rounding errors because all decimal fractions do not have binary equivalents in the negative powers of the base 2. The rounding errors occur with the least significant digits in a value (that is, the digits to the right of the decimal point), and because DOUBLE PRECISION increases the number of digits, this has the effect of pushing the rounding error further and further to the right of the value. The third main advantage of DOUBLE PRECISION pertains to the storage of alphabetic characters. The increased size of a storage location doubles the number of alphabetic characters which may be stored in one string. Therefore, if a processor has a 4 character storage capacity in single precision, it will have an 8 character capacity in DOUBLE PRECISION.

The primary disadvantages of DOUBLE PRECISION are the expanded memory space consumed for any one value and the object code inefficiencies introduced.

Input/Output and Processing Options in DOUBLE PRECISION

The DOUBLE PRECISION specification relates primarily to the arrangement of *internal memory locations* for the storage of values. DOUBLE PRECISION values are *always* in the *real mode*. These two facts raise a question about the relationships between single precision variables and DOUBLE PRECISION variables. The following sections will describe the use of DOUBLE PRECISION for input and output and in processing.

THE DOUBLE PRECISION (D) FORMAT Specifications

Earlier illustrations in this section used the F FORMAT specification for reading input values even though they were treated internally in DOUBLE PRECISION. An optional input specification for DOUBLE PRECISION values uses the D specification. Use of the D specification is always permissible for DOUBLE PRECISION input values and is required by some processors when input values are small.

The D specification is nearly identical to the exponential form (E code) discussed in Chapter 9. The only change is the use of the letter D where the letter E is used in the exponential form. Therefore an input FORMAT such as 10 FORMAT (D10.3) specifies a field 10 columns wide and has a three digit fractional portion. The use of a D specification means that the input value will be raised to the power of 10 indicated by the integer value following the letter D. All input values must contain the letter D as shown below:

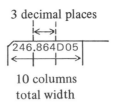

3 decimal places

246.864D05

10 columns
total width

FORMAT (D10.3)

Compare this example with the one on page 151.

When a decimal point is omitted from the input value, the FORMAT specification will provide the proper placement. Punched decimal points will override the FORMAT description. Blanks anywhere within the input field are converted to zeros. The digits following the letter D indicate the power of 10 to which the value preceding the D should be raised. This, of course, has the effect of moving the decimal point to the right (positive exponent) or to the left (negative exponent).

Table 11.6 shows the storage of several different D code values.

Table 11.6 Storage of DOUBLE PRECISION Input Values

Card Columns 1-9 Punched Values*	FORMAT	Stored Values**	Decimal Equivalence
1. −8.921D03	D9.2	$-8.921(10)^3$	−8921.0
2. +49412D02	D9.4	$+4.9412(10)^2$	494.12
3. −32248D−8	D9.3	$-32.248(10)^{-8}$	−.00000032248
4. 57834bD1b	D9.5	$+5.78340(10)^{10}$	57834000000.0
5. −bb.246D8	D9.1	$-.246(10)^8$	−24600000.0

*b = blank card columns
**The stored values in a binary computer may not be identical to the digits read. Items 2, 3, and 4 in the example will have the following approximations: (2) 494.119873046875, (3) −0.000000322479991154978, and (4) 57833996287.99999.

Note the following factors in handling the punched values:

Line 1: the punched decimal point overrode the D9.2 code.

Lines 2 and 3: the D9.4 and D9.3 codes provide the assumed decimal point placements.

Line 4: blanks which follow the integer digits are counted as part of the values when converted to zeros. In this case, both the precision portion and the exponent were raised beyond the intended values.

Line 5: blanks preceding a value do not change the size of the value, and the sign may appear anywhere in the field preceding the value.

The D code specification may be used in output FORMATs as well as input FORMATs. Printed values will be taken from memory and displayed in accordance with the width and fractional digit size given in the FORMAT statement. Of course, only DOUBLE PRECISION values may be displayed with the use of the D code. When a value is written, the computer will automatically determine the exponent size needed to state the value correctly. All values printed will be right justified in the output field. Table 11.7 shows the conversion of stored values to printed values under varying D codes.

Table 11.7   Conversion and Printing of Stored DOUBLE PRECISION Values

	Stored Values	FORMAT	Printed Values*
1.	$+1.23456(10)^0$	D15.6	bbb0.123456D+01**
2.	$-246.89(10)^4$	D16.9	-0.246890000D+07
3.	$+1.745(10)^{-2}$	D11.4	b0.1745D-01
4.	$-3567.42183(10)^0$	D14.7	-0.3567422D+04
5.	$+8.1623(10)^{25}$	D10.3	b0.816D+26
6.	$-.123456789(10)^6$	D20.13	-0.1234567890000D+06

*b = blank character position
**Some processors leave a blank after the letter D when the exponent is positive. A negative exponent will always have a minus sign.

The examples shown in Table 11.7 illustrate how the D code specifies the output characteristics of printed values. The letter D in the FORMAT statement indicates the DOUBLE PRECISION form. The digits following the letter D, and preceding the decimal point, indicate the total width of the printed value. The total width will include seven positions for: (1) a leading sign, (2) a zero prior to the decimal point, (3) the decimal point, (4) the letter D, (5) a sign following the letter D, (6) and (7) two positions for the exponent value. Finally, the digits following the decimal point, in the FORMAT statement, specify the number of significant digits which will follow the printed decimal point.

These points should be observed about the examples shown above:

Line 1:   to meet the total character width of 15, blanks had to be inserted preceding the printed value.

Line 2:   to meet the 9 decimal places, zeros had to be inserted after the significant digits, and the exponent had to be increased to indicate the proper placement of the decimal point.

Line 3:   to meet the 4 decimal places, the exponent had to be decreased to indicate the proper placement of the decimal point.

Line 4:   more significant digits existed than were called for in the FORMAT statement. The excess digits were dropped *after* rounding up to the least significant digit.

Line 5:   more significant digits existed than were called for in the FORMAT statement. The excess digits were dropped without rounding because of the small value of the dropped digits.

Line 6:   more decimal places were specified than significant digits were available to fill them. Zeros were inserted to fill the value to its overall width.

Errors are generated in a manner similar to the F code when fields, specified in output FORMATS, are too narrow for the stored values. The most common error encountered is specification of a D code for less than seven character positions. This causes the computer to generate an error condition indicating the skimpy field specification. Obviously, the best rule is to add 7 positions to the number of output digits desired.

DOUBLE PRECISION Constants

Variables that have been declared DOUBLE PRECISION may receive values through reading, as explained above, or by assignment in an executable statement. When the assignment method is used, the values are expressed in arithmetic statements as constants. An example of this assignment technique is:

PRIN = 5000.D00

In this case, the value 5000 has been assigned to the variable name PRIN as a DOUBLE PRECISION constant. Note that the value was written with all of the significant digits contained in the value. The D notation was set to D00 which meant that the exponent of 10 was zero. This same amount could have been written in any of the following ways and have been equally acceptable as DOUBLE PRECISION constants.

PRIN = 5000D00	no decimal point; it is assumed to precede the letter D
PRIN = 500D01	move assumed decimal point one place to the right
PRIN = 50D02	move assumed decimal point two places to the right
PRIN = 5.D03	move decimal point three places to the right
PRIN = .5D04	move decimal point four places to the right
PRIN = 50000.D−01	move decimal point one place to the left

DOUBLE PRECISION Variables/Constants in Arithmetic Statements

All DOUBLE PRECISION variables and constants are in the real mode. Therefore, it is permissible to mix these variables and constants with any other real mode values within an arithmetic statement. This means that mixing single precision and DOUBLE PRECISION values is permitted. The following statements would be legal if included within the same program.

```
DOUBLE PRECISION A,B
    .
    .
    .
A = 74.3
B = 825.3367D04
C = 283.4
D = − 55.827E −02
    .
    .
    .
E = A + B + C + D
    .
    .
    .
STOP
END
```

In this example, two variables are defined as DOUBLE PRECISION variables (A, B). Variable A is assigned the value 74.3 which appears to be a single precision constant. However, due to the DOUBLE PRECISION declaration at the beginning of the program, the 74.3 will be converted to DOUBLE PRECISION size and stored. Variable B is assigned a constant value written in the normal DOUBLE PRECISION form. Variable C is assigned the single precision amount of 283.4. Variable D is assigned a constant in the exponential form. This amount, of course, is in the real mode. Variable E is assigned the sum of variables A,B,C, and D. This statement is permitted because each of the variables being summed is in the real mode. Temporarily, during summing, all of these variables will be converted to the most complex mode represented, in this case, the DOUBLE PRECISION mode. The sum stored in E is in single precision. Any variables which were changed to DOUBLE PRECISION during summing will be returned to their original form after the sum is computed. If variable E had been included in the DOUBLE PRECISION declaration, at the beginning of the program, the result of summing would be stored in DOUBLE PRECISION.

The normal rules apply for changing modes when an integer variable name appears to the left of the equal sign, even though all of the items within the expression to the right of the equal sign are in the real mode. The result of all manipulations within the expression are truncated when assignment is made to the integer storage location. The following statements are legal and illustrate this point:

```
DOUBLE PRECISION A
A = 123.4D-01
NR = A+2.3D01
```

These statements result in the addition of 12.34 and 23.00. The sum is 35.34, but when assigned to NR it is truncated to 35.

```
DOUBLE PRECISION B
B = 53.22D00
MAX = B/2.5
```

These statements result in the division of 53.22 by 2.5. The quotient is 21.288, and it is stored in MAX as 21.

Conversion To/From the D Code for Input and Output

A last point concerning the DOUBLE PRECISION specification deals with its conversion during input and output. Programs 11.6-11.8 illustrate how conversion from the F code (single precision, real mode) for reading input was made to DOUBLE PRECISION. These programs declared the variable TEST as DOUBLE PRECISION. Therefore, when reading was executed, the F code values were converted to DOUBLE PRECISION and stored in location TEST. These same programs illustrate the conversion of DOUBLE PRECISION back to the F code. When the WRITE statement was executed, the values stored in TEST were printed in accordance with the F20.0 specification.

The basic point is that any real values may be read with F or E code FORMAT specifications and may be converted for storage in a DOUBLE PRECISION memory location. Conversely, any DOUBLE PRECISION value stored in memory may be written with an E or F code used in the FORMAT statement for output. In this case, the computer will make an automatic conversion of the DOUBLE PRE-CISION value to fit the E or F specification.

The following rules apply to the DOUBLE PRECISION specification:

1. All variables which are to be treated by the processor in DOUBLE PRECISION must be declared in a DOUBLE PRECISION statement at the beginning of the program.
2. All real mode values may be stored in a DOUBLE PRECISION location. The processor will convert all single precision values to DOUBLE PRECISION.
3. DOUBLE PRECISION constants must contain the letter D and specify an exponent value for the number.
4. Any instruction which uses real values may mix single and DOUBLE PRE-CISION variables within the expression.
5. When the D code is used with an input FORMAT, the input values must also contain the letter D and an exponent value.
6. It is permissible to read values with the E or F codes and store the values in DOUBLE PRECISION memory locations.
7. It is permissible to write output values with the E or F codes from DOUBLE PRECISION memory locations.

Programs 11.9 and 11.10 illustrate the DOUBLE PRECISION mode of process-ing. These programs calculate the cumulative sum which results from making an investment which earns compound interest. The principal amount invested plus the compound interest is referred to as the *compound amount*. The compound amount is calculated according to the formula:

$$a = p(1 + r)^n$$

where: a = compound amount
p = original principal invested
r = rate of interest for compounding
n = number of periods over which interest is compounded

Programs 11.9 and 11.10 compute the compound amount for a $5,000 principal over 15 years at a 5 percent interest rate. The amount is $10,394.53. Program 11.9 handles the computations in single precision while Program 11.10 uses DOUBLE PRECISION.

Programs 11.11 and 11.12 compute the compound amount over the same time period and at the same interest rate, but use a $5,000,000 principal. The compound amount is $10,394,525.53. Program 11.11 handles the computations in single pre-cision while Program 11.12 uses DOUBLE PRECISION. The difference between single precision and DOUBLE PRECISION is evident in these programs, and the advantages of DOUBLE PRECISION are illustrated.

Note the following points about Program 11.9.

1. All amounts in this program are handled in single precision. Therefore, all com-putations are carried out to a maximum of 7 significant digits.
2. Note that the compound amount contains a one cent ($.01) rounding error. This is due to the inherent limitation of single precision.
3. Adjustment for this rounding error could be made by inserting a +.005 factor:

AMT=PRIN * (1. + RATE) ** NYR + .005

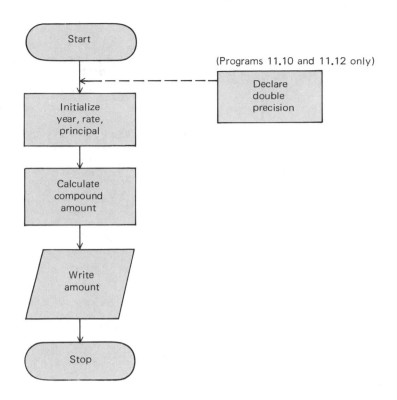

(Programs 11.10 and 11.12 only)

Program 11.9

```
      C
      C   CALCULATING COMPOUND AMOUNT
      C   USING SINGLE PRECISION
      C
1            NYR = 15
2            PRIN = 5000.00
3            RATE = .05
4            AMT = PRIN*(1.0+RATE)**NYR
5            WRITE (6,10) AMT
6         10 FORMAT (10X,16HSINGLE PRECISION/
             115X,15HCOMPOUND AMOUNT,2X,F8.2)
7            STOP
8            END


      SINGLE PRECISION
          COMPOUND AMOUNT   10394.52
```

rounding error

Program 11.10

```
      C
      C   CALCULATING COMPOUND AMOUNT
      C   USING DOUBLE PRECISION
      C
1           DOUBLE PRECISION AMT, PRIN
2           NYR = 15
3           PRIN = 0.5D04
4           RATE = .05
5           AMT = PRIN*(1.0+RATE)**NYR
6           WRITE (6,15) AMT
7        15 FORMAT (10X,16HDOUBLE PRECISION/
           115X,15HCOMPOUND AMOUNT,2X,D15.7)
8           STOP
9           END
```

```
      DOUBLE PRECISION
         COMPOUND AMOUNT     0.1039453D 05
```

1. This program uses the same numeric values as Program 11.9 but handles them in DOUBLE PRECISION. The number of significant digits is now increased to 16.
2. The compound amount is both calculated and written in DOUBLE PRECISION. The result appears as 0.1039453D+05. When the decimal point is realigned, the value will be 10394.53. DOUBLE PRECISION enabled the compound amount to be carried with enough singificant digits so that the result could be rounded up to the correct value when printed.

Program 11.11

```
      C
      C   CALCULATING COMPOUND AMOUNT
      C   USING SINGLE PRECISION
      C
1           NYR = 15
2           PRIN = 5000000.00
3           RATE = .05
4           AMT = PRIN*(1.0+RATE)**NYR
5           WRITE (6,10) AMT
6        10 FORMAT (10X,16HSINGLE PRECISION/
           115X,15HCOMPOUND AMOUNT,2X,F11.2)
7           STOP
8           END
```

```
      SINGLE PRECISION
         COMPOUND AMOUNT   10394520.00
```

rounding error

1. This program handles all amounts in single precision. Only 7 significant digits are retained even though the computed values will be much larger.

2. A significant rounding error of $5.53 is evident. This program illustrates how large values have rounding errors which grow to material amounts. In this case, the investor would expect receipt of his complete earned sum—including the $5.53!

Program 11.12

```
      C
      C  CALCULATING COMPOUND AMOUNT
      C  USING DOUBLE PRECISION WITH
      C  "D" AND "F" CODE OUTPUT
      C
 1        DOUBLE PRECISION AMT, PRIN
 2        NYR = 15
 3        PRIN = 0.5D07
 4        RATE = .05
 5        AMT = PRIN*(1.0+RATE)**NYR
 6        WRITE (6,15) AMT
 7     15 FORMAT (10X,16HDOUBLE PRECISION/
          115X,24HD CODE - COMPOUND AMOUNT,2X,D17.10)
 8        WRITE (6,20) AMT
 9     20 FORMAT (/15X,24HF CODE - COMPOUND AMOUNT,2X,F11.2)
10        STOP
11        END
```

```
DOUBLE PRECISION
      D CODE - COMPOUND AMOUNT   0.1039452553D 08

      F CODE - COMPOUND AMOUNT   10394525.53
```

1. This program uses the same $5 million principal as Program 11.11. All amounts are handled in DOUBLE PRECISION.

2. The increase in the number of significant digits carries the computation to the correct amount without rounding error.

3. Output is written in two forms. The D code displays the computed value in DOUBLE PRECISION output FORMAT. The F code has converted the value to decimal form.

Exercise 27

1. Prepare the necessary statements to initialize the following five constants. Each constant should be handled in DOUBLE PRECISION, and the numeric values should be written in the D code form. They are shown in decimal form below.
   a. A = 12.345
   b. N = 67
   c. B = 1500000000.0
   d. J = 225832.19
   e. C = 1

2. Read the following program and trace its processing logic. Indicate the values of each variable, shown to the right of the program, after the completion of processing. Show each variable's value carried to the number of significant digits inherent with the variable's use in the program. Assume single precision holds 7

significant digits and DOUBLE PRECISION holds 16 digits. Show all output values in decimal form.

```
       DOUBLE PRECISION X,Y,Z          A  _____
       DIMENSION Z(5)                  X  _____
       DO 5 J = 1,5                    Y  _____
     5 Z(J)=0.0                        Z(1)_____
       X=5.0                           Z(2)_____
       J=2                             Z(3)_____
       DO 10 K=1,5                     Z(4)_____
       A=X**2+.028365+Z(J-1)           Z(5)_____
       Z(K)=A                          N  _____
       X=X-1.0                         M  _____
       J=J+1
    10 CONTINUE
       Y=Z(4)/3.0
       N=X+3.4
       M=N+Y
       STOP
       END
```

3. Using the input FORMAT and input data values, shown below, indicate how these same values would be printed, according to the output FORMAT given. Use lowercase b's for any necessary blank output positions.

Input FORMAT (D12.2)	Output FORMAT (D15.8)
a. 123456789D00	a. _____
b. 12.345678D02	b. _____
c. .1234567D–03	c. _____
d. 12345678D–02	d. _____
e. 12345678.D05	e. _____

4. Compare the following input values with the FORMATs given. Identify any errors between the values and FORMATs and then rewrite the FORMATs to correctly describe the values. (b = blanks; assume values are punched beginning in column 1 and the values are correct.)

a. 12345D–02	FORMAT (D8.1)	_____
b. –123.45D+22b	FORMAT (D12.5)	_____
c. 12bb3.4D–02	FORMAT (D11.3)	_____
d. bb–12034D03	FORMAT (D10.1)	_____
e. +123.456D–04	FORMAT (D12.0)	_____

Questions

1. What advantages does the ability to manipulate subscripts offer the programmer?
2. What is a nested loop? Explain this concept.
3. What types of transfers are *illegal* within and around loops? Explain what conditions make these transfers illegal.
4. What is a PAUSE statement? What distinguishes this statement from the STOP and END statements?

5. Explain what advantage the DOUBLE PRECISION specification provides for handling data.

6. Prepare an example of a DOUBLE PRECISION number and accompanying FORMAT statement. Explain the detailed elements of both the number and FORMAT statement.

7. Write the decimal number 52489.30468 as a DOUBLE PRECISION constant in three different forms. Explain how the same number can be written in three ways but retain the same numeric value.

8. May integer values be mixed with DOUBLE PRECISION values in an arithmetic statement? Explain.

9. When single precision and DOUBLE PRECISION real values are mixed in an arithmetic statement, how is execution completed? Prepare an example to illustrate the addition of two numbers with one in single precision and one in DOUBLE PRECISION.

10. Why does the D code have to provide for more than seven characters when used to specify an output field?

12
Refining Input and Output

FORTRAN language elements presented in earlier chapters have enabled the computer to acquire data values either through the use of READ statements or arithmetic statements. Output values have been displayed on the line printer in accordance with the A, I, F, E, or D codes. These input/output options are adequate for most program uses. However, several additional methods for handling input/output are also available. These added techniques are refinements of the language elements already discussed and, in most instances, will make program preparation easier or more efficient or both.

The DATA Statement

Initialization is a simple process for inserting initial values in memory locations prior to processing. As discussed in Chapter 7, statements used to initialize values were arithmetic replacement statements, such as:

BIG = 5.6
COUNT = 1.0
LOW = 7

An alternative statement form, which also accomplishes this initialization, is the DATA statement. It appears as:

DATA BIG, COUNT, LOW/5.6, 1.0, 7/

This DATA statement accomplishes the same tasks as the previous three arithmetic replacement statements. The ability to initialize multiple memory locations in a single statement, of course, illustrates one substantial advantage of the DATA statement.

The primary elements within DATA statements are:

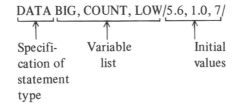

DATA BIG, COUNT, LOW/5.6, 1.0, 7/

Specification of statement type   Variable list   Initial values

218

A DATA statement is composed of the following elements:

1. DATA: each DATA statement must begin with the word DATA.
2. Variable list: each memory location which is to be initialized must have its variable name included within this list. All variables are separated by commas.
3. Initial values: each location's initial value is included in this list. The values are assigned, in a one-for-one order, to the variables in the variable list. All values are separated by commas.
4. Slashes: a single slash precedes the list of initial values, and another single slash follows the last value listed.

In addition to packing several variables and their data values into a single statement, the DATA statement enables the processor to initialize memory locations at the time *compilation* takes place. This offers an increase in processing efficiency. Initialization through the use of arithmetic statements requires the processor to *execute* them and thereby consumes processing time. Conversely, initialization during compilation eliminates the execution of arithmetic statements thereby saving processing time.

Another advantage of DATA statements is the reduced number of memory locations allowed by the eliminated arithmetic statements. Conservation of memory is critical for large programs and is a valid objective for all programs.

DATA statements normally appear at the beginning of a program but *must appear before any executable statements which use the variable names* being initialized. This requirement may become a minor drawback to the statement's use when reinitialization of values must be made within a program. In that event, the DATA statement may be used at the beginning of the program, and then separate arithmetic statements will be used within the body of the program.

The primary elements of the DATA statement, shown above, may also be used in several modified forms. Examples of these forms appear in the following list.

1. Single variable-value groups.

   DATA BIG/5.6/, COUNT/1.0/, LOW/7/

   Individual variables and the related values may be shown in successive groups. This alternative is more cumbersome to write but may more clearly relate the variables and values than when single lists of each are given.

2. Mixing real and integer values in one statement.

   DATA MAX, KAT, SUM, J/8, 1, 4.3, 0/

   Real and integer values may appear in any order within the DATA statement. The values are assigned to the variables in the order of their appearance in the listing. A variable name, and its mode, must be matched with a value and its mode. In this statement, for example, SUM and 4.3 are associated because each is the third item in its own list.

3. Use of the repeator symbol.

   DATA BLUES, SYS, SALES, CALL/4*0.0/

   If a number of variables are to have identical values, the use of an integer repetition value and an asterisk will result in the repeated use of the same value to initialize several variables. In the DATA statement shown, all four variable locations would be assigned the value 0.0.

4. Dimensioned variables.

DIMENSION GET(10)
DATA A, MO, GET/4.5, 2, 5*0.0, 5*1.0/

When an array is to be initialized, the DATA statement *must follow* the DIMEN-SION which establishes the size of the array. The array name is written without subscripts in the DATA statement. The DATA statement may initialize large portions of the array by use of the repetition value. In the above statement, the first 5 locations of GET are assigned the value of 0.0 and locations 6-10, the value of 1.0.

5. Subscripted dimensioned variable.

DIMENSION A(3), J(5)
DATA ROT, A(1), NUM, J/2.3, 1.0, 2, 5*0/

When a dimensioned variable is written with a subscript in the DATA statement, an initial value will be assigned *only* to the *single* array *location* specified by the subscript. A(1) will be assigned 1.0, in the example, while the entire J array will be initialized at zero.

6. Initializing E and D constants.

DOUBLE PRECISION ABLE
DIMENSION DP(3)
DATA ABLE, MAX, RMD, DP/ - 5.8D03, 0, 2.3E - 02, 1.0, 2.0, 3.0/

Variables may be initialized in double precision (D code) and the exponential (E code) as well as in single precision (F code) and the integer (I code). The example shows D and E code constants and shows how an array (DP) may have each element initialized to a different value. The DATA statement shown would make the same assignments as the following arithmetic statements:

ABLE = - 5.8D+03
MAX = 0
RMD = 2.3E - 02
DP(1) = 1.0
DP(2) = 2.0
DP(3) = 3.0

The DATA statement *must follow* the DOUBLE PRECISION specification so that the declared variable (ABLE) will have the proper storage reserved prior to assignment of its value (- 5.8D03).

7. Alphabetic data initialization. (b = a blank character)

DIMENSION NAME(4)
DATA NR, NAME/0, 4HJOHN, 4HSONb, 4HR.bJ, 1H./

Alphabetic data may be initialized, as well as numeric data, as illustrated above. This example assumes a processor which will hold a maximum of four alphabetic characters in one memory location. The NAME array is dimensioned to hold a maximum of 16 alphabetic characters. The assignment of the name JOHNSON R. J. is made through use of the Hollerith (H) code to the following array elements:

NAME(1) = JOHN
NAME(2) = SONb   (b = a blank character)
NAME(3) = R.bJ
NAME(4) = .bbb

8. Implied DO loop within the DATA statement.

DIMENSION NAME(4)
DATA NR, (NAME(K),K=1,4)/0, 4HJOHN,4HSONb,4HR.bJ,1H./

Some versions of FORTRAN permit the use of implied loops within the DATA statement. The statement shown in (7) is rewritten with the use of an implied loop in this illustration. The effect is the same in both DATA statements, and little advantage is gained with use of the implied loop for one dimensional arrays. If the loop is used, all index parameters must be integer constants. Integer variables are illegal.

Programs 12.1 and 12.2 provide an illustration of the DATA statements ability to accomplish the initialization of several arithmetic statements. This illustration is based on Program 11.10 in Chapter 11. The purpose of each program is to calculate the compound amount which will result from an investment of $5 million, at 5 per cent interest, for 15 years. Program 12.1 executes without use of the DATA statement. Program 12.2 uses a DATA statement which combines the action of three arithmetic replacement statements and illustrates the initialization of integer, real (single precision), and DOUBLE PRECISION (D code) values.

Program 12.1

```
C
C   CALCULATING COMPOUND AMOUNT
C
C   *** INITIALIZATION USING
C       EXECUTABLE STATEMENTS ***
C
      DOUBLE PRECISION AMT, PRIN
      NYR = 15
      PRIN = 0.5D07        Initialization using three
      RATE = .05           arithmetic statements
      AMT = PRIN*(1.0+RATE)**NYR
      WRITE (6,15) AMT
   15 FORMAT (10X,16HDOUBLE PRECISION/
     115X,24HD CODE - COMPOUND AMOUNT,2X,D17.10)
      WRITE (6,20) AMT
   20 FORMAT (/15X,24HF CODE - COMPOUND AMOUNT,2X,F11.2)
      STOP
      END
```

```
DOUBLE PRECISION
    D CODE - COMPOUND AMOUNT   0.1039452553D 08

    F CODE - COMPOUND AMOUNT   10394525.53
```

Program 12.2

```
C
C   CALCULATING COMPOUND AMOUNT
C
C   *** INITIALIZATION USING
C       A DATA STATEMENT ***
C
        DOUBLE PRECISION AMT, PRIN
        DATA NYR, PRIN, RATE/15, 0.5D07, .05/
        AMT = PRIN*(1.0+RATE)**NYR
        WRITE (6,15) AMT
    15  FORMAT (10X,16HDOUBLE PRECISION/
       115X,24HD CODE - COMPOUND AMOUNT,2X,D17.10)
        WRITE (6,20) AMT
    20  FORMAT (/15X,24HF CODE - COMPOUND AMOUNT,2X,F11.2)
        STOP
        END
```

Initialization
using one DATA
statement

```
DOUBLE PRECISION
      D  CODE - COMPOUND AMOUNT     0.1039452553D 08

      F  CODE - COMPOUND AMOUNT    10394525.53
```

Both programs compute identical results. In Program 12.2, the variable data name NYR is assigned (initialized) the integer value 15 by the DATA statement. Similar assignments are made for the other variables with PRIN set to 0.5D07 and RATE set to .05. These values are assigned when the program is compiled from FORTRAN into object code. This process saves the time which would be required to execute the three arithmetic statements, as required in Program 12.1, and is a more compact and convenient way to write the initialization instructions.

Exercise 28

1. Write a single DATA statement which will initialize the following variables and values:
   a. A = 7.5
   b. B = 3.2
   c. C = 5.4
   d. J = 9
2. Write the necessary statements to accomplish the following:
   a. establish an array named NIX which has 38 memory locations
   b. initialize all locations in the array with the value 3. Use a DATA statement to initialize.
3. Rewrite your DATA statement in (2) above to initialize the NIX array as follows:
   a. locations 1-22 with the value of 3
   b. locations 23-30 with the value of 0
   c. locations 31-38 with the value of 7
4. Analyze the following variable names and associated values. Then write the necessary statements to establish memory locations for storage and initialize all locations with the use of a DATA statement.

Variable Names	Data Values
AB	0
JAC	15
ELEC	10.3D−02
SOME(1)	8.0
SOME(2)	0
SOME(3)	8.0
SOME(4)	2.0
SOME(5)	2.5
CT	2.2E+07
ID(1)	CAN
ID(2)	YOU
ID(3)	DO
ID(4)	IT?

The G Code for Input/Output

Normally, the format specifications for data that the computer reads or writes are carefully tailored to match the format codes (I, F, E, D) with appropriate values. As a matter of fact, errors will arise when a value does not agree with the format code specified. An example of this condition is shown below:

$$\lceil 3.45 \rceil$$

FORMAT (I4)

An attempt to read a field containing a decimal point (real value) when the FORMAT specifies an integer (I4) results in an error condition.

The FORTRAN language does provide a format code which will accept integer or real data[1] without knowing, at the time the program is written, which data type will be used in processing. This generalized code is appropriately designated as the G code. An example of a FORMAT statement containing a G code specification is shown below:

15 FORMAT (F8.2, I5, G10.4)

The elements of the G code are:

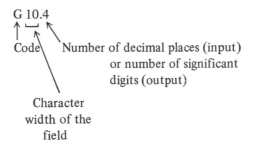

G 10.4

Code

Number of decimal places (input)
or number of significant
digits (output)

Character
width of the
field

---

[1] Complex and logical data may also be handled in the G mode. These data types are explained in Chapter 13.

1. The letter G specifies data handling using the generalized code.
2. Character width (10 in the example):
   a. Input: when input is in punch card form, this specification indicates the number of card columns in the input field. Any blank input columns are converted to zeros.
   b. Output: the character width specification for printed output indicates the number of character print positions in the output field.
3. Number of decimal places or digits (.4 in the example):
   a. Input: for input, this specification serves the same function as it does with the F, E, or D codes. When the decimal point is punched, this specification is ignored. When the decimal point is not punched, this specification will place (insert) the assumed decimal point. If the G code is used for integer input, this specification is ignored.
   b. Output: this specification indicates the total number of significant digits to be displayed as output. This means that with real values zeros may be added to a value so that the specified number of digits is printed. For integer values, all output values are right justified in the output field, with leading zeros suppressed.

The fact that the G code may be specified for values which are *either* real or integer makes its use advantageous. The *implied mode* of the *variable name* used with an input/output value determines whether the value will be treated in the real or integer mode. For instance, the following data values, FORMAT statements, and READ statements treat the same sequence of digits in opposite modes:

	REAL Mode	INTEGER Mode
Input card	56802	56802
FORMAT	5 FORMAT (G5.2)	5 FORMAT (G5.2)
READ	READ (5,5) A	READ (5,5) K
Stored value	568.02	56802

This example illustrates how the use of a G code specification handles an input value in the real mode when the READ statement variable is in the real mode (A in this case). The same G code specification treated an identical input value in the integer mode when the READ statement contained the integer variable name K.

Several additional characteristics of the G code should be noted. First, the G code may *not* be used for input/output of alphabetic data or special characters. Second, when an input/output value is in the integer mode, the specification for decimal places or digits is ignored. This may be seen in the example above. Third, output of real values is normally printed in a format equivalent to the F code (that is, without an exponent). However, this is true only when the size of the output value falls within the range .1 to $10^{**}d$ (where d = number of significant digits in the G code). When values are outside this range, the output will be displayed in the E code format (that is, with an exponent).

Table 12.1 illustrates the use of the G code with several different real values. Column 1 shows the input values and a G code used to read them. Column 2 contains the values as they would be stored after reading. Column 3 shows how the stored values, from column 2, are printed when the G20.9 FORMAT is used.

Table 12.1

	FORMAT (G8.2) Input Values	Internal Storage	FORMAT (G20.9) Output Values
1.	1234567.	1234567.	1234567.00
2.	12345678	123456.7	123456.700
3.	12.34567	12.34567	12.3456700
4.	1234E-02	12.34E-02	0.123400000
5.	12.34E03	12.34E03	12340.0000
6.	1234D-02	12.34D-02	0.123400000
7.	12.34D03	12.34D03	12340.0000
8.	1234bbbb*	123400.0	123400.000
9.	bbbb1234	00012.34	12.3400000
10.	000.0001	000.0001	0.100000000E-03

*b = blank column

1. The above table shows all values in single precision. We have assumed a maximum of 7 digits stored in single precision. When a field contains more than 7 digits, the excess digits are dropped. Example 2 shows this conversion.
2. The input FORMAT (G8.2) will insert the decimal point when it is not punched with the input value. This can be seen in examples 2, 4, 6, 8, and 9.
3. In examples 4, 5, 6, and 7, the E and D codes both indicate appropriate powers of 10.
4. Blanks are converted to zeros in examples 8 and 9.
5. The output FORMAT (G20.9) causes 9 significant digits to be printed as output. All examples have 9 digits and, when necessary, 0's are added to fill the output fields.
6. All values which fall in the range .1 to 10^9 are printed in the F code. This means that the input E and D codes are converted in this example (4, 5, 6, and 7).
7. When a value is less than .1, output is converted to the E code as shown in example 10. Care must be taken to provide sufficient room for the 7 required positions of the E code (see page 152).

The conversion of a G code value when it exceeds 10**d on output is illustrated below.

FORMAT (G12.0) Input Value	Internal Storage	FORMAT (G20.9) Output Value
123456789012	123456700000.	0.123456700E12

The input value contains 12 digits. The value has no decimal point punched, but the FORMAT assumes a decimal point to the right of the twelfth digit. When the value is stored, only 7 digits are retained. Zeros are shown to represent the digits dropped. The value is actually 1234567E05, indicating that the decimal point is 5 places to the right of the digit 7.

This value is very large and actually exceeds 123 billion (123,456,700,000). To determine the code to be used for output, it must be determined whether the value exceeds 10^9. $10**9$ is 1 billion. Hence, the output value will be shown using the E code. To print the E code, the decimal point is shifted seven places to the left. This causes the exponent to be raised from 5 to 12 (5 + 7) in order to express the correct value for the printed amount.

The G code characteristics closely resemble the E and D codes. The most significant advantages of the G code are the ability to use a single code type for both real and integer data and the ability to specify the number of digits to be printed regardless of the internal size of values. In the appropriate situation, the G code may permit the use of a single FORMAT statement with several READ statements. The READ statements could each contain different mixtures of real and integer variable names. However, use of this language element requires the same careful considerations as do all other FORTRAN elements.

Input/Output Control: FORMAT versus Punched Decimal Point

A simple, though very important, point must be made about priorities when input is in punched card form. The priorities concern the potential conflicts between the decimal point specifications in a FORMAT statement and the actual punched decimal points in an input card. Of course, when the FORMAT and the data cards agree, no problem exists. But what if they do not agree? Which input element takes precedence? The general rule is: *a punched decimal point overrides any FORMAT specification for real mode values.* This means that the decimal point alignment portion of the FORMAT is ignored. The field width portion of the FORMAT specification must still agree between the FORMAT and data card. The decimal override provision of FORTRAN applies to all real mode data whether expressed in the F, D, E, or G codes.

The following illustrations will demonstrate this point.

1. Input data card   2468

   Input FORMAT   (F4.0)

   This value is handled as 2468.0. The FORMAT and data card assume that the decimal point follows the 8.

2. Input data card   24.68

   Input FORMAT   (F5.2)

   This value is handled as 24.68. The punched decimal point and the FORMAT specification agree.

3. Input data card   2468

   Input FORMAT   (F4.3)

   This value is handled as 2.468. No decimal point is punched so the FORMAT specifies location of the point.

4. Input data card   2.468

   Input FORMAT   (F5.1)

   This value is handled as 2.468. The punched decimal point overrides the FORMAT specifications.

5. Input data card   67.89E02

   Input FORMAT   (E8.2)

   This value is handled as 67.89E02. The FORMAT and the punched decimal point agree.

6. Input data card   6.789E02

   Input FORMAT   (E8.1)

   This value is handled as 6.789E02. The punched decimal point overrides the FORMAT specification.

If all input data is punched with decimal points, the input FORMAT statements may be written in a form of shorthand. For instance, if the fields are six columns wide, the FORMAT specification may be written as F6.0. This FORMAT specification indicates no decimal places. However, the punched decimal points in the data cards will override this specification and cause the computer to allow the proper number of decimal places.

No conflict over decimal points exists with output FORMAT statements. The computer will automatically align the internal storage of a value and the output FORMAT prior to printing. The number of decimal places specified by an output FORMAT are always printed.

Input/Output Control: READ/WRITE Lists versus FORMAT Specification

A control question arises when the length of the list in a READ or WRITE statement does not agree with the number of value specifications in the FORMAT statement. Does the computer stop reading or writing when the FORMAT is exhausted or is some other technique available to continue reading or writing? The rule in this case is: *a READ/WRITE list must be executed in full even when the FORMAT is exhausted.* When a FORMAT is exhausted and variables remain in a READ or WRITE list, the computer will reuse the FORMAT beginning at the last opening parenthesis. The READ/WRITE list is controlling. When a FORMAT is reused, the computer accesses a new record. If the processor is reading, a new card is read. When the processor is writing, a new line is printed. A FORMAT statement may be discarded without using all of its specifications, but a READ/WRITE list must be filled.

The following examples illustrate this point. The examples show READ statements, but the rules are the same for WRITE statements. In each example, the word WRITE could be substituted for READ and illustrate the same points.

1. 15 FORMAT (8F5.3)
   READ (5,15) A,B,C,D,E,F,G,H

   The FORMAT statement indicates that eight data values are on one card. The READ statement has 8 variable names. Both statements agree.

2. 20 FORMAT (8F5.3)
   READ (5,20) A,B,C,D

   The FORMAT statement describes eight data values, but the READ statement reads only 4 values. The extra 4 FORMAT specifications are discarded.

3. 25 FORMAT (3F6.2)
   READ (5,25) A,B,C,D,E

   The FORMAT statement describes 3 data values, while the READ statement calls for 5 values. The first 3 values will be read from 1 card and the last 2 from a second card.

4. 30 FORMAT (4F10.0)
   READ (5,30) (Z(K),K=1,8)

   The array Z is loaded from 2 cards. Each card contains 4 values read by the implied DO loop. The variables Z(1)-Z(4) are read from card 1, variables Z(5)-Z(8) from card 2.

5. 35 FORMAT (F9.3)
   DO 40 N=1,5
   READ (5,35) Y(N)
   40 CONTINUE

The array Y is loaded from 5 separate cards. The FORMAT statement describes 1 value per card, and the explicit DO loop causes the READ statement to be reexecuted 5 times.

6. 45 FORMAT (F10.2)
   READ (5,45) (X(L),L=1,5)

The X array is loaded from 5 separate cards. The implied DO loop is unable to cause reading across a card because the FORMAT statement indicates that only 1 value is on each card. The FORMAT specification is reused 5 times and causes a new card to be read with each reuse.

7. 50 FORMAT (2F6.3/F4.1/(2F8.3))
   READ (5,50) (W(M),M=1,10)

Card	Array Values
1	W(1), W(2)
2	W(3)
3	W(4), W(5)
4	W(6), W(7)
5	W(8), W(9)
6	W(10)

The W array is loaded from 6 cards. The implied DO loop reads the first 2 values from card 1. The slash then causes a second card to be read. The third value is read from this card. The second slash causes a third card to be read. The remaining values will be read two-at-a-time from successive cards. The summary on the left shows which values are related to the 6 cards read.

The Short List Convention for Input

An additional refinement in dealing with data arrays is known as the short list convention. This refinement permits the reading or writing of an *entire* array without having to specify subscript values within the READ or WRITE statements. For example, assume an array is DIMENSIONed as SAMPLE(10) and that ten input data values are punched in one card under a 10F5.2 FORMAT specification. The statements necessary to read these values would normally be written:

```
DIMENSION SAMPLE(10)
15 FORMAT (10F5.2)
   READ (5,15) (SAMPLE(K),K=1,10)
```

The short list convention option permits the READ statement to be rewritten as:

READ (5,15) SAMPLE

When an array name is written *without a subscript*, the computer interprets it as a command to read as many values as necessary to fill the *entire* array. This technique provides a powerful shorthand method for input but has a possible drawback in that reading *must* continue until the entire array has been filled. Obviously, this will not be an appropriate technique when a program's requirements call for less than a full array to be read.

The following three examples provide further illustrations of the short list convention's use in a READ statement. In each of the program segments which follow, it is assumed that a one dimensional array named LOT is to be filled with the integer values 11, 22, 33, 44, and 55.

Example 1. In each example given, the use of LOT without a subscript accomplishes the same input task as would the following implied loop: (LOT(J), J=1,5)

	LOT Array
1	11
2	22
3	33
4	44
5	55

Input Data Card

11	22	33	44	55

```
    DIMENSION LOT (5)
10 FORMAT (5I2)
    READ (5,10) LOT
    .
    .
    .
    END
```

Example 2. In this example, the FORMAT specification has been adjusted from that shown in Example 1 to accommodate the reading of five values from five consecutive cards.

	LOT Array
1	11
2	22
3	33
4	44
5	55

Input Data Cards

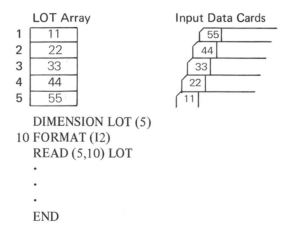

```
    DIMENSION LOT (5)
10 FORMAT (I2)
    READ (5,10) LOT
    .
    .
    .
    END
```

Example 3. This FORMAT specification has been adjusted from that shown in previous examples so that a maximum of three values will be read from a single data card.

	LOT Array
1	11
2	22
3	33
4	44
5	55

Input Data Cards

44	55

11	22	33

```
    DIMENSION LOT(5)
10 FORMAT (3I2)
    READ (5,10) LOT
    ·
    ·
    ·
    END
```

If the available input data values are either greater or less than the dimensioned size of the array, several possible steps may be taken by the computer. These are shown in Examples 4-6.

Example 4. When the number of values to be read is less than the array size, zeros will be placed in the array to fill its locations.

	LOT Array
1	11
2	22
3	33
4	0
5	0

Input Data Card

11	22	33

```
DIMENSION LOT(5)
10 FORMAT (5I2)
    READ (5,10) LOT
    ·
    ·
    ·
    END
```

Example 5. When the number of values to be read are less than the array size and the FORMAT calls for reading consecutive cards, two possible actions may result:

1. If additional cards (either blank or with some values punched) follow the array values being read, these cards will be loaded into the LOT Array. With the five cards shown below, zeros would be stored in the LOT array.
2. If no additional cards follow the array values being read, the computer will attempt reading, but an error condition will result.

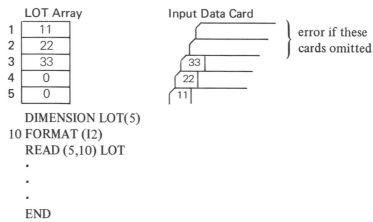

```
    DIMENSION LOT(5)
10 FORMAT (I2)
    READ (5,10) LOT
    ·
    ·
    ·
    END
```

Example 6. When input cards contain more values than the dimensioned size of the array, the excess values will be ignored.

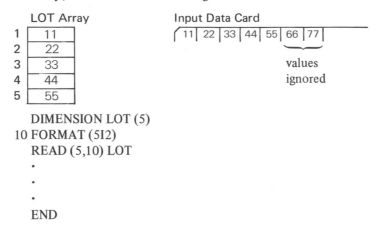

LOT Array

1	11
2	22
3	33
4	44
5	55

Input Data Card

| 11 | 22 | 33 | 44 | 55 | 66 | 77 |

values
ignored

```
    DIMENSION LOT (5)
10 FORMAT (5I2)
    READ (5,10) LOT
    .
    .
    .
    END
```

The Short List Convention with Output

The same short list convention is available when writing from an array. Listing an array name, without subscripts, in a WRITE statement will cause the computer to print the *entire* array. The entire array will be printed regardless of whether or not values have been stored in all array locations. Zeros will be printed when empty locations are written. The following illustration shows how an array named **TOTAL** will be written using the short list convention.

TOTAL Array

1	10.5
2	20.6
3	30.7
4	0.0
5	0.0
6	0.0

Program Statements

```
    DIMENSION TOTAL(6)
25 FORMAT (2(2X, F4.1))
    WRITE (6,25) TOTAL
    .
    .
    .
    END
```

Printed Output

10.5	20.6
30.7	0.0
0.0	0.0

Use of the short list convention is equivalent to writing the WRITE statement with an implied loop:

WRITE(6,25) (TOTAL(K),K=1,6)

Several other examples of the short list convention with WRITE statements are shown below.

Example 1.

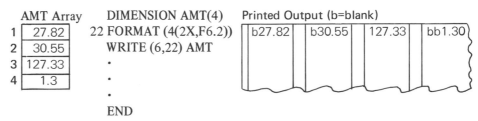

AMT Array

1	27.82
2	30.55
3	127.33
4	1.3

```
    DIMENSION AMT(4)
22 FORMAT (4(2X,F6.2))
    WRITE (6,22) AMT
    .
    .
    .
    END
```

Printed Output (b=blank)

| b27.82 | b30.55 | 127.33 | bb1.30 |

Example 2.

AMT Array		Dimension AMT(4)	Printed Output (b=blank)
1	27.82	22 FORMAT (2X, F6.2)	b27.82
2	30.55	WRITE (6,22) AMT	b30.55
3	127.33	·	127.33
4	1.3	·	bb1.30
		·	
		END	

Example 3.

AMT Array		DIMENSION AMT(4)	Printed Output (b=blank)
1	27.82	22 FORMAT (2(2X, F6.2))	b27.82 b30.55
2	30.55	WRITE (6,22) AMT	127.33 bb1.30
3	127.33	·	
4	1.3	·	
		·	
		END	

The short list convention provides a compact command for the input/output of entire arrays but must be used with caution. It does not apply where less than a complete array is being read or written.

Exercise 29

1. Assume that the five values shown below are stored in the processor's memory. If a program contains the G code FORMAT specifications shown, how will the printed output values appear?

	Stored Values	G Code FORMAT	Printed Value
a.	5678.23	G14.7	_____
b.	567.E-02	G5.3	_____
c.	567 (integer)	G6.2	_____
d.	567.E-02	G9.3	_____
e.	INTY	G4.0	_____

2. A series of input data cards are shown below with related FORMAT and READ statements. After studying each combination, indicate how each value would be stored in memory (b = blank).

a. | 1234 | .68bb | 12.3D-05 | 0 | 5678 |
   DOUBLE PRECISION C
   5 FORMAT (F4.2,F5.2,D8.3,I1,I3)
   READ (5,5) A,B,C,J,K

A _____
B _____
C _____
J _____
K _____

b. | .123 | 68bbb | 1234D-05 | b | 567.8 |
   DOUBLE PRECISION C
   5 FORMAT (F4.2,F5.2,D8.3,I1,I3)
   READ (5,5) A,B,C,J,K

A _____
B _____
C _____
J _____
K _____

c. | 1.23 | 68bbb | 1234D –05 | 0 | 5678 |

DOUBLE PRECISION C
5 FORMAT (F4.0,F5.0,D8.0,I1,I3)
READ (5,5) A,B,C,J,K

A _____
B _____
C _____
J _____
K _____

3. The following data card has its values stored with the variables shown below it. The variables and values are shown in the order they were taken from the data card. Prepare the FORMAT which must have been used to input the values shown. Assume that *no* card columns were skipped with the X code.

| 123b456bbb2b9b.789b

FORMAT_____

A = 12.3   N = 9
B = .045   D = 0
K = 600   E = 7.8
C = 20.

4. The following input data cards will be used in each of the questions given below:

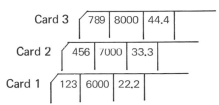

Card 3 | 789 | 8000 | 44.4 |
Card 2 | 456 | 7000 | 33.3 |
Card 1 | 123 | 6000 | 22.2 |

Each of the following program segments is intended to read the three data cards shown above. After studying each program segment, indicate the values which each variable would have upon *completion* of processing of *all* of the segment's statements. Also show the number of the card from which the values came.

a. 5 FORMAT (I3,F4.2,F4.1)
    50 READ (5,5) N,A,B
        .
        .
        .
        GO TO 50

Variable	Value	Card
N	_____	_____
A	_____	_____
B	_____	_____

b. DIMENSION N(3),A(3),B(3)
    10 FORMAT (I3,F4.2,F4.1)
    READ (5,10) (N(K), A(K), B(K),K=1,3)

Variable	Value	Card	Variable	Value	Card
N(1)	_____	_____	A(3)	_____	_____
N(2)	_____	_____	B(1)	_____	_____
N(3)	_____	_____	B(2)	_____	_____
A(1)	_____	_____	B(3)	_____	_____
A(2)	_____	_____			

c. DIMENSION N(3),A(3),B(3)
    15 FORMAT (I3)
    READ (5,15) (N(K),K=1,3)

Variable	Value	Card	Variable	Value	Card
N(1)	____	____	A(3)	____	____
N(2)	____	____	B(1)	____	____
N(3)	____	____	B(2)	____	____
A(1)	____	____	B(3)	____	____
A(2)	____	____			

d. DIMENSION N(3),A(3),B(3)
    20 FORMAT (I3)
      READ (5,20) N

Variable	Value	Card	Variable	Value	Card
N(1)	____	____	A(3)	____	____
N(2)	____	____	B(1)	____	____
N(3)	____	____	B(2)	____	____
A(1)	____	____	B(3)	____	____
A(2)	____	____			

e. DIMENSION N(3),A(3),B(3)
    25 FORMAT (I3, F4.2)
      I = 1
    50 READ (5,25) N(I), A(I)
         .
         .
         .
      I = I+1
      GO TO 50

Variable	Value	Card
N(1)	____	____
N(2)	____	____
N(3)	____	____
A(1)	____	____
A(2)	____	____
A(3)	____	____
B(1)	____	____
B(2)	____	____
B(3)	____	____

Use of the Single Quotation Mark (') in Place of the H Code

The H code is used to print alphanumeric characters as output. We have used this code for headings and captions. While all systems permit the use of the H code, most FORTRAN systems also allow a second method for indicating alphanumeric strings. The majority of these sytems use single quotation marks (or "break" characters) which are placed at the beginning and the end of the alphanumeric string. When the quotation marks are used, it is not necessary to indicate the number of characters in the message. The following examples *compare* the use of quotation marks, and the H code. In the last example, note how carriage control characters may also be enclosed within single quotation marks.

12 FORMAT (2X, 10HTHE SUM IS,2X,F7.3)
12 FORMAT (2X,'THE SUM IS',2X,F7.3)

14 FORMAT (5X, 4HX = ,3X, I9)
14 FORMAT (5X,'X = ', 3X, I9)

16 FORMAT (30X, 14HPAYROLL SUMMARY)
16 FORMAT (30X, 'PAYROLL SUMMARY')

18 FORMAT (1H1, 5X, 16HCODE NUMBER 3 = , I3)
18 FORMAT ('1', 5X, 'CODE NUMBER 3 = ', I3)

Scale Factor P for Decimal Point Alignment

We have not yet considered the alignment of decimal points when moving data either into storage or from storage to printed form. The calculation of a percentage is a situation where decimal alignment might be of concern to a programmer. Let us assume that we wish to calculate the percentage which Cost of Goods Sold is of Sales. This percentage (assume a variable name PCT) is derived by dividing Cost of Goods Sold (assume a variable name CGS) by Sales (assume a variable name SALES). The following FORTRAN statement would calculate the percentage.

PCT = CGS / SALES

If we assume the following values for these variables: CGS = 786,150 and SALES = 900,000, division of these two values results in a quotient of .8735. Of course, this will be the value assigned to PCT. If we print this value, it could be shown in fractional form as .8735. However, it may be preferable to show the percentage as 87.35. Up to this point, movement of the decimal point two places to the right would have necessitated the following alteration in our statement:

PCT = CGS / SALES * 100.0

Use of the FORMAT scale factor P in displaying PCT could directly accomplish the decimal alignment movement. This technique would eliminate the multiplication required in the above statement. If the FORMAT for printing PCT is F5.2, the addition of the specification 2P in front of the F5.2 will indicate that the value of PCT is to have the decimal point moved two places to the right. The statements with and without the scale factor would appear as:

Without the Scale Factor	With the Scale Factor
PCT = CGS / SALES	PCT = CGS / SALES
20 FORMAT (5X, F5.4)	20 FORMAT (5X, 2PF5.2)
WRITE (6,20) PCT	WRITE (6,20) PCT
Output	Output
.8735	87.35

The letter P indicates the movement of the decimal point in a data value. The digit preceding P specifies how many places the decimal point should be moved. If the scale factor is preceded by a *minus sign*, the decimal point is moved to the *left*. When a *sign* is *omitted*, the scale factor indicates a decimal point movement to the *right*. This discussion of the scale factor has been related to *output* and is summarized below:

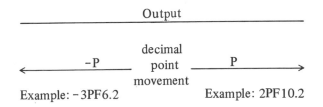

It should be noted that use of the P scale factor *applies only to real data values.* No decimal point is printed for integer values but is assumed to exist to the right of the right-most digit in an integer number. It may not be moved by the P scale factor, but, of course, the size of an integer value may be increased or decreased by either multiplication or division. The P scale factor, therefore, applies only to F, E, D and G code values.

Several examples of the scale factor for output are given below:

	Stored Value	Output FORMAT	Output Value
F Code	2.468	(2PF5.1)	246.8
	−2345.6	(−4PF8.5)	−0.23456
	.1357	(3 PF5.1)	135.7
	68.905	(−1PF6.4)	6.8905
E Code*	.12345E+03	(2PE12.5)	12.345E+01
	.33772E+01	(−1PE12.6)	0.033772E+02
	−.2566E+03	(3PE15.6)	−256.600000E+00
	−.12478E+03	(−1PE12.6)	−0.012478E+04

*The D code is handled identically to the E code with the exception that the letter D appears where the letter E is shown here.

The P scale may be used for *input* as well as output. The scale factor permits an input value which contains a decimal point to be altered, prior to its storage in memory. For example, a program may make use of data which was prepared for use with some other program. In this situation the punched FORMAT specification usually will not agree with the requirements of the current program. To change decimal point positions, either a series of executable instructions will have to be written (to multiply or divide the values) or the P scale factor may be included in the FORMAT statement. Assume that an input data card contains the value 62.834, but the desired value is 6283.4. This change in decimal point location can be made with the following FORMAT statement:

22 FORMAT (−2PF6.3)

Note that movement of an *input* decimal point to the *right requires a minus sign* with the P scale factor. *This is the exact opposite of the sign used for output.* Of course, omission of a sign specifies movement of the decimal point to the left. This movement is summarized below:

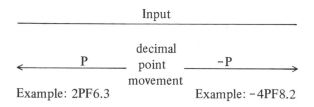

Several examples of the scale factor for input are shown below:

Data Card Value	Input FORMAT	Stored Value
8023.4	(3PF6.1)	8.0234
15.35E−02	(−2PE9.2)	.1535E00
−323.37	(−1PF7.2)	−3233.7
89286.4	(4PG7.1)	8.92864
−27.802D03	(−3PD10.3)	−.27802D05

A repeater symbol may be used in FORMAT specifications which contain P scale factors, just as it is used in any FORMAT statement. Suppose 4 values were to use the same scale factor. If each value was described as F8.3, FORMAT statements with and without the repeater would appear as shown below:

Without the repeater symbol

12 FORMAT (−3PF8.3,−3PF8.3,−3PF8.3,−3PF8.3)

With the repeater symbol

12 FORMAT (−3P4F8.3)

A Word of Caution in Using the P Scale Factor

Once the P scale factor has been listed in a FORMAT specification, it *remains in effect for all other real mode values in the same FORMAT specification.* Two methods exist for changing this condition. Another P scale factor may be encountered or the use of a 0P scale factor will turn off the decimal point adjustment. Consider the following statements:

7 FORMAT (F6.2,2PF8.1,F4.1,−3PF7.2,0PF5.2,F6.4)

READ (5,7) A, B, C, D, E, F

Variable

A: no decimal point adjustment

B: decimal point moved 2 places to the left

C: decimal point moved 2 places to the left; the adjustment remains in effect because it was turned on with variable B

D: decimal point moved 3 places to the right

E: turn off of the decimal point adjustment; no decimal point adjustment for this variable

F: no decimal point adjustment

The T Code for Output[2]

We have used the X code in FORMAT statements to skip character positions on a printed line. A similar provision for character skipping is achieved by use of the T

[2] Many systems do not permit the use of this language element. Check the manufacturer's manual before you use it in a FORTRAN program.

code. This code, called the *transfer code,* specifies the line position where a written message or value should begin. Spacing with the X code is limited only to movement across a line from left to right; the T code, however, is *not.* Consider the following FORMAT:

19 FORMAT ('1', 7X, 'DEPT NO.', 2X, 14)

This FORMAT specifies a printed line which appears as:

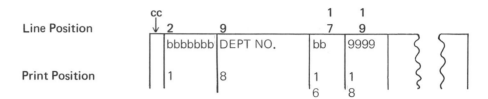

Recall that a line has a maximum 121 (or 133) positions. The first position is used only for carriage control, and nothing will be printed in that position. Therefore, there are only 120 (or 132) actual print positions. The T code specifies the *line position* where a printed item should begin. The FORMAT statement above could be written with the T code as:

19 FORMAT ('1', T9, 'DEPT NO.', T19, I4)

Note the relationship between the T code specifications and the line positions shown above. The following FORMAT statement would specify printing the same line, but it illustrates the fact that individual line items do not have to be specified from left to right when using the T code.

19 FORMAT (T19, I4, T1, '1', T9, 'DEPT NO.')

The T code may be used with any type of output code. The T code merely specifies where an output field begins on a printed line.

Exercise 30

1. Convert the following FORMAT statements from their use of the H code to the use of single quote marks (b = blank).
   a. FORMAT (5X,12HTOTAL VALUES, I12) _____
   b. FORMAT (3X,F8.1,3HX =,I2,3HY = I2) _____
   c. FORMAT (//1H1,2X,7HSUMMARY,2X,I3) _____
   d. FORMAT (5H-bbbb,9HMAX VALUE,2X,I7) _____
   e. FORMAT (3(2X,14HRESIDUAL VALUE,I3)) _____

2. The four following exercises deal with the P scale factor. The first two exercises give an input data card and the value as it should be stored. You are to prepare the FORMAT statement which would appropriately alter the values for storage. The second two exercises give input cards and FORMAT statements. Indicate the values as they would be stored.

a. | 456.78 | 2468 | 334.4 |

Variable   A   B   C

FORMAT _____

To Be Stored As:

A   45.678
B   24680.
C   3.344

b. $\overline{\mid 4567.8 \mid 246.8 \mid 33.44 \mid}$

Variable   A   B   C

FORMAT _____

To Be Stored As:

A 45678.

B 246.8

C 3.344

c. $\overline{\mid 123.45 \mid 67.890 \mid 2468 \mid}$

Variable   A   B   C

FORMAT (2PF6.2,0PF6.3,2PF4.2)

Stored As:

A _____

B _____

C _____

d. $\overline{\mid .12345 \mid .6789 \mid 2468 \mid}$

Variable   A   B   C

FORMAT (-3PF6.5,2PF5.0,-1PF4.4)

Stored As:

A _____

B _____

C _____

3. In the following exercise, you are given values as they were stored. In addition, you are given the printed values as they would have appeared. Assume that these values would have appeared on a single printed line and would have required a single FORMAT statement. You are to write the FORMAT statement which must have been used to convert the stored values to printed values. Ignore the requirements for line spacing (X code).

Stored Values	Printed Values
A 18.345	1.8345
B 19.456	19.456
C 20555.	.20555
D .21689	2168.9
E .22765	.0022765

FORMAT _____

4. In this exercise, you are given several stored values and FORMAT specifications for printing the values. Indicate how the printed values would have appeared.

Stored Value	FORMAT	Printed Value
A 22.222	1PF6.2	A _____
B 34.567	-2PF4.3	B _____
C 4321.9	-6PF6.4	C _____
D 555.12	4PF2.1	D _____
E 6.7891	0PF4.2	E _____

5. Based on the following FORMAT and WRITE statements, in what *print* positions will each of the output values or literals begin?

a. 5 FORMAT (T7,F8.3,T1,'1',T20,'TOTAL DOLLAR VALUE')
   WRITE (6,5) VAL

   Print Position _____   Item _____

   Print Position _____   Item _____

   Print Position _____   Item _____

b. 6 FORMAT (T50,6HSUM IS,T5,'LEVEL NUM,',T20,I3,T1,'-',T60,F8.3)
   WRITE (6,6) KT, TOT

Print Position _____   Item _____
Print Position _____   Item _____
Print Position _____   Item _____
Print Position _____   Item _____
Print Position _____   Item _____

Input/Output with the NAMELIST Statement[3]

An optional technique for entering and/or displaying data without requiring FORMAT statements is the NAMELIST statement. This statement declares one or more variable names to be within a NAMELIST group and automatically adjusts to the format sizes required to handle the input or output data values. The following simple program reads a series of values through a NAMELIST statement and immediately displays the values using the same NAMELIST declaration.

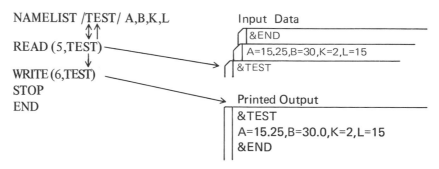

1. Note how the special group name TEST is used in place of a FORMAT statement number in both the READ and WRITE statements.
2. The list of variable names, following the right slash, appear in the input or output with their associated values.

The NAMELIST statement contains the following elements:

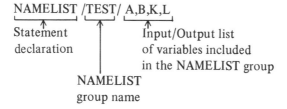

The following rules apply to the NAMELIST statement:

1. The NAMELIST declaration must appear first in this statement. The statement must appear before its use in any READ or WRITE statement using the group name.
2. The group name is constructed in the same manner as any FORTRAN data name and must be preceded and followed by a single slash (that is, /TEST/).

[3] This provision of the FORTRAN IV language is rather recent and many earlier versions of the language do not include the NAMELIST element. Refer to the appropriate manufacturer's manual.

3. The list of variables following the group name:
   a. Must be separated by commas,
   b. May be variable names of locations storing integer, real, logical, or complex values.
   c. May be array names but must be shown without subscripts.
4. Any array variables used in the NAMELIST statement must have been DIMENSIONed in a prior statement.
5. More than one NAMELIST group may be shown in a single NAMELIST statement. It is only necessary to specify another group name and variable name list. An example might be:

NAMELIST /ONE/A,B,K/TWO/C,A,N/TREE/X,Y,N

               Group 1   Group 2   Group 3

6. The same variable name may appear in several NAMELIST variable name lists.

Input data and printed output have an unusual form to permit its flexible use with this statement. Consider the input and output shown in the previous example.

Punched Input	Printed Output
&END	&TEST
A = 15.25, B = 30, K = 2, L = 15	A = 15.25,B=30.0,K=2,L=15
& TEST	&END

The following rules apply to input:

1. The first column of *all* input cards is left blank.
2. The first card in a NAMELIST group must contain the special group name preceded by the ampersand character *(&)* (that is, &TEST).
3. The second and succeeding cards show the variables in the group list with the data values to be assigned. An equal sign relates each variable and its value. Each variable *must be separated* from the following variable by a comma. Blanks are optional.

   Some systems permit variables to follow the special group name on the first card. In this case, at least one blank must be left after the group name.
4. The *order* in which variables and values are listed on the data cards does not have to be the same as the order in the NAMELIST statement.
5. *Simple variable names* and their related values appear as follows:

   ABLE = 22.4   XYZ = 15.27E02
   ITEM = 3   RUN = 22.435D - 04

   Subscripted variables may refer to a single element in an array. In this case, the subscript must be an integer constant and not an integer variable name. For instance:

   MAX(4) = 147   LG(1) = .96027E - 22
   FOX(2) = 88.26   KAR(8) = 6.2115D01

   An *entire array* may be referenced by listing the array name without subscripts. The array values are then listed consecutively with each value separated from the others by a comma. Where several array locations are to be given the same value, a repeater symbol may be used. For instance:

(Assume: DIMENSION INPUT(10))

INPUT = 2,4,6,8,0,5*3

When an array is more than one dimensional, the values are assigned and written in *column order by row*.

(Assume: DIMENSION SMALL(3,2))

SMALL = 1.,2.,3.,4.,5.,6.

This list will be read and written as:

SMALL(1,1)=1.0
SMALL(2,1)=3.0
SMALL(3,1)=5.0
SMALL(1,2)=2.0
SMALL(2,2)=4.0
SMALL(3,2)=6.0

6. The number of variables in the data card list must be *less than or equal to* the number of variables in the NAMELIST statement.
7. Trailing *blanks* are converted to *zeros* in integer values and in the exponents of E or D code values. For instance (b = blank):

MIN = 15b, (read as 150, not 15)
BIG = 12.3E-2b, (read as E-20, not E-2)

8. The end of a NAMELIST data list is signaled by the *&END* word. This word may be separated from the last data value by either a space or comma, though neither is required, or may appear on a separate card.

The following rules apply to output:

1. All output is printed with automatic allowance for the appropriate number of significant digits. The programmer has no control over the specific form in which the values will be displayed. The output will be shown with the appropriate *&(group name)* at the beginning of the output list. This name is followed by the *list* of variable data names and values and is terminated by the *&END* word.
2. Output is printed in a form suitable for punching as input to another program. Of course, if the program directs the output to be punched, it will be available immediately for further processing.
3. Each output line leaves the first column blank (the first card column is blank if output is punched) and therefore avoids carriage control complications.

The following problem illustrates a program using the NAMELIST statement.

1. A corporation has three divisions and each division has three subsidiaries.
2. Summary data from each subsidiary is sent monthly to its division headquarters. Each division then sends summary data to corporate headquarters.
3. Each subsidiary sends summary data in the NAMELIST form as output from its own processing.

4. The following program has been simplified to handle only two items of information:
   a. Number of Units Produced
   b. Number of Units Sold
5. The subsidiaries send the production and sales figures (expressed with 000 omitted).
6. This program is used at the division level. It accumulates the year-to-date amounts for each subsidiary and for the division. A schedule is printed for use at the division level, and the division summary data is punched in the NAME-LIST form for transfer to corporate headquarters. Punched output has 000 added.

A flowchart for our problem appears in Figure 12.1; input data (assumes March data) appears in Figure 12.2; the program and output appear in Program 12.3.

Figure 12.1

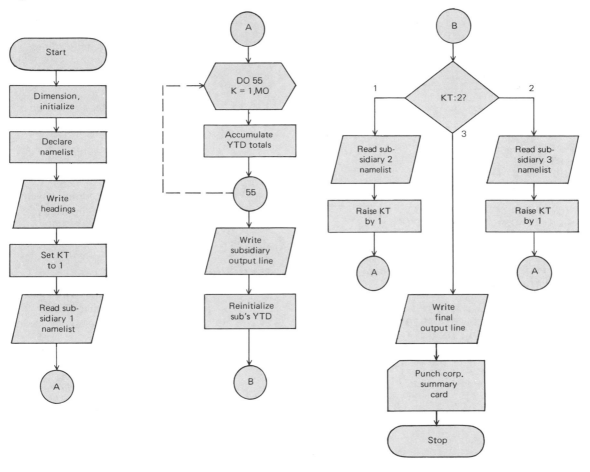

Figure 12.2

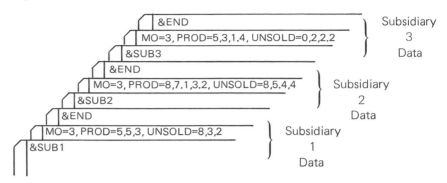

Program 12.3

```
NAMELIST PROGRAM USED AT DIVISION LEVEL

      DIMENSION PROD(12), UNSOLD(12)
      DATA PROD,UNSOLD,SPYTD,SSYTD,DPYTD,DSYTD /28*0.0/
      NAMELIST /SUB1/ MO,PROD,UNSOLD
      NAMELIST /SUB2/ MO,PROD,UNSOLD
      NAMELIST /SUB3/ MO,PROD,UNSOLD
      NAMELIST /DIVA/ DPYTD,DSYTD
   10 FORMAT (//19X,'PRODUCTION/SALES SCHEDULE (IN 000)'/12X,
     1'YTD JAN FEB MAR APR MAY JUN JUL AUG SEP OCT NOV DEC'//)
      WRITE (6,10)
      KT=1
      READ (5,SUB1)
      GO TO 50
   40 READ (5,SUB2)
      KT=KT+1
      GO TO 50
   45 READ (5,SUB3)
      KT=KT+1
   50 DO 55 K=1,MO
      SPYTD=SPYTD + PROD(K)
      SSYTD=SSYTD + UNSOLD(K)
      DPYTD=DPYTD + PROD(K)
      DSYTD=DSYTD + UNSOLD(K)
   55 CONTINUE
   60 FORMAT (2X,'SUB',1X,I1/4X,'PROD',3X,F4.1,1X,12(F3.1,1X)/
     14X,'SALES',2X,F4.1,1X,12(F3.1,1X))
      WRITE (6,60) KT,SPYTD,(PROD(N),N=1,12),SSYTD,(UNSOLD(N),N=1,12)
      SPYTD=0.0
      SSYTD=0.0
      IF (KT-2) 40,45,70
   65 FORMAT (//2X,'DIVISION YTD PRODUCTION',2X,F6.1/
     12X,'DIVISION YTD UNIT SALES',2X,F6.1//)
   70 WRITE (6,65) DPYTD, DSYTD
      DPYTD=DPYTD * 1000.0
      DSYTD=DSYTD * 1000.0
      WRITE (7,DIVA)
      STOP
      END
```

Dimension, initial-
ize, declare
NAMELIST

Write headings

Read subsidiaries
NAMELIST input

Accumulate year-
to-date totals

Reinitialize sub-
sidiary YTD

Raise division YTD
by 1000

Punch division
summary for
corporation HQ

Program Data Names

DIVA:	Division A—NAMELIST output group name	SSYTD:	Subsidiary Sales Year To Date
DPYTD:	Division Production Year To Date	SUB1:	Subsidiary 1—NAMELIST input group name
DSYTD:	Division Sales Year To Date	SUB2:	Subsidiary 2—NAMELIST input group name
KT:	Counter to determine which READ to execute	SUB3:	Subsidiary 3—NAMELIST input group name
PROD:	Array—units produced by subsidiary	UNSOLD:	Array—units sold by subsidiary
SPYTD:	Subsidiary Production Year to Date		

Printed Program Output

```
           PRODUCTION/SALES SCHEDULE (IN 000)
    YTD JAN FEB MAR APR MAY JUN JUL AUG SEP OCT NOV DEC


SUB 1
  PROD   13.0 5.0 5.0 3.0 0.0 0.0 0.0 0.0 0.0 0.0 0.0 0.0 0.0
  SALES  13.0 8.0 3.0 2.0 0.0 0.0 0.0 0.0 0.0 0.0 0.0 0.0 0.0
SUB 2
  PROD   18.3 8.0 7.1 3.2 0.0 0.0 0.0 0.0 0.0 0.0 0.0 0.0 0.0
  SALES  17.4 8.0 5.4 4.0 0.0 0.0 0.0 0.0 0.0 0.0 0.0 0.0 0.0
SUB 3
  PROD    4.9 0.5 3.0 1.4 0.0 0.0 0.0 0.0 0.0 0.0 0.0 0.0 0.0
  SALES   4.2 0.0 2.0 2.2 0.0 0.0 0.0 0.0 0.0 0.0 0.0 0.0 0.0


DIVISION YTD PRODUCTION    36.2
DIVISION YTD UNIT SALES    34.6
```

Punched Program Output

```
    /    | &END
   /     | DPYTD = 36200.000, DSYTD = 34600.000
  /   | &DIVA
```

Input/Output: A Variable FORMAT Statement[4]

Occasions may occur when a program is written for data which has an unknown FORMAT. While this condition is somewhat unusual, the FORTRAN language provides a technique for substituting, at the time the program is prepared, a variable FORMAT for the customary explicit FORMAT. The variable FORMAT technique allows a FORMAT specification to be read as data at the time the program is being executed. Of course, this means that the variable FORMAT statement will have to precede the actual data in the data deck. The following program statements compare an explicit FORMAT with a variable FORMAT specification.

Assume that data cards are punched in an F8.2, I8, F6.2 form. The following explicit FORMAT and READ statement would serve to input the data:

```
5 FORMAT (F8.2, I8, F6.2)
  READ (5,5) ABLE, NUM, FOX
```

[4] This language feature is not available on all computing systems. Refer to the appropriate manufacturer's manual.

However, suppose that at the time of program preparation, we know only that three variables in the ABLE, NUM, FOX order will be processed. Their specific FORMATs are unknown.

The variable FORMAT technique will handle this situation as follows:

1. An array is included in the program and is used to store the variable FORMAT read at the time the program is executed.
2. READ statement(s) which input all actual data values will have the customary FORMAT reference number replaced with the name of the array holding the variable FORMAT.
3. When the altered READ statement is executed, the processor will substitute the stored FORMAT for the missing explicit FORMAT statement. All data cards will then be read in accordance with the variable FORMAT specification.

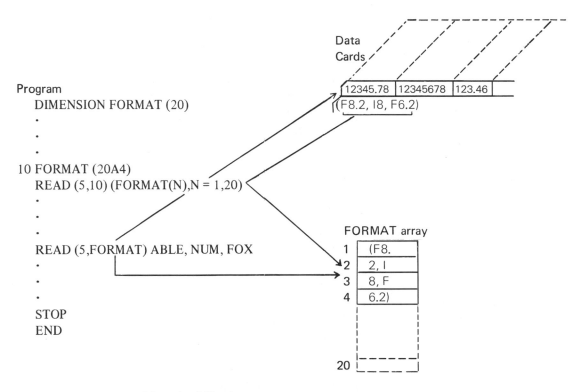

Note the following:

1. This program creates an array called FORMAT. It is large enough to hold up to eighty characters of FORMAT specification (20A4) from one card.
2. The first data card contains all of the normal specifications of a FORMAT statement except for the statement number and the word FORMAT. All other specifications *must* be included.
3. First, the program reads the variable FORMAT and stores it in the FORMAT array.
4. Subsequent data cards are then read with the implied specifications in the FORMAT array.

The variable FORMAT *must* be read with the *A code.* This same variable FORMAT could also be used for output by writing:

WRITE (6,FORMAT) ABLE, NUM, FOX

Where more than one variable FORMAT is to be used, an array for each expected FORMAT will have to be reserved. Variable FORMATS are permitted for both input and output, and any one FORMAT does not have to be used for both input and output.

Exercise 31

1. Write the necessary FORTRAN statements to accomplish the following:
   a. Create a NAMELIST group called FIRST
   b. Include variables ONE, NUM, and XYZ in the group
   c. After writing the statement for parts a and b, outline the data cards which would be read by the NAMELIST statement. In preparing these cards, assign:
      (1) the value 1.0 to ONE
      (2) the value 3 to NUM
      (3) the value 0.0 to XYZ
   d. Assume that the input values were written with the NAMELIST statement. How would the printed output appear?
2. Write the necessary statements to accomplish the following:
   a. Dimension MIN at 10 and MAX at 3
   b. Create a NAMELIST statement with two groups: SECOND and THIRD
   c. Include the variables A, B, and MIN in SECOND
      Include the variables MAX, X, and Y in THIRD
   d. Outline data cards which have the following values assigned:

      X has a value of 10.0
      Y has a value of 5.0
      A has a value of 0.0
      B has a value of 2.0
      MIN(1) – MIN(5) have values of 3
      MIN(6) has a value of 4
      MIN(7) – MIN(10) have values of 0
      MAX—all locations have the value of 12

   e. If this NAMELIST data is printed, how would it appear?
3. For this exercise, refer to the program in the example on page 246.
   a. Prepare a WRITE statement which will take the data values read and display them in the same form in which they were read.
   b. How would this printed line appear?
4. Write the necessary statements to read in a variable FORMAT which has the following specifications:

   (3X,F8.2,2X,I8,2X,F6.2)

   Read this FORMAT into an array called SAMPLE. This array has 20 memory locations of size A4. Sketch how this array will look after it is loaded with the FORMAT.

   FORTRAN Statements   Array Sketch

5. If your statements from exercise 4 were inserted into the program on page 246, how would the data values read from the first card appear if they were printed using your FORMAT (in array SAMPLE)? Write the necessary WRITE statement to display the values and also illustrate the printed line.

FORTRAN Statement   Printed Line

1. What are the major advantages gained from the use of the DATA statement?
2. What advantage can be gained by using the G Code for input/output of data values?
3. What type of data *cannot* be handled by the G Code?
4. Explain the meaning of each element in a G8.3 Code: (a) for use with input and (b) for use in displaying output.
5. Explain how conflicts between FORMAT specifications and punched decimal points are resolved when handling input values.
6. What is meant by the statement that "a READ/WRITE list must be executed in full?" What relationship exists between a READ or WRITE command and its FORMAT statement when each specifies handling a different number of variables?
7. What is the short list convention? Explain.
8. What is the purpose of the scale factor P? How does its use vary between input and output?
9. What advantages are gained through use of the NAMELIST statement? Explain carefully.
10. Explain how program flexibility is gained through use of the variable FORMAT provision. Cite an example in which a variable FORMAT statement would be advantageous.

13
Alternative Data Specifications

A large part of the computing needs in business may be satisfied, through the FORTRAN language, by using the data handling specifications discussed in earlier chapters. In those chapters, we discussed the requirements of FORTRAN for handling integer, real (including DOUBLE PRECISION), alphabetic, and special character data. This chapter presents two new data types and several alternative specifications for special treatment of the data types that we covered earlier. These alternative data specifications are mainly extensions or refinements of the FORTRAN language. Therefore, they may be omitted until you have gained a comfortable familiarity with FORTRAN.

The COMPLEX Mode[1]

A complex number is composed of two parts:

1. a *real* part, plus
2. an *imaginary* part

We can express a complex number algebraically as $a + bi$, where a and b are real numbers and i, which represents $\sqrt{-1}$, is the imaginary number. Obviously, both parts of a complex value must be available to the computer if it is to process the value. A COMPLEX constant is written with the real and imaginary parts enclosed within parentheses; for example,

$X = (8.462, 5.25)$ represents $x = 8.462 + 5.25\,i$.

Note that both parts are separated by a comma. The variable X, shown above, is a complex variable, and it must be declared as such in the program, because the computer must arrange for two storage locations to be associated with the complex variable name. One location will hold the real part of the complex value, and the second location will hold the imaginary part. To declare the variable X as being COMPLEX, the following statement would be included at the very beginning of the program:

COMPLEX X

[1] A familiarity with the mathematical use of complex numbers is necessary for use of the COMPLEX mode. The reader may skip this section without detracting from the language. Business applications requiring the use of the COMPLEX mode are not as prevalent as is true in mathematics. In addition, not all FORTRAN systems allow complex values to be handled.

All of the standard mathematical manipulations are available for complex numbers. When complex values are manipulated, the FORTRAN language will use stored routines for accomplishing the manipulations. These routines automatically handle the two memory words used to store the real and imaginary parts of the complex value. The programmer need only indicate the type of manipulation desired by using the standard operators (+, -, *, /, **). The following examples illustrate several of the mathematical operations which may be performed using complex numbers.

COMPLEX A,B,C,D,E,F,G,H

A = (5.0, -6.2)
B = (3.4, 1.0)
C = A + B
D = (3.2, -3.4) + C
E = A/B
F = C- B*(1.2, 4.5E01) (any type real value [in the FORTRAN sense] may be used)
G = A**2
H = B*(0.0,1.0)

Mixed mode conditions may arise in the complex mode. There are two different meanings to the term "mixed mode." One meaning relates to the integer-real mixing of values. This mixing of values normally is not permissible. Consider the following example:

COMPLEX Z, X, A
Z = (5, 3.1)
X = I/A

In the first executable statement, 5 is in the integer mode. This value could not be assigned to Z. There are some processors, however, which would convert the number 5 to the real mode and then permit the assignment. In the second executable statement, the variable I is in the integer mode and is illegal for use here unless the processor is permitted to convert the I to the complex mode by assigning a zero imaginary part.

A second type of mixed mode relates to the mixing of F, E, and D real-mode specifications. It is permissible to mix these types of real values. The processor will convert any necessary items to the complex mode before completing the execution required.

A last caution deals with the type of variable receiving the results of a complex mode calculation. The variable to the left of the equals sign *must* be declared as a COMPLEX variable. While it is permissible to mix real modes in the expression to the right of the equal sign, it is not permissible to do so to the left of the equal sign.

Initialization of complex values may be made by arithmetic replacement statements, as shown above, or through the use of the DATA statement. Values for both parts of the complex value must be shown. This may be illustrated as follows:

COMPLEX HI,TOP
DATA HI/3.4,-6.1/, TOP/1.23E-2, 6.7/

Input and output of complex values is accomplished through standard FORMAT statements, with accompanying READ/WRITE statements. The FORMAT statements indicate real input values by using the F, E, or D codes as they do for any other real values. The only difference with complex numbers is the need to provide for two separate values. One value, of course, pertains to the real part of the complex number, and the other value pertains to the imaginary part. Examples of input and output FORMATs are shown below:

Input
   COMPLEX RD
10 FORMAT (F9.2, F3.1)
   READ (5,10) RD

Output
   COMPLEX WRT
20 FORMAT (//5X, F10.2, F10.1)
   WRITE (6,20) WRT

Logical Mode

The concept of logical testing was introduced in Chapter 10. The FORTRAN language element that we use to accomplish logical testing is appropriately labeled the "logical IF" statement. Logical IF statements use two types of operators to execute test comparisons. These operators are called relational operators (.EQ., .GE., .LT., etc.) and logical operators (.NOT., .AND., and .OR.). The outcome from testing a logical IF statement is determination of the binary result true or false.

Logical IF statements use relational and logical operators to compare arithmetic expressions. For example,

IF (SUM − 3.7 .EQ. TOT .OR. TOT / 5.0 .LT. 4.2) MAX=NUM

      Expression 1   Expression 2

This test causes execution of the statement MAX = NUM when either expression 1 or expression 2, or both, is true. Of course, if both are false, the next sequential statement is executed.

The hierarchy for all operations was presented in Chapter 10. Note that logical operators are given the lowest priority in the processing order. Within the logical operators, however, the following order is observed:

.NOT.   highest
.AND.   intermediate
.OR.   lowest

To illustrate this order, assume that a statement is written as follows:

S = R .AND. S .OR. T .AND. .NOT. V

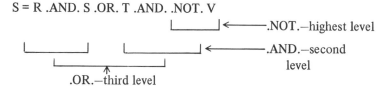

The order in which the logical operations would be processed is shown by the brackets.

This order may, of course, be altered by the use of parentheses. The previous statement could be rewritten with parentheses and have a processing order as follows:

S = R .AND. (S .OR. T) .AND. .NOT. V

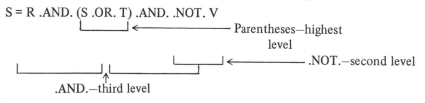

Note how the use of parentheses has elevated .OR. to the highest processing level in this last example.

The concept of binary logic may be extended beyond the logical IF statement. The FORTRAN language contains a data mode which allows variable names to be assigned the values of either true or false. This data mode is called the logical mode and, as is true of all data modes, contains variable data names and constants. However, it is necessary to declare a variable name as being in the logical mode at the *beginning* of a program. This declaration is made by specifying that certain variable names are of logical type as follows:

LOGICAL FIRM, MGT, LOG

The word LOGICAL establishes the type for all variable names listed. A variable name may begin with *any letter,* because there is no mode distinction related to specific alphabetic letters.

Once a variable is declared as LOGICAL, the *only* values which it may hold are true or false. No numerical or alphanumeric values may be used with a logical variable name. A LOGICAL variable receives its value in one of the following three ways:

1. An assignment statement may set the value through the use of the *constants* .TRUE. or .FALSE. The statements below assign a constant to each variable name.

   LOGICAL COUNT, LIMIT
   COUNT = .TRUE.
   LIMIT = .FALSE.

   Note the construction of logical constants. There are only two logical values, and, when used, each is written with a leading and trailing period. A DATA statement may be used for logical mode assignments in the same way it is used for other modes.

   DATA COUNT, LIMIT/.TRUE.,.FALSE./

2. One logical variable may have its value assigned to another logical variable. For example,

   LOGICAL FIRST, SECOND
   FIRST = .TRUE.
   SECOND = FIRST

   After executing this sequence of statements, both FIRST and SECOND will have the value of .TRUE.

3. A value of either TRUE or FALSE may be read into memory as an input data value. Handling logical data as input will require the use of the *L Code*.

L Code. The L FORMAT code consists of the letter L and a digit, indicating the number of characters in the input field. The following examples illustrate this code:

5 FORMAT (L4)   ⌐ TRUE ⌐

This FORMAT indicates that the input field is four characters (columns) wide.

5 FORMAT (L5)   ⌐ FALSE ⌐

This FORMAT specifies a five character field.

There is a peculiar characteristic associated with use of the L code. The computer will take only the *first letter* of the input field into storage. The remaining characters will be ignored. The first character, therefore, *must be* either *T or F*. All other characters may be any alphanumeric. The following examples demonstrate this point.

15 FORMAT (L7)   ⌐ TROUBLE ⌐

This FORMAT calls for a seven character field. However, only the letter T (true) will be stored.

20 FORMAT (L3)   ⌐ FOX ⌐

This FORMAT specifies a three character field but only F (false) will be stored.

A READ statement to input the last example (FOX) would be accompanied by a LOGICAL declaration and FORMAT as follows:

    LOGICAL NO
20 FORMAT (L3)
    READ (5,20) NO

If the input card contains FOX in columns 1-3, these statements will cause the value F (false) to be stored in memory location NO. The L code may be mixed in a FORMAT with any of the other FORMAT codes (I, F, E, D, etc.).

Exercise 32

1. Identify the following COMPLEX statements which are incorrect and explain why they are incorrect. Assume that all variables have been defined as COMPLEX.
   a. CT = (3,2)
   b. FOX = (4.2 + 8.3)
   c. JM = (8.23, 1427.)
   d. A = 4.0, 0.0
   e. TOT = FOX * (2.3, 4.7
   f. SIG = TOT ** 3.4
   g. WW = 4.2 − (8.3, 4.8)
   h. Z = SIC / A **3
   i. KI = KI − ((8.0, 0.0) * (4.2, 5.6))
   j. DATA X,Y,Z/ 0.0,2.8,6.2,1.4,0.0,0.0/

2. Write the necessary statements to accomplish the following:
   a. Declare HIGH, AND, and MIGHTY as being of logical type.
   b. Set each of the above variables to a value of "true." Use separate statements for each variable.
   c. Set each of the variables in (a) to the value "false." Use one DATA statement for all three variables.

3. Four independent data cards appear below. Write the necessary statements to:
   a. Establish a logical variable of your choice for each data value shown.
   b. Write a FORMAT and READ statement to input the data on each card, also, indicate the value which your variables will have after reading each card.

1. ⌠TRUE⌡

    Variable Name _____ Value _____

2. ⌠TROUBLE IS EVERYWHERE⌡

    Variable Name _____ Value _____

3. ⌠FIRST COUNT⌡

    Variable Name _____ Value _____

4. ⌠FALSE⌡

    Variable Name _____ Value _____

Logical Mode: Processing

When logical values are used in a program, the statements permitted for processing these values are not as varied as are the statements for numeric values. Logical values are restricted to either true or false and may not be manipulated in any numeric sense. The arithmetic operations of addition, subtraction, multiplication, etc., are *not permitted* with logical values and, furthermore, logical values may not be mixed with non-logical values in a statement.

There are two basic processing operations which may be performed with logical values:

1. Testing for the true or false value of a logical variable through the use of the logical IF statement.
2. Writing an arithmetic type statement which sets a logical variable (to the left of the equal sign) equal to the true/false result of a logical expression (to the right of the equal sign).

The following flowchart (in Figure 13.1) and program (Program 13.1) illustrate these processing operations.

Figure 13.1

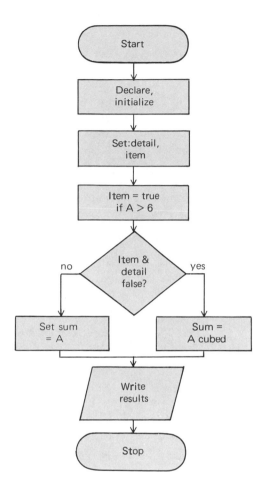

Program 13.1

```
      C
      C   PROGRAM USING LOGICAL VALUES
      C
1          LOGICAL ITEM, DETAIL
2          DATA A,ITEM/8.0,.FALSE./
3          DETAIL = ITEM
4          ITEM = A.GT.6.0
5          IF (ITEM.AND.DETAIL) GO TO 10
6          SUM = A
7          GO TO 51
8       10 SUM = A**3
9       50 FORMAT (15X,'ITEM =',L3,' DETAIL =',L3/
           115X,'SUM = ',F5.1)
10      51 WRITE (6,50) ITEM, DETAIL,SUM
11         STOP
12         END
```

```
      ITEM =  T DETAIL =  F
      SUM =    8.0
```

Statement 1. This statement declares the variables ITEM and DETAIL as being of logical type.

Statement 2. The DATA statement initializes variable A (real mode) with the numeric value of 8.0 and sets the logical variable ITEM to false.

Statement 3. The third statement transfers the false value of ITEM to the variable DETAIL. Both ITEM and DETAIL will now have values of false.

Statement 4. This statement illustrates one of the processing operations using logical values. It is in a form similar to an arithmetic statement. The logical variable ITEM will be set to true or false based on the results from processing the logical expression on the right of the equal sign.

In this program, we know that A has been initialized as 8.0 and will be greater than 6.0. Therefore, ITEM will be changed from its original value of false to a value of true. This, of course, results from the fact that the logical expression is true: A (8.0) is greater than 6.0.

Note that the logical expression used a relational operation (.GT.). All logical expressions used in this fashion *must* use either relational or logical operators so that a true/false condition will result. A logical expression may contain arithmetic variables and/or constants as explained in Chapter 10 (see the discussion of the logical IF statement).

Examples of other more complex statements are:

```
LOGICAL TOTAL, NUM
TOTAL = X.NE.0.0 .AND. CAT.LT.GO/(B-5.7)
NUM = LIMIT.EQ.MAX .OR. J.LT.K .AND. J.NE.N
```

Statement 5. This IF statement tests the logical variables to determine their true/false values. If *both* ITEM and DETAIL are true, then the statement GO TO 10 will be executed. If *either* (or both) ITEM or DETAIL is false, then statement 6 will be executed.

A logical IF statement is the second type of processing statement which may be used with logical variables. When logical variables are being tested, a *logical operator must be used*. This statement, under different test assumptions, could have been written as:

```
IF (ITEM.OR.DETAIL) GO TO 10
IF (ITEM.AND..NOT.DETAIL) GO TO 10
```

The first IF statement indicates that if either ITEM or DETAIL is true, or if both are true, transfer should be made to statement 10. The second IF statement indicates that when ITEM is true and DETAIL is false, transfer should be made to statement 10.

Statements 6, 7, and 8. These are standard arithmetic and transfer statements.

Statements 9 and 10. This FORMAT statement describes two lines. The first line will display the logical values of ITEM and DETAIL. This output function is discussed in the following section. The second line displays the numeric value of SUM.

Statements 11 and 12. STOP and END are familiar statements.

Logical Constants. In processing logical values, the use of logical constants within expressions is *illegal*. This limitation is contrary to the use of arithmetic constants which may be included within arithmetic expressions. The following statement illustrates the *illegal* use of logical constants.

50 IF (FIRM .EQ. .TRUE. .OR. MGT .EQ. .FALSE.) GO TO 60

Variables which hold the true or false values may be tested within IF statements, but the constants themselves are not permitted.

Logical Mode: Output

Logical values may be displayed as output. The L code is used in output FORMATs to specify the number of character print positions to be used in writing the logical value. Several unusual conditions relate to the printing of logical values. First, in most systems only the letter T or F will be printed.[2] This condition prevails regardless of the number of print positions specified in the L FORMAT code. Second, the T or F is right justified in the output field. This, of course, means that the letter T or F is printed in the rightmost field position, and all preceding positions are left blank.

Three examples are given below which illustrate the relationship between the L FORMAT code and the form in which the output will appear. In these examples, assume that the variable NUM has been declared as **LOGICAL** and that the value of NUM is **FALSE**.

Statements	Printed Output (b=blank)

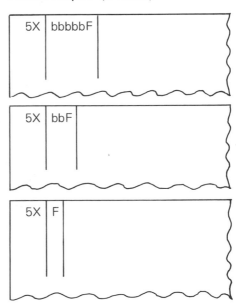

5 FORMAT (5X, L6)
  WRITE (6,5) NUM

Six positions specified in the FORMAT will result in five blank print positions.

5 FORMAT (5X, L3)
  WRITE (6,5) NUM

Three positions specified in the FORMAT will result in two blank print positions.

5 FORMAT (5X, L1)
  WRITE (6,5) NUM

A single print position is specified in this FORMAT and will result in no excess spacing.

[2] Several systems use alternative output techniques. The two most common alternatives either print the full words TRUE/FALSE or display a numeric 1 for TRUE and a numeric 0 for FALSE.

The following example will demonstrate the use of the logical mode. Assume that a firm maintains its personnel records in punch card form. Among the records maintained is the personnel history for each employee. Management is interested in finding those employees who meet certain criteria for filling an open position. A program, with sample output, to search the personnel records appears in Program 13.2 on page 260, and a flowchart for the search program appears in Figure 13.2.

The program reads an employee's history record and tests it to determine whether the employee meets the stated criteria. Assume management sets the following selection criteria:

1. age 35 through 45, inclusive.
2. must have had experience in 4 of the following five departments: 10, 15, 33, 47, and 56.
3. must satisfy one of the following:
   a. worked for the firm 8 or more years.
   b. attained a management level position of 6 through 10, inclusive.
4. would like to know whether employee currently is located in corporate marketing areas 6, 7, 8, or 9.

Input cards appear as follows:

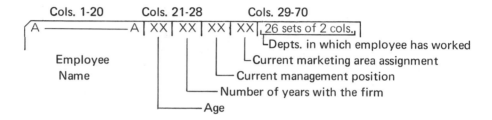

Exercise 33

1. Read the following program. After determining its logic, determine what the values of the five variables (shown to the right) would be after completion of the program's execution.

```
        LOGICAL A,B,C,D,E                          A _____
        DATA A,B/ .TRUE.,.FALSE./G/6.8/            B _____
     10 C = .TRUE.                                 C _____
        D = .NOT.A                                 D _____
        E = 15.2+G.LT.22.0                         E _____
        IF (C.AND.D) GO TO 20
        A = .FALSE.
     20 STOP
        END
```

2. Assume that the IF statement in the program in problem 1 was written as IF (C.OR.D) E = .TRUE. If this IF statement replaced the one appearing in the original program, what would the value be for each variable after executing the program?

   A _____ B _____ C _____ D _____ E _____

Figure 13.2

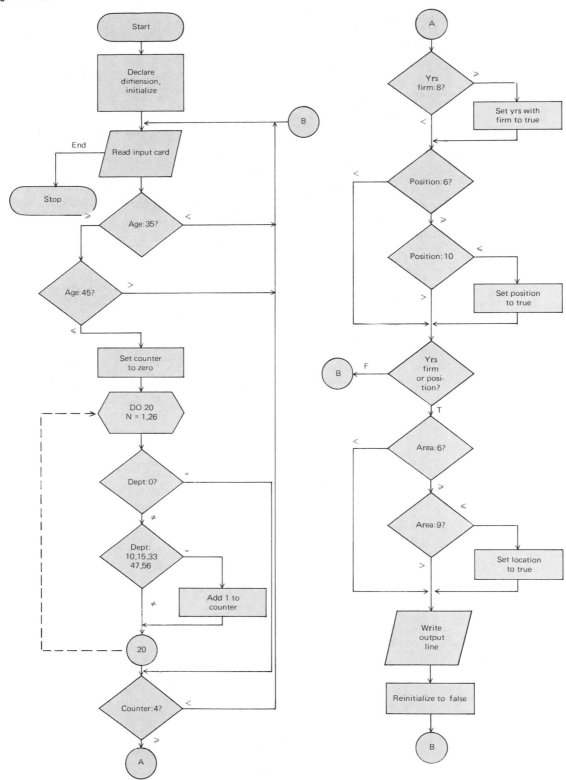

Program 13.2

```
      LOGICAL FIRM, MGT, LOC
      DIMENSION NAME(20), DEPT(26)
      DATA FIRM,MGT,LOC/3*.FALSE./
   5  FORMAT (8X,'EMPLOYEE   NAME',5X,'8 YRS    MGT   AREA'/
     128X,'FIRM  6-10   6-9')
      WRITE (6,5)
  10  FORMAT (5A4,4F2.0,26F2.0)
  15  READ (5,10,END=100) (NAME(K),K=1,5),
     1YRS, TIME, POS, AREA, (DEPT(J),J=1,26)
      IF (YRS.LT.35.OR.YRS.GT.45) GO TO 15
      KOUNT=0
      DO 20 N=1,26
      IF (DEPT(N).EQ.0) GO TO 25
      IF (DEPT(N).EQ.10) KOUNT=KOUNT+1
      IF (DEPT(N).EQ.15) KOUNT=KOUNT+1
      IF (DEPT(N).EQ.33) KOUNT=KOUNT+1
      IF (DEPT(N).EQ.47) KOUNT=KOUNT+1
      IF (DEPT(N).EQ.56) KOUNT=KOUNT+1
  20  CONTINUE
  25  IF (KOUNT.GE.4) GO TO 30
      GO TO 15
  30  IF (TIME.GE.8) FIRM=.TRUE.
  40  IF (POS.GE.6.AND.POS.LE.10) MGT=.TRUE.
  50  IF (FIRM.OR.MGT) GO TO 60
      GO TO 15
  60  IF (AREA.GE.6.AND.AREA.LE.9) LOC=.TRUE.
  80  FORMAT (/ 5X,5A4,L5,2X,L5,1X,L5)
  85  WRITE (6,80) (NAME(K),K=1,5) ,FIRM,MGT,LOC
      FIRM=.FALSE.
      MGT=.FALSE.
      LOC=.FALSE.
      GO TO 15
 100  STOP
      END
```

Logical Declaration,
Dimension,
Initialization,
Write Headings

Read Data Card

Age Test

Test for required
experience in 4 of
5 departments

Test for time with
firm and management
position level

Test of marketing
area

Write output line
Reinitialize

EMPLOYEE NAME	8 YRS FIRM	MGT 6-10	AREA 6-9
ABLE, JOHN	T	F	F
ADAMS, HERBERT	T	T	T
WILLIS, HARVEY	F	T	T

Computed Output

3. Indicate the value of L which would result from executing each of the following statements. Assume that the program which contains these statements begins with the following declarations:

LOGICAL J, K
J = .TRUE.
K = .FALSE.   Value of L

  a. L = J+K   _____
  b. L = J.OR.K   _____
  c. L = J.AND.K   _____
  d. L = .NOT.J.OR.K   _____
  e. L = J.AND..NOT.K   _____
  f. L = J.OR..NOT.K   _____
  g. L = .NOT.J.AND.K   _____
  h. L = .NOT.J.OR..NOT.K   _____
  i. L = .NOT.J.AND..NOT.K   _____

4. The following statements make use of parentheses to alter the implied hierarchy for handling logical operations. Read each statement and determine the value which would be assigned to variable A. Assume the program began with the following declarations:

LOGICAL W,X,Y,Z
DATA W,X/2*.TRUE./Y,Z/2*.FALSE./

  a. A = (W.AND.X).OR.(Y.OR.W)   A _____
  b. A = (Y.OR.Z) .AND. X .AND. W   A _____
  c. A = .NOT.(Z.AND.Y).OR. W .AND. X   A _____
  d. A = .NOT.(Z.AND.X) .AND. Z .OR.W   A _____
  e. A = .NOT.(Z.AND.Y).AND.(Z. OR.W)   A _____

5. Indicate the spacing and contents of the output line for each of the following FORMAT/WRITE combinations. Assume the variables BEG and END have logical values of TRUE and FALSE, respectively.

  a. 10 FORMAT (5X,'THE ANSWER IS',L3)
       WRITE (6,10) BEG

  b. 20 FORMAT (10X,'TEST ONE',L2,2X,'TEST TWO',L2)
       WRITE (6,20) BEG, END

  c. 30 FORMAT (15X,'ITEM 1 =',L4/15X,'ITEM 2 =',L4)
       WRITE (6,30) BEG, END

d. 40 FORMAT (2X,'1 =',L2,2X,'2 =',L2)
        WRITE (6,40) END, END

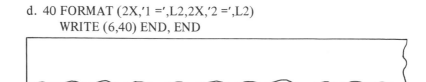

Alternative Specification for Memory Size—Standard versus Optional Length

A number of the commonly used processors (notably the IBM System 360) store data in memory locations, each with a standard size referred to as 4 bytes. 4 bytes will store up to a maximum of 8 binary digits (or approximately 7 decimal digits). These same systems normally allow adjustments to increase or decrease the standard size of memory locations. The programmer may specify memory sizes which will store larger or smaller amounts of data than handled by the standard size inherent in the computer's design. The allowable adjustments are listed below.

Data Mode	Standard Size	Optional Size
Real	4 bytes	8 bytes (DOUBLE PRECISION)
Integer	4 bytes	2 bytes
Logical	4 bytes	1 byte
Complex	8 bytes	16 bytes

The complex mode requires 8 bytes as the standard size because the real and imaginary parts are each stored in 4 bytes. The real and complex modes may be optionally doubled in size. This option allows for the storage of values which are approximately twice the standard size (identical size as given by the DOUBLE PRECISION specification for real mode values).

Integer storage may not be increased but may be reduced. Many integer values are small and do not require 4 bytes. Reduction of storage size to 2 bytes conserves memory locations and allows additional variables to use the freed locations.

Logical mode values may be stored in 1 byte memory locations. A logical value is composed of only the numeric equivalent of the letters T or F. These values do not require more than 1 byte for storage. Use of the optional size for these values also frees memory locations for use by other variables.

The FORTRAN language technique for specifying optional memory size requires the use of statements referred to as *type specifications*. Type specifications are also used to alter the implied mode of variable data names and are explained below.

REAL Type Specification

In previous chapters, we have associated real values with real variable data names by beginning the variable name with a letter from the A-H or O-Z groups. This technique employed an *implied* association of real values and real variable data names by reference to the beginning letter of the variables' names. In addition, it is *implied* that the size of each real storage location is 4 bytes. We may alter both of these implied conditions.

The first alteration will increase the storage size of a real value. To accomplish this, we must write a *REAL statement,* such as

REAL*8 COUNT

This statement, located at the *beginning* of the program, will cause the processor to allocate 8 bytes to the variable COUNT rather than the standard 4 bytes. Any real variable may use 8 bytes of storage if it is included in a REAL*8 statement. Furthermore, any other variable listed in the REAL*8 statement will be allocated 8 bytes of storage. For example:

REAL*8 COUNT, CAR, ABLE

Each of these variables will be associated with 8-byte memory locations. All other real variables used in a program will use the standard 4-byte storage. It might also be noted that REAL*8 storage is the same size as a variable declared in DOUBLE PRECISION.

It is possible to include a real variable, listed at its standard size, in the REAL*8 statement. However, if a variable begins with an implied real mode letter, this seems to be an unnecessary procedure. Such a statement would appear as:

REAL*8 COUNT, FOX*4, CAR,ABLE

The three variables COUNT, CAR, and ABLE will be size REAL*8 while FOX will be stored at the standard size of 4 bytes.

A second important alteration in a variable may also be made with the REAL type specification. We can change an implied integer variable into a real variable by including it in a REAL type statement. The following example illustrates this point:

REAL ITEM

Normally ITEM would be treated as an integer variable. Including it within the REAL statement *overrides* the implied integer mode, and the program will handle ITEM as a real variable. ITEM may be stated at the optional 8-byte length by rewriting the statement as:

REAL*8 ITEM

In addition to the change in storage size and the *explicit* alteration of a variable's implied mode, the REAL type specification may also include DIMENSION specifications and DATA initialization specifications.[3] These four language elements would appear as shown in the following example:

REAL*8 BAKER/3.0/, SALES*4/0.0/, NUM(100)/100*0.0/

This statement specifies:

1. BAKER: real, 8 bytes, initialized with value 3.0
2. SALES: real, 4 bytes, initialized with value 0.0
3. NUM: array of 100 locations, each location real, 8 bytes, all locations initialized with value 0.0

[3] Smaller versions of FORTRAN do not allow the DATA statement type of specification within a type statement. Refer to the manufacturer's appropriate manual.

This statement demonstrates the use of four types of specification (real type, size, dimension, and initialization) which would require four separate statements if done as follows:

REAL NUM
DOUBLE PRECISION BAKER, NUM
DIMENSION NUM(100)
DATA BAKER/3.0/, SALES/0.0/, NUM/100*0.0/

INTEGER Type Specification

An *explicit* type specification for integer mode variables is also a part of the FORTRAN language. Except for the fact that the mode and optional storage sizes are different, this statement is constructed in the same manner as the REAL statement discussed in the preceding section. For example:

INTEGER*2 TOP, MAX, KT*4, ABLE

This statement specifies that TOP and ABLE are not to be handled in the real mode, but in the integer mode, and that TOP, MAX, and ABLE are to store values in the optional integer size of 2 bytes. KT is to handle data in the standard integer 4-byte size.

We can also include DIMENSION and DATA specifications with the INTEGER statement. For example:

INTEGER*2 ABC(25)/25*1/, KOUNT/0/, SIZE*4/5/, J*4(5)/5*0/

LOGICAL Type Specification

The LOGICAL type specification is very similar to the REAL and INTEGER type specifications. The primary alteration is from standard 4-byte storage to optional 1-byte storage. Of course, when we include the DATA initialization specification, we would use the logical constants .TRUE. and .FALSE. Several LOGICAL statement examples are shown below:

LOGICAL LOG, MEN*1/.FALSE./, TOPSY(5)/5*.TRUE./
LOGICAL*1 WILL,TEST, RUN/.TRUE./
LOGICAL*1 COT*4(15)/10*.TRUE.,5*.FALSE./,A

COMPLEX Type Specification

The COMPLEX mode may have storage locations increased from the standard 8 bytes to 16 bytes. A statement that increases the storage size for COMPLEX variables and, at the same time, explicitly types a variable COMPLEX would appear as follows:

COMPLEX*16 STORE(5)/10*0.0/

The use of these explicit type statements is very convenient when preparing a FORTRAN program. Care must be exercised, however, to be certain that variables are of the correct size desired. In addition, *when a variable is changed from its implied mode or implied size, this change will be carried through the complete program.* The explicit use of REAL, INTEGER, LOGICAL, and COMPLEX statements will *override* any other implied or stated specifications in the program. This type of statement is *first* in the hierarchy for establishment of data modes.

IMPLICIT Type Specification

The previous type specifications contained complete variable data names with applicable alterations for size, dimension, initialization, etc. One other option is available to alter the specifications for variable names. This type of alteration uses the IMPLICIT statement and is available to specify the mode that will be associated with the *first letter* of variable names. For example, if all variable names beginning with the letter J were to be in the real mode, the following statement would accomplish this alteration:

IMPLICIT REAL(J)   (note the use of parentheses)

The IMPLICIT specification may list either individual letters in parentheses or list a range of letters. When the letters are listed *individually, they must be separated by commas.* A range of letters is shown by *separating the first and last letter in the range with a hyphen.* Each method is illustrated in the following example:

IMPLICIT REAL(K,N), INTEGER(A-D, P-S)

This statement indicates that any variable name beginning with K or N is to be handled in the real mode, and variable names beginning with A, B, C, D, P, Q, R, or S are to be handled in the integer mode.

We can also specify storage size options in the IMPLICIT statement. Array dimensions and data initialization are *not* permitted. The following example illustrates the inclusion of size options:

IMPLICIT REAL*8(J-N), INTEGER*2(X,Z)

The IMPLICIT statement is *second* in the hierarchy of type specifications. It does override the implied mode (first letters) in variable names but does not override the explicit REAL, INTEGER, LOGICAL, or COMPLEX specifications.

With proper and careful use, all of these specifications may add efficiency to a program and compact the size of the program by combining several elements in single statements.

In summary, the hierarchy for specifying the mode for a variable data name is:

Level 1 (highest)—*explicit* typing

REAL
INTEGER   } Each of these explicit
LOGICAL   } types has equal stature
COMPLEX   } within Level 1

Level 2 (second)—*implicit* typing
IMPLICIT

Level 3 (lowest)—*implied* typing
A-H, O-Z (REAL mode)
I-N (INTEGER mode)

Exercise 34

1. Write a statement for each of the following items. The statements should specify the appropriate memory size for the variables listed.
   a. variable named BLK, 8 bytes
   b. variable named WIL, 4 bytes

c. variable named NMR, 2 bytes
d. variable named JKS, 4 bytes
e. logical variable named TST, 1 byte

2. Write a statement to set the appropriate type for each of the following descriptions:

	Variable	Mode	Size	Dimension	Initial Value
a.	NUM	real	4	—	—
b.	CNT	integer	2	—	—
c.	CAT	real	8	—	—
d.	JAK	integer	2	—	—
e.	KAL	real	4	10	5
f.	BEG	integer	4	8	0
g.	RUN	logical	1	—	false
h.	ABC	complex	16	4	0
i.	LOK	real	8	25	2
j.	XEQ	logical	4	10	true

3. Write IMPLICIT statements for the following specifications:
   a. letters A through J = integer, K = real
   b. letters A through C = integer with 2 bytes, M, N = real
   c. letters X through Z = real with 4 bytes
   d. letters H through K, Q = integer with 4 bytes
   e. letters M, N, O = real with 8 bytes, P = integer with 2 bytes

Questions

1. Explain the differences between values handled in the complex mode and other real mode values.
2. What is the logical mode? What operators are associated with this mode?
3. Explain the differences among the following statements.
   a. N = (J.OR.K)
   b. N = (J.AND.K)
   c. N = (.NOT.J.AND.K)
4. What purpose is served by declaring a variable to be of LOGICAL type?
5. What are the logical constants?
6. Prepare an example and explain how the L code is used for input and output.
7. What are type specifications? What are their purposes? Illustrate.
8. What distinguishes the IMPLICIT statement from other type statements?
9. What is the advantage gained from the use of the optional memory size specifications?
10. What is the hierarchy for variable data name modes? List and explain each level within the hierarchy.

14
Two- and Three-Dimensional Arrays

Review of One-Dimensional Arrays

Arrays are a series of memory locations that are identified by a common (single) data name. Subscripts are used to identify specific array locations. As a brief illustration of a one-dimensional array, let us assume that we wish to total a series of sales amounts and find the average sale value. If the program provides for an array of 100 locations (named SALES), we can visualize the array as shown below:

SALES Array

1	100.00
2	200.00
3	300.00
4	400.00
5	500.00
6	999.99

100

When the following six data cards are read, the SALES array will store values in the first six locations as shown above.

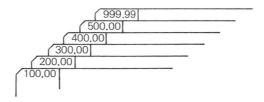

In this sample, the sixth input card serves as a trailer card.

The program to process these input cards is shown in Program 14.1. The computed output appears immediately below the program and a flowchart for the program appears in Figure 14.1.

Figure 14.1

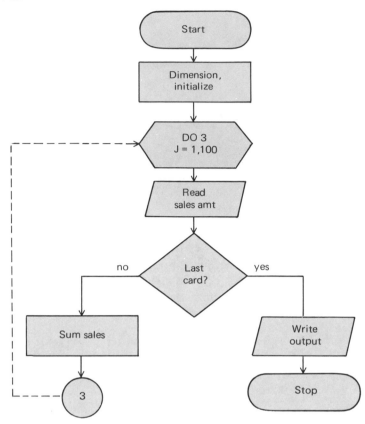

Program 14.1

```
      C
      C*******************************************************************
      C STATEMENT TO RESERVE MEMORY SPACE FOR THE SALES ARRAY
      C AND SECOND STATEMENT TO INITIALIZE THE VARIABLE "TOTAL"
      C*******************************************************************
      C
1           DIMENSION SALES(100)
2           TOTAL = 0.0
      C
      C*******************************************************************
      C PROGRAM STATEMENTS TO LOAD MEMORY AREAS
      C*******************************************************************
      C
3         5 FORMAT (5F6.2)
4           DO 3 J = 1,100
5           READ (5,5) SALES(J)
      C
      C*******************************************************************
      C TRAILER CARD TEST
      C*******************************************************************
      C
6           IF (SALES(J) - 999.99) 2,4,4
      C
```

```
C*****************************************************************
C STATEMENTS TO SUM SALES AND CALCULATE AVERAGE SALES
C*****************************************************************
C
7          2 TOTAL = TOTAL + SALES(J)
8          3 CONTINUE
9          4 J = J-1
10           AVE = TOTAL / J
C
C*****************************************************************
C STATEMENTS TO WRITE INDIVIDUAL, TOTAL, AND AVERAGE SALES
C*****************************************************************
C
11        10 FORMAT (//' SALES AMOUNTS', 5(2X, F6.2))
12           WRITE (6,10) (SALES(K), K=1,J)
13        15 FORMAT (//' TOTAL SALES', 4X, F10.2/
          1' AVERAGE SALES', 2X, F10.2)
14           WRITE (6,15) TOTAL, AVE
15           STOP
16           END
```

```
SALES AMOUNTS  100.00  200.00  300.00  400.00  500.00


TOTAL SALES        1500.00
AVERAGE SALES       300.00
```

The use of arrays and subscripts gives the programmer a powerful tool in data handling. In a very real sense, the task of assigning and finding memory locations is turned over to the computer. The array depicted on page 267 is shown as a single column with a maximum of 100 rows. This is a useful way to visualize the computer's storage of an array. However, internally, the computer stores the array as a series of consecutive memory locations which probably is not vertical in its physical alignment.

Two-Dimensional Arrays

Frequently, processing requirements call for the storage and manipulation of two, or more, directly related types of data, such as employee labor costs classified by department. Labor costs may be divided into several categories, two of which are direct labor and indirect labor.

This simple example of labor classification will be illustrated for a firm that has only two operating departments. A report for these combinations of cross-classification can be prepared as follows:

Labor Type	Dept. 1	Dept. 2
Direct Labor	$xxxxx	$xxxxx
Indirect Labor	$xxxxx	$xxxxx

We are accustomed to reading reports (or tables) which combine several rows and columns of data. In this example, we have two rows representing types of labor and one column for each of the two departments. When writing a program, we must give careful consideration to the storage of a numeric data which will be used in the eventual preparation of a report like that illustrated above. Based on the material discussed earlier, it would seem logical to use two single-dimensional arrays. If we visualize two arrays placed side-by-side, they would appear as:

	Array 1	Array 2
	DEPT1	DEPT2
Row 1 (direct labor)	xxxxx	xxxxx
Row 2 (indirect labor)	xxxxx	xxxxx

These two arrays (DIMENSIONed as DEPT1(2) and DEPT2(2)) would each store the labor data in identical fashion. Row 1 would store direct labor data, and Row 2 indirect labor data. Of course, each array would be composed of a single column.

Handling this labor information with two one-dimensional arrays is only one method available. An alternative method also exists. With two arrays, the programmer has to keep track of each array and its subscripts. In the FORTRAN language, it is possible to couple two arrays and to call the total storage area by one array name. This arrangement of storage is called a two-dimensional array. The two dimensions refer to an array with multiple rows (one dimension) and multiple columns (the second dimension).

If we continue with the previous example and combine the two arrays, the result would be the relationships illustrated in Figure 14.2.

Figure 14.2 Computer Storage of a 2 × 2 Array

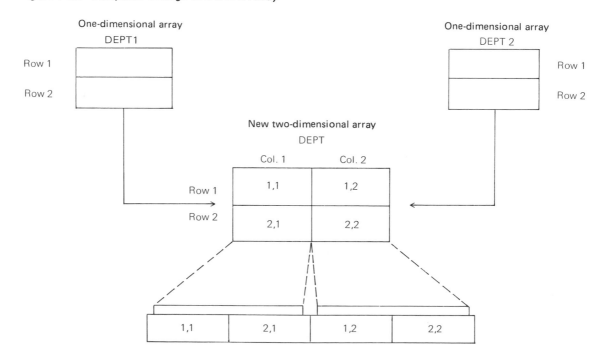

We can make several observations about the illustration in Figure 14.2.

1. The two original arrays (DEPT1 and DEPT2) are now coupled, but their individual row elements remain in the same relative position.
2. The new array is identified by a single name (DEPT) which applies to all four cells in the new two-dimensional array.
3. It is now necessary to identify both rows and columns, and each cell in the array is identified by its row and column number.
4. The schematic drawing, at the bottom of Figure 14.2, indicates the order in which a two-dimensional array is stored in computer memory. The computer stores consecutive columns of the array. Each row is stored in order within the columns. Due to this arrangement, multiple-dimensional arrays are said to be stored *columnwise by rows.*

Changes in the DIMENSION Statement

When we use two-dimensional arrays, we must modify the DIMENSION statement and the handling of subscripts from that used with one-dimensional arrays.

A DIMENSION statement is still necessary to establish array memory size requirements. Recall that a one-dimensional array requires a single integer number which indicates the storage locations that will be reserved. For a two-dimensional array, we must specify the number of storage locations for *both* the *rows* and *columns.* We accomplish this by writing the DIMENSION statement to indicate *first, row* size, and *then, column* size. To illustrate this specification, a DIMENSION statement for the previous example would be written as:

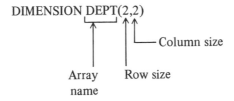

This DIMENSION statement would reserve a total of four memory locations which is equivalent to an area two rows high and two columns wide.

When arrays are expanded to two dimensions, we will need a variable name (that is, an index) for specifying row subscripts and another variable name for column subscripts. In the previous example, if we use the variables J and K for the rows and columns, respectively, then a statement to write one value from the array would appear as:

WRITE (6,25) DEPT (J,K)

The *first index* (J) applies to the *row* subscript specification. The *second index* (K), of course, applies to the *column* subscript specification. The indices within parentheses are always written in row-column order.

It is also possible to specify subscripts by use of numeric digits for row-column combinations. The first memory location in the DEPT array would be written as DEPT(1,1) and the last location as DEPT(2,2). However, a more general usefulness is found in using symbolic subscript names like J and K. When the processor encounters symbolic subscript names, it substitutes the existing numeric values of the subscript names to indicate specific row-column intersections. In the DEPT example, the following range of subscript relationships exists:

| Array Name | Value of Index | | Row-Column Intersection |
	J	K	
DEPT	(1,	1)	row 1, column 1
DEPT	(1,	2)	row 1, column 2
DEPT	(2,	1)	row 2, column 1
DEPT	(2,	2)	row 2, column 2

Expansion of this two-dimensional concept for larger arrays is accomplished by merely reserving more internal storage through the DIMENSION statement. The maximum value of the array subscripts must also increase to handle the increased number of storage location references.

Suppose that an array named GO is specified as having three rows and four columns. The DIMENSION statement will appear as:

DIMENSION GO(3,4)

Note how added storage is specified by increasing the row and column values. In this case the DIMENSION statement reserves twelve memory locations (3×4). Assume that the symbolic subscript K designates the row values and that the subscript L indicates the columns. The schematic in Figure 14.3 shows the 3×4 GO array with its row/column subscript values printed in each array cell.

Figure 14.3 Schematic of 3 X 4 GO ARRAY

Array GO (K,L)

	Col. 1	Col. 2	Col. 3	Col. 4
Row 1	1,1	1,2	1,3	1,4
Row 2	2,1	2,2	2,3	2,4
Row 3	3,1	3,2	3,3	3,4

Subscript K

Subscript L

The range of subscript relationships for this array would appear as:

Array Name	Value of Index K	L	Row-Column Intersection
GO	(1,	1)	row 1, column 1
GO	(1,	2)	row 1, column 2
GO	(1,	3)	row 1, column 3
GO	(1,	4)	row 1, column 4
GO	(2,	1)	row 2, column 1
GO	(2,	2)	row 2, column 2
GO	(2,	3)	row 2, column 3
GO	(2,	4)	row 2, column 4
GO	(3,	1)	row 3, column 1
GO	(3,	2)	row 3, column 2
GO	(3,	3)	row 3, column 3
GO	(3,	4)	row 3, column 4

Expansion of this storage concept can be continued by adding rows and columns. Array sizes are limited only by the size of the available computer memory. Regardless of the array size, however, there are only two dimensions involved: rows and columns.

Two illustrations of two-dimensional arrays appear in Figure 14.4. Each of these arrays reserves 24 memory locations, but the number of rows and columns are reversed. The importance of knowing the exact number of rows and columns should be obvious. When close attention is not paid to these parameters, it is easy to write a program statement which will attempt to access inaccurate row-column intersections.

Figure 14.4 Schematic of 6 × 4 and 4 × 6 Arrays

DIMENSION LOG(6,4)   DIMENSION BIG(4,6)

	1	2	3	4
1	1,1	1,2	1,3	1,4
2	2,1	2,2	2,3	2,4
3	3,1	3,2	3,3	3,4
4	4,1	4,2	4,3	4,4
5	5,1	5,2	5,3	5,4
6	6,1	6,2	6,3	6,4

	1	2	3	4	5	6
1	1,1	1,2	1,3	1,4	1,5	1,6
2	2,1	2,2	2,3	2,4	2,5	2,6
3	3,1	3,2	3,3	3,4	3,5	3,6
4	4,1	4,2	4,3	4,4	4,5	4,6

Recall that the first letter in an array name sets the *mode* for the values stored in the array. In the above examples, the LOG array will store only integer numeric values and the BIG array will store only real values.

Exercise 35   1. Indicate how many rows and columns will be reserved for the following arrays.

	Rows	Columns
a. DIMENSION ONE(3,4)	_____	_____
b. DIMENSION NUM(8,12)	_____	_____
c. DIMENSION XYZ(7,25)	_____	_____
d. DIMENSION COUNT(100,3)	_____	_____
e. DIMENSION KOUNT(6,4)	_____	_____

2. Refer to the arrays DIMENSIONed in question 1. How many total storage locations were reserved for each array and what will the mode be for the numeric values stored in each array?

	Total Storage	Data Mode
a.	_____	_____
b.	_____	_____
c.	_____	_____
d.	_____	_____
e.	_____	_____

3. Several sets of program instructions are given below. Draw a schematic outline of each array DIMENSIONed. Then identify the proper array location (that is, cell), and its contents, which will result from executing the program statements.

a. DIMENSION TEST(8,5)
   N = 6
   J = 3
   A = 3.4
   TEST(N,J) = A

b. DIMENSION SAMPLE(5,6)
   L = 4
   K = L+2
   B = 25.32
   SAMPLE(L,K) = B

c. DIMENSION NUM(7,8)
   J = 4
   NN = (J+3)/2
   N = NN
   NUM(NN,J) = N

Nested DO Loops and Two-Dimensional Arrays

At this point, it seems appropriate to reconsider the two FORTRAN concepts of looping and arrays. DO loops enable the programmer to instruct the computer to cycle through a series of instructions several times. Chapter 11 discussed the use of nested DO loops. Essentially, nesting means that for each cycle of an outer DO loop, one or more inner DO loops are being cycled. This relationship is shown below.

.
.
.

DO 20 N = 1,5 ⟵
.
.
.

DO 15 J = 1,4 ⟵
          inner   outer
          loop   loop
.
.

15 CONTINUE ⟵
.
.
.

20 CONTINUE ⟵
.
.
.

In this illustration, the inner DO loop (DO 15) will be completed four times for *each cycle of the outer loop (DO 20)*. When the computer first encounters the outer DO loop it will set N = 1. It will then process the second DO loop (through 15 CONTINUE) *four times before moving down to 20 CONTINUE*. The computer then returns to the outer loop and increments N by one. It will *again process the inner DO loop four times* before returning to the outer loop. The result of these nested loops will be the completion of the inner loop 20 times when the outer loop has been completed 5 times. This, of course, assumes that no abnormal exit has been made from either loop (GO TO or IF statements).

This illustration shows the extremely powerful concept of nesting. The *main rule* to remember is that the *inner loop cycles most rapidly* and will be completed prior to the completion of the outer loop. Each loop is controlled by its own index. The degree to which nesting may be exercised is very substantial. Two, three, four, or more levels of DO loops may be nested. The computer will always complete the innermost loop before moving to the next outermost loop. Outward progress will continue until the final outer loop has been executed.

One example which usefully joins the looping capability and the concept of arrays relates to programs which require either reading data into arrays or printing from arrays.

Consider the simple case where five cards are read into the one-dimensional STORE array. Assume that the input cards, program, and array appear as follows:

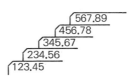

Program

Computer Memory
for Array STORE

DIMENSION STORE(5)
DO 20 K = 1,5
READ(5,5) STORE(K)
5 FORMAT (F6.2)
20 CONTINUE
 ·
 ·
 ·
END

1	123.45	Card 1
2	234.56	Card 2
3	345.67	Card 3
4	456.78	Card 4
5	567.89	Card 5

This program uses the DO loop to cycle through the READ statement five times. Each loop causes a value to be read from a new data card and to be stored in the next location of the STORE array.

The use of DO loops may also be applied easily to the handling of items in two-dimensional arrays. In this case the nesting characteristics of DO loops may be related to the two subscript requirement of two-dimensional arrays. Each of the loops in the nest will control one of the array's subscripts. Assume that we continue to have data cards appearing in the F6.2 FORMAT shown above. In the following illustration, twelve cards are read and placed in a 4 × 3 array (4 rows, 3 columns) called STORE. The program and array appear as follows:

Program

Computer Memory-Array STORE

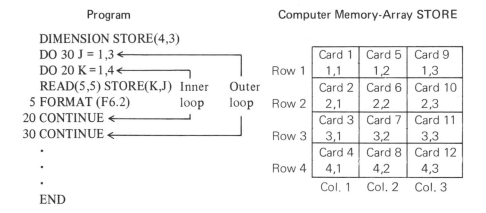

DIMENSION STORE(4,3)
DO 30 J = 1,3 ←
DO 20 K = 1,4 ←
READ(5,5) STORE(K,J)   Inner   Outer
5 FORMAT (F6.2)   loop   loop
20 CONTINUE ←
30 CONTINUE ←
 ·
 ·
 ·
END

	Col. 1	Col. 2	Col. 3
Row 1	Card 1 1,1	Card 5 1,2	Card 9 1,3
Row 2	Card 2 2,1	Card 6 2,2	Card 10 2,3
Row 3	Card 3 3,1	Card 7 3,2	Card 11 3,3
Row 4	Card 4 4,1	Card 8 4,2	Card 12 4,3

The array is shown above with both the card number and row/column cross-reference in each cell. Of course, when the program is executed the array would store the actual *values* read from each input card.

It is important to recall that the order of K and J in the symbolic name STORE (K,J) causes the subscript K to identify rows and the subscript J to identify columns.

Progress through each DO loop cycle is shown in the following summary:

Number of Loop Cycle		Value of Index		Card Number Read	Places Data Value in Array Location Number
Outer Loop	Inner Loop	J	K		
1	1	1	1	1	STORE (1,1)
	2		2	2	STORE (2,1)
	3		3	3	STORE (3,1)
	4		4	4	STORE (4,1)
2	1	2	1	5	STORE (1,2)
	2		2	6	STORE (2,2)
	3		3	7	STORE (3,2)
	4		4	8	STORE (4,2)
3	1	3	1	9	STORE (1,3)
	2		2	10	STORE (2,3)
	3		3	11	STORE (3,3)
	4		4	12	STORE (4,3)

Columns — Rows — Rows — Columns

Implied Nested Loops in Two Dimensions

The implied DO loop for reading and writing data is an alternative to the explicit DO loop. The implied loop places the loop indices within READ or WRITE statements. A comparison of the explicit loop method illustrated above and this alternative implied loop method is made below:

Original example—Explicit DO loop

```
DIMENSION STORE (4,3)
  .
  .
  .
DO 30 J = 1,3
DO 20 K = 1,4
   READ(5,5)STORE(K,J)
 5 FORMAT  (F6.2)
20 CONTINUE
30 CONTINUE
  .
  .
  .
```

Alternative method—Implied DO Loop

```
DIMENSION STORE (4,3)
  .
  .
  .
READ(5,5)((STORE(K,J),K=1,4),J=1,3)
 5 FORMAT (F6.2)
  .
  .
  .
```

The implied loop contains several similarities, as well as dissimilarities, to the explicit loop, and these should be examined carefully. It is obvious that the implied loop is more compact, but extreme care must be exercised to be sure that the computer will perform exactly what the programmer desires.

Note that the FORMAT statements are *identical*. In this illustration, the FORMAT tells the computer to anticipate data cards with only *one data item* punched *per card*.

The construction of the alternative READ statement breaks down into the following elements:

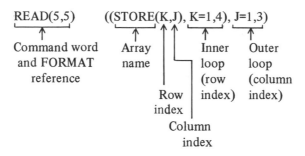

It is often difficult to understand the implied DO loop when more than one loop index is included, as shown above. The form of the loops' construction is quite logical, and the illustration below may aid your understanding of the relationship of the inner and outer loops.

If the two examples of the explicit and implied loops are compared, we can see the following relationships:

Explicit DO Loop

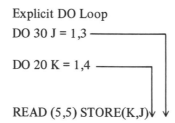

Implied DO Loop

If the explicit outer and inner DO loops were rotated on their sides, the implied loop would have the same outer/inner relationship as the explicit loop. Therefore, the statement containing the implied loop becomes:

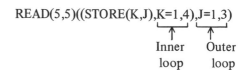

Changing the FORMAT Statement for Implied Looping

Our previous example assumed that input data was read from twelve separate cards. The FORMAT used was (F6.2). Of course, with this FORMAT, either the explicit or implied loops would cause cards to be read continuously with one value taken from each card.

If, alternatively, the data was punched *across* 12 fields of F6.2, this would necessitate a change in the FORMAT specification. The FORMAT would change *from* FORMAT (F6.2) *to* FORMAT (12F6.2). The computer would read the data as twelve items per card and read across the card. This form of reading could be accomplished *only* with the *implied loop*. The explicit loop would not work because it causes a new record to be read each time it cycles through a loop. Explicit looping causes the READ statement to be encountered over and over. With each encounter of the READ statement, a new record (that is, data card) would be read. Therefore, only the implied loop can satisfy the requirement to read across an input card.

The implied loop and the correct FORMAT statement for reading *twelve values from one card* are shown below.

DIMENSION STORE(4,3)
   •

5 FORMAT (12F6.2)
  READ(5,5) ((STORE(K,J),K=1,4),J=1,3)

Note the use of commas
and parentheses in the
READ statement

In this example, the first field from the data card will be assigned array location 1,1 (that is, row 1, column 1), the second field location 2,1, the third 3,1, and so on.

The combination of (1) DO loops and (2) the expansion of storage through the use of two-dimensional arrays gives the programmer a sizable capability for handling large quantities of data with few program steps. Although we have discussed only the reading of data into arrays, the concepts are equally applicable to writing data from arrays. Essentially, the only change needed would be substitution of the command word WRITE for the word READ. Naturally, the FORMAT statement might also require change in order to describe an output line. The use of subscript indices would be the same, however.

A Word of Caution. It is important to exercise extreme caution in writing subscript indices *in the correct order*. The concept of an inner and outer loop cannot be ignored. If the intended inner and outer loops are reversed, data will be read or printed, but the order will be changed so that references will be made to the wrong array locations. The following example demonstrates the problems generated by lack of attention to proper indexing.

Let us assume the following facts: (1) we wish to create a 3 × 3 array named KOOL, (2) nine data cards are to be read to fill the array, and (3) the data cards each have an I2 format and contain the following values:

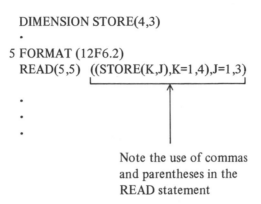

Card 1	10		Card 4	40		Card 7	70
Card 2	20		Card 5	50		Card 8	80
Card 3	30		Card 6	60		Card 9	90

The program segment to fill the array *as desired* appears below:

```
    DIMENSION KOOL(3,3)                              Implied Loop
5 FORMAT (I2)

    DO 20 J = 1,3                                row        column
    DO 30 K = 1,3
    READ (5,5) KOOL(K,J)       or     READ(5,5) ((KOOL(K,J),K=1,3),J=1,3)
30 CONTINUE
20 CONTINUE
    .
    .
    .
```

The above program would store the data in the following row, column order:

1,1	2,1	3,1	1,2	2,2	3,2	1,3	2,3	3,3

Note how the inner loop (subscript K which applies to rows) cycles most rapidly. The KOOL array would now contain:

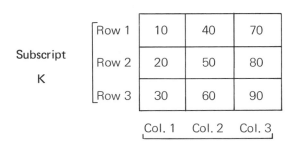

Subscript K

	Col. 1	Col. 2	Col. 3
Row 1	10	40	70
Row 2	20	50	80
Row 3	30	60	90

Subscript J

Now assume that the DO statements were inadvertently written in the reverse order. The input cards would continue to have the same format, but the program would appear as:

```
    DIMENSION KOOL(3,3)                              Implied Loop
5 FORMAT (I2)

    DO 30 K = 1,3                                row        column
    DO 20 J = 1,3
    READ (5,5) KOOL(K,J)       or     READ(5,5) ((KOOL(K,J),J=1,3),K=1,3)
20 CONTINUE
30 CONTINUE
    .
    .
    .
```

This program will store the data in the following row, column order:

1,1	1,2	1,3	2,1	2,2	2,3	3,1	3,2	3,3

Note that the inner loop (J) in this program relates to the column subscript. This loop cycles most rapidly and causes the values to be stored in an order opposite to that of the previous program.

The KOOL array will now contain:

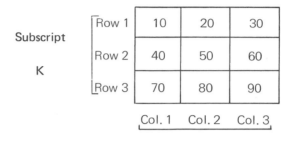

	Col. 1	Col. 2	Col. 3
Row 1	10	20	30
Row 2	40	50	60
Row 3	70	80	90

Subscript K

Subscript J

This program illustrates that while the values would be stored in the KOOL array, they would be located in an *order which was not intended.*

The Short List Convention and Two-Dimensional Arrays

The short list convention's use with one-dimensional arrays was discussed in Chapter 12. This language element allows the use of a nonsubscripted array name within a READ or WRITE statement and results in the reading or writing of an entire array. The short list convention applies equally well to two-dimensional arrays.

When a two-dimensional array name is used without subscripts in READ or WRITE statements, the computer will either load or print the entire array in a column-wise by row order. This order of array handling is taken automatically. The restrictions which apply to the short list convention are: (1) an entire array is read or written, and (2) the order of array handling is always column-wise by rows.

To illustrate, assume that a simple program is to read and store twelve values in a 3 X 4 array named SAVE. After reading the values, the program will then write all twelve values. The following program illustrates the use of the short list convention for both input and output.

Assume the twelve data values will appear on three cards. Each card holds four values, and a FORMAT of 4F2.0 is used. The cards and program appear as follows:

Card 3 | 09 | 10 | 11 | 12 |
Card 2 | 05 | 06 | 07 | 08 |
Card 1 | 01 | 02 | 03 | 04 |

DIMENSION SAVE(3,4)
10 FORMAT (4F2.0)

READ (5,10) SAVE ⟵————————— This READ statement will cause the SAVE array to be loaded with twelve values in the following locations:

20 FORMAT ((5X, 5(F4.1,2X))/)

WRITE (6,20) SAVE

STOP
END

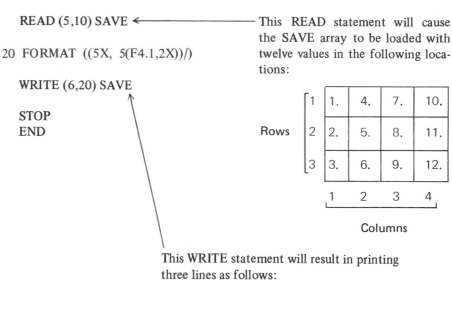

Rows

This WRITE statement will result in printing three lines as follows:

```
1.0    2.0   3.0   4.0    5.0
6.0    7.0   8.0   9.0   10.0
11.0  12.0
```

Note how the short list convention causes the array to be filled column by column (column-wise) with all rows filled before moving from one column to the next (column-wise by rows). Writing the array, under control of the short list convention, also causes the values to be taken from the array column-wise by rows.

Exercise 38

1. Take the following two-dimensional array and fill in the row-column numbers which apply to each cell in (a). After completing the first step, fill in the row-column numbers for each cell in (b) to show how the array would be stored in the computer's memory.

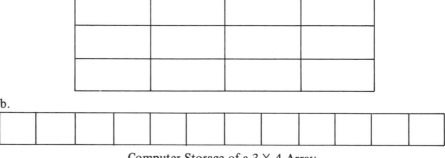

Computer Storage of a 3 × 4 Array

2. What values will be in the cells of the A array after the instructions shown below are executed? Assume that the array was initially set to zeros.

```
      DO 500 I = 1,4
      DO 500 J = 1,4
      IF (I- J) 50,500,50
50    A(I,J) =J
500 CONTINUE
      .
      .
      .
      END
```

A Array

3. After the following statements have been executed, what values will be in the MAX and MIN arrays? Assume the arrays were originally set to zero.

```
      DIMENSION MAX (4,4),MIN(4)
      DO 500 K = 1,4
500 MIN (K) = K
      DO 800 J = 2,4
      DO 800 N = 2,4
800 MAX (J,N) = N+2
      IF (MIN(2) .GE. MAX(2,1)) GO TO 300
      MIN(4) = 7
300 MAX(1,1) = 9
      MIN(2) = 11
      .
      .
      .
      END
```

MIN Array

MAX Array

Adding Mileage to a Program

The discussion in this chapter has dealt with two-dimensional arrays primarily in terms of reading or writing values. While multiple-dimensional arrays add significant data handling ability for input and output, these arrays may also be used to increase computing efficiency within a program. However, to increase the efficiency of a program, careful thought must be given to the preparation of the statements in the program. The following program illustration makes multiple use of the subscripts from a two-dimensional array to reduce the number of program statements which would be required if the two-dimensional array were omitted.

Program Efficiency Using Table (Array) Lookup

For this example, assume the following facts:

1. A firm allows specific commission rates, to its salesmen, on sales of the company's products.
2. The commission rate will vary depending on the product sold and will also vary with the model (or class) of each product sold.
3. A commission table will be read into computer memory and will hold the rates for reference in computing sales commissions.
4. The commission table will be a 3 X 4 array called COMTAB. Each row in the array represents a product class (that is, product model). Each column represents one product of the firm. Therefore, commission rates will vary in accordance with the class and the type of product sold.
5. The program will first read in the commission table. After the table (array) has been read (that is, loaded), cards with sales transaction data will be read. These cards will contain (a) the salesman's number, (b) sales amount (before commission), and (c) the product sold (identified by product and class).

The program will read the data card shown below to load the commission table. The applicable instructions to load the table appear below the data cards.

Commission Rate Card

.050.075.100	.060.080.090	.080.085.090	.090.100.120
Product 1	Product 2	Product 3	Product 4
Class 1,2,3	Class 1,2,3	Class 1,2,3	Class 1,2,3

```
DIMENSION COMTAB(3,4)
5 FORMAT (12F4.3)
READ (5,5) ((COMTAB(K,N),K=1,3),N=1,4)
```

After reading, the commission array will appear in memory as:

COMTAB

Rows = Class   (Commission Table)

Subscript K

	1	2	3	4
1	.050	.060	.080	.090
2	.075	.080	.085	.100
3	.100	.090	.090	.120

Columns = Products
Subscript N

Note that the array is used to hold *real* numeric data and is named COMTAB. The name of the array must begin with a real alphabetic character. By contrast, the rows and columns are identified through the use of *integer* numbers and hence are named with integer alphabetic characters (that is, K and N).

A sample sales transaction card containing salesman number, sales amount, product class, and product number is shown below. A READ and a FORMAT statement to read this card is also shown.

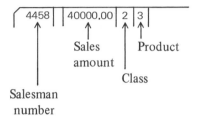

```
15 FORMAT (I4,2X,F8.2,2X,I1,1X,I1)
   READ (5,15) NUM,AMT,KLAS,IPROD
```

After reading a sales transaction card, the program would have to identify the class and product values in order to enter the commission table to find the applicable commission rate. At this point in the program, there are essentially two alternative methods for entering the commission table. The first method requires a series of IF tests to determine the class and product values on the transaction card. This method is discussed immediately below. The second method, which is significantly more efficient, makes use of the class and product values for direct entry into the commission table. This method is shown on page 289.

Method 1 for Entering the Commission Table. After reading a sales transaction card, it would seem logical to test for the class and product values in the transaction card. The applicable portion of a flowchart and the program steps to accomplish this testing are shown on page 286.

This method of testing and setting integer indices (which will be used as subscripts for entering the commission table) requires fifteen program statements. After completion of this testing, the variable K will hold the value corresponding to the class number, and the variable N will correspond to the product number.

The example salesman's card shows the class as 2 and the product as 3. Therefore, entering the COMTAB array at row 2 and column 3 indicates that the $40,000 sale amount should have a commission rate of 8.5 per cent. The commission would be $3,400 (40,000 $\times$ .085).

The program step to compute the commission is:

```
30 COMM = AMT*COMTAB(K,N)
```

The commission is equal to the sale amount (AMT) multiplied by the commission rate COMTAB(K,N). This result is stored in variable location COMM.

[1] An alternative discussed in Chapter 13 would allow the use of subscript variable names CLAS and PROD. To have the computer handle these variables in the integer mode, they would have to be declared in a statement: INTEGER CLAS, PROD.

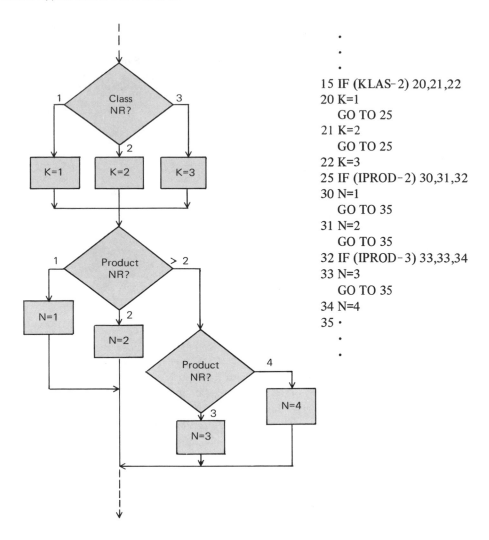

```
          .
          .
          .
15 IF (KLAS-2) 20,21,22
20 K=1
   GO TO 25
21 K=2
   GO TO 25
22 K=3
25 IF (IPROD-2) 30,31,32
30 N=1
   GO TO 35
31 N=2
   GO TO 35
32 IF (IPROD-3) 33,33,34
33 N=3
   GO TO 35
34 N=4
35 •
   •
   •
```

A flowchart for the complete program which loads the commission table, reads transaction cards, tests, and computes the applicable sales commission appears in Figure 14.5. The data used in this example is shown below. The program and computed commissions are shown in Program 14.2.

Input Card	Sample Input Data Values
1	.050.075.100.060.080.090.080.085.090.090.100.120
2	4458 40000.00 2 3
3	5162 30000.00 1 2
4	8034 50000.00 3 1
5	9988 20000.00 3 4
6	9999

Figure 14.5

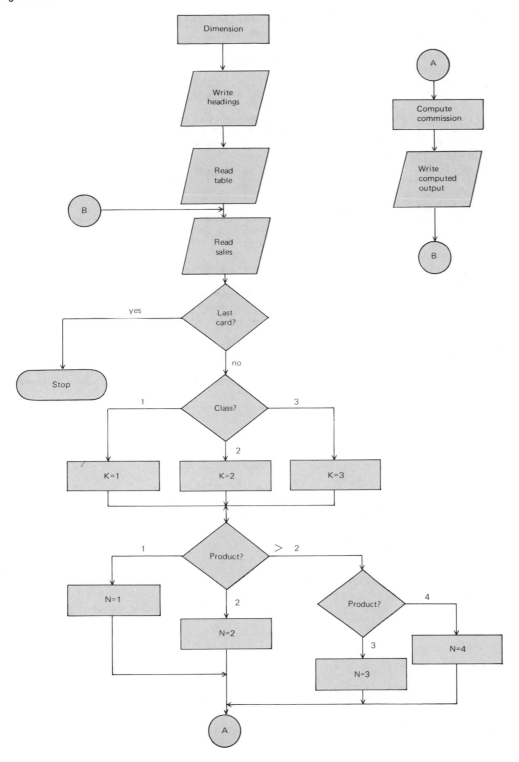

Program 14.2

```
      C**********************************************************************
      C ESTABLISH MEMORY AREA FOR COMMISSION TABLE
      C WRITE OUTPUT HEADINGS
      C**********************************************************************
 1          DIMENSION COMTAB(3,4)
 2       40 FORMAT ('1',4X,'SALES-  PRO-',11X,'SALES  COMM    COMM'/7X,'MAN'
           13X,'DUCT  CLASS   AMOUNT  RATE   AMOUNT'/)
 3          WRITE (6,40)
      C**********************************************************************
      C READ COMMISSION RATES INTO COMMISSION TABLE
      C**********************************************************************
 4        5 FORMAT (12F4.3)
 5          READ (5,5) ((COMTAB(K,N), K=1,3), N=1,4)
      C**********************************************************************
      C READ SALES DATA
      C LAST CARD TEST
      C**********************************************************************
 6       10 FORMAT (I4,2X,F8.2,2X,I1,1X,I1)
 7       12 READ (5,10) NUM, AMT, KLAS, IPROD
 8          IF (NUM-9999) 15,50,50
      C**********************************************************************
      C TEST FOR CLASS
      C**********************************************************************
 9       15 IF (KLAS-2) 20,21,22
10       20 K=1
11          GO TO 25
12       21 K=2
13          GO TO 25
14       22 K=3
      C**********************************************************************
      C TEST FOR PRODUCT
      C**********************************************************************
15       25 IF (IPROD-2) 30,31,32
16       30 N=1
17          GO TO 35
18       31 N=2
19          GO TO 35
20       32 IF (IPROD-3) 33,33,34
21       33 N=3
22          GO TO 35
23       34 N=4
      C**********************************************************************
      C COMPUTE COMMISSION AMOUNT
      C WRITE SALES REPORT
      C**********************************************************************
24       35 COMM = AMT * COMTAB(K,N)
25       45 FORMAT (6X,I4,2(5X,I1),4X,F8.2,1X,F5.3,1X,F8.2)
26          WRITE (6,45) NUM, IPROD, KLAS, AMT, COMTAB(K,N), COMM
27          GO TO 12
28       50 STOP
29          END
```

SALES- MAN	PRO- DUCT	CLASS	SALES AMOUNT	COMM RATE	COMM AMOUNT
4458	3	2	40000.00	0.085	3400.00
5162	2	1	30000.00	0.060	1800.00
8034	1	3	50000.00	0.100	5000.00
9988	4	3	20000.00	0.120	2400.00

Method 2 for Entering the Commission Table. An alternative to the program shown above lends greater computing power to the programmer and accomplishes the same objective while requiring fewer statements.

You will recall that when the test for class was made in the above example, the test measured whether the value stored at KLAS was 1, 2, or 3. When the computer determined the value, it set the index K to 1, 2, or 3. In the example transaction card, KLAS held a value of 2, and K was correspondingly set to a value of 2.

When the array name COMTAB(K,N) was used in statement 30, the computer referred back to variable name K and used the value 2 as the first subscript. But was not this a redundant value? KLAS already had stored 2 as a value. Would it not be more logical to use KLAS as the first subscript for COMTAB? The answer is yes, and COMTAB(K,N) would be written COMTAB(KLAS,N). Row 2 in the commission table is indicated just as accurately by using KLAS for a subscript as it is when using K.

Naturally, the same relationship exists between IPROD and N. IPROD stores the value 3, in the above example, as will N after the test instructions are completed. Why not use IPROD as a subscript and omit the use of N? If this is done, the reference to the COMTAB array will appear as COMTAB(KLAS, IPROD) and still mean COMTAB(2,3).

The relationships between the input card, array, and a revised program segment are shown in Figure 14.6.

Figure 14.6

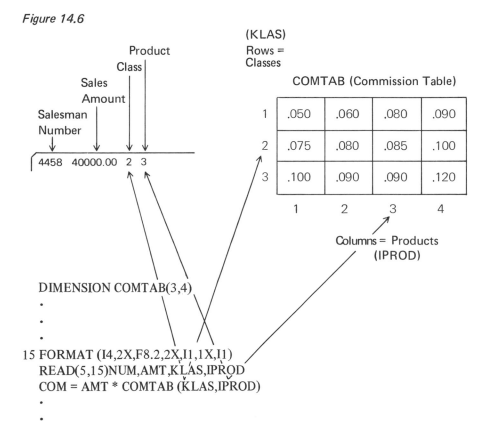

```
       DIMENSION COMTAB(3,4)
       .
       .
       .
   15  FORMAT (I4,2X,F8.2,2X,I1,1X,I1)
       READ(5,15)NUM,AMT,KLAS,IPROD
       COM = AMT * COMTAB (KLAS,IPROD)
       .
       .
       .
```

Note that in the program segment above, one line achieves the same computation as did the 15 lines of FORTRAN statements shown on page 286.

The flowchart shown in Figure 14.5 would still be applicable for this amended program. The complete amended program appears in Program 14.3

This illustration indicates how a programmer may reduce the number of FORTRAN statements if he spends time selecting the combination of statements which accomplishes the greatest amount of computing with the fewest number of statements.

Previous examples of DO loops, multi-line FORMATS, and the inclusion of implied looping characteristics within the READ and WRITE statements also illustrate ways to achieve large quantities of computing with minimum numbers of program statements. Programs designed to use these techniques will add a great deal of mileage to your program instructions.

Program 14.3

```
      C*********************************************************************
      C ESTABLISH MEMORY AREA FOR COMMISSION TABLE
      C WRITE OUTPUT HEADINGS
      C*********************************************************************
1           DIMENSION COMTAB(3,4)
2        40 FORMAT (/5X,'SALES- PRO-',11X,'SALES   COMM     COMM'/7X,'MAN    DUC
           1T  CLASS   AMOUNT  RATE    AMOUNT'/)
3           WRITE (6,40)
      C*********************************************************************
      C READ COMMISSION RATES INTO COMMISSION TABLE
      C*********************************************************************
4         5 FORMAT (12F4.3)
5           READ (5,5) ((COMTAB(K,N), K=1,3), N=1,4)
      C*********************************************************************
      C READ SALES DATA
      C LAST CARD TEST
      C*********************************************************************
6        10 FORMAT (I4,2X,F8.2,2X,I1,1X,I1)
7        12 READ (5,10) NUM, AMT, KLAS, IPROD
8           IF (NUM-9999) 15,50,50
      C*********************************************************************
      C COMPUTE COMMISSION AMOUNT
      C*********************************************************************
9        15 COMM = AMT * COMTAB(KLAS, IPROD)
      C*********************************************************************
      C WRITE SALES REPORT
      C*********************************************************************
10       45 FORMAT (6X,I4,2(5X,I1),4X,F8.2,1X,F5.3,1X,F8.2)
11          WRITE (6,45) NUM, IPROD, KLAS, AMT, COMTAB(KLAS,IPROD), COMM
12          GO TO 12
13       50 STOP
14          END
```

SALES- MAN	PRO- DUCT	CLASS	SALES AMOUNT	COMM RATE	COMM AMOUNT
4458	3	2	40000.00	0.085	3400.00
5162	2	1	30000.00	0.060	1800.00
8034	1	3	50000.00	0.100	5000.00
9988	4	3	20000.00	0.120	2400.00

Three-Dimensional Arrays[2]

With two-dimensional arrays, the computer stores the equivalent of two or more one-dimensional arrays. The computer uses two subscripts, and each subscript identifies one dimension of the array. The two dimensions correspond to the storage of several rows and several columns.

The example on page 269 illustrates the classification of labor as direct or indirect (one dimension) and by department 1 or 2 (the second dimension). All labor costs that appear in the two-dimensional classification are assumed to be actual costs. Most firms would also be vitally interested in matching these actual costs with their budgeted labor costs.

The addition of the budgeted cost factor is, in fact, the introduction of a third dimension. Budgeted costs for labor will also have to be broken down by direct, indirect, department 1, and department 2, if a meaningful comparison is to be made with the actual costs.

The cross-classification for actual and budgeted labor costs is:

Labor Type	Budgeted		Actual	
	Dept 1	Dept 2	Dept 1	Dept 2
Direct	$XXXX	$XXXX	$XXXX	$XXXX
Indirect	$XXXX	$XXXX	$XXXX	$XXXX

Observe that for each major classification of labor (actual and budgeted), there are four storage areas required. As a matter of fact, the only difference between the two sets of cross-classifications is the use of one classification for budgeted costs and the other for actual costs. It would seem logical to handle these labor types in two 2×2 arrays. Rows would be used for direct and indirect labor and columns for departments. To illustrate this type of storage, actual costs would be stored in an array named ACT and budgeted costs in the BUD array. These arrays are shown below with the row-column indices in each array cell.

Rows = Labor Type		BUD Array		Rows = Labor Type		ACT Array	
Direct	1	1,1	1,2	Direct	1	1,1	1,2
Indirect	2	2,1	2,2	Indirect	2	2,1	2,2
		1	2			1	2

Columns = Departments   Columns = Departments

Examination of each array shows that the storage locations are in identical array position with respect to direct/indirect and department cross-classifications. For

[2] Nearly all computer systems will permit the use of at least two-dimensional arrays. The majority of computers will also handle three-dimensional arrays. In addition, a few will accept more than three dimensions. Refer to the manufacturer's manuals for array limitations.

instance, the BUD array direct labor-department 1 position (cell 1,1) is in the same position in its array as the direct labor-department 1 position (cell 1,1) in the ACT array. The only difference is the name of the array. Of course, the numeric quantities stored in each array probably would be different because one array reflects actual costs while the other reflects budgeted costs.

Although it is possible to use two arrays to reflect these costs, it would probably be more efficient to use a single array which contained all three dimensions of information. The creation of a three-dimensional array is relatively simple. It requires only the assignment of an additional subscript for the third dimension and the use of one name for all of the data stored in the array.

To visualize a three-dimensional array, refer to the illustration in Figure 14.6. The essential change from a two-dimensional array is the addition of a dimension for array depth. This is shown in Figure 14.6 by imagining that the ACT array is slipped behind the BUD array. This alignment would give the three-dimensional array height, width, and depth. In this illustration, the new three-dimensional array is given the name EXP.

A computer requires subscript references to keep the array elements properly controlled. For three-dimensional arrays, the programmer must add a third subscript to indicate whether the front array (the previous BUD array) or the back array (the previous ACT array) is being referenced. Each of the array groups (front and back) is called a *plane* (or slice or segment), and the third subscript value will indicate the plane being referenced. In this illustration, the former BUD array is designated as plane 1 and the former ACT array as plane 2. Each cell in the EXP array is shown in Figure 14.6 with its three subscript reference values. The new plane subscript is circled.

Figure 14.6   Computer Storage of a Three-Dimensional Array with a Total of Eight Cells

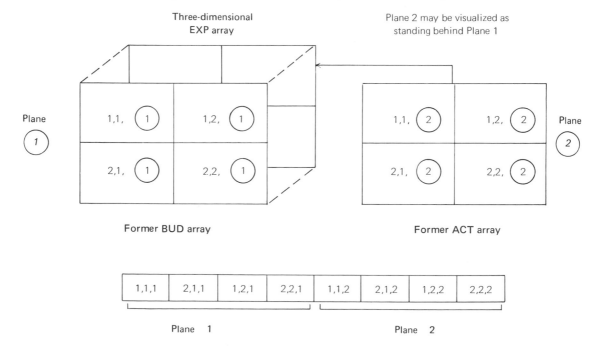

At the bottom of Figure 14.6, the illustration shows how the computer actually stores a three-dimensional array. Consecutive memory positions are allocated to the first plane, then additional consecutive positions are reserved for the second plane. Within each plane, the array is stored column-wise by rows, as is true for two-dimensional arrays.

Changes in the DIMENSION Statement

When we use three-dimensional arrays we must reserve memory locations as we do for one- and two-dimensional arrays. The change necessary for specifying three-dimensional storage is the addition of an integer number to indicate the depth of the planes used. In the example given above, the DIMENSION statement for the EXP array would be:

DIMENSION EXP(2,2,2)

This statement reserves eight consecutive memory locations (2 X 2 X 2) under the EXP array name.

Two other examples of three-dimensional arrays are given below. The schematic drawing for each array is in outline form. The size of each plane is listed in the first plane of each array. The correct DIMENSION statement for each array appears below the array drawing.

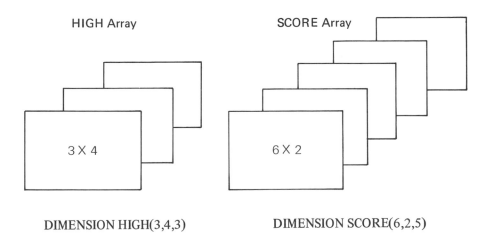

HIGH Array

3 X 4

DIMENSION HIGH(3,4,3)

SCORE Array

6 X 2

DIMENSION SCORE(6,2,5)

Subscripts and Nested Loops (Implied) for Three-Dimensional Arrays

Three-dimensional arrays have requirements for subscripting which are extensions of the subscripting specifications related to one- and two-dimensional arrays. In addition to the row and column subscripts, we must specify a third subscript when we refer to any three-dimensional array name. The third subscript identifies the appropriate plane number. This new subscript must adhere to the same requirements that were given for previous subscripts. In summary, these requirements are: (1) a subscript must be a positive non-zero integer; (2) it may be either a number or variable name; (3) it may not itself be a subscripted variable; (4) it may be an expression using +,- , or * symbols.

For example, the following statements are correct array references to cell (2,1,2) in the EXP array:

EXP(2,1,2)
EXP(K,1,J)   Assuming: K=2 and J=2
EXP(L,M,N) Assuming: L=2, M=1, and N=2

The order of reference in a three-dimensional array name is:

Subscript 1: row
Subscript 2: column
Subscript 3: plane

Looping is changed somewhat with three-dimensional arrays. This change relates to the third subscript. For example, assume that a program is to read eight values into an array called COST. The array is DIMENSIONed as (2,2,2). The data cards, array schematic, flowchart segment, and program segment to accomplish reading are shown in Figure 14.7.

Figure 14.7

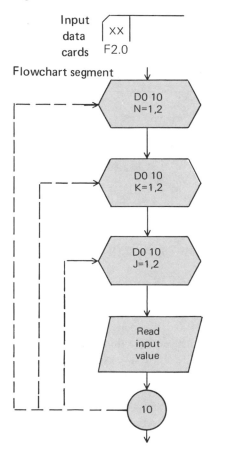

Card Value
1   10
2   20   Location
3   30   of input
4   40   Values in
5   50   the COST
6   60   Array
7   70
8   80

Program Segment
```
      DIMENSION COST(2,2,2)
    5 FORMAT (F2.0)
      DO 10 N=1,2
      DO 10 K=1,2
      DO 10 J=1,2
      READ(5,5) COST(J,K,N)
   10 CONTINUE
```

The steps in the Figure 14.7 program segment are summarized below.

| Loop Indices | | | | |
Inner J	Middle K	Outer N	Array Subscript Order (J,K,N)	Values Stored
1	1	1	COST (1,1,1)	10.
2			COST (2,1,1)	20.
1	2		COST (1,2,1)	30.
2			COST (2,2,1)	40.
1	1	2	COST (1,1,2)	50.
2			COST (2,1,2)	60.
1	2		COST (1,2,2)	70.
2			COST (2,2,2)	80.

Rather than use three explicit DO loops, the READ statement could have included implied looping specifications written as:

READ(5,5) (((COST(J,K,N),J=1,2),K=1,2),N=1,2)

In this case, N is still shown as the outer loop, K the middle loop, and J the inner loop. Naturally, combinations of explicit and implicit DO loops are possible. The following example illustrates such a combination.

The budget/actual example presented earlier in this section is modified below to illustrate data handling with three-dimensional arrays. For this example, assume that a firm maintains budgeted and actual expense data on operating expenses for three operational departments. These departments have ten expense categories (that is, accounts). A computer program is written to do the following processing:

1. Dimension a three-dimensional array (named EXP) to hold the budgeted and actual figures. Plane 1 will be used for budget amounts and plane 2 for actual. The other dimensions are 10 rows (expense accounts) and 3 columns (three departments).
2. Initialize the names of the expense accounts by storing them in an array. This requires storage of alphabetic data.
3. Read and test data cards. If a data card is:
   a. a *budget* card, store the budget figures in plane 1 of the EXP array.
   b. an *actual* card, accumulate the actual expense in the appropriate expense account in plane 2 of the EXP array.
   c. a *last card,* transfer to program steps which will accumulate expense totals.
4. Accumulate budget and actual expense totals for each department.
5. Accumulate budget and actual expense totals for all departments.
6. Write a report comparing budget and actual expenses.

The EXP array is schematically shown below. A flowchart for this program is presented in Figure 14.8 and contains an explanation of the data cards processed. The program appears in Program 14.4. The computed output follows the program. Exercise 35 relates to the program and should aid your understanding of the FORTRAN instructions used.

Scehmatic of the EXP Array

EXP(10,3,2)

The data names used are:

ACTTOT: a variable name used to store the sum of all actual expenses from departments 1, 2, and 3.

BUDTOT: a variable name used to store the sum of all budgeted expenses from departments 1, 2, and 3.

DATA: a one-dimensional array which temporarily stores data values from an input data card as it is read.

DEPACT: a one-dimensional array which stores the separate total of each department's actual expenses.

DEPBUD: a one-dimensional array which stores the separate total of each department's budgeted expenses.

EXP: a three-dimensional array which stores the budgeted and actual expenses for all departments by expense account, department, and budget/actual classifications.

ID: a variable name used to store temporarily the card code of a data card when it is read.

KODDEP: a variable name used to store temporarily the department code from a data card when it is read.

KODEXP: a variable name used to store temporarily the expense code from a data card when it is read.

NAME: a two-dimensional array used to store the alphabetic characters necessary to write out the expense account titles.

All input cards will have the same FORMAT. There will be three budget cards (card code 1). Only budget cards will have all ten data values punched. These ten values correspond to the ten expense account budgets for the department being read. Actual expense cards (card code 2) will contain only one data value. This value will be for one expense account for the department read. There may be any number of actual expense cards. The last data card will be punched with a card code of 3.

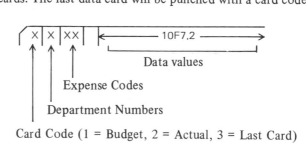

Card Code (1 = Budget, 2 = Actual, 3 = Last Card)

Figure 14.8

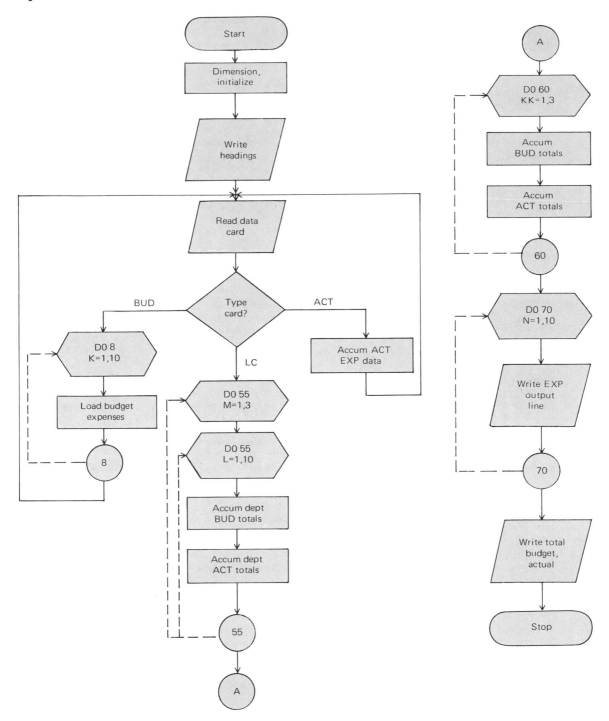

Program 14.4

```
      C*********************************************************************
      C DIMENSION AND INITIALIZE MEMORY AREAS
      C*********************************************************************
 1          DIMENSION NAME(10,5), DATA(10), EXP(10,3,2), DEPBUD(3), DEPACT(3)
 2          DATA EXP,DEPBUD,DEPACT,BUDTOT,ACTTOT/68*0.0/
 3          DATA ((NAME(K,L),L=1,5),K=1,10)/ 'SAL','ARI','ES',2*' ',
           1'SUP','PLI','ES',2*' ','MAI','NTE','NAN','CE',' ','POS','TAG','E',
           22*' ','UTI','LIT','IES',2*' ','TRA','VEL',3*' ','TEL','EPH','ONE',
           32*' ','DAT','A P','ROC','ESS','ING','EQU','IP ','PUR','CHA','SES',
           4'ENT','ERT','AIN','MEN','T'/
      C*********************************************************************
      C WRITE HEADINGS
      C*********************************************************************
 4        1 FORMAT (1H1,31X,'DEPARTMENTAL EXPENSE REPORT'
           1//28X, 'DEPARTMENT ', I1, 2(11X, 'DEPARTMENT ' I1)
           2/8X, 'EXPENSES   ', 3(7X, 'BUDGET      ACTUAL'))
 5          WRITE (6,1) (I,I=1,3)
      C*********************************************************************
      C READ DATA AND TEST FOR CARD TYPE
      C*********************************************************************
 6        3 FORMAT (2(I1,1X), I2, 1X, 10F7.2)
 7        4 READ (5,3) ID,KODDEP, KODEXP, (DATA(J), J=1,10)
 8          GO TO (6,10,50), ID
      C*********************************************************************
      C LOAD BUDGET ARRAY
      C*********************************************************************
 9        6 DO 8 K=1,10
10        8 EXP(K,KODDEP,1) = DATA(K)
11          GO TO 4
      C*********************************************************************
      C ACCUMULATE ACTUAL EXPENSE DATA
      C*********************************************************************
12       10 EXP(KODEXP,KODDEP,2) = EXP(KODEXP,KODDEP,2) + DATA(1)
13          GO TO 4
      C*********************************************************************
      C ACCUMULATE TOTALS
      C*********************************************************************
14       50 DO 55 M=1,3
15          DO 55 L=1,10
16          DEPBUD(M) = DEPBUD(M) + EXP(L,M,1)
17       55 DEPACT(M) = DEPACT(M) + EXP(L,M,2)
18          DO 60 KK=1,3
19          BUDTOT = BUDTOT + DEPBUD (KK)
20       60 ACTTOT = ACTTOT + DEPACT (KK)
      C*********************************************************************
      C WRITE OUTPUT
      C*********************************************************************
21       65 FORMAT ( /5X, 5A3, 3(5X,F8.2,2X,F8.2))
22          DO 70 N=1,10
23       70 WRITE (6,65) (NAME(N,M), M=1,5), ((EXP(N,N2,N3),N3=1,2),N2=1,3)
24       75 FORMAT (//11X, 'TOTALS ', 5X, 3(2F10.2, 3X))
25          WRITE (6,75) (DEPBUD(N), DEPACT(N), N=1,3)
26       80 FORMAT (///5X, 'TOTAL BUDGET - ALL DEPTS', 2X, F10.2/ 5X,
           1'TOTAL ACTUAL EXP TO DATE', 2X, F10.2)
27          WRITE (6,80) BUDTOT, ACTTOT
28          STOP
29          END
```

DEPARTMENTAL EXPENSE REPORT

EXPENSES	DEPARTMENT 1		DEPARTMENT 2		DEPARTMENT 3	
	BUDGET	ACTUAL	BUDGET	ACTUAL	BUDGET	ACTUAL
SALARIES	20000.00	5000.00	30000.00	10000.00	40000.00	15000.00
SUPPLIES	5000.00	2500.00	4000.00	2000.00	3500.00	1275.00
MAINTENANCE	3000.00	1000.00	2500.00	500.00	4000.00	2000.00
POSTAGE	1000.00	800.00	800.00	200.00	400.00	150.00
UTILITIES	5500.00	4000.00	3000.00	3000.00	900.00	500.00
TRAVEL	200.00	50.00	1000.00	850.00	800.00	625.00
TELEPHONE	250.00	70.00	400.00	375.00	600.00	300.00
DATA PROCESSING	30000.00	12000.00	3000.00	1500.00	8000.00	4350.00
EQUIP PURCHASES	10000.00	500.00	5000.00	2000.00	4000.00	600.00
ENTERTAINMENT	800.00	600.00	1000.00	500.00	1200.00	800.00
TOTALS	75750.00	26520.00	50700.00	20925.00	63400.00	25600.00

```
TOTAL BUDGET - ALL DEPTS    189850.00
TOTAL ACTUAL EXP TO DATE     73045.00
```

The Short List Convention and Three-Dimensional Arrays

The use of the short list convention with three-dimensional arrays is merely an extension of its use with two-dimensional arrays, as discussed earlier in this chapter. When a three-dimensional array is either read into or written from memory using the short list convention, the order of automatic sequencing is column-wise by row *by plane.* For example, reading values into a 3 X 3 X 2 array would have the array locations filled in the following order:

1. column 1, rows 1 through 3, plane 1
2. column 2, rows 1 through 3, plane 1
3. column 3, rows 1 through 3, plane 1
4. column 1, rows 1 through 3, plane 2
5. column 2, rows 1 through 3, plane 2
6. column 3, rows 1 through 3, plane 2

Adding columns, rows, or planes to the size of an array would not alter the order in which the array was filled.

Of course, writing from a three-dimensional array results in the extraction of stored data values in the same order as specified above for loading an array.

Exercise 37   This exercise contains a series of questions related to the example on pages 295 through 299. It will be helpful to refer to the flowchart, list of data names, and the output. The questions will refer to specific lines in the program by citing *compiler* line numbers rather than program statement numbers. The compiler line numbers are found along the extreme left border of the program on page 298.

1. How many storage locations are reserved for the EXP array?
2. How many storage locations are reserved for all the arrays listed (including the EXP array)?
3. DATA statements are used to initialize values in the program.
   a. What is the function of the DATA statement in compiler line 2?
   b. What is the function of the DATA statement in compiler line 3?
4. Draw a schematic of the NAME array showing the correct number of cells. Fill the array with values in accordance with the DATA statement in compiler line 3.
5. Why was the implied DO loop included in the DATA statement on compiler line 3?
6. Review the FORMAT and WRITE statements on compiler lines 4 and 5. What function does the WRITE statement perform?
7. What is the function of each of the following data names as they are used in the READ statement in compiler line 4?
   a. ID   c. KODEXP
   b. KODDEP   d. DATA(J)
8. What types of value will each of the following data names have when each input data card is read?
   a. Budget card:
       (1) ID value   (3) KODEXP value
       (2) KODDEP value   (4) DATA(J) values
   b. Actual expense card:
       (1) ID value   (3) KODEXP value
       (2) KODDEP value   (4) DATA(J) values
   c. Last card:
       (1) ID value   (3) KODEXP value
       (2) KODDEP value   (4) DATA(J) values
9. Explain what happens when the computer encounters the statement in compiler line 8.
10. Explain what processing occurs in compiler lines 9, 10, and 11.
11. Where does the computer find values for the EXP array's three subscripts in compiler line 10?
12. Explain the processing which occurs in compiler line 12.
13. Where does the computer find values for the EXP array's three subscripts in compiler line 12?
14. Explain the processing which occurs in compiler lines 14, 15, 16, and 17.
15. Explain the processing which occurs in compiler lines 18, 19, and 20.
16. Explain how the computer writes the line in accordance with the WRITE statement in compiler line 23.
17. Where does the computer find values for the EXP array's three subscripts in compiler line 23?
18. Explain what processing occurs in compiler lines 25 and 27.

Questions

1. What advantages can be gained by using two-dimensional arrays rather than several one-dimensional arrays?

2. What is meant by the term "column-wise by rows" as it relates to the reading and writing of arrays?

3. Create your own two-dimensional array example and specify its name and dimensions. Write a DIMENSION statement for your array and explain how it specifies column, row, and total memory space to be reserved.

4. Create your own example and explain how nested loops can be used to advantage with two-dimensional arrays.

5. What is the importance of knowing that with nested loops, the inner loop cycles most rapidly? What relationship does this looping concept have with two-dimensional arrays?

6. Explain the relationship between the structure of nested explicit DO loop statements and the structure of implied nested loop statements.

7. Explain the advantage gained through the use of the short list convention as it applies to two-dimensional arrays.

8. What important feature of the short list convention must be planned for when using this language element with two-dimensional arrays?

9. Explain the conceptual difference between two- and three-dimensional array storage.

10. What change is necessary in DIMENSION statements and implied DO loops when arrays are expanded from two to three dimensions?

15

FORTRAN Subprograms

Program instructions explained in earlier sections assumed that completed programs would result from the efforts of a single individual and that programs would read data, process the data, and write information as the end product of a single computer run. Many programs are prepared and processed in this manner. However, there is also the very real possibility that major segments of one program will be needed again, in the same program, or will be useful in other programs. In such situations, the programmer must decide whether to rewrite the same program steps or to find some method for reusing the original program segments.

A second situation which calls for program segmentation relates to the exceedingly large size of some programs. Large programs often require that many programmers work independently on portions of the program and that, upon completion, the individual segments are grouped into a comprehensive program. A master program, called the main program, is then written, and it controls the individual segments. The separate program components are known as *subprograms*. Main programs, by definition, control overall processing and, under this control, call upon subprograms to make available their special processing steps.

The relationship between a main program and two subprograms is shown graphically at the top of page 303.

When a main program calls for the processing capabilities of a subprogram, the computer transfers control to the subprogram and begins executing. Return from the subprogram results in branching back to the main program at the point where the original call was made. The illustration on page 303 shows two separate subprograms being called. It is also possible and appropriate for a main program to repeatedly call the same subprogram for processing.

Subprograms are classified as follows:

1. functions
   a. open (built-in) functions
   b. closed (library) functions
   c. arithmetic statement functions
2. function subprograms
3. subroutine subprograms

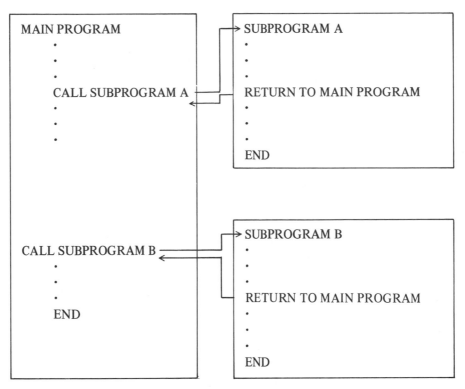

Functions and function subprograms are explained in this chapter. Subroutine subprograms are discussed in Chapter 16.

Functions

Functions are the most easily used members of the subprogram group and are of two types: (1) manufacturer supplied functions and (2) arithmetic statement functions. Functions supplied by a computer manufacturer are included in the FORTRAN compiler. On the other hand, arithmetic statement functions are written by the programmer.

Open or Built-in Functions

The first type of function we will discuss is the *open, or built-in, function.* See Table 15.1 for a list of these functions.

Let us look at an example of these functions, and of functions in general. Suppose that a program requirement calls for computing the *absolute value* of a variable named A. An absolute value is defined as the magnitude of a number without regard to the number's sign (that is, the absolute value of -6.23 is 6.23). Therefore, a computation to find the absolute value of A would require a series of instructions to test and remove the sign. This sequence of instructions could be written by the programmer, but a function is available to complete this task easily. To call the function, a simple statement like that shown below would determine the absolute value.

RESLT = ABS(A)

This statement directs the computer to determine the absolute value of variable A and to store it in a location named RESLT. RESLT, of course, is a variable data name created only for this example. ABS is a special name used to call the function.

Examination of the statement calling the absolute value function shows the following elements:

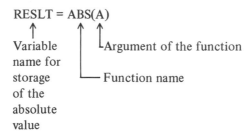

This statement introduces two new elements: the function name and the function argument.

Function Name. Functions supplied by computer manufacturers have standard designated names, as shown in Table 15.1. When the computer compiles a FORTRAN program and encounters a function name, such as ABS, the compiler branches to its stored functions (that is, subprograms) and automatically inserts the function's instructions into the compiled (object) FORTRAN program. Technically, functions are subprograms because they reside outside of the written FORTRAN program. However, when a function is used, it results in the insertion of instructions within the compiled object program. Therefore, it appears that there is no distinction between the main program and the subprogram.

Note the programming power associated with the use of a function name. The programmer needs to write only a single function name, and the result is the generation of several program instructions. Also, to use this subprogram, the programmer does not have to set up any special linkages to the subprogram. This task is handled automatically.

Function Argument. The parentheses following a function name are used to enclose the function argument. In the example above, the argument was the single variable data name (A). An argument may be a variable data name, constant, valid FORTRAN expression, and may also include other functions. As an example of another argument, the following statement would be a legal call for the absolute value function.

RESLT = ABS((A+3.5)/(B*(-8.2)))

> Outer parentheses
> enclose the function
> argument

Several other points may be noted about functions.

1. A function returns only *one value* to the calling program. The value will be the result of applying the function's statements to the argument.

2. The mode of the value returned and its memory location size depend upon the function name used and the size of the variables and constants in the argument. For instance, with absolute value functions the following combinations of mode and size exist:

Function Name	Mode of Function	Mode and Size of Argument	Mode and Size of Returned Value
ABS	real	Real *4	Real *4
IABS	integer	Integer *4	Integer *4
DABS	double precision	Real *8	Real *8

3. Most functions require only one argument within parentheses. A few require more than one argument. When more than one argument is listed, commas must separate them.
4. Any values or expressions which appear within the argument of a function are used only temporarily in executing the function. Any changes in mode or size of values are not permanent and are not saved by the computer.
5. A function may be used only in the expression to the right of the equal sign. A function may never be placed to the left of the equal sign.

Table 15.1 FORTRAN Open Functions

FORTRAN Function Name	Function Meaning	Number of Arguments	Type of Argument	Type of Value Returned
FLOAT	Convert an integer value to	1	Integer *4	Real *4
DFLOAT	a real value	1	Integer *4	Real *8
IFIX	Convert a real value to an	1	Real *4	Integer *4
HFIX	integer value	1	Real *4	Integer *2
SIGN	Give the sign of argument$_2$	2	Real *4	Real *4
ISIGN	to argument$_1$	2	Integer *4	Integer *4
DSIGN		2	Real *8	Real *8
INT	Give the sign of the argument	1	Real *4	Integer *4
AINT	to the largest integer which is	1	Real *4	Real *4
IDINT	$\leqslant$ the argument	1	Real *8	Integer *4
IABS*	Determine the absolute value	1	Integer *4	Integer *4
ABS	of the argument	1	Real *4	Real *4
DABS		1	Real *8	Real *8
MOD	Determine the remainder from	2	Integer *4	Integer *4
AMOD	the division: argument$_1$/argument$_2$	2	Real *4	Real *4
DMOD		2	Real *8	Real *8
DIM	Determine the positive differ-	2	Real *4	Real *4
IDIM	ence if argument$_1$ is $>$ argument$_2$ —otherwise result is 0.	2	Integer *4	Integer *4

Table 15.1 FORTRAN Open Functions (continued)

FORTRAN Function Name	Function Meaning	Number of Arguments	Type of Argument	Type of Value Returned
SNGL	Determine the most significant part of a Real *8 argument	1	Real *8	Real *4
REAL	Obtain the real part of a complex argument	1	Complex *8	Real *4
AIMAG	Obtain the imaginary part of a complex argument	1	Complex *8	Real *4
DBLE	Change a Real *4 argument to Real *8	1	Real *4	Real *8
CMPLX	Express real arguments in the	2	Real *4	Complex *8
DCMPLX	complex mode	2	Real *8	Complex *16

*Two absolute value functions are of the closed type. They appear in Table 15.2.

Table 15.2 FORTRAN Closed Functions

FORTRAN Function Name	Function Meaning	Number of Arguments	Type of Argument	Type of Value Returned
EXP	Calculate the antilogarithm	1	Real *4	Real *4
DEXP	(base e) of the argument	1	Real *8	Real *8
CEXP		1	Complex *8	Complex *8
CDEXP		1	Complex *16	Complex *16
ALOG	Calculate the natural logarithm	1	Real *4	Real *4
DLOG	(base e) of the argument	1	Real *8	Real *8
CLOG		1	Complex *8	Complex *8
CDLOG		1	Complex *16	Complex *16
ALOG10	Calculate the common loga-	1	Real *4	Real *4
DLOG10	rithm (base 10) of the argument	1	Real *8	Real *8
ARSIN	Calculate the arc sine of the	1	Real *4	Real *4
DARSIN	argument	1	Real *8	Real *8
ARCOS	Calculate the arc cosine of the	1	Real *4	Real *4
DARCOS	argument	1	Real *8	Real *8
ATAN	Calculate the arc tangent of the	1	Real *4	Real *4
DATAN	argument	1	Real *8	Real *8
ATAN2	Calculate the arc tangent of	2	Real *4	Real *4
DATAN2	$argument_1$ divided by $argument_2$	2	Real *8	Real *8
SIN	Calculate the trigonometric	1	Real *4	Real *4
DSIN	sine of the argument (argument	1	Real *8	Real *8
CSIN	in radians)	1	Complex *8	Complex *8
CDSIN		1	Complex *16	Complex *16

Table 15.2 FORTRAN Closed Functions (continued)

FORTRAN Function Name	Function Meaning	Number of Arguments	Type of Argument	Type of Value Returned
COS	Calculate the trigonometric	1	Real *4	Real *4
DCOS	cosine of the argument (argu-	1	Real *8	Real *8
CCOS	ment in radians)	1	Complex *8	Complex *8
CDCOS		1	Complex *16	Complex *16
TAN	Calculate the trigonometric	1	Real *4	Real *4
DTAN	tangent of the argument (argu- ment in radians)	1	Real *8	Real *8
COTAN	Calculate the trigonometric	1	Real *4	Real *4
DCOTAN	cotangent of the argument (argument in radians)	1	Real *8	Real *8
SQRT	Calculate the square root of the	1	Real *4	Real *4
DSQRT	argument	1	Real *8	Real *8
CSQRT			Complex *8	Complex *8
CDSQRT			Complex *16	Complex *16
AMAX0	Determine the largest (maximum)	$\geqslant 2$	Integer *4	Real *4
AMAX1	value from the arguments listed	$\geqslant 2$	Real *4	Real *4
MAX0	$(arg_1, arg_2, \ldots, arg_n)$	$\geqslant 2$	Integer *4	Integer *4
MAX1		$\geqslant 2$	Real *4	Integer *4
DMAX1		$\geqslant 2$	Real *8	Real *8
AMIN0	Determine the smallest (mini-	$\geqslant 2$	Integer *4	Real *4
AMIN1	mum value from the arguments	$\geqslant 2$	Real *4	Real *4
MIN0	$(arg_1, arg_2, \ldots, arg_n)$	$\geqslant 2$	Integer *4	Integer *4
MIN1		$\geqslant 2$	Real *4	Integer *4
DMIN1		$\geqslant 2$	Real *8	Real *8
CABS	Determine the absolute value	1	Complex *8	Real *4
CDABS	of the complex argument	1	Complex *16	Real *8

Note: the following functions have been omitted from this table and may be found in the manufacturers' manuals.

hyperbolic tangent
hyperbolic sine
hyperbolic cosine
error function
complemented error function
gamma
log-gamma
conjugate of a complex argument

The term *open* or *built-in* function describes the compiler's technique for insert-ing these functions in the object program. Each time an open function is called, the compiler will insert the function's instructions in the object program. Open func-tions individually do not require many instructions, and their insertion in the object program does not add significantly to the object program's length. However, this does mean that when the same function is used several times in a program, the compiler will make several insertions of the same instructions.

Closed or Library Functions

The second type of function is called a *closed or library function*. These functions (listed in Table 15.2) are called in the same way as are open functions, but the compiler does not insert repeated sets of instructions for each function call. In this case, the compiler will insert only one copy of the function instructions, and if repeated calls for the function are given, reference to the single copy will be made. The compiler automatically takes care of establishing the necessary linkages so that proper cross-references may be made to the function. Closed functions generally require more instructions than open functions.

An often used closed function is the call to calculate the *square root* of a value. This function is called by using the function name SQRT and an argument in parentheses immediately following it. The SQRT function accomplishes the same mathematical result as exponentiating a value to the .5 power. If the variable REP was to have its square root taken, the following instruction would make the calculation:

ANS=SQRT(REP)

Note that the instruction calling for this function has the same construction as the example using the open function on page 304. Closed functions also adhere to the same five points discussed for open functions on page 305.

The following program will illustrate the use of closed functions. We will use the square root (SQRT) function and two additional functions, one open and one closed.

Assume that a firm wants to calculate the economic order quantity for purchasing several types of inventory and that a computer program is written to make these calculations. Let us assume that the firm has less than 50 inventory products.

The economic order quantity (EOQ) for a product is the optimum number of units which will balance inventory usage, costs of ordering and storing, and the purchase price of the inventory units. The following formula is used to calculate EOQ:

$$EOQ = \sqrt{\frac{2 \times \text{annual demand} \times \text{cost @ order}}{\text{unit cost} \times \text{carrying cost as a \% of inventory value}}}$$

The flowchart for finding the EOQ appears in Figure 15.1. The data card format is shown below, and the program's data names appear on page 310. The program and computed output appear in Program 15.1.

The input data card has the following format:

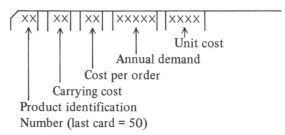

Figure 15.1

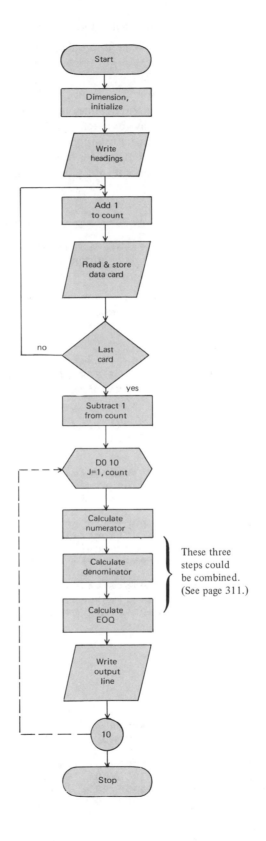

The data names used in the program are:

ID: variable for product identification
CARCST: array for carrying cost of inventory expressed as a per cent of inventory
             value
ORDCST: array for cost of ordering inventory (to nearest dollar)
ANNDMD: array for annual usage of inventory (in units)
UNTCST: array for purchase price per unit for inventory
ANUMR: numerator in formula
DENOM: denominator in formula
EOQ: economic order quantity (in units)

Program 15.1

```
C**************************************************************************
C DIMENSION MEMORY AREAS
C**************************************************************************
1         DIMENSION CARCST(50), ORDCST(50), ANNDMD(50), UNTCST(50), EOQ(50)
C**************************************************************************
C WRITE HEADINGS
C**************************************************************************
2      2 FORMAT (//14X,'CARRYING',2X,'ORDER',3X,' ANNUAL',3X,' UNIT',6X,
          1'ECON-'/5X,'PRODUCT',4X,'COST',5X,'COST',3X,' DEMAND',3X,' COST',
          25X,'ORD-QTY'/)
3         WRITE (6,2)
C**************************************************************************
C READ AND COUNT CARDS, TEST FOR LAST CARD
C**************************************************************************
4         KT = 0
5       4 KT = KT+1
6       5 FORMAT (I2,2X,F2.2,2X,F2.0,2X,F5.0,2X,F4.2)
7         READ (5,5) ID, CARCST(ID), ORDCST(ID), ANNDMD(ID), UNTCST(ID)
8         IF (ID-50) 4,6,6
9       6 KT = KT-1
C**************************************************************************
C CALCULATE EOQ - USE OF "SQRT" FUNCTION (LIBRARY/CLOSED)
C**************************************************************************
10        DO 10 J=1,KT
11        ANUMR = 2.0 * ANNDMD(J) * ORDCST(J)
12        DENOM = UNTCST(J) * CARCST(J)
13        EOQ(J) = SQRT(ANUMR/DENOM)
C**************************************************************************
C WRITE EOQ RESULTS
C**************************************************************************
14      9 FORMAT (7X,I2,7X,F4.2,5X,F3.0,4X,F8.2,2X,F5.2,2X,F10.2)
15        WRITE (6,9) J, CARCST(J), ORDCST(J), ANNDMD(J), UNTCST(J), EOQ(J)
16     10 CONTINUE
17        STOP
18        END
```

PRODUCT	CARRYING COST	ORDER COST	ANNUAL DEMAND	UNIT COST	ECON- ORD-QTY
1	0.18	8.	2000.00	12.25	120.47
2	0.12	22.	3000.00	5.00	469.04
3	0.05	10.	10000.00	1.00	2000.00
4	0.25	15.	8000.00	4.00	489.90
5	0.10	7.	8000.00	2.00	748.33

Note the following items in the above program:

1. The use of the SQRT function in compiler line 13. This call for the closed function appears identical to a call for an open function. The use of this function name results in the automatic calculation of a square root.
2. The three statements on compiler lines 11, 12, and 13 could have been written in a single statement with an extensive argument. This statement would be:

EOQ(J) = SQRT((2.*ANNDMD(J)*ORDCST(J))/(UNTCST(J)*CARCST(J)))

As another illustration using functions, let us extend the assumptions about the EOQ example shown above. In addition to computing the EOQs for each inventory item, the program should find the largest single EOQ. With the sample of 5 EOQs shown above, we see that product 3 with 2000 units is the largest. Actually, the 2000 figure, in a binary machine such as the System 360, is a rounded figure. The actual number of units is 1999+ units. To find the largest EOQ, and have it expressed as an integer value, requires the use of the following two functions:

1. MAX0: to select the largest value (EOQ)
2. IFIX: to convert the EOQ, expressed as a real mode value, to the integer mode

The statements shown in the following program segment (Program 15.2) will accomplish the required EOQ selection and the writing of this value.

Program 15.2

```
C******************************************************************************
C FIND THE LARGEST EOQ - USE OF "MAX0" (CLOSED) FUNCTION.
C CONVERT EOQ TO INTEGER MODE - USE OF "IFIX" (OPEN) FUNCTION.
C******************************************************************************
      LARGE = 0
      DO 12 N=1,KT
   12 LARGE = MAX0(IFIX(EOQ(N)+.05),LARGE)
   15 FORMAT (//5X, 'THE LARGEST EOQ = ', I10)
      WRITE (6,15) LARGE
```

Statement 12 in the above program segment illustrates several important aspects of functions.

LARGE = MAX0 (IFIX (EOQ(N) + .05), LARGE)

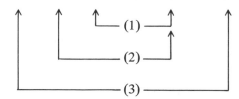

(1) EOQ(N)+.05: this portion of the statement takes each EOQ from the EOQ array and rounds up to the nearest whole value.
(2) IFIX(EOQ(N)+.05): the IFIX function and its argument convert each EOQ to the integer mode. Any fractional value is truncated.
(3) MAX0 (IFIX(EOQ(N) + .05),LARGE): the MAX0 function compares the current value of LARGE with the integer value of EOQ. The largest of these values is stored in LARGE. Note how the function IFIX is executed both as a function and as an argument of the second function (MAX0).

This statement shows how the multiple use of functions may be incorporated into a single statement. In addition, one function may call other functions by listing them in the argument list.

A complete program for computing the EOQs and selecting the largest EOQ appears in Program 15.3 (page 313). This program illustrates the use of three functions: SQRT, MAX0, and IFIX.

Exercise 38

1. Write a FORTRAN statement for each of the following items. In writing these statements, use FORTRAN functions wherever appropriate and possible.
   a. Set variable A to the quotient from dividing the whole value portions of variables X and Y.
   b. Store the remainder from dividing X1 by X2 in variable C.
   c. Store the remainder from dividing N1 by N2 in variable K.
   d. Store the square root of the double precision expression F/G+B**2 in the double precision variable RR.
   e. Store the square root of variable N in variable S.
   f. Select the largest value from the WRONG array (dimensioned at 5000) and store this value in variable NUM. (Hint: use a DO loop in this case.)
   g. Select the smallest value from the MID array (dimensioned at 300 × 200) and store this value in variable KT.
2. Functions are designed to deal with data modes in two important respects: the mode of the function's argument(s) and the mode of the final value returned by the function. These modes determine the function name selected. Indicate the applicable modes for each of the functions listed below.

Mode of Argument	Mode of Argument	Mode of Returned Value
a. DFLOAT	_____	_____
b. IABS	_____	_____
c. ABS	_____	_____
d. EXP	_____	_____
e. DSQRT	_____	_____
f. DEXP	_____	_____
g. SQRT	_____	_____
h. MAX0	_____	_____
i. AMIN1	_____	_____
j. MAX1	_____	_____

3. Identify the errors in each of the following statements.
   a. SQRT(A) = FLOAT(N-3)
   b. NUM = EXP(NCOL)
   c. DD3 = SQRT(FLOAT(N,M))
   d. SMALL = AMIN0(A)
   e. KEEP(K) = ABS(AMOD(FLOAT(N),FLOAT(M)))

Arithmetic Statement Functions

A third type of function is called the *arithmetic statement function*. These functions are written by the programmer; they are not supplied by the computer manufacturer. This distinguishing characteristic sets the arithmetic statement function apart from the open and closed functions discussed above.

Program 15.3

```
      C*******************************************************************
      C DIMENSION MEMORY AREAS
      C*******************************************************************
1           DIMENSION CARCST(50), ORDCST(50), ANNDMD(50), UNTCST(50), EOQ(50)
      C*******************************************************************
      C WRITE HEADINGS
      C*******************************************************************
2         2 FORMAT (//14X,'CARRYING',2X,'ORDER',3X,' ANNUAL',3X,' UNIT',6X,
            1'ECON-'/5X,'PRODUCT',4X,'COST',5X,'COST',3X,' DEMAND',3X,' COST',
            25X,'ORD-QTY'/)
3           WRITE (6,2)
      C*******************************************************************
      C READ AND COUNT CARDS, TEST FOR LAST CARD
      C*******************************************************************
4           KT = 0
5         4 KT = KT+1
6         5 FORMAT (I2,2X,F2.2,2X,F2.0,2X,F5.0,2X,F4.2)
7           READ (5,5) ID, CARCST(ID), ORDCST(ID), ANNDMD(ID), UNTCST(ID)
8           IF (ID-50) 4,6,6
9         6 KT = KT-1
      C*******************************************************************
      C CALCULATE EOQ - USE OF "SQRT" FUNCTION (LIBRARY/CLOSED)
      C*******************************************************************
10          DO 10 J=1,KT
11          ANUMR = 2.0 * ANNDMD(J) * ORDCST(J)
12          DENOM = UNTCST(J) * CARCST(J)
13          EOQ(J) = SQRT(ANUMR/DENOM)
      C*******************************************************************
      C WRITE EOQ RESULTS
      C*******************************************************************
14        9 FORMAT (7X,I2,7X,F4.2,5X,F3.0,4X,F8.2,2X,F5.2,2X,F10.2)
15          WRITE (6,9) J, CARCST(J), ORDCST(J), ANNDMD(J), UNTCST(J), EOQ(J)
16       10 CONTINUE
      C*******************************************************************
      C FIND THE LARGEST EOQ - USE OF "MAX0" (CLOSED) FUNCTION.
      C CONVERT EOQ TO INTEGER MODE - USE OF "IFIX" (OPEN) FUNCTION.
      C*******************************************************************
17          LARGE = 0
18          DO 12 N=1,KT
19       12 LARGE = MAX0(IFIX(EOQ(N)+.05),LARGE)
20       15 FORMAT (//5X, 'THE LARGEST EOQ = ', I10)
21          WRITE (6,15) LARGE
22          STOP
23          END
```

PRODUCT	CARRYING COST	ORDER COST	ANNUAL DEMAND	UNIT COST	ECON- ORD-QTY
1	0.18	8.	2000.00	12.25	120.47
2	0.12	22.	3000.00	5.00	469.04
3	0.05	10.	10000.00	1.00	2000.00
4	0.25	15.	8000.00	4.00	489.90
5	0.10	7.	8000.00	2.00	748.33

THE LARGEST EOQ =   2000

Arithmetic statement functions are *declared* at the very beginning of a program. The declaration must precede the first executable statement in the program and specifies the function names, arguments, and the manipulation that will be executed when the program makes use of the function. The purpose of the arithmetic statement function is to return *one value* to the program, as is true with open and closed functions. In this case, however, the programmer can tailor the function to the specific requirements of his program.

Discussion of the arithmetic statement function is best pursued in the context of an example. Consider the following situation. Assume that a program is to calculate a customer's account receivable balance at the end of a monthly billing period. In calculating the ending account balance, a service charge is to be computed on any unpaid amount remaining from the prior period. For this example, the service charge will be based on the dollar balance remaining from the beginning balance of the period after deducting any amount paid. An assumed service charge of 1.5 percent per month will be used.

If we assume the following facts for a customer:

1. beginning balance of $500
2. purchases during the month of $100
3. payments during the month of $300

then the calculations for his account are:

Service Charge		Ending Balance	
beginning balance	$500.00	beginning balance	$500.00
payments	−300.00	payments	−300.00
remaining balance	$200.00	remaining balance	$200.00
interest rate	× .015	purchases	+100.00
service charge	$ 3.00	service charge	+ 3.00
		ending balance	$303.00

In this example, the instructions to calculate the monthly service charge will be declared as a function in the program. The flowchart for this example appears in Figure 15.2, and the computer program is shown in Program 15.4. The format for the input data card is:

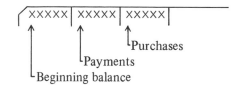

The data names used in the program are:

BBAL: Beginning balance of customer account
PAY: Payments during the month
PUR: Purchases during the month
EBAL: Ending balance of customer account
SCHG: Service charge

Figure 15.2

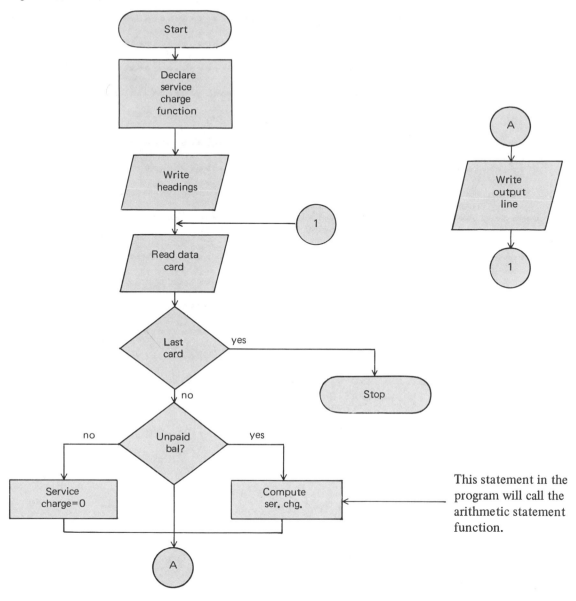

Several new concepts are introduced with the use of an arithmetic statement function. We will discuss these concepts in terms of the service charge example.

The first new concept is the location of a function name to the *left* of the equal sign. This occurs in the statement appearing in compiler line 1. The statement is:

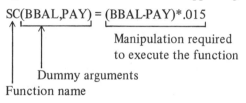

SC(BBAL,PAY) = (BBAL-PAY)*.015

Function name

Dummy arguments

Manipulation required
to execute the function

Program 15.4

```
      C*************************************************************************
      C DECLARE ARITHMETIC STATEMENT FUNCTION
      C*************************************************************************
1           SC(BBAL,PAY) = (BBAL-PAY)*.015
      C*************************************************************************
      C WRITE HEADINGS
      C*************************************************************************
2           WRITE (6,10)
3        10 FORMAT (/1X,'BEG BAL ',2X,'PAYMENTS',2X,'PURCHASES',2X,'SV CHG',
           12X,'END BAL'//)
      C*************************************************************************
      C READ DATA AND TEST FOR UNPAID BALANCE
      C*************************************************************************
4         4 READ (5,5,END=20) BBAL,PAY,PUR
5         5 FORMAT (3F5.0)
6           IF(BBAL-PAY) 7,7,6
      C*************************************************************************
      C CALCULATE SERVICE CHARGE USING THE ARITHMETIC
      C STATEMENT FUNCTION
      C*************************************************************************
7         6 SCHG = SC(BBAL,PAY)
8           GO TO 8
9         7 SCHG = 0.0
      C*************************************************************************
      C CALCULATE ENDING BALANCE
      C*************************************************************************
10        8 EBAL = BBAL - PAY + PUR + SCHG
      C*************************************************************************
      C WRITE RESULTS
      C*************************************************************************
11          WRITE (6,11) BBAL,PAY,PUR,SCHG,EBAL
12       11 FORMAT (1X,3(F8.2,2X),1X,F6.2,2X,F8.2)
13          GO TO 4
14       20 STOP
15          END
```

BEG BAL	PAYMENTS	PURCHASES	SV CHG	END BAL
500.00	300.00	100.00	3.00	303.00
10000.00	8000.00	4000.00	30.00	6030.00
20000.00	21000.00	1000.00	0.00	0.00
60000.00	48000.00	10000.00	180.00	22180.00

This function is known to the program as SC, and, because it was created by the programmer, it had to be *declared* as the first step in the program. Obviously, this is necessary because, unlike the open and closed functions included within the compiler, the computer has no prior reference to the SC function.

Another new concept is the inclusion, within parentheses, of the variables which are to be manipulated when the function is executed. These variables are known as *dummy arguments or variables* in the function declaration statement. The term dummy is used because these variables have no numeric value at the time the declaration is written. When the program is being executed, actual values will be inserted in the function. In summary, the function name (SC) and the variables which the function will use (BBAL, PAY) are listed to the left of the equal sign in the function declaration statement.

The third new concept deals with the specification of the manipulation required of the function. This specification appears to the right of the equal sign. The factors in the manipulation appear to be identical to any executable FORTRAN statement. Generally, this is correct, but actual execution takes place only when the function is called. The declared expression, to the right of the equal sign, must indicate how the dummy variables are to be manipulated.

Several other elements that relate to the use of an arithmetic statement function are:

1. This is the *only time* a function name appears to the left of an equal sign within a main program.
2. A function name may be one to six characters in length. The first character must always be alphabetic, and no special characters may be used in the function name.
3. The name of the function determines whether the value returned is in the real or integer mode. The first letter in the function name establishes the mode. The mode of a function may be altered by using a REAL or INTEGER type statement or by using an IMPLICIT statement. These statements are discussed in Chapter 13.
4. The function will return *one value* to the main program.
5. The dummy arguments (variables) must not be subscripted. As many dummy arguments as are necessary in the function may be listed after the function name.
6. The arguments in a function do not have to be in the same mode as the function.
7. The variables in the expression to the right of the equal sign may not be subscripted.

The SC function in Program 15.4 is called for execution in compiler line 7. This line appears as:

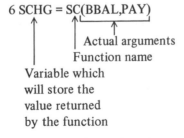

Note how the arithmetic statement function is called by simply using the function name. The service charge calculation in this example is not complicated, but the ease with which its execution may be called illustrates the advantage gained by using a function. This advantage would be compounded if a program required the same execution in several different places.

The statement which *calls* a function also has some specific requirements. The variable data name on the left of the equal sign may be any simple or subscripted variable data name used in the program. It is constructed in accordance with the normal rules for FORTRAN data names. The function name on the right of the equal sign must be identical to the function declared at the beginning of the program. The variable names in parentheses, following the function name, are called *actual arguments*. At the time a function is called, these variables will have actual values. In the program example above, BBAL and PAY have values assigned by the READ statement in compiler line 4. These actual values will be transferred to the arithmetic statement function and will be used in executing the function.

It is critically important to understand the technique for passing data values to a function. This technique is also used with function subprograms and subroutine subprograms. The relationship between a function and its calling statement can be illustrated as:

SC(BBAL,PAY) = (BBAL-PAY)*.015
.
.
.
6 SCHG = SC(BBAL,PAY)

When the program executes statement 6, the actual arguments' values are transferred to the dummy arguments. The actual arguments are transferred to the SC function on a one-for-one basis and in the order of their appearance in the calling statement. In this case, the actual value of BBAL will be transferred to the dummy argument BBAL, and the actual value of PAY will be sent to the dummy PAY. The function is then executed using the actual values transferred to it. In this example, PAY is subtracted from BBAL and the result multiplied by .015. The final product is transferred back to the calling statement and stored in variable data name SCHG.

Program 15.4 used a single function with dummy and actual arguments that had identical names. Neither of these conditions is required. The following program, Program 15.5, uses two arithmetic statement functions and note that the second function does not have dummy and actual argument names which are identical. The program computes customer account balances, as did the previous program, but a function is used to calculate the customer's ending balance.

For the ENDBAL function (compiler line 2), the principles of construction and use are identical to those previously covered. However, observe the relationship between the function and its calling statement.

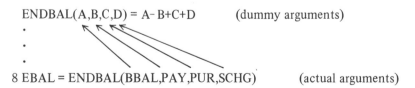

ENDBAL(A,B,C,D) = A-B+C+D   (dummy arguments)
.
.
.
8 EBAL = ENDBAL(BBAL,PAY,PUR,SCHG)   (actual arguments)

Several items should be noted:

1. The dummy argument names and the actual argument names do not agree.
2. Transfer of actual arguments to replace the dummy arguments is made in the order of their appearance, and it is the *values* which are transferred, *not* the names.

Program 15.5

```
      C********************************************************************
      C DECLARE TWO ARITHMETIC STATEMENT FUNCTIONS
      C********************************************************************
 1          SC(BBAL,PAY) = (BBAL-PAY)*.015
 2          ENDBAL(A,B,C,D) = A - B + C + D
      C********************************************************************
      C WRITE HEADINGS
      C********************************************************************
 3          WRITE (6,10)
 4       10 FORMAT (/1X,'BEG BAL ',2X,'PAYMENTS',2X,'PURCHASES',2X,'SV CHG',
           12X,'END BAL'//)
      C********************************************************************
      C READ AND TEST FOR UNPAID BALANCE
      C********************************************************************
 5        4 READ (5,5,END=20) BBAL,PAY,PUR
 6        5 FORMAT (3F5.0)
 7          IF(BBAL-PAY) 7,7,6
      C********************************************************************
      C CALCULATE SERVICE CHARGE USING "SC" FUNCTION
      C********************************************************************
 8        6 SCHG = SC(BBAL,PAY)
 9          GO TO 8
10        7 SCHG = 0.0
      C********************************************************************
      C CALCULATE ENDING BALANCE USING "ENDBAL" FUNCTION
      C********************************************************************
11        8 EBAL=ENDBAL(BBAL,PAY,PUR,SCHG)
      C********************************************************************
      C WRITE RESULTS
      C********************************************************************
12          WRITE (6,11) BBAL,PAY,PUR,SCHG,EBAL
13       11 FORMAT (1X,3(F8.2,2X),1X,F6.2,2X,F8.2)
14          GO TO 4
15       20 STOP
16          END
```

BEG BAL	PAYMENTS	PURCHASES	SV CHG	END BAL
500.00	300.00	100.00	3.00	303.00
10000.00	8000.00	4000.00	30.00	6030.00
20000.00	21000.00	1000.00	0.00	0.00
60000.00	48000.00	10000.00	180.00	22180.00

3. The function declaration specifies the manipulation which is to take place using the values transferred. This function accomplishes the same result as would the following statement:

EBAL = BBAL-PAY + PUR + SCHG

4. The actual arguments received their values either by assignment from the READ statement (variables BBAL, PAY, and PUR) or by a prior calculation (variable SCHG).

This program, of course, illustrates the fact that the same variable names do not have to be used for both actual and dummy arguments. The correct transfer of values will occur as long as the variable data names are listed in the proper order.

It should be apparent that arithmetic statement functions allow one or more arguments to be used, while open and closed functions generally allow only one argument. All functions are written within a main program though they technically are subprograms. Due to this fact, these functions, as a group, are sometimes referred to as "internal" functions. The implication is that they are internal to the main program.

Subprograms

Another major class of subprograms is "external" to a main or "calling" program. These subprograms actually have a series of statements which are physically located outside the main program. The two main classifications of external programs are:

1. function subprograms
2. subroutine subprograms

Each external subprogram has its own processing objective, but normally this objective is in direct support of a calling program. Each subprogram is linked to a calling program, and this usually requires the transfer of data values between them. Data transfer is necessary so that a subprogram may operate on the same values used by the calling program. Data values are *always* transferred to and from *function subprograms.* Subroutines usually will have data values transferred, but in some cases this is not required. The characteristics of subroutines are discussed in the next chapter.

Passing Data Values to and from a Subprogram

The concept of passing data values to a subprogram is very similar to that for functions, discussed on page 318. The rules are the same as those for arithmetic statement functions. The primary difference is that the data values are explicitly passed outside of the calling program. This data movement causes a *second copy* of the values to be stored in memory. The second copy is used by the function or subroutine subprogram. The original copy remains in memory for the calling program. Of course, this means that the amount of storage required for retaining the passed values is doubled.

An example showing the comparative techniques for passing data is shown on **page 321.**

The following important requirements relate to the use of dummy and actual arguments in calling programs and subprograms.

Dummy Arguments.

1. Dummy arguments must correspond to the actual arguments in these respects:
   a. the same *number* of arguments
   b. the same *mode* (though real and integer modes may be used in the same argument list)
   c. the same storage *size* (that is, length in bytes)
   d. the same *order* (that is, arguments are assigned in a one-for-one order between argument lists)

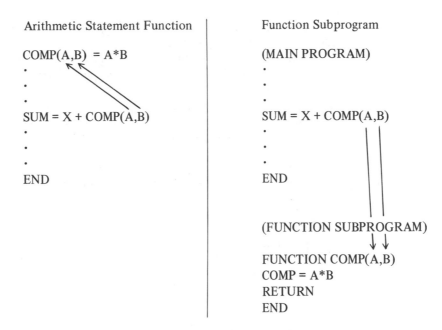

Arithmetic Statement Function

COMP(A,B) = A*B
.
.
.
SUM = X + COMP(A,B)
.
.
.
END

Function Subprogram

(MAIN PROGRAM)
.
.
.
SUM = X + COMP(A,B)
.
.
.
END

(FUNCTION SUBPROGRAM)
FUNCTION COMP(A,B)
COMP = A*B
RETURN
END

2. A dummy argument may be an array reference. When an array is used, an appropriate DIMENSION statement must appear in the function subprogram.

Actual Arguments.

1. An actual argument may be either a subscripted or non-subscripted variable data name.
2. Constants may be transferred as actual arguments.
3. Array names may be used providing that appropriate DIMENSION statements are used in both the calling program and subprogram.
4. An arithmetic expression or logical expression may be the actual argument.
5. An actual argument may be the name of another FUNCTION. In this case, the function name being passed must have been identified by an EXTERNAL statement. This statement is explained later in this chapter.

Function Subprograms

A function subprogram is a self-contained set of instructions. This type of program is subordinate to a main (or calling) program, and execution of a subprogram occurs only when a specific call has been made by the calling program. A function subprogram is composed of multiple statements. This is in sharp contrast to the functions discussed earlier which had only a single statement. However, *a function subprogram returns only one value* to the calling program. This factor corresponds directly with the functions discussed earlier.

A function subprogram is written by the programmer. There are no manufacturer supplied programs of this type. The advantages to using function subprograms fall into two categories. First, the calculation of a value for return to the calling program may require several instructions. This fact would rule out the use of an arithmetic statement function which is only a single statement. Second, when a function is used in several programs, it is possible to insert the function subprogram, intact, in another program.

To illustrate the preparation of a function subprogram, the ENDBAL arithmetic statement function from Program 15.5 will be converted to a function subprogram. This function calculates the ending balance of a customer's account by taking the beginning balance, deducting payments made, and adding any new purchases and/or service charges. The essential program statements for these two types of functions may be compared below.

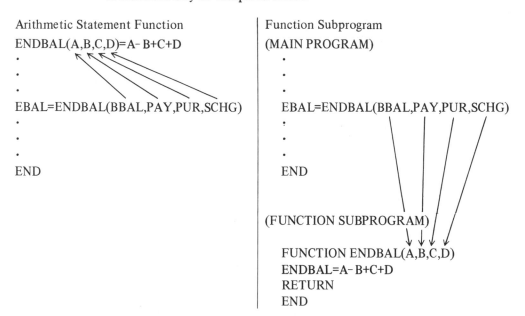

Arithmetic Statement Function
ENDBAL(A,B,C,D)=A-B+C+D
.
.
.
EBAL=ENDBAL(BBAL,PAY,PUR,SCHG)
.
.
.
END

Function Subprogram
(MAIN PROGRAM)
.
.
.
EBAL=ENDBAL(BBAL,PAY,PUR,SCHG)
.
.
.
END

(FUNCTION SUBPROGRAM)
FUNCTION ENDBAL(A,B,C,D)
ENDBAL=A-B+C+D
RETURN
END

The following elements are related to the function subprogram:

1. A function subprogram begins with the word FUNCTION.
2. Following FUNCTION, the name of the function subprogram is given with the non-subscripted dummy arguments shown in parentheses.
3. The function name must appear in the function subprogram to the *left* of an equal sign.
4. The computed value from the subprogram is transferred back to the calling program when the word RETURN (*not STOP*) is encountered. Multiple RETURN statements may appear in a subprogram.
5. An END statement must be located at the physical end of a subprogram.

As explained in the previous section, transfer of data values through related dummy and actual arguments is critical to the working relationship of the calling program and subprogram. Refer to pages 318-320 for a review of the requirements for specifying arguments.

The mode and size of the value returned from a function subprogram may be altered through the use of the REAL, INTEGER, IMPLICIT, and optional memory size specifications. The critical element is to be certain that the changes in mode and size are specified in both the calling program and subprogram. The following examples illustrate this point.

```
(MAIN PROGRAM)                          (MAIN PROGRAM)
   REAL NUM                                INTEGER*2 SUM,A,B
   .                                       .
   .                                       .
   .                                       .
XAX = XIN/NUM(J,K)                      KT= SUM(A,B)*JAX
   .                                       .
   .                                       .
   .                                       .
END                                    END

(FUNCTION SUBPROGRAM)                   (FUNCTION SUBPROGRAM)
   REAL FUNCTION NUM(M,N)                  INTEGER FUNCTION SUM*2(L,N)
   .                                       .
   .                                       .
   .                                       .
NUM=M*N/(J-6)                           SUM=L-(N**5)
   .                                       .
   .                                       .
   .                                       .
RETURN                                 RETURN
END                                    END
```

In this example, the calling program declares NUM in the real mode. This overrides the implied integer mode.

The same change in mode is indicated in the subprogram by declaring the FUNCTION as REAL.

Note that integer arguments are used with this function. After using these arguments, the function will convert the computed value to the real mode for return to the calling program.

In this example, not only is SUM declared in the integer mode, but the optional size of *2 is declared.

The function subprogram also makes these same adjustments by declaring the FUNCTION as INTEGER and the size of SUM as SUM*2.

Note that the calling program also declares A and B as integer mode. This causes them to match the dummy arguments L and N in the function subprogram.

As a final function subprogram example, the customer account balance illustration will be extended one step further. In this program, both the service charge function (SC) and the ending balance function (ENDBAL) will be shown as function subprograms. Therefore, the main program will have to make two separate calls to external subprograms when processing a customer's account. The SC (service charge) subprogram has been written to illustrate how more than one statement may be used in the subprogram. One statement subtracts the amount paid from the beginning balance, and the second statement computes the service charge. In all other respects, this program, which appears in Program 15.6, is identical to the previous program illustration.

Program 15.6

```
      C*****************************************************************
      C MAIN PROGRAM
      C*****************************************************************
      C WRITE HEADINGS
      C*****************************************************************
 1           WRITE (6,10)
 2        10 FORMAT (/1X,'BEG BAL ',2X,'PAYMENTS',2X,'PURCHASES',2X,'SV CHG',
             12X,'END BAL'//)
      C*****************************************************************
      C READ AND TEST FOR UNPAID BALANCE
      C*****************************************************************
 3         4 READ (5,5,END=20) BBAL,PAY,PUR
 4         5 FORMAT (3F5.0)
 5           IF(BBAL-PAY) 7,7,6
      C*****************************************************************
      C CALCULATE SERVICE CHARGE USING "SC" FUNCTION
      C*****************************************************************
 6         6 SCHG = SC(BBAL,PAY)
 7           GO TO 8
 8         7 SCHG = 0.0
      C*****************************************************************
      C CALCULATE ENDING BALANCE BY CALLING "ENDBAL" FUNCTION SUBPROGRAM
      C*****************************************************************
 9         8 EBAL=ENDBAL(BBAL,PAY,PUR,SCHG)
      C*****************************************************************
      C WRITE RESULTS
      C*****************************************************************
10           WRITE (6,11) BBAL,PAY,PUR,SCHG,EBAL
11        11 FORMAT (1X,3(F8.2,2X),1X,F6.2,2X,F8.2)
12           GO TO 4
13        20 STOP
14           END
      C
      C
      C*****************************************************************
      C FUNCTION SUBPROGRAM - "ENDBAL" FUNCTION
      C*****************************************************************


15           FUNCTION ENDBAL (A,B,C,D)
16           ENDBAL = A - B + C + D
17           RETURN
18           END
      C
      C
      C*****************************************************************
      C FUNCTION SUBPROGRAM - "SC" FUNCTION
      C*****************************************************************


19           FUNCTION SC(BBAL,PAY)
20           REMAIN = BBAL-PAY
21           SC = REMAIN*.015
22           RETURN
23           END
```

BEG BAL	PAYMENTS	PURCHASES	SV CHG	END BAL
500.00	300.00	100.00	3.00	303.00
10000.00	8000.00	4000.00	30.00	6030.00
20000.00	21000.00	1000.00	0.00	0.00
60000.00	48000.00	10000.00	180.00	22180.00

Use of the EXTERNAL Statement

Occasionally you will need to call one subprogram from another subprogram. In this circumstance, it is important to distinguish between a main program and a calling program. We can illustrate this relationship schematically as:

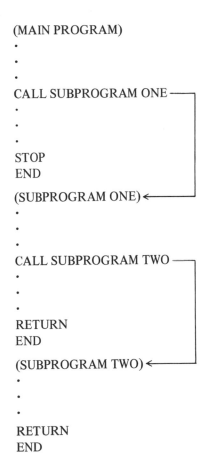

(MAIN PROGRAM)
.
.
.
CALL SUBPROGRAM ONE
.
.
.
STOP
END
(SUBPROGRAM ONE)
.
.
.
CALL SUBPROGRAM TWO
.
.
.
RETURN
END
(SUBPROGRAM TWO)
.
.
.
RETURN
END

In this example, the main program calls subprogram one. The main program is both a calling and a main program. It has ultimate control over all levels of subprograms and transfers this control *temporarily* when calling subprogram one.

Subprogram one is never the main program but does acquire temporary control when called by the main program. This subprogram, in turn, calls subprogram two. It transfers control temporarily to subprogram two with its call. Subprogram two executes its statements after the call from subprogram one. Control is then passed back to subprogram one, *not* to the main program. Finally, subprogram one will return control to the main program.

Nesting of subprogram calls has implications for both the transfer of control and the transfer of data values among programs. When transfer is made among several levels of function subprograms, data values are passed through the use of dummy and actual arguments in a manner nearly identical to the transfer explained earlier.

The essential program instructions taken from the previous example of a customer's account balance will serve to illustrate the transfer of control and data between subprograms. In this example, the main program will call the ENDBAL function subprogram to calculate the customer's ending account balance. This function subprogram will then call on the SC function subprogram to insert any service charge. The service charge is then included in the ENDBAL calculation which is returned, in turn, to the main program.

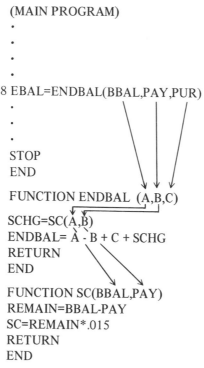

(MAIN PROGRAM)
.
.
.

8 EBAL=ENDBAL(BBAL,PAY,PUR)
.
.
.

STOP
END

FUNCTION ENDBAL (A,B,C)
SCHG=SC(A,B)
ENDBAL= A - B + C + SCHG
RETURN
END

FUNCTION SC(BBAL,PAY)
REMAIN=BBAL-PAY
SC=REMAIN*.015
RETURN
END

Transfer of control among these programs is identical to that described on page 325. Note how the actual arguments in the main program are transferred through the dummy arguments A, B, and C to the ENDBAL subprogram. The main program's actual values of BBAL and PAY are then transferred as the ENDBAL subprogram's actual arguments A and B through the dummy arguments BBAL and PAY to the SC subprogram. The SC subprogram will calculate the service charge and return it to the variable SCHG in the ENDBAL subprogram. This value is then included in the ending balance returned to the main program.

Following the alternating changes between dummy and actual arguments in the above example should clearly illustrate that it is the *values transferred* which are *important*. The particular *variable data names* used are *immaterial*.

A function subprogram name may be transferred as an actual argument between programs. This transfer does present a minor problem, however. The difficulty relates to the fact that the computer is unable to distinguish between a simple variable name and a subprogram name, in an argument list, without some assistance. For instance, using the previous example, if we wrote the calculation for the ending balance as:

8 EBAL=ENDBAL(BBAL,PAY,PUR,SC)

it would appear that SC was an actual argument variable name with a value, as is the case for BBAL, PAY, and PUR. This, of course, is not true. SC is another subprogram. Furthermore, SC is being transferred to the function subprogram ENDBAL. This subprogram has no indication that SC is another external subprogram. To avoid this type of confusion, the *calling* program should indicate that the function subprogram name in the argument list is external to these programs. This indication is made simply by writing the following specification statement:

EXTERNAL SC

This statement will appear in the main program (that is, the calling program) prior to the use of SC in the calling statement.

The use of the EXTERNAL statement is shown below. The previous example has been altered to include the transfer of the SC function subprogram in the argument list calling for the calculation of the customer's ending account balance.

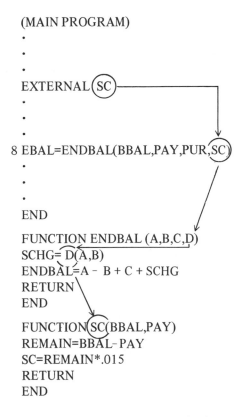

```
(MAIN PROGRAM)
  .
  .
  .
EXTERNAL SC
  .
  .
  .
8 EBAL=ENDBAL(BBAL,PAY,PUR,SC)
  .
  .
  .
END
FUNCTION ENDBAL (A,B,C,D)
SCHG= D(A,B)
ENDBAL=A - B + C + SCHG
RETURN
END
FUNCTION SC(BBAL,PAY)
REMAIN=BBAL-PAY
SC=REMAIN*.015
RETURN
END
```

In this illustration, the external subprogram name is circled. In the main program, the subprogram name (SC) is passed as an actual argument. It has been declared as external in this calling program. In the ENDBAL function subprogram, it takes on the reference name of D. The computer will retain the correct association of name, however. When the function D(A,B) is called, the computer will transfer to the SC function and pass the actual values of A and B as arguments. These values, of course, correspond to the original values of BBAL and PAY. After calculating the service charge, the service charge value and control will be returned to the ENDBAL function. Then, after computing the ending balance, control and the customer's balance will be transferred to the main program.

Exercise 39

1. Read the following sets of instructions. Assume that each set of instructions appears in a main program which also contains the following arithmetic statement function:

GIM(N,A,B)=N + (15.3*B – A/2.4)

In each of the following sets of instructions there is a call for the use of the function. Identify any errors which you find in the instructions and explain what the errors are.

a. REAL N
   SAVE=GIM(N,A,B)

b. INTEGER A,B
   SAVE2=GIM(A,B)

c. INTEGER A,B
   SAVE3=G(N,J,K)

d. REAL N
   DIMENSION N(5)
   SAVE4=GIM(N(1),R,S)

e. REAL N
   SAVE5=GIM(N,ABS(A),T)

f. INTEGER C,F,H
   DIMENSION H(5)
   REAL N,K,M
   SAVE6=GIM(H(15),F,M)

g. INTEGER V,Z
   SAVE7=GIM((J- 3/2,V**2,Z+V- J)

h. EXTERNAL X2
   REAL N
   SAVE8=GIM(X2,G*H,H+G)

i. INTEGER A,B
   DIMENSION N(10)
   SAVE9=GIM(N(1),N(2),N(3))

j. SAVE10=GIM(2,4,6)

2. For each of the following situations, write a single arithmetic statement function to accomplish the necessary computing.

   a. Write a function named COMP which uses three variables A, B, and C. The function is to multiply A and B and then add 4.7 to the product of the multiplication. This total is then divided by C.

   b. Write a function which will calculate the discount (stored in DISC) to be given on all customers' sales orders which are over \$600.00. Use the variables QTY (quantity) and PRICE (sales price per unit) to calculate the sales values. The discount rate is 5 per cent.

   c. Write a function to calculate the result from the following formula:

$$\sqrt{\frac{N(K)}{J - 3.4}}$$

The result should be stored in RESLT, and the variables supplying values for the formula are N, K, and J.

   d. A television station has completed an extensive amount of marketing research to find viewers' preferences. A survey of TV viewers was made, and it is now necessary to determine which station in the area had the highest percentage of viewers at different times during the day. Assume that there are three stations in the area and that they have data on the number of viewers stored in separate arrays named CH2, CH4, and CH5. Each element in an array applies to one hour of the day (therefore, each array is dimensioned at 24) and stores the number of viewers watching the channel during that hour. Write a function to compute the percentage of total viewers which the station with the highest number of viewers had in any one hour. Store the result in TOPS.

3. Take the four situations described in question 2 and, for each, write a function subprogram to make the same computations. Also write the calling statement which would have to appear in the calling program so that access could be made to these subprograms.

4. Write function subprograms for the following situations.
   a. A function named COMP is to have an array (A), dimensioned at 10, summed (totaled), and sent back to the calling program.
   b. A function is to calculate the net cash flows from a proposed investment project. The function named CSHFLO receives three values from the calling program:
      (1) inflows of cash (variable IN)
      (2) outflows of cash (variable OUT)
      (3) a count of the number of periods over which the inflows and outflows have been measured (variable K)

   IN and OUT are arrays with each element storing one period's inflow and outflow of cash, respectively. Assume an equal number of inflows and outflows. Dimension IN and OUT at (50).

   The function subprogram should compute the *net* cash flow (that is, IN—OUT) for all periods and return this value to the calling program.

Questions

1. Under what circumstances are subprograms both necessary and advantageous to program preparation?
2. Explain the conceptual relationship between a calling program and a subprogram.
3. What are functions? Explain the difference between the following types of functions:
   a. open functions
   b. closed functions
   c. arithmetic statement functions
4. What is the significance and purpose of a function's argument(s)?
5. Why do arithmetic statement functions have to be declared? What purpose is served by the declaration?
6. What are dummy and actual arguments? What is their purpose?
7. What distinguishes a function subprogram from a function?
8. How many values are returned to a calling program from functions and function subprograms? How are the mode and size of the value(s) determined?
9. What is the purpose served by STOP, END, and RETURN statements in calling and function subprograms?
10. Explain what an EXTERNAL statement is and when its use is required.

16
FORTRAN Subroutines

Function subprograms discussed in Chapter 15 were labeled as "external" because they were explicitly written as self-contained program units outside of a calling program. The subroutine subprogram is a second type of external subprogram. Its construction is very similar to that of the function subprogram. The subroutine subprogram:

1. is written by the programmer
2. is composed of multiple statements
3. is called by a main program or other subroutines
4. may have data values transferred through arguments
5. returns control to the calling program with a RETURN statement
6. uses an END statement to demark the final statement in the program

Of course, subroutines and functions subprograms are different in several ways:

1. More than one value may be returned from a subroutine.
2. While values are normally returned, this is not a requirement. A subroutine does not have to return a value to the calling program.
3. A subroutine does not have a mode associated with its name. The individual values within a subroutine will have associated modes, but the subroutine itself is neutral.
4. Subroutines are called by a statement explicitly using a CALL command.

A subroutine, like a function subprogram, is a self-contained set of instructions which may be called for execution by another program (that is, main program or other subroutine). A subroutine is written once and is compiled as a separate FORTRAN program unit. Only one copy of a subroutine is stored in memory, and transfer is made to this copy each time the subroutine is called. Because of this characteristic, subroutines are classified as one type of "closed" subprogram. Subroutines may then be viewed as "packaged" subprograms available for multiple use by one calling program and also available for use in different programs by incorporating them as complete units. Schematically, a main program which uses one subroutine several times would appear as:

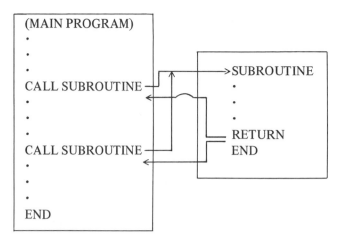

A calling program uses the CALL statement to initiate transfer of control to the subroutine. The subroutine returns control when a RETURN statement is encountered. Control is returned to the *first executable statement following the CALL* statement which originally caused branching to the subroutine. This same channel of control transfer to and from a subroutine is used with each CALL to the subroutine.

From the diagram above, we see that there are two critical action commands included within calling (main) programs and subroutines. These commands enable one program to *call* the subroutine and provide the subroutine with a way to *return* to the calling program. Appropriately, the command words used for these actions are CALL and RETURN. In addition, two other important FORTRAN words are used in all subroutines: SUBROUTINE and END.

The CALL Command

When one program needs to use a subroutine, it calls the subroutine by using the command word CALL coupled with the name of the subroutine to be called. For example, if a subroutine is named CALC, we must use the following CALL statement in the calling program:

CALL CALC

When the computer encounters a CALL command, transfer of control is made to the subroutine, and processing is continued in accordance with the program steps in the subroutine.

In addition to the call for a named subroutine, when data values are to be passed to the subroutine, the use of dummy and actual arguments are employed. (See Chapter 15.) Arguments are used in the same manner as described in Chapter 15 with *one important exception:* A subroutine and calling program may exchange *multiple* values *to and from* each program through the argument lists. In addition, a calling program and subroutine do not have to exchange any values (that is, they may have the argument lists omitted). This exception is, of course, in direct contrast to the use of argument lists with functions and function subprograms. At least one argument is required with those types of subprograms.

In summary, a CALL statement is composed of the following elements:

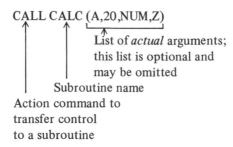

CALL CALC (A,20,NUM,Z)

List of *actual* arguments;
this list is optional and
may be omitted

Subroutine name

Action command to
transfer control
to a subroutine

The SUBROUTINE Name Statement

When a subroutine is called, the subroutine name in the CALL statement is matched with the same name in a SUBROUTINE statement. A subroutine name is restricted only in that it must fit the allowable number of characters for a FOR-TRAN variable name. The name may begin with any alphabetic character, but no mode is related to it. Data modes are related to each variable used within a subroutine but not to the subroutine name. The word SUBROUTINE *must* be used to identify a subroutine unit, and this identification, along with the assigned subroutine name, *must* be the *first* statement in the subroutine. The following relationship exists between a CALL statement and SUBROUTINE name:

Calling Program	Subroutine
CALL CALC(A,20,NUM,Z)	SUBROUTINE CALC(A,20,NUM,Z)

The calling (main) program contains *actual* arguments in its argument list. The subroutine contains a list of *dummy* arguments. The dummy arguments will be replaced by the values of the actual arguments when the subroutine is called. Furthermore, the calling program has access to *all* of the arguments *after* the subroutine has finished executing. This is a major and significant difference between function subprograms and subroutines. A subroutine may use any or all of its arguments to return values to the calling program. In other words, any argument in the subroutine's list has its value available for the calling program when control is returned from the subroutine. In this fashion, a free flow of values moves between a calling program and a subroutine.

Consider the following simple example.

```
(MAIN PROGRAM)
  B = 0.0
  A = 5.0
  CALL MULT(A,B)
5 FORMAT (5X,F10.2)
  WRITE (6,5) B
  STOP
  END

(SUBROUTINE SUBPROGRAM)
  SUBROUTINE MULT(A,B)
  B = A * 2.0
  RETURN
  END
```

The main program initially sets variable A to a value of 5.0 and B to 0.0. A call is then made to subroutine MULT, and the actual arguments A and B are transferred to the subroutine. The subroutine replaces its dummy argument A with the actual value of 5.0 and dummy argument B with 0.0. A is then multiplied by 2.0, and the value of B is set at 10.0. The values of A and B are then transferred back to the main program through the argument list and are available for use in the calling program. The value of 10.0 is displayed as output by writing B. A, which still has a value of 5.0, is not used by the main program.

The explanation of dummy and actual arguments in Chapter 15 indicated that the argument lists must match with respect to:

1. number of arguments
2. mode of arguments
3. length (size) of arguments
4. order of arguments

The following four examples each illustrates an *error* with respect to one of these requirements.

Calling Program   Subroutine Subprogram

1. CALL ABC(X,Y,Z)   SUBROUTINE ABC(A,B,C,D)

   Error: number of arguments in each list does not match.

2. CALL NUM(A,J,X)   SUBROUTINE NUM(N,M,Z)

   Error: modes of first argument in each list do not match (A and N).

3. DIMENSION P(5)   SUBROUTINE ZIP(K,KP,P)
   CALL ZIP(20,P,JAX)   DIMENSION P(5)

   Error: the order does not match (array P occupies positions 2-6 in the calling program and positions 3-7 in the subroutines).

4. INTEGER*2 NN   SUBROUTINE KAT(SS,KT)
   CALL KAT(NN,50)   INTEGER*2 SS,KT

   Error: length of arguments does not match (50 in calling program is of the implied length of integer *4, but its matching argument KT in the subroutine is declared as integer *2).

Note that the same names *do not* have to be used in both dummy and actual argument lists.

In summary, the SUBROUTINE statement possesses the following components:

SUBROUTINE CARDS(NIT,22.5,X,NUM)

List of *dummy* arguments;
this list is optional and
may be omitted.

Subroutine name

FORTRAN specification
used to indicate the
beginning of a group
of instructions to be
handled as a subroutine

The RETURN Statement

When a subroutine has been executed, the use of a RETURN command directs the computer to return control and the value(s) computed to the main or calling program. This command causes the computer to resume processing with the *first executable statement* following the CALL command which called the subroutine. The RETURN statement indicates the *logical conclusion* of a subroutine. Therefore, the RETURN statement results in transfer of both control and data values to the calling program.

The END Statement

All subroutines must have an END statement as the last statement in the program. This is a non-executable statement and signals the *physical end* of the subroutine to the compiler.

A Subroutine Illustration

We will use the following example to illustrate the development of a main program and several supporting subroutines. Assume that a program is to sort several values which are in no specific order. The program will sort the values into ascending order and will write the ordered values. This situation is similar to one where data items, such as inventory numbers, customer account numbers, product numbers, insurance policy numbers, or employee numbers, need sorting prior to further processing. For simplicity, only five numbers will be used in this initial example.

This program will initialize the five data values rather than inputing them through a READ statement. The algorithm employed for sorting the values uses the "exchange" technique. This technique allows the smallest values to rise to the top of a list by making repeated passes through the original list of values.

The sorting technique requires the following steps:

1. The first value in the unsorted list is compared with all others in the list, one at a time.
2. When a value is found which is less than the first value in the list, the two values will be exchanged.
3. After passing through the complete list, the smallest value will work up to the first position in the list.
4. The process is then repeated by comparing the second value in the list to all the remaining values.
5. When a value smaller than the second value is found, the two values will be exchanged.
6. After completing a second pass through the list, the second smallest value will move up to the second position in the list.
7. This process is then repeated comparing all remaining values to the third value and so on.

The diagram on page 335 shows the exchanges required with each "pass," or comparison, to move from the original unsorted list to the sorted list.

The final value which has risen to the top of the list after each pass is circled in the diagram. The first pass through the list required two exchanges. These were exchanges of the values 9 and 3 and of 3 and 1. The second pass exchanged 9 and 7,

Original List	Compare to Position 1	Compare to Position 2	Compare to Position 3	Compare to Position 4	Sorted List
9	3				1
3	9	7 5 3			3
7	7 9	9 9 9	7 5		5
5	5 7	5 7 7	9 9	7	7
1	1 5	3 3 5	5 7	9	9
	3				
	(Two Exchanges)	(Three Exchanges)	(Two Exchanges)	(One Exchange)	

7 and 5, and 5 and 3. The third pass exchanged 9 and 7 and 7 and 5. The last pass exchanged 9 and 7.

Note that with five values only four passes through the list were required. This, of course, is related to the fact that after the fourth pass only the fifth number remains from the original list. It has no other values to be compared with and automatically assumes the last position in the sorted list.

The detailed steps used to exchange any two values are:

Step 1.   Move one value to a temporary storage area.
Step 2.   Move the other value into the position previously held by the first value.
Step 3.   Move the temporarily stored original value into the position of the second value.

Each of these steps is shown below to illustrate the first exchange made in "pass" 1.

Step 1 Original List		Step 2 List		Step 3 List		Adjusted List
9	9	3	9	3	9	3
3		3		9		9
7	TEMP	7	TEMP	7	TEMP	7
5		5		5		5
1		1		1		1

A flowchart and program to sort the values and write the sorted values are shown in Figure 16.1 and Program 16.1.

Essentially, there are four sections to the program:

1. initialization (compiler lines 1 through 3)
2. writing headings (compiler lines 4 through 5)
3. the sorting routine (compiler lines 6 through 13)
4. writing the sorted list (compiler lines 14 through 17)

Figure 16.1

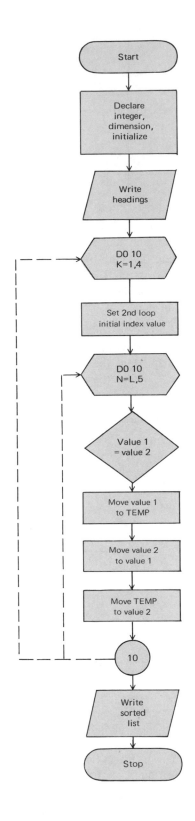

Program 16.1

```
C***********************************************************
C MAIN PROGRAM
C***********************************************************
1           INTEGER TEMP
2           DIMENSION LIST(5)
3           DATA LIST/9,3,7,5,1/
4         5 FORMAT (//10X,'SORTED LIST'/
          110X,'ITEM',2X,'VALUE'/)
5           WRITE (6,5)
6           DO 10 K=1,4
7           L = K+1
8           DO 10 N=L,5
9           IF (LIST(N).GE.LIST(K)) GO TO 10
10          TEMP = LIST(K)
11          LIST(K) = LIST(N)
12          LIST(N) = TEMP
13       10 CONTINUE
14       20 FORMAT (12X,I1,5X,I1)
15          WRITE (6,20) (J,LIST(J),J=1,5)
16          STOP
17          END
```

```
SORTED LIST
ITEM  VALUE

 1     1
 2     3
 3     5
 4     7
 5     9
```

To illustrate the use of subroutines, we will alter the program in Program 16.1 so that a subroutine is called to write the headings. This subroutine will require *no* transfer of data values and appears in Program 16.2

Note that the subroutine shown in Program 16.2 executes only the printing of output headings. Therefore, it is not necessary to share data values between the main (calling) program and the subroutine. The CALL and SUBROUTINE statements contain no arguments. This illustrates a major difference between subroutines and function subprograms. Function subprograms always require the return of one value.

Let us expand our example by further segmenting the program into other subroutines. In Program 16.3, an altered program presents the use of three subroutines. These subroutines will write headings, sort the data values, and write the values. The two new subroutines require the transfer of data values. In these cases, the LIST array is used as an argument in calling both the sort subroutine and the subroutine which writes the sorted list.

Several items are worthy of note in Program 16.3.

1. The main program serves only as a controller over the three subroutines. The main program contains three successive CALL statements. When the first CALL is completed, control is transferred directly to the second CALL statement

Program 16.2

```
      C***************************************************
      C MAIN PROGRAM
      C***************************************************
 1           INTEGER TEMP
 2           DIMENSION LIST(5)
 3           DATA LIST/9,3,7,5,1/
 4           CALL HEAD
 5           DO 10 K=1,4
 6           L = K+1
 7           DO 10 N=L,5
 8           IF (LIST(N).GE.LIST(K)) GO TO 10
 9           TEMP = LIST(K)
10           LIST(K) = LIST(N)
11           LIST(N) = TEMP
12        10 CONTINUE
13        20 FORMAT (12X,I1,5X,I1)
14           WRITE (6,20) (J,LIST(J),J=1,5)
15           STOP
16           END
      C***************************************************
      C SUBROUTINE TO WRITE HEADINGS

17           SUBROUTINE HEAD
18         5 FORMAT (//10X,'SORTED LIST'/
           110X,'ITEM',2X,'VALUE'/)
19           WRITE (6,5)
20           RETURN
21           END
```

This CALL statement causes control to be transferred to the subroutine named HEAD. No indication is given that data values are to be transferred. This is evident by the absence of an argument list in the CALL statement.

Control is returned from the subroutine to the first executable statement following the CALL.

The SUBROUTINE HEAD statement is the point to which control is transferred from the main program.

The RETURN statement causes control to be returned to the main program.

```
      SORTED LIST
      ITEM   VALUE

        1      1
        2      3
        3      5
        4      7
        5      9
```

sending the computer to the second subroutine. After completing the second CALL, control is again sent out from the main program to the third subroutine.

2. The LIST array is shared with the second and third subroutines through the argument lists. While the main program specifies a DIMENSION of 5 locations for LIST, subroutines two and three also provide for DIMENSIONs of five locations. This results in a total of 15 memory locations being reserved for the data in the passed array.

3. The SORT subroutine is now the only program using the variable TEMP. Therefore, it is necessary to move the INTEGER declaration statement from the main program to the SORT subroutine. This change illustrates the independent nature of subroutines. If the implied mode of the variable TEMP is not overriden *in the subroutine,* the subroutine would handle TEMP in the real mode. This INTEGER declaration could not have been transferred through the argument lists.

Program 16.3

```
      C**************************************************
      C MAIN PROGRAM
      C**************************************************
1           DIMENSION LIST(5)
2           DATA LIST/9,3,7,5,1/
3           CALL HEAD
4           CALL SORT(LIST)
5           CALL OUTPUT(LIST)
6           STOP
7           END
      C**************************************************
      C SUBROUTINE TO WRITE HEADINGS

8           SUBROUTINE HEAD
9         5 FORMAT (//10X,'SORTED LIST'/
           110X,'ITEM',2X,'VALUE'/)
10          WRITE (6,5)
11          RETURN
12          END
      C**************************************************
      C SUBROUTINE TO SORT VALUES

13          SUBROUTINE SORT(LIST)
14          INTEGER TEMP
15          DIMENSION LIST(5)
16          DO 10 K=1,4
17          L = K+1
18          DO 10 N=L,5
19          IF (LIST(N).GE.LIST(K)) GO TO 10
20          TEMP = LIST(K)
21          LIST(K) = LIST(N)
22          LIST(N) = TEMP
23       10 CONTINUE
24          RETURN
25          END
      C**************************************************
      C SUBROUTINE TO WRITE OUTPUT

26          SUBROUTINE OUTPUT(LIST)
27          DIMENSION LIST(5)
28       20 FORMAT (12X,I1,5X,I1)
29          WRITE (6,20) (J,LIST(J),J=1,5)
30          RETURN
31          END
```

These successive CALL statements cause the main program to serve only as a controller for transferring control to the subroutines.

This subroutine functions only to write output headings. No data values need to be transferred. Therefore, arguments are omitted.

This RETURN transfers control back to the main program. Control is then immediately given to the subroutine SORT.

This subroutine sorts the input values. These values are sent down from the main program through the LIST argument.

This RETURN sends control to the main program. The main program will have access to the sorted values through the LIST argument shared with the SORT subroutine. This transfer results in an immediate switching of control to the subroutine OUTPUT.

This subroutine writes the sorted list of values. The values are sent to the subroutine through the LIST argument.

This is the final RETURN to the main program. After this transfer is made, the STOP command is executed, and processing is complete.

```
      SORTED LIST
      ITEM  VALUE

        1     1
        2     3
        3     5
        4     7
        5     9
```

Let us consider another example of subroutine use. Assume that a main program is to read data cards containing inventory information. The purpose of the program is to compute the final dollar balance for each inventory item. The data cards contain inventory identification numbers and dollar values for beginning balances, receipts, and shipments during one month. Output will be listed in ascending order by inventory number. The data cards, however, are not in ascending order when read, and a sort subroutine is called to put them in order. After sorting, the ending balances will be calculated and printed.

We will use the sorting algorithm illustrated on page 335. However, a two-dimensional array will be used for storing the input values. This necessitates a modification in the sorting subroutine so that, when an exchange is made, all four elements (inventory number, beginning balance, receipts, and shipments) will be exchanged. If only the inventory numbers were sorted, the inventory dollar values would be associated with the wrong inventory numbers.

This program passes a two-dimensional array to the subroutine as well as a count of the inventory cards read. This count is used to calculate the DO loop parameters in the sorting subroutine.

The data card format and a schematic of the two-dimensional array are shown below. A flowchart and program for this example are presented in Figure 16.2 and Program 16.4, respectively.

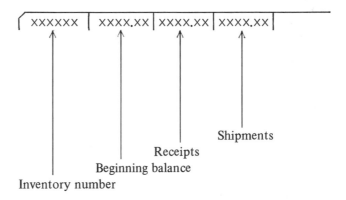

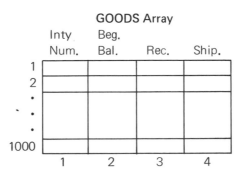

Figure 16.2

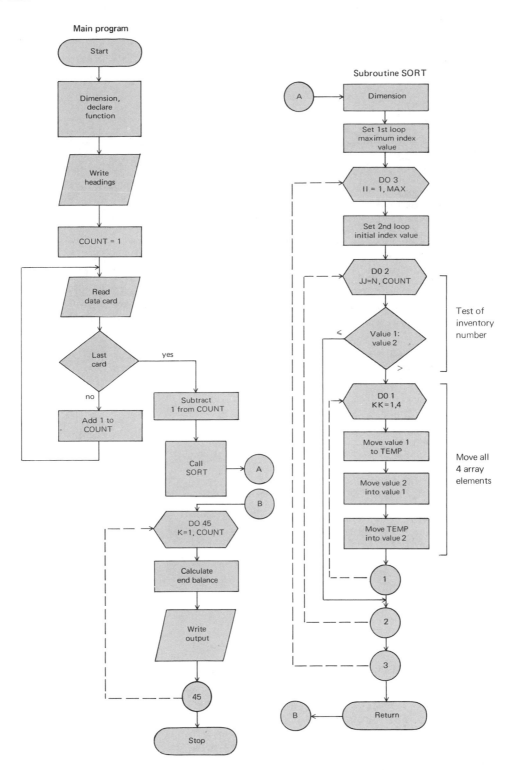

Program 16.4

```
C***************************************************************
C MAIN PROGRAM
C***************************************************************
      DIMENSION GOODS(1000,4)
      ENDBAL(BB,REC,SHIP) = BB + REC - SHIP
   10 FORMAT(/9X,'INTY NR',2X,'BEG BAL ',2X,'RECEIPTS',
     12X,'SHIPMENTS',2X,'END BAL'//)
      WRITE (6,10)
      KOUNT = 1
   15 FORMAT (F6.0, 3(2X,F7.2)) ·
   16 READ (5,15) (GOODS(KOUNT,N), N=1,4)
      IF (GOODS(KOUNT,1).EQ.9.0) GO TO 25
   20 KOUNT = KOUNT + 1  ◄─────────────────────────── This statement counts the
      GO TO 16                                        data cards read.
   25 KOUNT = KOUNT - 1
C***************************************************************
C CALL SUBROUTINE TO SORT INVENTORY NUMBERS
C IN ASCENDING ORDER
C***************************************************************
      CALL SORT (GOODS, KOUNT) ◄────────────────────── The CALL statement trans-
      DO 45 K = 1,KOUNT                                fers both the data array and
      EBAL = ENDBAL(GOODS(K,2), GOODS(K,3), GOODS(K,4))  the count of inventory items
      WRITE (6,41) (GOODS(K,N), N=1,4), EBAL          read through the actual argu-
   41 FORMAT (9X, F7.0, 4(2X, F8.2))                  ment list.
   45 CONTINUE
      STOP
      END
C***************************************************************·
C SUBROUTINE SUBPROGRAM - SORT
C***************************************************************
                                                       The subroutine receives the
                                                       array and data count through
      SUBROUTINE SORT(DUMMY, KOUNT) ◄──────────────    the dummy list.
      DIMENSION DUMMY(1000,4)
      MAX = KOUNT - 1  ◄─────────────┐                 Note how the data count is
      DO 3 II=1,MAX                  │                 used to calculate the DO loop
      NN = II + 1                    ├───────────────  parameters.
      DO 2 JJ = NN,KOUNT  ◄──────────┘
      IF (DUMMY(II,1) - DUMMY(JJ,1))2,2,4
    4 DO 1 KK=1,4                         ┐            This interior loop exchanges
      TEMP = DUMMY(II,KK)                 │            all four elements related to an
      DUMMY(II,KK) = DUMMY(JJ,KK)  ◄──────┤            inventory number.
      DUMMY(JJ,KK) = TEMP                 ┘
    1 CONTINUE
    2 CONTINUE
    3 CONTINUE
      RETURN
      END
```

INTY NR	BEG BAL	RECEIPTS	SHIPMENTS	END BAL
22345.	98000.50	50000.00	58000.00	90000.50
123456.	10000.00	20000.00	25000.00	5000.00
135790.	15000.00	0.00	12750.50	2249.50
552468.	530.00	620.00	1000.00	150.00

Exercise 40

1. For each of the following subroutine CALL statements, write an appropriate subroutine name statement.
   a. CALL ONCE (R,2,S,5.6)
   b. CALL COMPAR (N(1),P-Q,Q)
   c. CALL NUMBR (J,K,Z,J2)
   d. CALL TEAM (GLE,WNG,CNTR)
   e. CALL WHEN (MEX,ABLE)

2. Read each of the following subroutine name statements. Identify and explain any errors in these statements.
   a. SUBROUTINE AA(1.5,S,L)
   b. SUBROUTINE Z1(J2,K(5))
   c. SUBROUTINE (J,P,L)
   d. SUBROUTINE STP(R**2,S,V)
   e. SUBROUTINE ABC(ON,THE,AIR)

3. The following subroutine contains seven errors. What are they?

SUBPROGRAM TEST X,Y,Z	Errors
DO 10 K 5,20,3	
X Y*Z+K	1 _____
A=A+X**2	
CONTINUE	
3 FORMAT (5X,F10.2)	2 _____
WRITE (6,3) A	3 _____
CALL TEST	
END	

4 _____

5 _____

6 _____

7 _____

4. Write a subroutine to compute the balance in a checking account. Assume these facts:
   a. The subroutine name is BANK.
   b. The beginning balance is in variable BBAL which is sent to the subroutine by the calling program.
   c. All deposits are stored in the DEP array in the calling program. The array is dimensioned at 20.
   d. Checks paid by the bank are stored in the CHK array, in the calling program, dimensioned at 50.
   e. A count of the number of deposits is in variable K and a count of the checks in variable N. Both are in the calling program.
   f. The service charge for the period is in variable SC in the calling program.
   g. The ending balance should be sent back to the calling program through variable EBAL.

The COMMON Statement

All previous examples which required programs to share data values have used actual and dummy arguments to accomplish data transfer. One characteristic of this transfer technique is the allocation of memory locations once for data values in the calling program and a second allocation of an equal amount of memory for storing the values in the subprogram. This use of memory is illustrated below:

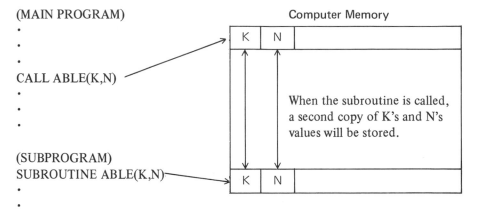

Obviously, the number of memory locations used with argument lists is twice as large as the number of variables and/or array locations specified. An alternative approach to sharing data values is available. This alternative eliminates the multiple storage of the same values and uses a specification statement identified by the word COMMON. A COMMON statement which would be used to replace the argument lists shown in the illustration above is written as follows:

COMMON K,N

Following the word COMMON, the shared variables and/or array names are listed. These variables are now *deleted* from the CALL and SUBROUTINE name statements. Each program which is to share data values must contain a COMMON statement. The previous illustration, modified to use COMMON statements, would appear as follows:

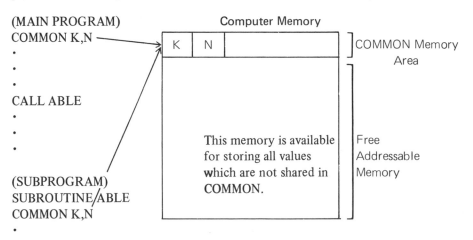

The COMMON memory area is a special portion of computer memory containing variables and arrays whose values are shared by several programs. Use of COMMON memory provides data sharing without the need to recopy data values.

When a COMMON statement is encountered, memory locations are assigned, for each variable and/or array, beginning with location one in the COMMON memory area. Memory locations are assigned consecutively until the list of variables in the COMMON statement is exhausted.

When COMMON statements are encountered in subprograms, the variable and/or array names in these programs are also assigned to the COMMON memory area *beginning with location one*. This assignment technique makes it critical that all variables and/or arrays shared in COMMON memory conform to:

1. the same order
2. the same mode
3. the same size (in bytes) and array sizes
4. the same number of variables

Variable names used in COMMON statements are *not* subscripted and may be names from either the integer or real modes. Constants may *not* be listed in a COMMON statement. When a variable name represents an array, normally the size of the array will be specified in an accompanying DIMENSION statement. In this fashion, the compiler is able to allocate the appropriate number of consecutive memory locations for the array.

The following illustration shows how a main program and subroutine would allocate COMMON memory when both programs use the same variable and array names.

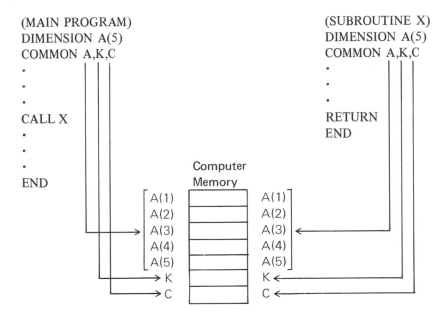

These programs use seven common memory locations. The order of names, mode of names, equal size of memory locations, and use of an equal number of variables meet the requirements cited earlier. The requirement for having an equal number of names could result in the need to force this equality. When one program does not require the use of all the variables in COMMON memory, dummy variable names may be inserted to align the memory locations properly. For instance, if a main program has declared the variables A, B, and C in a COMMON statement, the first three COMMON memory locations will be assigned to these variables. A subroutine, however, may need only the use of variable C (other subroutines may need all three variables). The subroutine cannot declare only variable C in a COMMON statement because it would be associated with the same memory location as variable A. This *incorrect* relationship between the COMMON allocations would appear as:

Main Program   COMMON A,B,C   mismatched variables

Subroutine   COMMON C

To force the *proper alignment* of the variables, the subroutine should have two dummy variables (X and Y in this example) inserted in the COMMON statement. The relationship between COMMON statements then becomes:

Main Program   COMMON A,B, C   matched variables

Subroutine   COMMON X,Y, C

It is not necessary to have the same variable names used in all COMMON statements. The important element is the sharing of memory locations and their contents, not the sharing of location names. The following illustration demonstrates the allocation of COMMON memory when programs use different variable and array names.

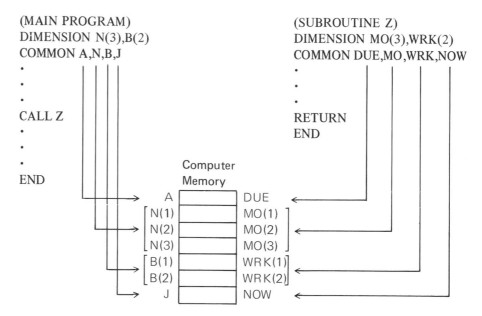

```
(MAIN PROGRAM)
DIMENSION N(3),B(2)
COMMON A,N,B,J
 .
 .
 .
CALL Z
 .
 .
 .
END
```

```
(SUBROUTINE Z)
DIMENSION MO(3),WRK(2)
COMMON DUE,MO,WRK,NOW
 .
 .
 .
RETURN
END
```

This illustration matches the order, mode, size, and number of variables in COMMON although neither program uses the same names.

Using the COMMON Statement to Dimension Arrays

A modification which may be made in the COMMON statement is the inclusion of array dimensions within the COMMON statement. This capability reduces the need for DIMENSION statements but gives the proper array size specifications needed for memory allocation. For example, the COMMON statements in the previous example could be modified as follows:

Main Program   Subroutine
COMMON A,N(3),B(2),J   COMMON DUE,MO(3),WRK(2),NOW

The only change necessary in the COMMON statements is inclusion of the array size, in parentheses, following each array name.

The final example in this chapter will be a payroll application which illustrates a program using several subroutines. Let us assume that this payroll application calls for a program which will:

1. read employee data on time, rates of pay, and deductions
2. calculate gross pay for the period
3. calculate the income tax to be withheld
4. calculate health insurance deductions (which are optional)
5. record any savings bond deductions (also optional)
6. calculate the total deductions for the period
7. calculate the net pay for the period
8. print payroll headings
9. print the payroll data calculated for each employee

This example will illustrate only an hourly payroll. However, several segments of the program can also be utilized for employees paid on other bases, such as salary or piece-rate. An illustration in Chapter 17 demonstrates this usage.

The program in this section exchanges a large amount of data between subroutines and, for this task, COMMON statements are used. The basic processing sequence in this program uses the main program to read the information for each employee and, then, calls two subroutines which calculate the gross pay and payroll deductions, respectively. After all employee data has been read, two additional subroutines are called. One writes headings for the payroll and the other displays the computed payroll information.

A flowchart for this program is shown in Figure 16.3 on pages 350-351. The format for input data cards is shown below, along with a sketch of the HOURLY array which stores the payroll information as it is calculated. The program assumes that no more than 1000 employees will be included on the payroll and that the data cards are in ascending order by employee number.

Input Data Card

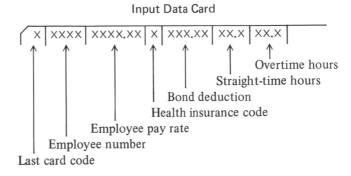

Assume:

1. last card has a 9 in column 1
2. health insurance code is: 1 = yes, 2 = no. The insurance deduction is 5 per cent of gross pay.
3. bond deduction is a dollar amount authorized by the employee
4. overtime is paid at a time and one-half rate
5. taxes are calculated at 20 per cent of gross pay.

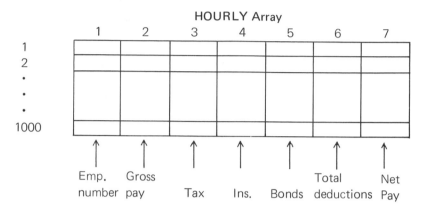

HOURLY Array

Emp. number | Gross pay | Tax | Ins. | Bonds | Total deductions | Net Pay

Program 16.5

```
C*******************************************************************
C MAIN PROGRAM
C*******************************************************************
      DIMENSION HOURLY(1000,7)                        DIMENSION,
      COMMON HOURLY,RATE,INS,BOND,ST,OT,J             COMMON
      DO 2 N=1,1000                                    Initialize
      DO 2 NN=1,7
    2 HOURLY(N,NN) = 0.0
      J = 1
    1 FORMAT (I1,I4,F7.2,I1,F6.2,2(F4.1))
   50 READ (5,1) KEY,NR,RATE,INS,BOND,ST,OT
      IF (KEY.EQ.9) GO TO 20            Last card test
      HOURLY(J,1) = NR
      CALL GROSS                       Subroutines to calculate gross
      CALL DEDUCT                      pay and deductions
      J = J+1
      GO TO 50
   20 J = J-1
      CALL HEADS                       Subroutines to write headings
      CALL PAYROL                      and payroll
      STOP
      END
C*******************************************************************
C SUBROUTINE GROSS
C*******************************************************************

      SUBROUTINE GROSS
      DIMENSION HOURLY(1000,7)
      COMMON HOURLY,RATE,INS,BOND,ST,OT,J
      HOURLY(J,2) = (ST + OT * 1.5) * RATE
      HOURLY(J,3) = HOURLY(J,2) * .20
      RETURN
      END
```

```
C****************************************************************************
C SUBROUTINE DEDUCT
C****************************************************************************

27          SUBROUTINE DEDUCT
28          DIMENSION HOURLY(1000,7)
29          COMMON HOURLY,RATE,INS,BOND,ST,OT,J
30          IF (INS-2) 10,12,12
31       10 HOURLY(J,4) = HOURLY(J,2) * .05
32       12 IF (BOND) 15,15,13
33       13 HOURLY(J,5) = BOND
34       15 HOURLY(J,6) = HOURLY(J,3)+HOURLY(J,4)+HOURLY(J,5)
35          HOURLY(J,7) = HOURLY(J,2) - HOURLY(J,6)
36          RETURN
37          END
C****************************************************************************
C SUBROUTINE HEADS
C****************************************************************************

38          SUBROUTINE HEADS
39       60 FORMAT (//25X,'HOURLY  PAYROLL'//)
40          WRITE (6,60)
41       62 FORMAT(5X,'EMPLOYEE    GROSS       TAX',
            14X,'HEALTH',5X,'BOND    TOTAL     NET'/
            26X,'NUMBER     PAY      WITHD     INS',
            35X,'DEDUC    DEDUC     PAY'/)
42          WRITE (6,62)
43          RETURN
44          END
C****************************************************************************
C SUBROUTINE PAYROL
C****************************************************************************

45          SUBROUTINE PAYROL
46          DIMENSION HOURLY(1000,7)
47          COMMON HOURLY,RATE,INS,BOND,ST,OT,J
48       62 FORMAT ( 6X,F5.0,3X,6(F7.2,2X))
49          DO 30 K = 1,J
50          WRITE (6,62) (HOURLY(K,N), N=1,7)
51       30 CONTINUE
52          RETURN
53          END
```

HOURLY PAYROLL

EMPLOYEE NUMBER	GROSS PAY	TAX WITHD	HEALTH INS	BOND DEDUC	TOTAL DEDUC	NET PAY
1234.	340.00	68.00	17.00	6.50	91.50	248.50
1357.	275.00	55.00	0.00	1.50	56.50	218.50
2345.	154.00	30.80	7.70	0.00	38.50	115.50
2468.	140.00	28.00	0.00	1.00	29.00	111.00

Figure 16.3

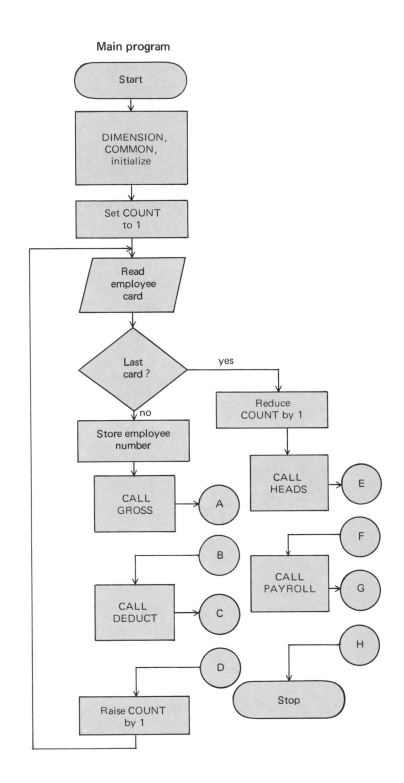

Main program

Figure 16.3 (Continued)

GROSS Subroutine

A

Dimension, common

Compute and store gross pay

Compute and store tax withheld

Return → B

HEADS Subroutine

E

Write payroll heading line

Return

F

PAYROL Subroutine

G

Dimension, common

DO 30 K = 1, J

Write payroll line

30

Return → H

DEDUCT Subroutine

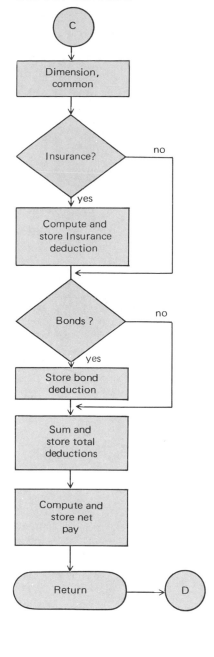

C

Dimension, common

Insurance? → no

yes

Compute and store Insurance deduction

Bonds ? → no

yes

Store bond deduction

Sum and store total deductions

Compute and store net pay

Return → D

Note the following points about Program 16.5:

1. A COMMON statement is used in each program, except HEADS, to pass data among the subroutines and main program.
2. The main program counts employee data cards read and passes this count to all subroutines through the variable J in the COMMON statements. J is then available for use as a subscript in subroutines GROSS and DEDUCT and as the DO loop maximum in compiler line 49.
3. All COMMON statements are identical. This causes a matching in order, mode, size, and number of variables. All COMMON variables are not used in each subroutine. However, inclusion of the variables in the COMMON statements assures proper memory alignment.

Exercise 41

1. Take each of the following sets of statements (MP = main programs and SR = subroutines) and rewrite the statements using COMMON statements to replace the use of argument lists.

    a. MP – DIMENSION NN(10)
                 CALL SUB1 (A,B,NN)

       SR – SUBROUTINE SUB1(A,B,NN)
                 DIMENSION NN(10)

    b. MP – REAL JACK, MAN
                 DIMENSION MAN(2,4)
                 CALL SUB2 (X,JACK,Y,MAN,Z)

       SR – SUBROUTINE SUB2 (A,B,C,D,E)
                 DIMENSION C(2,4)

    c. MP – REAL DP*8
                 INTEGER SM*2
                 CALL SUB3 (L,K,DP,SM)

       SR – SUBROUTINE SUB3 (A,B,C,D)
                 REAL C*8
                 INTEGER A,B,D*2

2. The following program is a simple example which takes an array of values, sums them, and sums the squares of the values. If the sum of the values is equal to or greater than 25, it writes the sum and sum of the squares. Rewrite this program so that:

    a. a main program will read the original values and then call a subroutine (named WORK) to do all of the computing and writing, if the qualifications are met.
    b. share all necessary values between programs in COMMON.

```
DIMENSION X(10)
1 FORMAT (F5.1)
READ (5,1) (X(K),K=1,10)
SUM=0.0
SUMXSQ=0.0
DO 5 J=1,10
```

continued on page 353

```
      SUM=SUM + X(J)
      SUMXSQ=SUMXSQ + X(J)**2
    5 CONTINUE
      IF (SUM.LT.25.0) STOP
   10 FORMAT (5X,'SUM',F20.2/
    15X,'SUMXSQ',F20.2)
      WRITE (6,10) SUM,SUMXSQ
      STOP
      END
```

3. Each set of instructions below pertains to the sharing of COMMON memory between a main program and a subroutine. Read each set of instructions and then fill in the sketch of COMMON memory locations to indicate which variables share location (MP = main program and SR = subroutine).

a. MP - COMMON A,B,C,D
          DIMENSION B(3)

   SR - COMMON A,B(3),C,D

b. MP - COMMON J,K,X,Y(3)
          DIMENSION J(2)

   SR - COMMON L,N(2),F,A
          DIMENSION F(3)

c. MP - COMMON R,J(2),M
          REAL J,M(4)

   SR - COMMON A,B(3),K
          REAL K(3)

Questions

1. What is the primary difference in the technique for calling a subroutine from that used to call a function subprogram?
2. What are the primary differences in the return of values (to a calling program) from a subroutine and a function subprogram?
3. What is the difference between the purposes of the RETURN and END statements in subroutines?
4. Why is a RETURN statement used in a subroutine rather than a STOP statement? What would be the result if a STOP statement was executed in a subroutine?
5. With one exception, the use of dummy and actual arguments is the same for subroutines as their use with function subprograms. What is the exception? Explain.
6. What data mode is associated with a subroutine name? Explain.
7. Explain the technique for transmitting a two-dimensional array between a calling program and a subroutine. Prepare an example to illustrate your explanation.
8. What purpose is served by use of the COMMON statement? Explain the relationship between COMMON memory and the memory assigned through the use of dummy and actual argument lists.

9. Does it seem logical that a calling program and a subroutine could contain both COMMON statements and dummy/actual argument lists? Explain your reasoning related to situations when it would be permissible to use both and when it would not be permissible.

10. A program may contain both DIMENSION and COMMON statements or have arrays dimensioned in COMMON statements directly. What characteristics do both of these statements have which makes this alternative construction seem logical?

17
Refining Subprograms

The language elements presented in Chapters 15 and 16 are completely adequate for developing subprograms. However, several optional refinements are available and may be used to conserve memory allocated for storage or to add flexibility to the subprograms written.[1]

Labeled COMMON Memory

The COMMON area of computer memory is a special area in which variables from different programs share memory locations. When the COMMON memory area is not further classified, it is known as *"blank" COMMON* memory. Because the allocation of memory is consecutive, the programmer cannot select portions of the COMMON area for sharing with some subprograms but not with others. The difficulty with sharing portions of COMMON memory is related to the possible misalignment of the shared common locations.

It is possible to avoid this problem by using a technique which subdivides the COMMON memory area into *segments* or *blocks*. When selective sharing of COMMON memory locations is desired, the memory segments may be identified and shared by specifying special names associated with the shared blocks. Therefore, two important steps in this technique are (1) division of memory and (2) labeling each block with an identifying name. This type of COMMON memory is called *"labeled" COMMON* storage.

Division of the COMMON memory area is handled automatically by the compiler when the COMMON statement is written as:

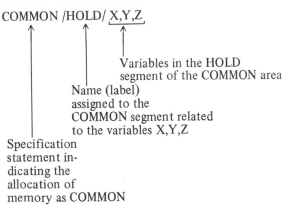

COMMON /HOLD/ X,Y,Z

Variables in the HOLD segment of the COMMON area

Name (label) assigned to the COMMON segment related to the variables X,Y,Z

Specification statement indicating the allocation of memory as COMMON

---

[1] All of the options discussed in this chapter are not available on *all* systems. This is most likely to be true on smaller computer systems. Refer to the applicable manufacturer's manual.

The requirements for specifying labeled COMMON blocks are:

1. The name of the segment must follow the rules for any FORTRAN variable name. No mode is associated with it.
2. The name of a COMMON segment must be enclosed in slashes.
3. The variables to be included in the labeled segment follow the closing slash of the segment name. These variables are listed in the same manner as used in blank COMMON lists.

More than one COMMON statement may be used in a subprogram to list both blank and labeled COMMON areas. For example:

COMMON A,B,C ←——————————— This statement indicates blank COMMON.
COMMON /HOLD/ X,Y,Z ←——————— This statement indicates labeled COMMON.
.
.
.

END

These two statements could be combined in a single COMMON statement (note the absence of commas before and after slashes):

COMMON A,B,C/HOLD/ X,Y,Z

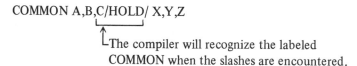

└The compiler will recognize the labeled
COMMON when the slashes are encountered.

An optional way to write this COMMON statement is:

COMMON /HOLD/ X,Y,Z//A,B,C

└The use of double slashes causes the compiler to
discontinue assigning variables to the labeled
COMMON area and to begin assigning variables to the
blank COMMON area.

We can visualize the assignment of variables to COMMON memory as:

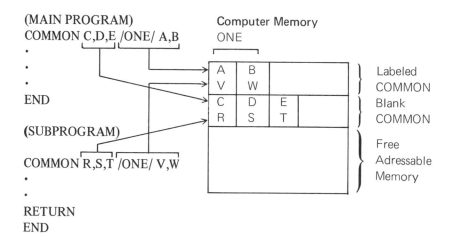

(MAIN PROGRAM)
COMMON C,D,E /ONE/ A,B

Computer Memory
ONE

.
.
.

END

(SUBPROGRAM)

COMMON R,S,T /ONE/ V,W
.
.

RETURN
END

Identification of a specific labeled segment of COMMON memory by two programs is made through the name used for the segment. In the example above, the labeled segment was named ONE. For both programs to share this memory area, both had to list the name ONE in COMMON statements. The names of the variables within the labeled segment do not have to have identical names, however.

To illustrate the advantage of labeled COMMON, we will use the payroll program developed in Chapter 16. In that program, each of the subroutines used an identical COMMON statement. This assured the proper alignment of memory, but all variables were not needed in every subprogram. The necessary variables for each program were:

Program	Variables Used
Main Program	HOURLY,J,ST,OT,RATE,INS,BOND
GROSS Subroutine	HOURLY,J,ST,OT,RATE
DEDUCT Subroutine	HOURLY,J, INS,BOND
PAYROL Subroutine	HOURLY,J

Examination of this listing shows that the variables HOURLY and J are used by all programs. These names can be listed in blank COMMON. The other variables are used in only two of the subroutines. They could be specified in labeled COMMON segments and shared selectively. A skeleton of the program and subroutines with COMMON statements to illustrate this subdivision of memory appears in Figure 17.1 on page 358.

BLOCK DATA Subprograms

The use of labeled COMMON specifications for transferring data values among programs is accompanied by one minor difficulty. This difficulty is the inability to use a DATA statement for the initialization of values in the labeled COMMON area. This difficulty extends to the initialization of all COMMON memory on some systems. Recall that the DATA statement initializes variables *during compilation* rather than requiring execution of statements when the program is processing. To circumvent this problem, a special type of subprogram is available which has *only one purpose:* to initialize COMMON areas. This program is called a BLOCK DATA subprogram.

A BLOCK DATA subprogram contains *no executable statements*. It lists the variables in COMMON memory with an accompanying DATA statement to initialize the memory area. The only statements which may appear in a BLOCK DATA program are:

1. DATA
2. COMMON
3. DIMENSION
4. EQUIVALENCE (see page 360)
5. type declarations (REAL, INTEGER, LOGICAL, etc.)

For example, assume that the following statements begin a main program:

```
DIMENSION A(10,B(20)
COMMON /ONE/A,B,C/TWO/K,N,Z
     .
END
```

Figure 17.1

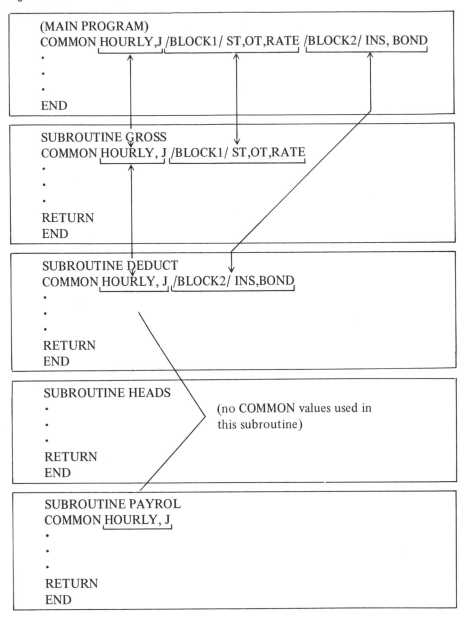

If the initialization of variable C at 2.4 and variable K at 3 is desired, the use of a DATA statement would not be permitted. The COMMON area contains two labeled segments, and a BLOCK DATA program must be used. This program would appear as follows:

```
BLOCK DATA
DIMENSION A(10),B(20)
COMMON /ONE/A,B,C/TWO/K,N,Z
DATA C/2.4/, K/3/
END
```

Several points should be observed about this program.

1. This type of program *always* begins with the name BLOCK DATA.
2. All of the variables in a COMMON segment *must* be listed even if they all are not to be initialized.
3. No STOP or RETURN statements are used in a BLOCK DATA program. *None* of the statements are executable.
4. Data may be placed in more than one segment in a single BLOCK DATA program.
5. Only one BLOCK DATA program may be used to place data in any one COMMON segment. However, more than one BLOCK DATA program may be used in one executable program.

As another example of a BLOCK DATA program, recall that the payroll program in Program 16.5 began with the following statements:

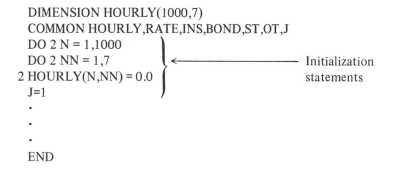

```
DIMENSION HOURLY(1000,7)
COMMON HOURLY,RATE,INS,BOND,ST,OT,J
   DO 2 N = 1,1000
   DO 2 NN = 1,7                        ←———————— Initialization
 2 HOURLY(N,NN) = 0.0                                statements
   J=1
   .
   .
   .
END
```

The purpose of the DO loops is to initialize the HOURLY array at zero, and, of course, the J = 1 statement set J equal to 1. These four statements require execution time rather than initialization of the variables when the program is compiled. The executable statements were used because J and the HOURLY array are listed in the COMMON statement. In systems which preclude the use of a DATA statement for initialization, there is no choice but to use executable statements. The BLOCK DATA subprogram can be used to overcome this problem. If it is written into this program, it would appear as shown below, and the executable statements would be eliminated.

```
BLOCK DATA
DIMENSION HOURLY(1000,7)
COMMON HOURLY,RATE,INS,BOND,ST,OT,J
DATA HOURLY/7000*0.0/ ,J/1/
END
```

Furthermore, if the COMMON statement in the main program uses labeled COMMON storage, as suggested earlier, the BLOCK DATA program would appear as:

```
BLOCK DATA
DIMENSION HOURLY(1000,7)
COMMON HOURLY,J /BLOCK1/ ST,OT,RATE /BLOCK2/ INS,BOND
DATA HOURLY/7000*0.0/, J/1/
END
```

EQUIVALENCE versus COMMON Statements

All previous discussions of the COMMON statement were intended to find ways for *different programs* to share memory locations for their variables and arrays. A related technique is available, and it will permit the sharing of memory locations for variables and arrays *within the same program.* This technique uses the EQUIVALENCE statement. Of course, the logic of a program must permit the use of a memory location by more than one variable. This means that one variable should be finished with the memory location prior to giving another variable its use. If this condition is not met, the original value will be destroyed.

An EQUIVALENCE statement is written in the following form:

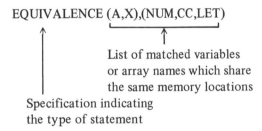

EQUIVALENCE (A,X),(NUM,CC,LET)

List of matched variables
or array names which share
the same memory locations

Specification indicating
the type of statement

The following points relate to the EQUIVALENCE statement:

1. The word EQUIVALENCE indicates the type of statement.
2. The variables or arrays to be matched are enclosed within their own set of parentheses.
3. Sharing of the same memory location by variables or arrays of different modes is legal. Only one variable or array will be using the memory location at one time.
4. The variables *share memory locations only, not* the *values* at the location.
5. Two or more variables in one labeled COMMON segment *cannot* be made equivalent. Also, variables in different COMMON blocks may *not* be made equivalent.
6. A variable in COMMON *can* be made equivalent to a variable which is not in COMMON storage.
7. The order of variables in parentheses is not important. EQUIVALENCE (A,B) is identical to EQUIVALENCE (B,A).
8. A subscripted variable can be made equivalent to other subscripted variables or to nonsubscripted variables. It is necessary to write the subscripted variable *with its subscript* in the EQUIVALENCE statement. The subscript *must* be an integer constant, not a variable.

Several examples of the EQUIVALENCE statement and its use are shown below:

EQUIVALENCE (A,B),(C,D)

In this case, the four original locations are compressed into two shared locations.

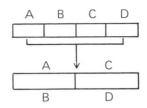

DIMENSION X(3),K(3)
EQUIVALENCE (X(1),K(1))

If the first subscript of each array is listed as equivalent, the other array locations are implied as equivalent.

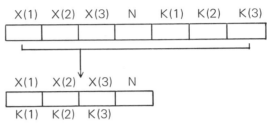

DIMENSION A(2,2)
EQUIVALENCE (A(2,1),X,Y)

This example indicates three variables share the same location with one variable subscripted.

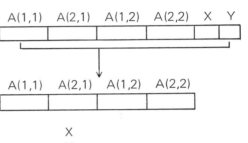

COMMON J
DIMENSION J(3,2), B(3)
EQUIVALENCE (J(1,2),X,B(3),N)

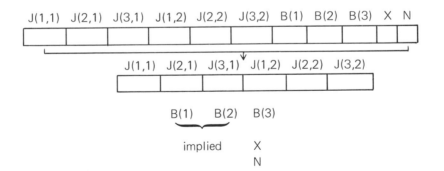

In this case, B(3) is listed in the EQUIVALENCE statement. Therefore, the lower numbered subscripts in the B array are implied as equivalent to the lower subscripted J locations. Note that a COMMON location was placed in EQUIVALENCE with a non-COMMON location.

Arrays are assigned consecutive storage locations, even when they are listed as multi-dimensional. Because of this sequential storage, the last EQUIVALENCE statement could have been written as:

EQUIVALENCE (J(4),X,B(3),N)

This illustrates the fact that location J(1,2) is the fourth memory location assigned to the J array. Equivalencing the J(4) location or the J(1,2) location specifies the same element in the array.

EQUIVALENCE Statement that Extends Memory

The use of EQUIVALENCE statements, involving arrays which are in COMMON, may result in implied extensions of the assigned memory. Implied extensions *beyond the end* of the common memory area are *legal*. However, implied extensions *prior to the COMMON area* are *illegal*. Each of these conditions is illustrated below.

COMMON N,M
DIMENSION N(5),R(3)
EQUIVALENCE (N(5),R(1))

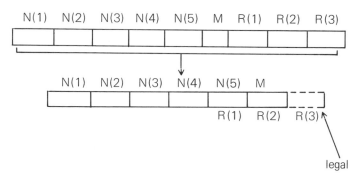

This EQUIVALENCE shows how the COMMON memory area may be extended *following* its last assigned location. R(2) is implied to share the memory location with M because of the consecutive nature in which COMMON memory is assigned.

COMMON Z
DIMENSION Z(4,2), Q(3)
EQUIVALENCE (Z(2,1),Q(3))

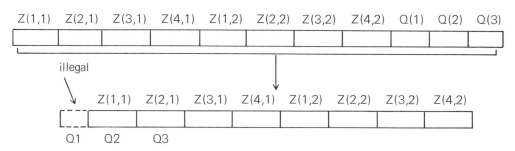

This EQUIVALENCE is illegal since it implies extending the COMMON memory area *prior* to its first location.

We can apply the EQUIVALENCE statement to the payroll example in Chapter 16. If we assume that the payroll program will be used for both hourly and salary wages, the following variables will be needed for processing each type of payroll data.

ST = straight-time hours worked by hourly employees
WK = number of weeks worked by salary employees
HOURLY = array holding payroll calculations for hourly employees
SALARY = array holding payroll calculations for salary employees

If the program is written so that all hourly data is processed before beginning the salary payroll, these variables can share the same memory locations. A second array for salary payroll calculations can be DIMENSIONed (that is, DIMENSION SALARY(1000,7)), but the amount of memory required can be reduced if arrays HOURLY and SALARY are made equivalent. The same reasoning applies to the amount of time an employee has worked. Variable ST represents the straight-time worked by hourly employees while WK holds the number of weeks salaried employees have worked. These memory locations can be made equivalent.

An amended DIMENSION statement and the new EQUIVALENCE statement would be:

DIMENSION HOURLY(1000,7), SALARY(1000,7)
EQUIVALENCE (ST,WK),(HOURLY(1,1),SALARY(1,1))

Specifying that the first location of the HOURLY and SALARY arrays are equivalent automatically implies that the other elements in both arrays will be equivalent.

Exercise 42

1. Write a single COMMON statement for each situation below. The statements should be written with the variables in the order shown.

	Blank COMMON Variables	Labeled COMMON Name	Variables	Blank COMMON Variables
a.	A, B, C	ALPHA	N, NN	—
b.	X, Y, Z	BETA	R, S	P, Q
c.	—	GAMMA	K	J,N
d.	F, G, H	SIGMA	H	—

2. For each set of statements given below, fill in the memory locations with the variables which will share the locations (MP = main (calling) program and SR = subroutine).

   a. MP— COMMON A1,A2,A3/FIRST/X,N,Q//B1
      SR— COMMON /TWO/L,S//B2,X/FIRST/A,J,T//B

} labeled COMMON

} blank COMMON

b. MP— COMMON P(3),Q/TREE/A,B,C//R(2)
    SR— COMMON/THREE/A,B,C//S(5)/TREE/Z

Remember, arrays
may be DIMENSIONed
in COMMON statements.

} labeled COMMON

} blank COMMON

c. MP— DIMENSION G(3),L(2)
        COMMON/NOW/G,R//L,X(2),W/THEN/Z
    SR1—COMMON/THEN/A//R,Q,P(3)/AGAIN/L1,L2
    SR2—COMMON/NOW/A,B/AGAIN/LL,L20//W,X,Y,Z

} labeled COMMON

} blank COMMON

3. Write a BLOCK DATA subprogram which properly initializes a main program having these specifications:

a. main program contains these statements:

    REAL LOW(6)
    DIMENSION NAME(8), HIGH(10)
    COMMON /FIRST/NAME//HIGH,LOW

b. NAME should be initialized with: WASHINGTON, GEO.

c. HIGH should be initialized with:

    locations (1) − (5) = 0
    locations (6) − (10) = 1

d. LOW should be initialized with:

    locations (1) − (3) = 5.2
    locations (4) − (6) = 6.4

4. Read the following BLOCK DATA subprogram. Identify and explain the errors which you find.

    BLOCK DATA SUBROUTINE
    DIMENSION A
    COMMON/CC/,B,B//D-2
    DATA A/5*3.2
    CC=3
    RETURN
    END

5. Assume the following three statements appear at the beginning of a main program.

REAL MAX(5)
COMMON SMALL(3,3)
DIMENSION BIG(4)

Use these statements, if necessary, and write an EQUIVALENCE statement for each of the situations given below. After writing a statement, fill in the sketch to show which values are equivalent.

a. Write a single statement to EQUIVALENCE:
   (1) variable A and MAX(1) and SMALL(2,2)
   (2) variable B and SMALL(3,2)
   (3) BIG(1) and SMALL(1,1)

b. Write a single statement to EQUIVALENCE:
   (1) MAX(5) and SMALL(3,2)
   (2) variable C and MAX(4)
   (3) MAX(4) and BIG(1)

c. Write a single statement to EQUIVALENCE:
   (1) variable D and MAX(3)
   (2) variable E and SMALL(2,3)
   (3) variable F and variable G
   (4) variable F and SMALL(1,3)
   (5) variable G and MAX(2)
   (6) BIG(2) and SMALL(1,3)

d. Write a single statement to EQUIVALENCE:
   (1) MAX(1) and SMALL(8)
   (2) variables K,L,M, and MAX(2)
   (3) variable R and SMALL(4)
   (4) variable S and variable R
   (5) BIG(2) and SMALL(6)

e. Write a single statement to EQUIVALENCE:
(1) SMALL(1,2), BIG(4), and MAX(5)

The ENTRY Statement

Subprograms used in prior examples have been called either by reference to a function name (for FUNCTION subprograms) or by a specific CALL statement (for SUBROUTINE subprograms). We have assumed that entry into these subprograms is made at the first statement in the program (that is, at the top). This form of entry is the most common and is referred to as normal entry. Occasions arise when we wish to enter a subprogram at a point other than at the beginning. A special statement is available which permits a calling program to gain access to the subprogram at a point other than the normal entry point. This statement is called an ENTRY statement.

The form of an ENTRY statement is:

ENTRY DRIVE

    ↑   ↑

    | Name of the entry point in

    | the subprogram

Special statement

indicating an

abnormal entry to

a subprogram

The ENTRY statement is *located in the subprogram* at the point where the entry is to be made. The calling program will use a CALL statement nearly identical to the call for a normal entry. The only difference will be the specification of the special entry point name following the word CALL. For instance, to call the ENTRY shown above, we write the following CALL statement:

CALL DRIVE

The ENTRY statement is *non-executable* and does not affect the logic of the subprogram in which it is located. When normal execution is taking place, if no branching statement is given to jump over the ENTRY statement, the processor will flow over the ENTRY statement and continue processing executable statements following it.

A subprogram may not transfer to its own ENTRY statement. This transfer is permitted only for a calling program. Furthermore, an ENTRY statement may not be located within the range of a DO loop.

A CALL statement and an ENTRY statement may have actual and dummy arguments which are used in the same manner as the argument lists in normal CALL statements. One important difference does exist, however. The order, mode, size, and/or number of arguments in the CALL/ENTRY statements may be different from those used in the normal CALL/Subprogram name statements. The only agreement required is between the CALL and the ENTRY statements. For example, consider the following skeleton main program and subroutine.

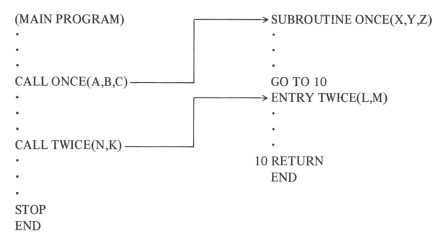

Note the change in the number of variables and the change in the modes of the variables between the two CALL statement executions in the above program. Each CALL to the subroutine would be returned from the 10 RETURN statement. The first return would be made to the statement following CALL ONCE, while the second return would be made to the statement following CALL TWICE.

When an ENTRY statement is used in a FUNCTION subprogram, the ENTRY may change the mode of the value returned from the mode which is returned from a normal entry to the function subprogram. This change is illustrated below.

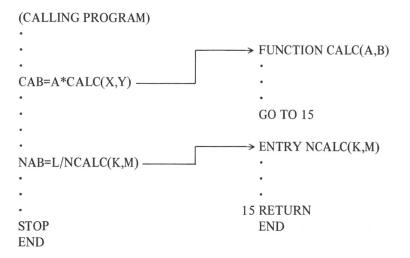

In the programs above, the first call, to the CALC function, will return a real mode value to the calling program. The second call, for NCALC, will return an integer mode value. The mode returned will be established by the last normal entry or ENTRY statement prior to returning from the function subprogram.

An Extended Example

We will now amend our payroll example to include several of the options discussed in this chapter. We will assume the following changes to the payroll problem:

1. Both hourly and salary wage data is to be processed in the same payroll run.
2. The input data for hourly wages is in a separate data deck from the salary data. The salary data is immediately behind the hourly data cards. One of the following codes is punched into column 1 of each input card (assigned the variable name KEY in the READ statement):

Code	Explanation
1	Hourly employee card
2	Salary employee card
7	Last card in the hourly data deck
8	Last card in the salary data deck
9	Last physical card in the total data deck

3. The addition of ENTRY statements permits the subroutines to be called at six different entry points. In addition to the previous subroutine calls, the GROSS subroutine and HEADS subroutine are entered at different points depending upon whether hourly or salary data is being processed.

   The six subroutine calls are each responsible for the following tasks:

   a. Subroutine GROSS: calculates hourly gross pay; then calculates income tax
   b. Entry GROSS2: calculates salary gross pay; then calculates income tax
   c. Subroutine DEDUCT: tests for and calculates deductions for insurance (medical) and bonds; then sums an employee's total deductions, and finally calculates an employee's net pay
   d. Subroutine HEADS: writes the heading for the hourly payroll
   e. Entry HEADS2: writes the heading for the salary payroll
   f. Subroutine PAYROL: writes the payroll record for both hourly and salary payrolls

4. Salary employee's gross pay is calculated by multiplying the number of weeks worked by the rate per week.
5. The EQUIVALENCE statement is used to reduce memory assignments. This results in the sharing of the ST (straight-time) and WK (number of weeks worked) locations as well as the array for payroll calculations. The arrays are named HOURLY and SALARY.
6. Labeled COMMON memory is used for sharing values among the programs. This memory is initialized through the use of a BLOCK DATA subprogram.

The flowcharts for this program appear in Figure 17.2. The program appears in Program 17.1.

Figure 17.1

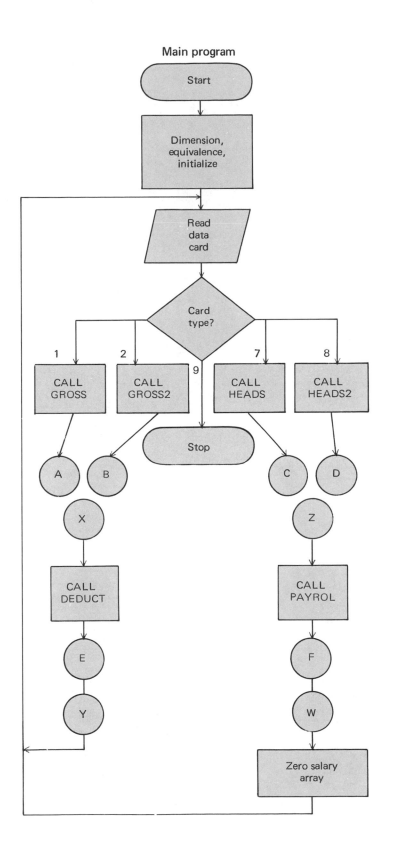

continued

Figure 17.1 (Continued)

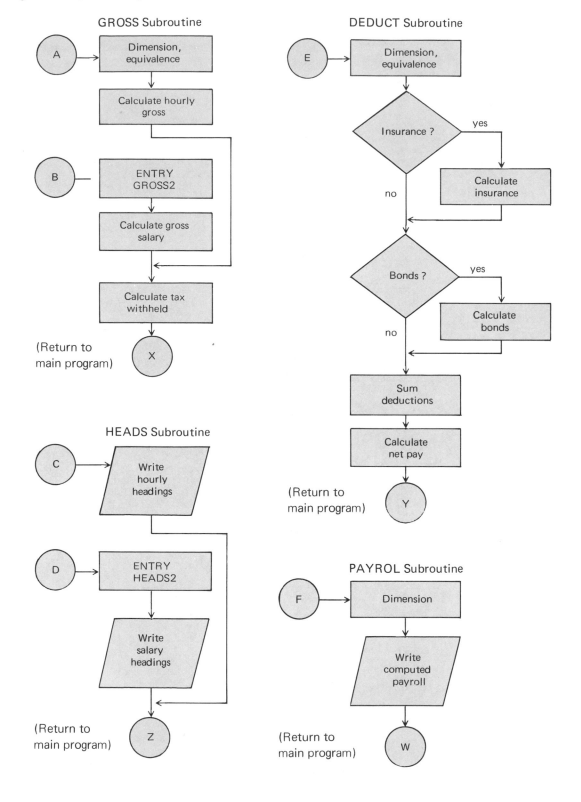

Program 17.1

```
C********************************************************
C MAIN PROGRAM
C ILLUSTRATES THE USE OF EQUIVALENCE,
C LABELED COMMON, AND BLOCK DATA
C********************************************************
      EQUIVALENCE (ST,WK), (HOURLY(1,1),SALARY(1,1))
      DIMENSION HOURLY(1000,7), SALARY(1000,7)
      COMMON HOURLY,J /BLOCK1/ ST,OT,RATE /BLOCK2/ INS,BOND
    1 FORMAT (I1,I4,F7.2,I1,F6.2,2(F4.1))
   50 READ (5,1) KEY,NR,RATE,INS,BOND,ST,OT
      GO TO (4,5,5,5,5,5,20,25,35), KEY
    4 HOURLY(J,1) = NR
      CALL GROSS
      GO TO 6
    5 SALARY(J,1) = NR
      CALL GROSS2
    6 CALL DEDUCT
      J = J+1
      GO TO 50
   20 J = J-1
      CALL HEADS
      GO TO 30
   25 J = J-1
      CALL HEADS2
   30 CALL PAYROL
      DO 41 N=1,1000
      DO 41 NN = 1,7
   41 SALARY(N,NN) = 0.0
      J = 1
      GO TO 50
   35 STOP
      END
C********************************************************
C SUBROUTINE GROSS
C********************************************************
```

EQUIVALENCE, blank and labeled COMMON	
Decision using a computed GO TO	
CALL for normal entry to GROSS	
CALL for optional entry to GROSS	
CALL for normal entry to HEADS	
CALL for optional entry to HEADS	
Use of executable statements to zero array—BLOCK DATA can *not* be used to *reinitialize* during execution	

```
      SUBROUTINE GROSS
      DIMENSION HOURLY(1000,7), SALARY(1000,7)
      EQUIVALENCE (ST,WK), (HOURLY(1,1),SALARY(1,1))
      COMMON HOURLY,J /BLOCK1/ ST,OT,RATE
      HOURLY(J,2) = (ST + OT * 1.5) * RATE
      GO TO 5
C********************************************************
C USE OF ENTRY STATEMENT
C********************************************************
      ENTRY GROSS2
      SALARY(J,2)= WK * RATE
    5 HOURLY(J,3) = HOURLY(J,2) * .20
      RETURN
      END
C********************************************************
C SUBROUTINE DEDUCT
C********************************************************
```

Normal entry

EQUIVALENCE, blank and labeled COMMON, Hourly gross pay

Optional entry

Salary gross pay and tax withheld

```
      SUBROUTINE DEDUCT ◄──────────────────────────              Normal entry
      DIMENSION HOURLY(1000,7), SALARY(1000,7)┐
      EQUIVALENCE  (HOURLY(1,1),SALARY(1,1))  │◄──              EQUIVALENCE, blank  and
      COMMON HOURLY,J /BLOCK2/ INS,BOND       ┘                 labeled COMMON
      IF (INS-2) 10,12,12
   10 HOURLY(J,4) = HOURLY(J,2) * .05
   12 IF (BOND) 15,15,13
   13 HOURLY(J,5) = BOND
   15 HOURLY(J,6) = HOURLY(J,3)+HOURLY(J,4)+HOURLY(J,5)
      HOURLY(J,7) = HOURLY(J,2) - HOURLY(J,6)
      RETURN
      END
C*********************************************************************
C SUBROUTINE HEADS
C*********************************************************************


      SUBROUTINE HEADS ◄───────────────────────────             Normal entry (no COMMON
   60 FORMAT (//25X,'HOURLY  PAYROLL'//)                        necessary)
      WRITE (6,60)
      GO TO 20
C*********************************************************************
C USE OF ENTRY STATEMENT
C*********************************************************************
      ENTRY HEADS2 ◄───────────────────────────                Optional entry
   61 FORMAT (//25X,'SALARY  PAYROLL'//)
      WRITE (6,61)
   62 FORMAT(5X,'EMPLOYEE    GROSS       TAX',
     14X,'HEALTH',5X,'BOND     TOTAL      NET'/
     26X,'NUMBER      PAY     WITHD    INS',
     35X,'DEDUC    DEDUC      PAY'/)
   20 WRITE (6,62)
      RETURN
      END
C*********************************************************************
C SUBROUTINE PAYROL
C*********************************************************************


      SUBROUTINE PAYROL ◄──────────────────────                Normal entry
      DIMENSION HOURLY(1000,7), SALARY(1000,7)┐
      EQUIVALENCE  (HOURLY(1,1),SALARY(1,1))  │◄──             EQUIVALENCE, blank  and
      COMMON HOURLY,J                         ┘                labeled COMMON
   62 FORMAT ( 6X,F5.0,3X,6(F7.2,2X))
      DO 30 K = 1,J
      WRITE (6,62) (HOURLY(K,N), N=1,7)
   30 CONTINUE
      RETURN
      END
C*********************************************************************
C BLOCK DATA SUBPROGRAM
C*********************************************************************


      BLOCK DATA
      DIMENSION HOURLY(1000,7)                                 BLOCK DATA to give origi-
      COMMON HOURLY,J /BLOCK1/ ST,OT,RATE /BLOCK2/ INS,BOND    nal initialization to the pay-
      DATA HOURLY/7000*0.0/,J/1/                               roll array
      END
```

		HOURLY	PAYROLL			
EMPLOYEE NUMBER	GROSS PAY	TAX WITHD	HEALTH INS	BOND DEDUC	TOTAL DEDUC	NET PAY
1234.	340.00	68.00	17.00	6.50	91.50	248.50
1357.	275.00	55.00	0.00	1.50	56.50	218.50
2345.	154.00	30.80	7.70	0.00	38.50	115.50
2468.	140.00	28.00	0.00	1.00	29.00	111.00

		SALARY	PAYROLL			
EMPLOYEE NUMBER	GROSS PAY	TAX WITHD	HEALTH INS	BOND DEDUC	TOTAL DEDUC	NET PAY
3456.	1000.00	200.00	50.00	50.00	300.00	700.00
3579.	900.00	180.00	0.00	100.00	280.00	620.00
4567.	800.00	160.00	40.00	5.00	205.00	595.00
4689.	562.50	112.50	0.00	100.00	212.50	350.00

Computed Output

The RETURN i Statement—An Option

We have used a RETURN statement in all of our subprograms to send control back to a calling program. A normal RETURN of this type transfers control to the first executable statement following the CALL to the subprogram. A variation in the RETURN statement is available in some systems. This RETURN statement allows transfer to any statement number in the calling program. The form of this altered RETURN statement is:

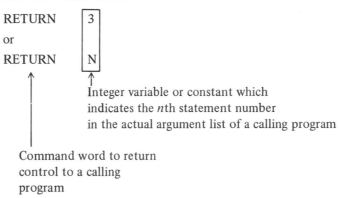

RETURN   3

or

RETURN   N

Integer variable or constant which indicates the nth statement number in the actual argument list of a calling program

Command word to return control to a calling program

The RETURN i statements shown above are interpreted as:

1. RETURN 3 means a subroutine should transfer control to the *third* statement number in the calling program's actual argument list.
2. RETURN N means a subroutine should take the numeric value of location N (1, 2, 3, 4, and so forth) and transfer control to the equivalent statement number in the calling program's actual argument list.

The fact that this RETURN statement is capable of causing control to be transferred to a variable number of statements in the calling program adds flexibility to the use of subroutines.

It should be noted that this statement is *used only in subroutines.* It is not used in FUNCTION subprograms which return only a single value to the calling program.

The RETURN i statement requires some changes in the CALL and SUBROUTINE name statements.

CALL Statement

The CALL statement provides a path for the return transfer of control by including in the actual argument list the *statement numbers* to which the subroutine may transfer at the time of its return. Any statement numbers listed are preceded by an ampersand symbol (&) to avoid confusion with integer constants which may be actual arguments. An example of a CALL statement including RETURN program statement numbers is:

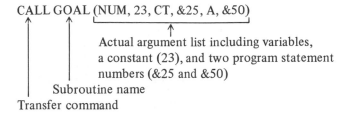

CALL GOAL (NUM, 23, CT, &25, A, &50)

Actual argument list including variables,
a constant (23), and two program statement
numbers (&25 and &50)
Subroutine name
Transfer command

SUBROUTINE Name Statement

An alteration in the SUBROUTINE name statement is necessary to indicate the path which corresponds to the statement numbers in the CALL statement's actual argument list. The use of *asterisks* (*) provides a symbol in the SUBROUTINE name's dummy argument list which corresponds with the ampersand symbols in the actual argument list. A SUBROUTINE name statement to complement the CALL statement shown above is:

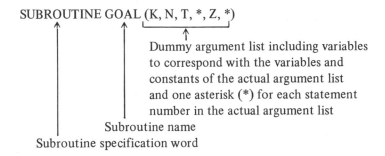

SUBROUTINE GOAL (K, N, T, *, Z, *)

Dummy argument list including variables
to correspond with the variables and
constants of the actual argument list
and one asterisk (*) for each statement
number in the actual argument list
Subroutine name
Subroutine specification word

In the statement shown above, the first asterisk will be associated with the statement number &25 and the second asterisk with &50.

The skeleton program on page 375 illustrates the use of the altered CALL, SUBROUTINE name, and RETURN *i* statements.

Note that the use of the RETURN *i* statement takes the integer value following the word RETURN and uses it to look up the correct statement number transferred in from the actual argument list. In the example, the integer value following RETURN should never be greater than 2 because there are only two statement numbers transferred through the argument lists. If the RETURN statements had been written as RETURN N, then the subroutine would have had to develop a value of 1 or 2, in a variable named N, prior to the execution of the RETURN *i* statements. The statement numbers transfered in from the calling program are always counted beginning with 1, 2, and so forth, and the RETURN *i* statement behaves very much like a computed GO TO in selecting the statement number to which it should return.

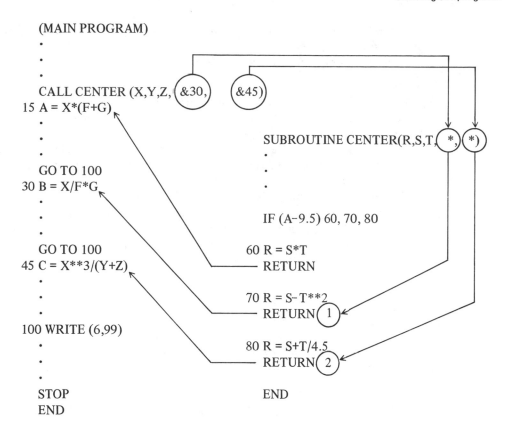

```
(MAIN PROGRAM)
      .
      .
      .
      CALL CENTER (X,Y,Z, (&30,) (&45))
 15 A = X*(F+G)
      .                         SUBROUTINE CENTER(R,S,T, (*,) (*))
      .                              .
      .                              .
      GO TO 100                      .
 30 B = X/F*G
      .
      .                         IF (A-9.5) 60, 70, 80
      .
      GO TO 100                 60 R = S*T
 45 C = X**3/(Y+Z)                 RETURN
      .
      .                         70 R = S- T**2
      .                            RETURN (1)
100 WRITE (6,99)
      .                         80 R = S+T/4.5
      .                            RETURN (2)
      .
      STOP                      END
      END
```

Argument References by Location versus References by Value

A standard method for transferring data values between a calling program and a subprogram is through actual and dummy argument lists. The earlier discussions of this method cited a potential drawback to this type of transfer. This drawback is related to the processor's technique of making a second copy of values transferred through argument lists. The copying of values already stored by the calling program doubled the amount of internal memory used for all values in the argument lists.

An option is available which permits the use of argument lists but which eliminates the creation of duplicate storage requirements. This option allows the processor to retrieve a transferred value by referring to its original *location* rather than copying its original value. Hence the term, "reference by location." In effect, this technique provides the same type of advantages gained by using COMMON statements.

This technique requires the enclosure of *dummy arguments only* in slashes when these arguments are to be referenced by location instead of by value. Both types of argument reference (location and value) may be used within a single dummy argument list. An example of this type of specification is:

FUNCTION CASH(/Q/,/R/,N,A,/L/)

Function dummy argument list showing:
a. reference by location for variables Q, R, and L
b. reference by value for variables N and A

The key to this technique is the fact that the program will reserve no storage for the dummy arguments in slashes. The actual argument's memory location will be used by the subprogram when it is called.

Specifying Variable DIMENSIONs

DIMENSION specifications are necessary for reserving appropriate amounts of memory to handle array storage. We have implied that all dimensions must be fixed prior to the execution of a program. This implication is only partially correct. A useful option is available to defer specification of an array's dimensions until the program is being executed (that is, at object time). This option requires the use of a calling program and at least one subprogram. With these two programs, the dimension sizes are determined by the calling program and are passed down to the subprogram. This allows the dimension sizes to be changed each time the subprogram is called, if necessary. The potential advantages to this method are the conservation of memory by eliminating fixed specifications for array storage which is not used and flexibility in writing subprograms which may be inserted into several different programs.

Two primary conditions must be met to use this technique:

1. A calling program and subprogram must exist. A single program cannot use variable DIMENSIONs.
2. An array which is to have variable DIMENSIONs must *not* be listed in a COMMON statement. Any variable name used to specify an array's dimensions may be in COMMON storage, however.

This dimensioning technique may be used with both FUNCTION subprograms and SUBROUTINE subprograms. In addition, DIMENSION sizes may be passed through more than one level of subprograms. The following skeleton outline of a main program and a subroutine illustrates the technique for specifying DIMENSIONs at object time.

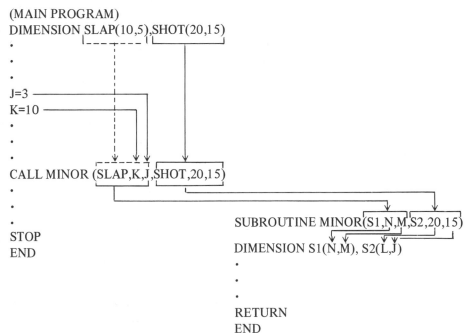

```
(MAIN PROGRAM)
DIMENSION SLAP(10,5),SHOT(20,15)
   .
   .
   .
J=3
K=10
   .
   .
   .
CALL MINOR (SLAP,K,J,SHOT,20,15)
   .
   .
   .
STOP                        SUBROUTINE MINOR(S1,N,M,S2,20,15)
END                         DIMENSION S1(N,M), S2(L,J)
                               .
                               .
                               .
                            RETURN
                            END
```

The following notes relate to the above example:

1. The dimensions for an array may be sent to a subprogram either as constants or as variables. Both are shown above. The SLAP array is initially dimensioned at 10 × 5. The dashed lines show its relationship to the CALL statement. The actual values sent to the subroutine were for a 10 × 3 array. These values were developed within the main program. The SHOT array had its original dimensions of 20 × 15 sent as constants to the subroutine.
2. The dimensions sent to a subprogram may be no larger than the original specifications but may be smaller.
3. A DIMENSION specification must be either an integer variable or an integer constant.
4. The subprogram receives the array dimensions through its dummy argument list and inserts the transferred array specifications in its DIMENSION statement. Note that the DIMENSION in the subroutine contains variables where constants would normally be found.
5. An array must have initial dimensions given in the first calling program. In this example, there was only one level of calling completed. When calls are made through several levels of programs, the initial program must have provided an array dimension.

Two illustrations are given below to show how array DIMENSIONs may be passed through several program levels.

Example 1

(MAIN PROGRAM)
DIMENSION XOUT(200,100)
COMMON K,N
·
·
·
K=50
N=50
·
·
·
CALL ABC(XOUT,K,N)
·
·
·
STOP
END

continued on page 378

Example 2

(MAIN PROGRAM)
DIMENSION NPLUS2(20,50)
·
·
·
J=20
M=10
·
·
·
CALL JACK(NPLUS2,J,M)
·
·
·
STOP
END

continued on page 378

```
SUBROUTINE ABC(XOUT,K,N)          FUNCTION JACK(M3,K,N)
COMMON K,N                        .
.                                 .
.                                 .
.                                 K=K-5
CALL XYZ(XOUT,K,N)                N=N+20
.                                 .
.                                 .
.                                 .
RETURN                            CALL NEXT(M3,K,N)
END                               .
                                  .
SUBROUTINE XYZ(XOUT,K,N)          .
COMMON K,N                        RETURN
DIMENSION XOUT(K,N)               END
.
.                                 SUBROUTINE NEXT (NOW,L,M)
.                                 DIMENSION NOW(L,M)
RETURN                            .
END                               .
                                  .
                                  RETURN
                                  END
```

This program passes the array dimensions through two subroutines.

The array XOUT is initially set at 200 × 100, but the main program establishes the dimensions to be passed at 50 × 50.

K and N pass the dimensions, and they are in COMMON with the subroutines.

The 50 × 50 dimensions flow through the first subroutine (ABC) and are used in the second subroutine (XYZ) to set the array dimensions.

The XYZ subroutine will pass the values back to the main program through the ABC routine.

This program passes the array dimensions through two subprograms but changes the dimensions in the first subprogram.

The NPLUS2 array is dimensioned 20 × 50 in the main program but is passed as 20 × 10 to the FUNCTION subprogram.

Note the change in variable names in the FUNCTION. Order, mode, size agree with the main program. The FUNCTION also changes the size of the array dimensions. The array is now changed to 15 × 30.

The NEXT subroutine receives the 15 × 30 array, uses it, and sends it back to the FUNCTION. Note the additional change in variable names in this subprogram. The FUNCTION, in turn, will send a single value to the main program.

Exercise 43

1. Write an ENTRY statement for each of the situations described below:
   a. enter subprogram SET with dummy variables of K, A, B, and N
   b. enter subprogram NIX with dummy variables of K2R, A, and ZZ
   c. enter subprogram CLASS with dummy variables of DEBIT, CREDIT, and BALNCE

2. Write a CALL statement to accompany each of your ENTRY statements in (1). Use the same variable names from (1) for the actual argument lists in your CALL statements.

3. Read the following programs and trace the CALLs among the programs. Indicate each CALL by listing the program name called and the value of variables A and B at the time each call is made. The first CALL is already entered to provide an example. After tracing the CALL statements, indicate the final values for A and B.

(MAIN PROGRAM)	SUBROUTINE SUB1(A,B)	SUBROUTINE PGM1(B)
B=0.0	A=(A+A)/2	IF (B-9.0) 5,10,15
A=5.0	ENTRY SUB2(A)	5 CALL SUB2(B)
CALL SUB1(A,B)	A=A+2.0	10 RETURN
B=A+A	CALL PGM1(A)	15 B=B*B
CALL SUB2 (B)	RETURN	RETURN
.	END	END
.		
.		
STOP		
END		

	Program CALL Statements	Value of A	B	
1.	CALL SUB1	5.0	0.0	
2.	_____	___	___	
3.	_____	___	___	
4.	_____	___	___	Final Value:
5.	_____	___	___	A_____
6.	_____	___	___	B_____

4. The RETURN *i* statement is used in conjunction with a special form of the CALL and SUBROUTINE name statements. Write the appropriate *CALL and SUBROUTINE name statements* for each of the following conditions. Use the SUBROUTINE name TEST in each case.
   a. actual arguments — A,B,C, statement number 22, X,Y, and statement number 40
      dummy arguments — X,Y,Z, statement number 22, A,B, and statement number 40
   b. actual arguments — K,L,M,N, statement number 50, and statement number 70
      dummy arguments — K2,L2,M2,N2, statement number 50, and statement number 70

c. actual arguments — statement number 75, statement number 85, A,N, and statement number 95

dummy arguments — statement number 75, statement number 85, R,J, and statement number 95

5. The RETURN i option permits multiple returns to a calling program. The program shown here is fairly simple but uses the RETURN i option. Read the program and indicate the value of X which will be written at the conclusion of processing.

```
(MAIN PROGRAM)                    SUBROUTINE SR(X,N,*,*)
 5 FORMAT (5X,F10.2)              N=2
   N=0                            IF (X-9.0) 10, 20, 30
   X=10.0                        10 RETURN
   CALL SR(X,N,&15,&25)          20 RETURN 1
   X=X**2                        30 RETURN N
   WRITE (6,5) X                  END
   GO TO 50
15 X=X+X
   WRITE (6,5) X
   GO TO 50
25 X=(X+X)/2.0
   WRITE (6,5) X
50 STOP                          Final Value of X: _____
   END
```

6. This is a somewhat more involved program than the one in the previous problem. Read the program and indicate what value of C will be written at the end of this program.

```
(MAIN PROGRAM)                    SUBROUTINE SUB1(J,Y,Z,*,*)
 5 FORMAT (5X,F10.2)              Z=Y+Z
   N=1                            IF (Z-6.0) 10,20,30
   A=2.0                        10 RETURN
   B=3.0                        20 RETURN J
   CALL SUB1(N,A,B,&10,&15)     30 J=J+1
10 C=B**2                          RETURN J
   WRITE (6,5) C                   ENTRY SUB2(J,C,*,*)
   CALL SUB2(N,C,&20,&25)          C=C-20.0
20 WRITE (6,5) C                   RETURN J
   GO TO 30                        END
25 WRITE (6,5) C
30 STOP
   END                            Final Value of C: _____
```

7. Explain the program purpose related to the following statements. Indicate in detail what will happen to each variable listed in these statements.

a. SUBROUTINE START(KEEP,SLOW,/LOW/,Z)

b. DIMENSION MATRIX(50,50)
   CALL JUMP(MATRIX,J,K)

c. CALL PASS(A,/B/,/C/)

d. FUNCTION COMP(G,/H/)

e. DIMENSION IRAY(10,10)
   N=2 $\left.\right\}$ from a calling program
   M=3
   CALL LEAD(IRAY,N,M)

   SUBROUTINE LEAD(KT,J,K) $\left.\right\}$ from a subprogram
   DIMENSION KT(J,K)

Questions

1. What is the difference between labeled COMMON memory and blank COMMON memory? Explain.

2. What is a BLOCK DATA subprogram? When is it necessary to use this program? What is its function?

3. What is the only executable statement permitted in a BLOCK DATA subprogram?

4. Explain the purpose of the EQUIVALENCE statement. How does its function compare with the function of the COMMON statement?

5. What purpose is served by the ENTRY statement? Explain.

6. Explain how the RETURN *i* statement compares with the simple RETURN statement.

7. Why is it true that argument reference "by location" gives the same advantages as the use of COMMON statements? Explain.

8. What are variable DIMENSIONs? Explain how they are used. What important requirement exists for their use?

Appendix A
Systems Control, Magnetic Tape, and Magnetic Disk

Computer system control (monitors and operating systems), the use of magnetic tape for input and/or output of problem data, and the similar use of magnetic disk storage (direct access) appear to be three diverse subjects, but they are, in fact, closely related. Understanding the concepts of system control is particularly critical when magnetic tapes or disks are included within a FORTRAN program. The basic concepts of control cards for punch card-to-printer programs were discussed in Chapter 6. This appendix develops those concepts more fully.

This appendix may be used either in separate sections or as an added chapter to the text. However, it is important that the section on system control be covered before the tape or disk sections.

System Control Cards, Monitors, and Operating Systems

Computing systems have always required users to specify control information in addition to the processing controls embodied in program instructions. The increasing complexity of control requirements has accompanied the increasing complexity of computer systems. Control instructions enable the system to accomplish FORTRAN program compilation, accumulation of accounting information on job execution time, specification of input/output units required by programs, allocation of required memory, display of error messages, maintenance of efficient program flow through the central processor, and the like.

The historical development of system control parallels the development of computing hardware. First generation computers were primitive in all respects. By comparison to today's processors, the speeds were slow, accuracy poor, memory capacity very limited, and system controls equally unsophisticated. Individuals ran their own programs by personally operating the computer. Computing facilities operated in this manner are described as *open shops* and are characterized by genuine "hands-on" operation and close man-machine interaction. Computers of that vintage (mid 1950s) had system controls which required each user to set switches on a console board and, during a single program's processing, all of the computer's components were committed to that one program. In addition, error messages were transmitted to the operator through console lights. Each job was expensive, in central processor time, as the computer sat idle while switches were set, cards loaded, programs unloaded, and so forth.

As user programs became more complex and the number of users increased, it became apparent that a better system was needed to raise the efficiency of processing. Second generation computing systems offered more capable hardware and the development of more capable system control software. *Supervisor* control programs were developed and, again, while elementary by today's standards, established the principle of automating computing systems' controls. Second generation hardware was faster, had larger memory, especially secondary external memory, and more capable control over input/output components. The supervisor program was a special program supplied by the computer manufacturer and was designed to:

1. centrally control input/output units
2. control programs so that as one program was completed another began processing
3. provide printed diagnostic messages
4. automatically compile or assemble programs

In other words, it supervised the operation of the computer system.

This step toward automating the system operation had the following consequences:

1. job processing efficiency increased (reduction in idle time of the central processor)
2. diagnostic messages were printed to aid system control
3. system input/output was better coordinated
4. human intervention was reduced by automating the functions formerly performed by the operator
5. computing operations changed from an open shop to a *closed shop* as users had less need to exercise hands-on control
6. programs were grouped into batches to take advantage of the processor's ability to perform continuous processing
7. certain penalties were invoked to gain these efficiencies
   a. it took longer to have program jobs returned (that is, "turnaround" times increased)
   b. the user was separated from the processor during the execution of his program (that is, man-machine interaction was sacrificed)

The growth of control programs extended to third generation computing equipment. Hardware became vastly more complex and so did the control systems. In addition to increasing the efficiencies of second generation controls, other abilities were added. The ability to load one processor with multiple programs at the same time (multiprogramming), simultaneous handling of input/output tasks and central processor execution, automatic priority scheduling and dynamic allocation of memory resources during processing, the addition of real-time processing capabilities, including time-sharing, input/output from locations geographically remote from the central processor, and the increasing ability to send computerized data over great distances via communications systems all required the development of highly sophisticated control systems.

All computers in use today have some system control requirements. Of course, the complexity varies among machines and these systems are referred to generally as operating systems. A user, such as a FORTRAN programmer, must submit not only his FORTRAN program for processing but also has to communicate appropriate system control information before executing his program. In more basic systems, the control instructions are conveyed by the use of *control cards*. Advanced control systems use an actual language generally called a *job control language* or JCL. JCL statements are given to the computing system via punch cards so the use of the term "control cards" broadly applies to all systems.

Specific control card formats have some variation from system to system but the principles of system control are very similar. Even among a single manufacturer's systems, specific system requirements will change because they are dependent upon the specifications given at the time the system is generated. Rather than attempt to discuss the details of every system in use, the remainder of this section will present a general description of operating system components. Specific requirements of any system may easily be acquired by consulting with the facility director. This discussion will be followed by an example from the IBM 360 Operating System.

Operating System Components

Operating systems (sometimes referred to as monitors or executives) are composed of three major components. These are an initial program loader, a supervisor program, and a job control program. These components have the following tasks:

Initial Program Loader (IPL).   When the operating system is initiated, this program clears memory and reads in the supervisor program.

Supervisor Program.   This program controls the computing system during the time a job is running. It executes all input/output operations, controls input/output devices, manages job execution, handles error conditions, and coordinates multiprogramming control on systems large enough to permit its use.

Job Control Program.   The job control program is loaded into memory when the supervisor program reads a JOB card (the first card in the deck submitted by a programmer). The job control program then reads the program cards. Functions related to job control include:

1. providing for the system options specified by the programmer
2. handling volume and label information related to the input/output of the program
3. program library control
4. establishing linkages (linkage editing) so that compiled programs may be placed in memory ready for execution
5. turning control over to the program to be executed

Communication with the operating system requires the programmer to specify the precise tasks which the operating system is expected to execute. Because an operating system is itself a program, the job control language instructions are given through a series of control cards. These cards are discussed in the following example.

Control Cards: A Card-to-Printer Example

A simple program will illustrate the preparation of job control language statements. Because the program merely reads and prints three data cards, we can highlight the control statements. A flowchart, program listing, and printed output are shown below.

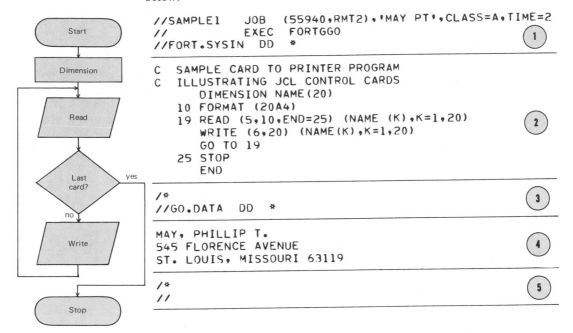

```
//SAMPLE1   JOB   (55940,RMT2),'MAY PT',CLASS=A,TIME=2
//          EXEC  FORTGGO                                  1
//FORT.SYSIN DD  *

C  SAMPLE CARD TO PRINTER PROGRAM
C  ILLUSTRATING JCL CONTROL CARDS
      DIMENSION NAME(20)
   10 FORMAT (20A4)
   19 READ (5,10,END=25) (NAME (K),K=1,20)    2
      WRITE (6,20) (NAME(K),K=1,20)
      GO TO 19
   25 STOP
      END

/*
//GO.DATA   DD  *                             3

MAY, PHILLIP T.
545 FLORENCE AVENUE                          4
ST. LOUIS, MISSOURI 63119

/*
//                                           5
```

Flowchart: Start, Dimension, Read, Last card? (yes/no), Write, Stop

Printed Output

MAY, PHILLIP T.
545 FLORENCE AVENUE
ST. LOUIS, MISSOURI 63119

The program listing has been divided into five basic sections:

1. control cards to identify the JOB, the type of compilation to execute (EXEC), and definition of the program data set (DD)
2. the FORTRAN source program
3. control cards to indicate the end of the program data set (/*) and definition of the data deck as another data set (DD)
4. the data deck
5. control cards for the end of the data set (/*) and end of the program (//)

Note that five types of control statements were used in the program. A sixth type of statement is in the job control language but it has a special purpose and will not be used in most basic FORTRAN programs. The six control statements are:

1. JOB—identifies a program and supplies accounting information
2. EXEC—indicates the type of program to be executed including the compiler needed, if necessary

3. DD—data definition which describes a program unit as a data set. This program unit may be a source program deck, a data deck, a magnetic tape file, a disk file, etc.
4. /*—delimiter statement which indicates the end of a data set
5. //—null statement indicating the end of a JOB
6. command statement—this type of statement indicates special options to the operating system

Before looking at these statements in detail, we should recognize that when an installation *generates an operating system* a wide choice of options may be included. This accounts for the near impossibility of finding two identical operating systems, even when the same manufacturer's equipment is being used. Generating an operating system involves placing the system control program into the computer system's memory. In this process, choices are made about which operating system options should be made available to users, specification of standard unit numbers (such as 5 for the card reader, 6 for the line printer, and 7 for the card punch), standard system unit names, etc. These choices dictate much of the form for the job control language statements used with the system. It may be concluded that each facility really designs its own control system by selecting those options which seem most appropriate for the types of processing to be executed.

The individual JCL statements explained below are used with an IBM 360 operating system. It should be noted that these statements begin either with double slashes (//) or with a slash-asterisk combination (/*). All IBM 360 systems use these characters but they are not standard among all manufacturer's systems, or even among all IBM computing systems for that matter. For example, some systems use a $ as the first character in control cards, others an * in the first card column, and some require no special character to begin control instructions. It is important to check these requirements before submitting a FORTRAN program.

Job Control Statements.

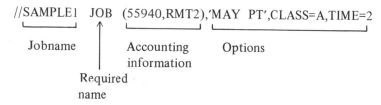

The JOB card is required as the first instruction for a specific job. This card identifies a new program and gives its name to the operating system. The jobname (created by the programmer) and word JOB are mandatory. The jobname may be from 1 to 8 characters and must begin with a letter. The spacing shown is also required.

All other information on the card is optional and will vary among installations. This card shows an account number (55940), the location to which the program is to be delivered (remote terminal 2), programmer's name ('MAY PT'), the portion of memory to be used for the program (CLASS=A), and the maximum amount of time which the system should allow for execution of the program (TIME=2). Numerous other options are available from the facility director.

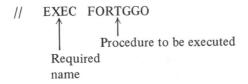

// EXEC FORTGGO

Required name — Procedure to be executed

The EXEC card instructs the operating system about which procedure to execute. The procedure may be a program compilation, a program being read in object code, any one of several procedures which have been catalogued by the system, etc. In this example, the procedure executed is a compilation of the FORTRAN source program. The word FORTGGO indicates the following to the operating system:

1. the FORTRAN compiler should be called into main memory for compilation.
2. The particular FORTRAN compiler to be used (most systems have several different compilers) will be the G level compiler.
3. After compiling, the object program should be loaded into memory and begin processing the data (that is, GO) without stopping. This procedure is referred to as compile-link-and-go.

Numerous other options are also available for use on the EXEC card and, like the JOB card, may be acquired from the computing facility.

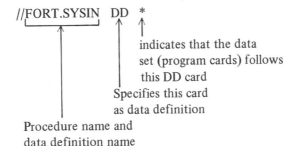

//FORT.SYSIN DD *

indicates that the data set (program cards) follows this DD card

Specifies this card as data definition

Procedure name and data definition name

The FORT.SYSIN data definition name is a catalogued procedure. It describes several system characteristics about the FORTRAN program data set which follows this card. These characteristics relate to the size of records read, their form, and the like. All of these specific details are prewritten and stored (that is, catalogued). Access to these details is gained by simply calling for the FORT.SYSIN procedure.

When an * is written after the letters DD, it indicates that a card data set (that is, FORTRAN program) follows this card.

/*

Delimiter card

Every data set (specified by a DD card) must have a /* instruction to indicate the end of the data set. In this program, FORT.SYSIN specified the FORTRAN program as a data set. Therefore, the /* is required after the FORTRAN program.

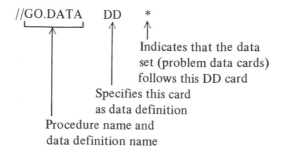

This card indicates that a second data set is being used in the program. This is a catalogued procedure in the same sense as the FORT.SYSIN described above. However, this procedure relates to execution of the FORTRAN program (that is, the GO. step) which processes the problem data. The name of this DD statement is DATA.

The use of DD and * are identical to the statement above. The data set following this card is composed of the problem data cards (that is, the data deck).

/*
↑
Delimiter card

This card indicates the end of a data set, as described with the /* card above.

//
↑
Null statement

This statement indicates the end of the job and signals the job control program to return responsibility for further processing to the supervisor program.

Magnetic Tape Input/Output

Punch cards serve as an inexpensive medium for handling data. Furthermore, punch cards offer an opportunity actually to see what is recorded in the cards. Major drawbacks to the use of punch cards are (1) an inability to store data in compact form, (2) slow reading and punching speeds, and (3) possible physical deterioration due to wear, humidity, and the like. The use of magnetic tape was developed in an attempt to overcome the shortcomings of the punch card. Computing systems record information on magnetic tape in much the same fashion as do home tape recorders. A tape unit (called a drive or transport) is attached to the computing system and is capable of both reading from and writing on magnetic tape.

A magnetic tape is a strip of plastic, normally one-half inch wide, which is covered with a metallic oxide. This coating can be magnetized to hold the binary representation of characters and numbers. The characters on a magnetic tape may be read repeatedly without destroying their magnetic properties. Writing over previous data is accomplished by first erasing the existing data, thus destroying it, and then writing the new data values. The reusable nature of magnetic tape makes it an economical medium for data storage and the high processing speeds make it a more efficient medium than punch cards.

Tape units move the tape past read/write heads (see Figure A.1) at high rates of speed. In this process, data is transferred to or from the tape at rates of 7,000 to 200,000 characters per second.

Figure A.1 Magnetic Tape Drive and Schematic of READ/WRITE Assembly

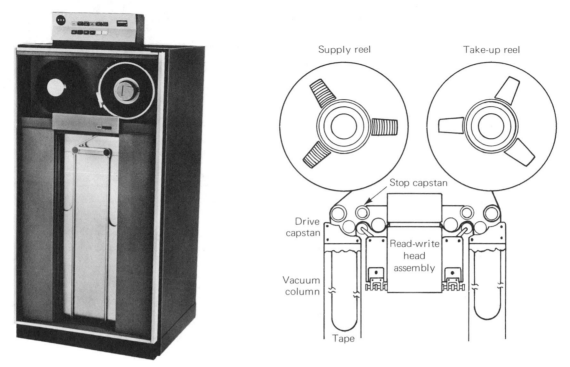

While tape of one-half inch width is widely used, other dimensions such as three-quarter and one inch are also used. Each magnetic tape is wound on a reel which is inserted in a plastic cover while not in use. This protects the tape from dust and physical damage. Tape lengths may vary in size, but tapes commonly come in 1200, 2400, or 3600 foot lengths. The amount of data which is recorded per inch of tape is referred to as tape density. Higher density tape holds more data than lower density tape with 200, 556, 800, and 1600 bytes per inch being the most common densities. Constant improvement in tape techniques has raised tape speeds and packing density significantly in recent years. The figures listed here will un-doubtedly change within a short period.

Magnetic tape has data coded along rows which run horizontally with the tape. Each row is called a track or channel. Two common channel sizes are in use today. Seven channel tape contains one parity, two zone, and four numeric positions. Nine channel tape has one parity, four zone, and four numeric positions. Each of these tape forms is shown in Figure A.2.

In each of the tape examples shown, a short line is used to represent magnetized spots on the tape. A tape drive magnetizes appropriate channel positions with the write head. When data is taken from a tape, the read head senses these magnetized positions. Each vertical column of magnetized spots (called a frame) represents an alphabetic, numeric, or special character. The parity channel is used to provide an accuracy check on a tape's data. In systems using even parity, each frame must contain an even number of magnetized spots. If a character lacks an even number of magnetized spots when written, the parity channel is magnetized to give the even parity. Any future handling of the character will be checked for its even parity. If

Figure A.2 Seven and Nine Channel Tape

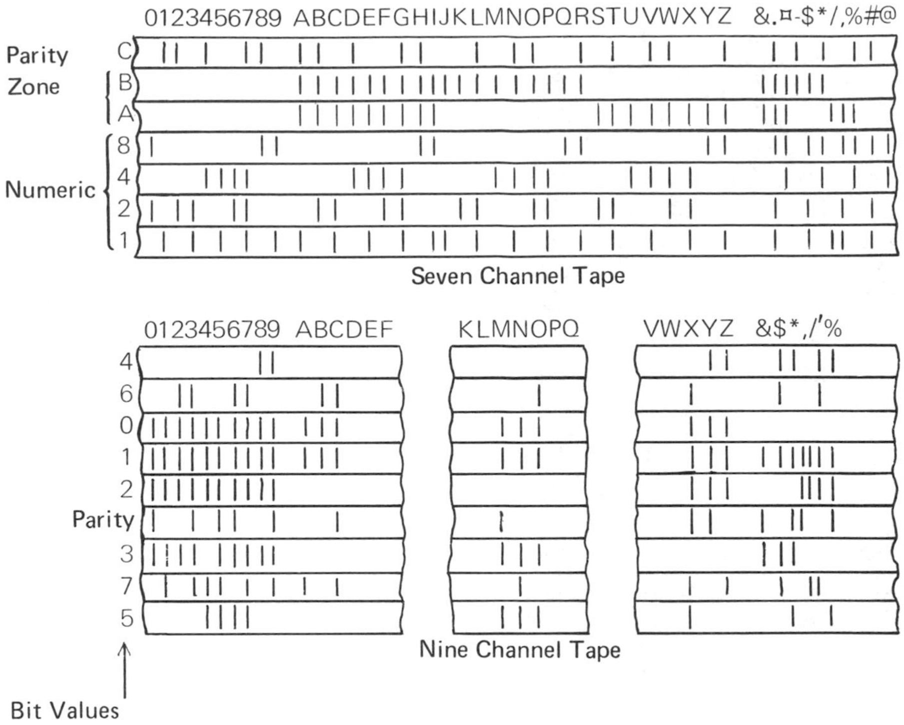

Seven Channel Tape

Nine Channel Tape

Bit Values

an absence of even parity is sensed, an error condition will be signaled. Some systems use odd parity. The principles are identical to even parity systems except that all characters carry an odd number of magnetized spots. A second type of parity check is also performed by a tape unit. A horizontal check is made of each channel to check for odd or even parity of all data along the channel. Recording and checking parity is done automatically by the system and is not directly under the programmer's control.

Data Records on Tape

Each tape reel contains a single continuous strip of tape which is processed sequentially. Data located at the end of a tape can be reached only by reading from the beginning of the tape, through the length of the tape, to the end. The sequential nature of magnetic tape does provide a drawback if processing calls for nonsequential data handling. No convenient and efficient method is available for moving back and forth at random among data values on a magnetic tape.

The sequential structure of tapes results in each tape holding records as shown in Figure A.3.

Each record on a tape is separated from previous and succeeding records by a blank section of tape about three-fourths of an inch long. This blank section is called an interrecord gap. Its function is to allow the tape drive enough space to slow down and stop after reading or writing a record and to gain speed before reading or writing the next record. The interrecord gaps preclude the loss of data while the tape drive is starting and stopping.

Figure A.3 Schematic of Magnetic Tape (Unblocked)

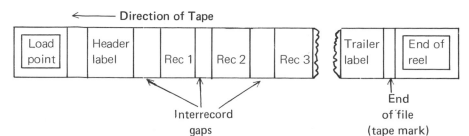

A magnetic tape also has several other important elements. The beginning of a tape contains a strip of reflective material known as the load point. When the tape is mounted, the tape drive will advance to the load point which indicates the beginning of the usable tape. Following the load point marker, the tape will have a header label. This label specifies control information which indentifies the tape, specifies record format, and so forth. In most systems, the programmer may either specify label information or, more conveniently, allow the system to attach its own standard label. A trailer label follows the last data record in a file. This label does not have to be at the physical end of the tape. Records may not fill the entire tape. Therefore, the trailer label may be found anywhere within the tape. A special end-of-file marker (called a tape mark) is placed on a tape to signal the end of a file. It also does not have to appear at the physical end of the tape. The end of each tape reel is indicated by a reflective strip similar to the load point marker. This strip is located at the physical end of the magnetic tape.

Records written on a tape require the use of many interrecord gaps when the records are numerous and are short. These gaps consume significant amounts of tape which cannot be used to hold data values. The technique of record blocking is available to reduce the interrecord gaps. This technique allows several records (called logical records) to be grouped (that is, blocked) into one physical record. Each block of records is separated by an interblock gap. The interblock gap is identical in purpose to the interrecord gap. This arrangement of records is shown in Figure A.4.

Figure A.4 Schematic of Magnetic Tape (Blocked)

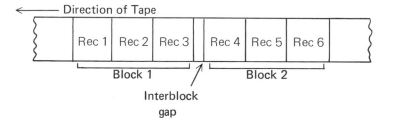

The use of blocked records speeds the reading of data as the tape unit is not required to start and stop as often as is necessary with unblocked records. An entire block is read into memory, and the program separates the blocked records into their individual logical components. Processing may then continue using the individual records. Therefore, blocking saves tape by allowing more data to be recorded per inch of tape and saves computer time because the central processor is not idle as often, waiting for the tape unit to read the next record.

Control Cards: A Card-to-Tape-to-Printer Example

This section illustrates a card-to-tape-to-printer program using the same data shown on page 385. This example shows a program which reads data from cards and writes the data on a magnetic tape. The program then reads the data from the magnetic tape and writes it on a line printer. A flowchart and program listing are shown below. The printed output is identical to that shown on page 385.

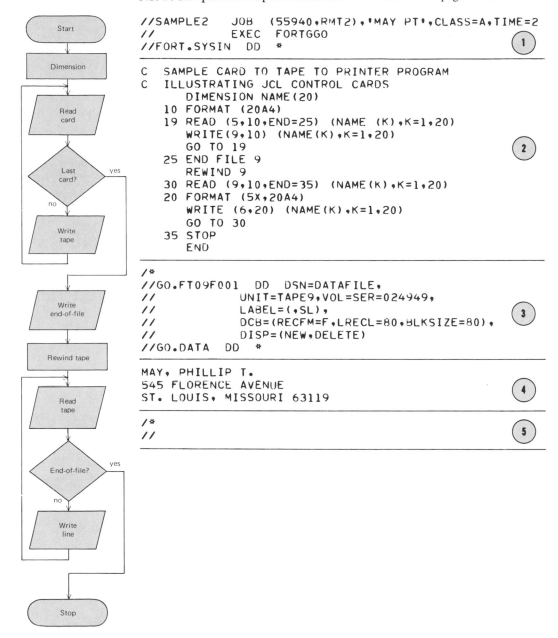

```
//SAMPLE2   JOB   (55940,RMT2),'MAY PT',CLASS=A,TIME=2
//          EXEC  FORTGGO
//FORT.SYSIN  DD   *                                            1

C  SAMPLE CARD TO TAPE TO PRINTER PROGRAM
C  ILLUSTRATING JCL CONTROL CARDS
      DIMENSION NAME(20)
   10 FORMAT (20A4)
   19 READ (5,10,END=25) (NAME (K),K=1,20)
      WRITE(9,10) (NAME(K),K=1,20)
      GO TO 19                                                  2
   25 END FILE 9
      REWIND 9
   30 READ (9,10,END=35) (NAME(K),K=1,20)
   20 FORMAT (5X,20A4)
      WRITE (6,20) (NAME(K),K=1,20)
      GO TO 30
   35 STOP
      END

/*
//GO.FT09F001  DD  DSN=DATAFILE,
//               UNIT=TAPE9,VOL=SER=024949,
//               LABEL=(,SL),                                   3
//               DCB=(RECFM=F,LRECL=80,BLKSIZE=80),
//               DISP=(NEW,DELETE)
//GO.DATA   DD   *

MAY, PHILLIP T.
545 FLORENCE AVENUE                                            4
ST. LOUIS, MISSOURI 63119

/*                                                              5
//
```

Note the following points about each section in the above listing.

Section 1—identical to section 1 on page 385

Section 2—three new elements appear:

1. two READ and WRITE commands call for unit 9, in addition to those using units 5 and 6
2. a new FORTRAN statement, END FILE
3. a new FORTRAN statement, REWIND

Section 3—a new data definition statement is included (GO.FT09F001). This statement defines the tape file as a data set.

Sections 4 and 5—identical to those on page 385.

Tape Job Control Statements

Section 3 of the program contains the only new control statement. This section defines the tape file as a data set. It appears as:

```
//GO.FT09F001    DD  DSN=DATAFILE,
//               UNIT=TAPE9,VOL=SER=024949,
//               LABEL=(,SL),
//               DCB=(RECFM=F,LRECL=80,BLKSIZE=80),
//               DISP=(NEW,DELETE)
```

The elements of this DD statement are:

1. GO.FT09F001

   F001 is a data set sequence number which indicates that this is the first reel in this tape data set.

   FT09 is a data set reference number which indicates that this tape will be on unit number 9. This number is selected by the programmer and must agree with the unit number in the tape READ and WRITE statements.

   GO. is a data definition name and indicates that this is a file used in the GO. or execution step of the program.

2. DSN=DATAFILE

   DSN means data set name.

   DATAFILE is a name created by the programmer and may be one to eight characters with the first character alphabetic.

3. UNIT=TAPE9 indicates that the data set will use a nine track tape.

4. VOL=SER=024949 indicates that the tape file will be on one tape (VOL) which has a serial number (SER) of 024949.

5. LABEL=(,SL) indicates that the system is to write standard labels (SL) on the tape. The comma implies that the tape contains one data set.

6. DCB(RECFM=F,LRECL=80,BLKSIZE=80)

   DCB means data control block.

   RECFM=F means record format, and it specifies fixed length (F) records (80 characters in this case). If these records were blocked, FB would be specified.

   LRECL=80 means the logical record length is 80 bytes (equivalent to 80 characters or columns).

   BLKSIZE=80 means the block size is 80 bytes. These records are *un*blocked. Therefore, each record is a block and block size is the same length as the record length. If this example had used blocks of ten records, for example, the LRECL and BLKSIZE would have been LRECL=80,BLKSIZE=800.

7. DISP=(NEW, DELETE) means disposition or status of the data set (tape) before and after processing.

NEW indicates that this is a new tape file being created in this job.

DELETE indicates that, after execution is completed, the tape is to be rewound for dismounting from the tape drive.

This control statement illustrates the large number of specifications which must be given to the operating system when using a tape data set. A wide variety of other options are available in defining tape files. Refer to the manufacturer's manual for full coverage of these options.

FORTRAN Tape Commands

Three FORTRAN command words apply only to the use of magnetic tape. Two of these commands were used in the example on page 392. Each command is explained below.

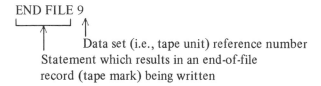

END FILE 9

        Data set (i.e., tape unit) reference number

Statement which results in an end-of-file record (tape mark) being written

A tape mark, written when an END FILE statement is executed, permits a subsequent READ statement to include the END= option. The computer reads the tape until the tape mark is sensed. A branch is then made to the statement number listed with the END= option.

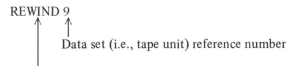

REWIND 9

        Data set (i.e., tape unit) reference number

Statement which causes a magnetic tape to be rewound and positioned at the first record on the tape

The REWIND command causes the control program to position a magnetic tape so that a subsequent READ/WRITE statement will apply to the first record on the tape.

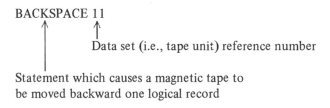

BACKSPACE 11

        Data set (i.e., tape unit) reference number

Statement which causes a magnetic tape to be moved backward one logical record

This command positions the magnetic tape so that the last logical record read, or written, may be accessed again. A BACKSPACE command used with unblocked records moves the tape backward one record. With blocked records, backward spacing moves the tape back over one block.

Direct Areas (Magnetic Disk) Input/Output

Current computing systems support a rapidly growing storage medium called direct access, or more popularly known as magnetic disk, in addition to punch cards and magnetic tape. Magnetic disks offer the following advantages:

1. high density, compact storage
2. rapid access to stored data
3. an ability to directly (randomly) access data regardless of its position in the disk file

Figure A.5 Removable Disk Pack and Magnetic Disk Drive Storage Unit

Figure A.5 shows an IBM 2311 Magnetic Disk Storage Unit. The disks on this unit may be removed and interchanged with other *disk packs*. This feature expands disk storage. Some systems use permanent disk units which have a fixed amount of storage.

A magnetic material covers both sides of a disk. Data is recorded on either disk side by magnetizing the surface. Each disk side is divided into concentric circles or tracks. In turn, the tracks are divided into sectors. Each sector can be addressed separately by positioning the disk unit's read/write heads over the sector. A key advantage to this read/write technique is that all sectors can be retrieved in an equal amount of time. Therefore, a disk file may be *randomly* accessed, by sector, rather than being sequentially read like tape and card files. Records on a disk file may be fixed or variable length and blocked or unblocked. It is the random access feature which is the key difference between disk and tape.

A disk unit spins the disks on a spindle at fifteen- to eighteen-hundred revolutions per minute. Each side of a disk is accessed by its own read/write head (see Figure

A.6). The heads move in and out on arms which position the heads over the track desired. Figure A.6 also shows a schematic drawing of a disk side. The storage dimensions listed relate to the more popular but smaller disks found in disk packs. Storage of two million characters is typical of this disk size. By comparison, permanent disk units have 50 or more disks which will hold 20 million or more characters.

Figure A.6 Schematic of Magnetic Disk Storage

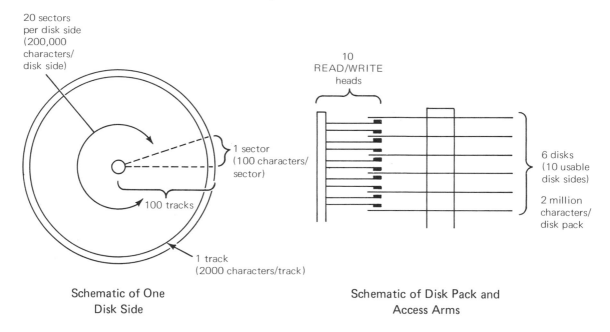

20 sectors per disk side (200,000 characters/disk side)

1 sector (100 characters/sector)

100 tracks

1 track (2000 characters/track)

Schematic of One Disk Side

10 READ/WRITE heads

6 disks (10 usable disk sides)

2 million characters/disk pack

Schematic of Disk Pack and Access Arms

Control Cards: A Card-to-Disk-to-Printer Example

This example uses FORTRAN instructions for disk input/output which are IBM extensions of the FORTRAN IV language. These instructions will not be standard among all manufacturers' systems using disk storage media. However, the example does give an illustration of the considerations necessary when using disk files.

The basic processing problem given on page 385 will be used again in this example. This program reads from cards, writes on a disk file, reads from the disk file, and writes on the line printer. Output from the program execution will be identical to the output shown on page 385. A flowchart and program listing appear on page 397.

This program contains specifications which permit reading and writing on a disk file. The primary elements in these specifications are (1) control statement parameters identifying the disk unit and the space requirements, and (2) program statements which define the file to be used and specify READ/WRITE commands using the disk file. Each of these elements is examined below.

Note the following points about the five sections in this program.

Section 1—identical control instructions to section 1 on page 385

Section 2—three new elements are introduced:

1. two READ and WRITE statements use disk unit 22, in addition to the READ/WRITE statements using units 5 and 6

2. a new FORTRAN statement, DEFINE FILE

3. a new FORTRAN statement, FIND

Section 3—GO.FT22F001 control statement describes the disk file

Sections 4 and 5—identical data deck and control instructions as sections 4 and 5 on page 385

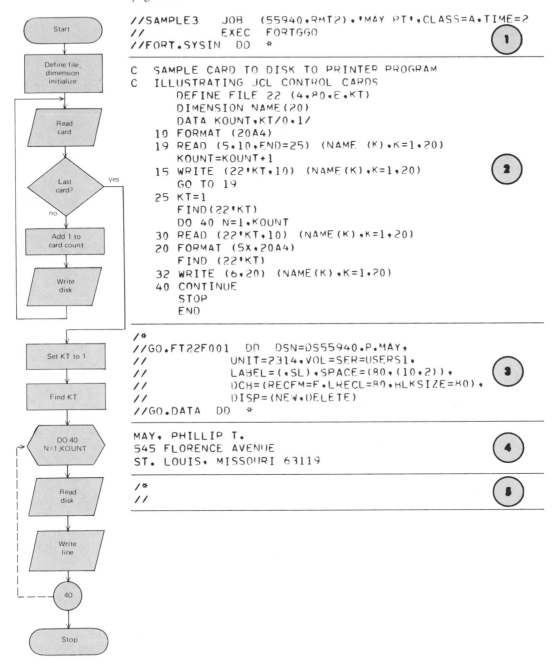

```
//SAMPLE3    JOB   (55940.RMT2).'MAY PT'.CLASS=A.TIME=2
//           EXEC   FORTGGO
//FORT.SYSIN  DD  *
```
(1)

```
C   SAMPLE CARD TO DISK TO PRINTER PROGRAM
C   ILLUSTRATING JCL CONTROL CARDS
        DEFINE FILE 22 (4.80.E.KT)
        DIMENSION NAME(20)
        DATA KOUNT.KT/0.1/
   10 FORMAT (20A4)
   19 READ (5.10.END=25) (NAME (K).K=1.20)
        KOUNT=KOUNT+1
   15 WRITE (22'KT.10) (NAME(K).K=1.20)
        GO TO 19
   25 KT=1
        FIND(22'KT)
        DO 40 N=1.KOUNT
   30 READ (22'KT.10) (NAME(K).K=1.20)
   20 FORMAT (5X.20A4)
        FIND (22'KT)
   32 WRITE (6.20) (NAME(K).K=1.20)
   40 CONTINUE
        STOP
        END
```
(2)

```
/*
//GO.FT22F001  DD   DSN=DS55940.P.MAY.
//            UNIT=2314.VOL=SER=USERS1.
//            LABEL=(.SL).SPACE=(80.(10.2)).
//            DCB=(RECFM=F.LRECL=80.BLKSIZE=80).
//            DISP=(NEW.DELETE)
//GO.DATA    DD  *
```
(3)

```
MAY. PHILLIP T.
545 FLORENCE AVENUE
ST. LOUIS. MISSOURI 63119
```
(4)

```
/*
//
```
(5)

Job Control Statements. The job control statements for disk files are quite similar to those for tape files. The following elements are required changes in the GO. - DD statement.

1. GO.FT22F001

   FT22 is a data set (that is, disk unit) reference number which must match the reference number in the program READ/WRITE statements and DEFINE FILE statement.

2. UNIT=2314 indicates the type of disk unit to be used. In this case, a disk drive numbered by the manufacturer as 2314.

3. VOL=SER=USERS1 indicates the system name used to identify the specific disk pack on which the data file will reside.

4. SPACE=(80,(10,2)) indicates the space to be reserved for the disk file.

   80 represents the *units of measurement* in which storage is assigned. In this example, 80 is the average length of the records to be stored.

   10 represents the *primary* amount of *space* allocated for the disk file. In this example, 10 records.

   2 represents the *secondary* amount of *space* allocated when the primary allocation is exhausted. In this example, 2 records. This secondary allocation would be made a maximum of 15 times, if needed.

   It is of key importance that the space allocation, made in this control statement, agree with the space designation in the DEFINE FILE statement.

5. LABEL=(,SL) this statement may be omitted because the operating system will *only* assign standard labels to disk files.

FORTRAN Disk Commands

Two new statements are needed when magnetic disk is used for data storage. These statements are the DEFINE FILE and FIND statements. In addition, an adjustment is required in the READ/WRITE statements using disk files.

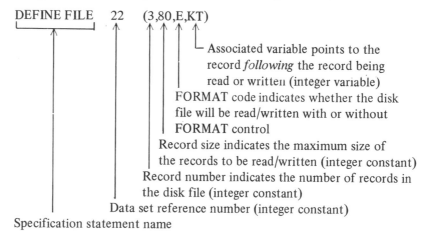

```
DEFINE FILE    22    (3,80,E,KT)
```

Associated variable points to the record *following* the record being read or written (integer variable)

FORMAT code indicates whether the disk file will be read/written with or without FORMAT control

Record size indicates the maximum size of the records to be read/written (integer constant)

Record number indicates the number of records in the disk file (integer constant)

Data set reference number (integer constant)

Specification statement name

A disk file must be defined prior to its use. The DEFINE FILE statement specifies a file's characteristics and must appear prior to any use of the file for input or output. The *data set reference number* is used in the READ/WRITE statements using the file. The *number of records* in the file must be specified in this statement.

A number larger than the records actually used may be specified but not the reverse. Record size must agree with the DD statement in the system control cards which describe this disk file. The *FORMAT code* may be one of these three:

E—the file is to be read and/or written with the use of a FORMAT statement and the record size is measured in numbers of characters or bytes.

U—the file is to be read/written without the use of a FORMAT. The record size is measured in storage units or words.

L—the file may be read/written either with or without the use of a FORMAT. Record size is measured in number of storage locations or bytes.

The *associated variable* is incremented automatically each time a READ/WRITE statement is executed. This variable points to the file record which immediately follows the record just read or written. This enables the next READ/WRITE statement to handle the records in a sequential order. The associated variable is subject to manipulation like any other variable, and records may be handled in a non-sequential order by altering the associated variable between READ/WRITE executions. This manipulation overrides the inherent incrementing of the associated variable. See the READ/WRITE statements below for an example of this manipulation.

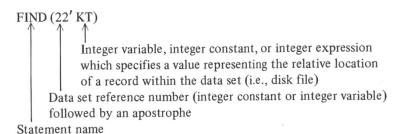

FIND (22′ KT)

          Integer variable, integer constant, or integer expression
          which specifies a value representing the relative location
          of a record within the data set (i.e., disk file)
     Data set reference number (integer constant or integer variable)
     followed by an apostrophe
Statement name

This statement directs the system and direct access unit to FIND a specific record in the disk file. Normally, this statement precedes a READ command. While a current record is being handled, the FIND statement is locating the next record to be read. This process increases the execution speed of a direct access program.

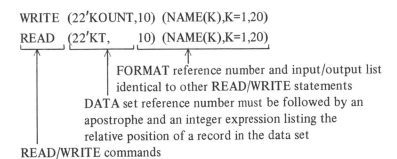

WRITE (22′KOUNT,10) (NAME(K),K=1,20)
READ   (22′KT,   10) (NAME(K),K=1,20)

          FORMAT reference number and input/output list
         identical to other READ/WRITE statements
     DATA set reference number must be followed by an
     apostrophe and an integer expression listing the
     relative position of a record in the data set
READ/WRITE commands

Direct access units require an indicator or pointer to specify the relative position of file records which are being read or written. This indicator appears in READ and WRITE statements using the disk file. The above examples show the inclusion of the pointer following the data set reference number. An apostrophe is required after the data set number. Following the apostrophe is the pointer. It may be an integer constant, variable, or expression.

Review of the program on page 397 illustrates how disk instructions are used.

1. DEFINE FILE: this statement describes the disk file used in the program.
2. The 15 WRITE statement places a record in the disk file. KT specifies the relative position of each record on the disk file. This variable was initialized at one in the DATA statement. After each execution of the WRITE statement, KT is automatically incremented by one. Thus, it points to the next record in the file.
3. Statement 25 reinitializes KT to one. This allows the FIND statement to access the first record for reading from the file.
4. When the 30 READ statement is executed, the first record will have been found and is immediately accessible for reading. KT will be incremented automatically by one.
5. The second FIND statement will access the next record while the 32 WRITE statement is printing a line. When the next cycle is made through the DO loop, the record to be read will be available.

This series of steps illustrates how a record can be accessed while another statement is being executed. This overlapping of functions adds efficiency to a program using a disk storage medium.

Appendix B
Suggested Answers to Exercises

1. a. Desired result: a single dollar figure expressing the average sales (both cash and credit sales) for one calendar month.
   b. Data elements: (1) individual sales (cash & credit) for the month, and (2) count of the number of sales during the month.
   c. Processing Factors: (1) summation of sales for the month, and (2) division of the sales total by the count of sales during the month.

3. Prior to specifying the desired results, some definitional questions should be answered. This illustrates that, even with a seemingly simple problem, there is a great need for understanding the problem *before* jumping to some computerized attempt at a solution.

   (1) What is an average student?
       (a) full-time or part-time?
       (b) full-time equivalent?
   (2) What is an average credit hour measure?
       (a) full-time? how many hours?
       (b) part-time?
       (c) full-time equivalent?
       (d) full-time defined as an absolute number of hours (such as 15) or as a range (such as 12-15 hours)?
   (3) What is tuition paid?
       (a) tuition charged and paid without regard to sources of funds?
       (b) paid measured after deducting payments resulting from tuition remission, scholarships, assistanceships, etc.?
   (4) What period of time is being measured?
       (a) semester?
       (b) quarter?
       (c) year?

   Assumptions used in this answer:
   (1) Full-time means the student is taking 15 hours (assume no student takes more than 15 hours).
   (2) Part-time figures will be converted to a full-time equivalent.
   (3) A semester is the time period for measurement
   (4) Paid tuition is equal to that charged, for some calculations, and is adjusted for other calculations (i.e., measures only the "new" funds flowing in to the college).

a. Desired result:
A single figure expressing the average dollar size of tuition paid, regardless of source, per full-time equivalent student.
A single figure expressing the average dollar size of tuition paid, regardless of source, per credit hour for each full-time equivalent student.
Two dollar figures identical to those above except that the tuition paid is adjusted to remove scholarships, etc. which do not represent "new" funds flowing in to the college.
Total tuition paid, regardless of source, to the college.
Total adjusted tuition paid to the college.
Average number of credit hours taken, per full-time equivalent student.
Average number of credit hours taken, per student (not adjusted for full-time equivalency).

b. Data elements:
Total tuition paid by student.
Number of credit hours taken, by student.
Tuition paid, by student, by fund source.

c. Processing factors:
Using number of credit hours taken, determine part-time students and convert to a full-time equivalent.
Accumulate the following:

(1) total tuition paid (from all funds sources)
(2) total tuition paid (adjusted sources)
(3) total credit hours taken by full-time equivalent students
(4) total credit hours taken (without adjustment for full-time equivalency)

Divide the following:

(1) by (5) average tuition paid, full-time, all sources
(2) by (5) average tuition paid, full-time, adjusted sources
(3) by (5) average number of credit hours taken, full-time equivalent
(4) by (6) average number of credit hours taken, no adjustment for full-time equivalency
(1) by (6) average tuition paid, all sources, not adjusted for full-time equivalency
(2) by (6) average tuition paid, adjusted sources, not adjusted for full-time equivalency
(1) by (3) average tuition paid @ credit hour, full-time, all sources
(1) by (4) average tuition paid @ credit hour, all sources, not adjusted for full-time equivalency
(2) by (3) average tuition paid @ credit hour, full-time, adjusted sources
(2) by (4) average tuition paid @ credit hour, adjusted sources, not adjusted for full-time equivalency

---

Exercise 2

1. Note these elements:
   a. use of a decision to determine when the last card is read
   b. counting and summing must be finished *before* division takes place
   c. writing may not take place *until* the calculation of average sales is made

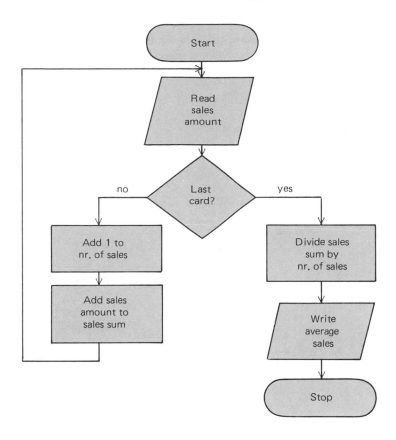

3. Note these elements:
   a.   use of the *notation* symbol opposite the READ step
   b.   accumulation of totals *prior* to calculations

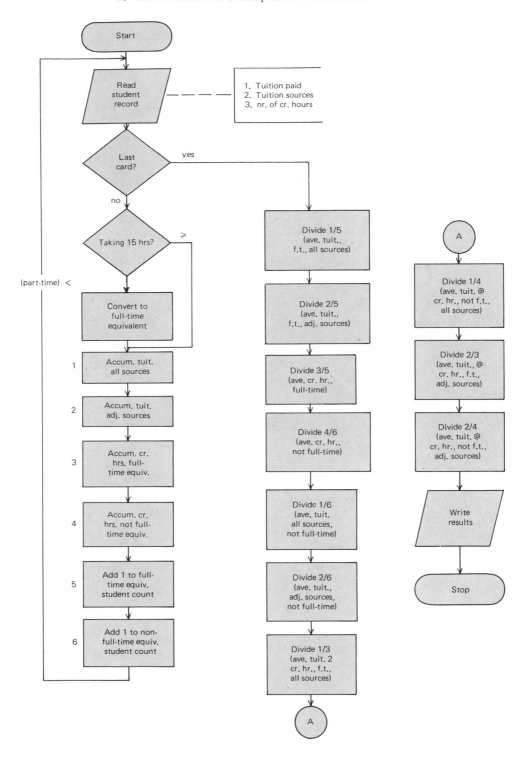

Exercise 3

1. Numbers *not* in real mode do not have decimal points.
   a. 287   b. -5   e. 137   f. 42   h. 2

3. Numbers *not* in integer mode have decimal points.
   a. -0.28   b. 3.7   c. 28.   f. 72.0   i. 0.4   j. +15.6

Exercise 4

1. Names *not* in the integer mode begin with the letters A-H or O-Z.
   b. ABC   c. GOGO   e. P   f. WASH   g. UNIV   h. BOOK
   i. C12   j. ZIM

3. Conversion can be accomplished by placing any letter from the opposite mode at the beginning of an existing data name.
   a. IA or JA, etc.   b. AIJK or BIJK, etc.   c. IRACK   d. NZ37   e. CMEE
   f. MC1F2   g. IHAM   h. ALOW   i. KS28R   j. DNUM

Exercise 5

1. Any appropriate combination of characters may be used. The following names are suggestions rather than absolute answers.
   a. YEAR   b. DEPR   c. SALES   d. INTY   e. EXP
   f. NUMBER   g. EQUIP   h. SALRY   i. LIFE   j. TOTAL

Exercise 6

1. a. 4.25
   b. 50
   c. 37.0—stored in real mode because variable data name begins with "D."
   d. 16—stored in integer mode because variable name begins with "I." Storage of a real mode value at a location having an integer mode variable name causes the value's mode to be converted. Conversion is accomplished by *truncating* (dropping) the fractional value.

   e. 15.8

3. Conversion can be accomplished by beginning the data name with one of the letters from the opposite mode.
   a. IBYE   b. CIBA   c. AJAZ   d. KZAP   e. MABI
   f. JB2   g. MH4G   h. DKA2   i. ZNOT   j. LTON

Exercise 7

   a. 10   FORMAT (I3, I2, F6.2, F3.0, I1)
   b. 5   FORMAT (2I3, F4.1, F4.2, F3.0, F3.2)
   c. 200 FORMAT (5I1, F2.1, I3)
   d. 50   FORMAT (2F8.2)
   e. 100 FORMAT (I2, F3.0, F4.0, F6.2, 2I1, F2.0)
   f. 32   FORMAT (F4.1, 2F3.1, I1, 2F3.1)

Exercise 8

1. a. 10   FORMAT (I3, I2, F6.2, F3.0, I1)
          READ (5,10) I, J, A, B, K

   b. 5   FORMAT (2I3, F4.1, F4.2, F3.0, F3.2)
          READ   (5, 5) I, J, A, B, C, D

   c. 200 FORMAT (5I1, F2.1, I3)
          READ (5, 200) I, J, K, L, M, A, N

   d. 50   FORMAT (2F8.2)   [remember, changing any character gives a
          READ (5,50) A1, A2   different data name]

   e. 100 FORMAT (I2, F3.0, F4.0, F6.2, 2I1, F2.0)
          READ (5,100) I, A, B, C, J, K, D

   f. 32   FORMAT (F4.1, 2F3.1, I1, 2F3.1)
          READ (5,32) A, B, C, I, D1, DD

Exercise 9

1. a.   I = 2(or I = 2.0,* I = 2.64, etc.)
   b.   G = 27.0(or G = 27*)
   c.   Y = 32.5
   d.   M = 400(or M = 400.*,M = 400.38, etc.)
   e.   A = S + T
   f.   J = X * 2.4*
   g.   K = M / N
   h.   H = V – 3.264
   i.   A2 = R**2 – A
   j.   Z = L**3 + LL – LLL*

*The mode of an arithmetic expression will be converted to the mode of the variable storage location shown to the left of the equals sign. Real mode expressions have any fractional values truncated when storage is made at an integer location. Integer expressions stored in real mode locations, in effect, have a decimal point added.

Exercise 10

1. 25   FORMAT (8X, 15HCURRENT QUARTER, 2X, I2, 4X,
               112HSALES VOLUME, 2X, F9.2)
            WRITE (6,25) IQTR, VOL

Note: any FORMAT number could be used here, spacing could have been included in the H codes, and variable names in the WRITE statement can be any of your choice but they must be in the correct mode.

2. b.   2 FORMAT (5X, 24HTHIS IS EXERCISE NUMBER, I2)
   c.   3 FORMAT (1X, 16HNEGATIVE ITEMS = , 2X, I3)
   e.   5 FORMAT (2X, 18 HERROR - STATEMENT ,I3, 13H IS TO LARGE)

3. b. WRITE (6,2) NUMBER   c. WRITE (6,3) NEG   e. WRITE (6,5) LARGE

Exercise 11

1. a.   S = A+2.0*R**2
   b.   H = A/(B+4.0*S**2)
   c.   N = K**3/(IA+IB)+2
   d.   B =B*(B+C*D) – (S*C – W*D)
   e.   Y = .0015*((P+A*BM)/(P–A*BM))
   f.   C = –I +J
   g.   T = A+(B*C)/D+CM**2–G*H
   h.   I = C*(A+B)/D+E**5*((A+B)/C)

Exercise 12

1. a.   L = 1
   c.   N = –3
   e.   E = 1.875
   g.   A = 5. (do you have the order of operations correct?)
   h.   M = 1 (fractions are truncated)
   l.   H = 121.5 (exponentiate first)
   m.   Z = 7.105556 (processing order-the key)
   o.   X = –405.4625

2. a.   OK
   b.   A+3.0 (more than one variable to left of equal sign)
   c.   I+ – D (two arithmetic operators in succession)
   d.   OK
   e.   4 (only variable names allowed to left of equal sign)
   f.   OK
   g.   DOLLARS (too long; NICKL—mixed mode on some computers)
   h.   OK (accomplishes nothing, however)

Exercise 13

1. Three statement numbers must follow the parentheses. For example:
   IF(A) 10,20,30

3. O.K.

5. For some computers, mixed mode in test expression. Illegal comma after parentheses. It should be: IF(AI−.9)44,45,46

7. Missing right parentheses. It should be: IF(A**3/B/(C−D))50,51,50

9. Incomplete test expression.

Exercise 14

1. This program reads data cards one at a time. As each value is read, it tests the value to determine whether it is larger than the previous largest value (see instruction 10). After reading all data cards, the largest value will be written (see instruction 15).

3. The trailer card will have 90000 punched in it. The instruction following the READ statement tests for this last card value. Any value less that 90000 will cause a transfer to instruction 10. When the trailer card is encountered, transfer will be made to instruction 15.

5. Output line: bbbbbTHIS IS ITbbXXXXX

              5X   10H   2X   I5

Exercise 15

1. Any valid read and integer variable names may be used as counters.

Real	Integer
a. A = A + 1.0	I = I + 1
b. B = B + 3.0	J = J + 3
c. C = C − 2.0	K = K − 2
d. D = D * 2.0	L = L * 2
e. E = E + 5.7	(not possible due to fractional value)

Exercise 16

1. DIMENSION ABC(200)
   DIMENSION IBIC(15)
   DIMENSION R2(99)
   DIMENSION XYZ(12)

3.   DIMENSION NOW(20)
   10 FORMAT (I5)
        J = 0
   20 J = J + 1
        READ (5,10) NOW(J)
        IF (NOW(J)−99999)20,25,25
   25   .
          .
          .

Exercise 17

1. a.   DO75 I = 1,4,1 (the last 1 could be omitted)
   b.   DO75 J2 = 7,12,3
   c.   DO75 KI = 3,N,2
   d.   DO75 LMN = K,N,L
   e.   DO75 IJK = 1,29,5

3. a.   Illegal comma follows statement number 10.
   b.   Index must be an integer variable (A=real mode).
   c.   No errors but senseless as loop will be completed only once.
   d.   Values in the index must not be signed numbers.
   e.   Index parameters must be in the integer mode and may not be arithmetic expressions.

Exercise 18

1. a.   Illegal comma after 6; should be closing parenthesis after 6.
   b.   Illegal comma after 7; should be closing parenthesis after 7; should be opening parenthesis before either J, K, or L (I); A is not an integer index.
   c.   O.K.
   d.   Illegal comma after (6,10).
   e.   Illegal comma after first J; should be closing parenthesis.
   f.   Should be opening parenthesis before IJ or K(M).

3. a.   25 FORMAT(5X,4(I2,3X))
             WRITE(6,25) (IJ(L),L=1,4)
   b.   N = 1
             M = 2
             DO 40 I=1,50
             WRITE(6,30) (A(K),J(K),K=N,M)
         30 FORMAT(5X,2(F6.2,3X,I2,3X))
             N = N+2
             M = M+2
         40 CONTINUE
   c.   45 FORMAT(5X,2(I1,2X),F5.2,2X,3(I1,2X),F5.2,2X,I1)
             WRITE(6,45)I,J,A(1),NO(1),I,J,A(1),NO(2)

Exercise 19

1. a.   8 FORMAT(I3,2F4.2,I2,I1,F5.1,2I1)
   b.   10 FORMAT(I3)
             READ(5,10) K
   c.   12 FORMAT(I3,4X,F4.2,2X,I1,5X,2I1)⎤ be sure to match the mode between
             READ(5,12) K,A,L,M,N   ⎦ your variable names and FORMAT

3.   30 FORMAT(1H1,24X,19HWASHINGTON COMPANY ///
             123X,23HMONTHLY SALES SUMMARY//10X, 10HDISTRICT A,
             25X,10HDISTRICT B,5X,10HDISTRICT C,5X,10HDISTRICT D)
             WRITE (6,30)

Exercise 20

	Stored		Printed (b = blank)
1. a.	1234	2. a.	1234
b.	−560	b.	bbb56
c.	7	c.	*** (error condition)
d.	−8900	d.	bbb−90
e.	0	e.	b2468

	Stored		Printed (b=blank)
3. a.	123.4	4. a.	−12.46
b.	567.		b28.903000
c.	−892.46	c.	*** (error condition)
d.	−3.500	d.	b−35.79
e.	78.401	e.	bb321.00

Exercise 21		FORMAT	Decimal Value		Printed Value
	1. (1)	E9.0	5438090000.	2. (1)	bbbb0.54381E+06
	(2)	E11.1	−.3125	(2)	bb−0.312500E+08
	(3)	E10.2	1234000.	(3)	bb0.1234000E−01
	(4)	E11.7	7284317000.	(4)	b0.72843170E+06
	(5)	E5.0	.01	(5)	***************

(field too small, takes 16 positions)

Exercise 22

1. a. No parentheses; IF(X.GE.Y)GO TO 15
   b. O.K.
   c. Operators may not appear in sequence (except .NOT.)–IF (N.LE.K) STOP
   d. Expressions to left and right of logical operator (.AND.) must be logical expressions; also, IN used erroneously and B/2 is mixed mode–
       IF(A+5.0.EQ.C.AND.B/2.0.EQ.C)GO TO 50
   e. No comma after parentheses, CONTINUE not an executable statement, and logical expression following .NOT. must be in parentheses–
       IF(L.NE.M.AND..NOT.(J+2.EQ.K)) [executable statement]

2. a. IF(CAR.GT.SMALL)MAX = NUM**3
   b. IF(AMT.EQ.SUM.OR.AMT.LT.SUM**2)AMT = 0.0
   c. IF(NUM.NE.KTOT.AND.K.LE.L.OR.M2−5.GE.N) STOP
   d. IF((TOP+A)/B.LT.6..OR.(TOP+A)/B.GT.12.0)GO TO 808
   e. IF(TOTAL*TOTAL3.LE.BUNCH.AND.DD+EE.LE.BUNCH) N = 3

Exercise 23

1.

	J	ONE	TWO	TREE	FOR	FIVE	SIX
1st	1	5.0	10.0	15.0	0.0	0.0	0.0
2nd	2	5.0	10.0	15.0	0.0	0.0	125.0
3rd	3	5.0	10.0	15.0	0.0	5.0	125.0

(after the third execution, transfer to statement 80 will result in FOR being set to a value of 20.0.)

3. a. GO TO (2,4,2,9,2,8,2,8), KEY
   b. GO TO (1,5,3,4,5,6,7,8), KEY
   c. GO TO (1,7,2,7,4,7,8,7,16,7), KEY

Exercise 24

1.
```
   10 FORMAT (I1, 4I3)
   15 READ (5,10,END=50)LC,N1,N2,N3,N4
      IF (LC.EQ.9) GO TO 30
   20 ·
      ·                          (These statements will now process
      ·                          either Market Area 1 or Market
      ·                          Area 2 data.)
      GO TO 15
   30 WRITE (results of Market Area 1 processing)
      GO TO 15
   50 WRITE (results of Market Area 2 processing)
      ·
      ·
      STOP
      END
```

3. A has a value of 3, KT a value of 23, MAC a value of 40.

Exercise 25

1. a. TOTAL(2)   b. TOTAL(17)   c. TOTAL(5)   d. TOTAL(4)
   e. This will result in an error. The calculation calls for a negative subscript
      (−5). Negative subscripts are illegal.

3. For machines which allow division within subscripts, the following algorithm
   (formula) could be used: (N/2+1). Remember the rules of integer arithmetic.
   The DO loop would now appear as:
   DO 25 N = 1,100,2
   SUM (N/2+1)=UNITS(N)+UNITS(N+1)
   25 CONTINUE

Exercise 26

1. a. Error: two loops cannot begin with the same statement and end at two
      different statements.
   b. Error: overlapping ranges are illegal.
   c. Error: overlapping ranges are illegal.
   d. O.K.
   e. Error: overlapping ranges are illegal.

3. a. No logical end; (STOP) is not a legal message form, however.
   b. No logical end; STOP will be displayed on the console.
   c. No logical end; END will be displayed on the console.
   d. STOP causes a logical end; the PAUSE and its message will never be dis-
      played as the program will have stopped processing.
   e. STOP is misplaced; it must appear prior to the END statement. The END
      statement will cause a logical end to the program though, technically, this is
      an error condition.

Exercise 27

1. DOUBLE PRECISION A,N,B,J,C
   A = .12345D02
   N = .67D02
   B = .15D10
   J = .22583219D06
   C = .1D01

3. a. b0.12345679Db07
   b. b0.12345678Db04
   c. b0.12345670D−03
   d. b0.12345678Db04
   e. b0.12345678Db13

Exercise 28

1. DATA A,B,C,J/7.5,3.2,5.4,9/

3. DATA NIX/22*3,8*0,8*7/

Exercise 29

1. a. 5678.23
   b. Error: not enough character positions (need 7 plus the value).
   c. 567
   d. 5.67 (this value is in the range for converting to decimal.)
   e. Error: no alpha in G mode.

3. FORMAT(F3.1,F3.3,I3,F3.0,I1,F2.0,F2.1)

Exercise 30

1. a. FORMAT (5X,'TOTAL VALUES',I12)
   b. FORMAT (3X,F8.1,'X = ',I2,'Y = ',I2)
   c. FORMAT (//' 1 ',2X,'SUMMARY',2X,I3)
   d. FORMAT ('–',4X,'MAX VALUE',2X,I7)
   e. FORMAT (3(2X,'RESIDUAL VALUE',I3))

3. FORMAT (–1PF6.4,0PF6.3,–5PF6.5,4PF6.1,–2PF8.7)

5.   Position   Item*
   a.   6   F8.3–variable VAL will be written
        0   carriage control character 1 (page restore)
        19   literal message–TOTAL DOLLAR VALUE

*Recall the differences: print and line positions.

   b.   49 literal message–SUM IS
        4 literal message–LEVEL NUM.
        19 I3–variable KT will be written
        0 carriage control character–(triple space)
        59 F8.3–variable TOT will be written

Exercise 31

1. a. b.   NAMELIST/FIRST/ONE,NUM,XYZ

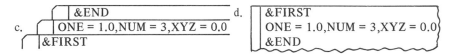

c.
```
  &END
  ONE = 1.0,NUM = 3,XYZ = 0.0
  &FIRST
```
d.
```
&FIRST
ONE = 1.0,NUM = 3,XYZ = 0.0
&END
```

3. a. WRITE (6,FORMAT) ABLE,NUM,FOX (See page 247.)
   b. (carriage control: the 1 in 12345.78 would cause page restore)

```
 b | 2345.78 | 12345678 | 123.46 |
```

5. WRITE (6,SAMPLE) ABLE,NUM,FOX

```
         ┌── [cc]
         ↓
  | 2X | 12345.78 | 12345678 | 123.46 |
  |    |   F8.2    |    I8    |  F6.2  |
  3X           2X         2X
```

Exercise 32

1. a. (3,2) are integer values and are illegal except for processors which auto-
      matically convert to the real mode.
   b. + should be a comma.
   c. O.K.
   d. Parentheses missing–(4.0,0.0).
   e. Missing closing parenthesis after 4.7.
   f. Exponents must be integers–3.4 is in the real mode.
   g. O.K.
   h. O.K.
   i. KI is in integer mode giving mixed mode condition.
   j. O.K.

3.   Card 1
         LOGICAL ONE
      5 FORMAT (L4)
         READ (5,5) ONE
      Variable name: ONE
      Value: T (true)

     Card 2
         LOGICAL TWO
     10 FORMAT (L21)
         READ (5,10) TWO
     Variable name: TWO
     VALUE: T (true)

     Card 3
         LOGICAL THREE
     15 FORMAT (L11)
         READ (5,15) THREE
     Variable name: THREE
     Value: F (false)

     Card 4
         LOGICAL FOUR
     20 FORMAT (L5)
         READ (5,20) FOUR
     Variable name: FOUR
     Value: F (false)

Exercise 33

1. A = F   B = F   C = T   D = F   E = F

3. a. Error: Illegal operation.
   b. L = T
   c. L = F
   d. L = F
   e. L = T
   f. L = T
   g. L = F
   h. L = T
   i. L = F

5. (In all answers b=blank)

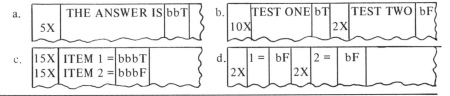

   a.
   | 5X | THE ANSWER IS | bbT |

   b.
   | 10X | TEST ONE | bT | 2X | TEST TWO | bF |

   c.
   | 15X | ITEM 1 = | bbbT |
   | 15X | ITEM 2 = | bbbF |

   d.
   | 2X | 1 = | bF | 2X | 2 = | bF |

Exercise 34

1. a. REAL*8 BLK
   b. No need to write this one; 4 bytes are standard.
   c. INTEGER*2 NMR
   d. No need to write this one; 4 bytes are standard.
   e. LOGICAL*1 TST

3. a. IMPLICIT INTEGER (A-H), REAL(K) [I and J assumed INTEGER]
   b. IMPLICIT INTEGER*2(A-C) REAL(M-N)
   c. No need to write this; assumed real *4 already.
   d. IMPLICIT INTEGER (H,Q) [I,J, and K assumed INTEGER]
   e. IMPLICIT REAL*8(M,N,O), INTEGER*2(P)

Exercise 35

1. | | Rows | Columns |
     |---|---|---|
     | a. | 3 | 4 |
     | b. | 8 | 12 |
     | c. | 7 | 25 |
     | d. | 100 | 3 |
     | e. | 6 | 4 |

3.
a.
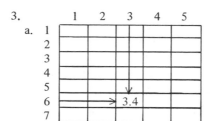

b.
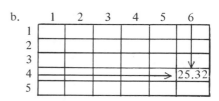

c.
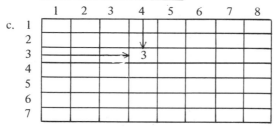

This is an example of integer arithmetic. Calculating the row subscript resulted in:

(J + 3)/2 or
(4 + 3)/2 = 7/2 = 3

The fractional value is truncated.

Exercise 36

1.

1,1	1,2	1,3	1,4
2,1	2,2	2,3	2,4
3,1	3,2	3,3	3,4

1,1	2,1	3,1	1,2	2,2	3,2	1,3	2,3	3,3	1,4	2,4	3,4

3.

1	9	0	0	0
11	0	4	5	6
3	0	4	5	6
4	0	4	5	6

Exercise 37

1. 60 locations (10 X 3 X 2)

3. a.   To initialize arrays at zero.
   b.   To intialize NAME array with expense account titles.

5. So the array was initialized *across each row* rather than down each column which is the assumed operation of subscripts unless otherwise specified.

7. a.   ID: holds identification values from input cards.
   b.   KODDEP: holds the department code.
   c.   KODEXP: holds the department expense code.
   d.   DATA: holds all numeric values read.
   All of these variables temporarily capture input data and store it until further processing directs the use for the data.

9. A decision is made, depending on the ID code, whether to transfer to the budget, actual, or last card processing instructions.

11. K comes from the DO loop.
    KODDEP comes from the input data card.
    1 is a constant written into the program.

13. KODDEP comes from the input data card.
    KODEXP comes from the input data card.
    2 is a constant written into the program.

15. The total budgeted and total actual expenses for all three departments are summed.

17. N comes from the DO loop.
    N2 and N3 are each loop indices in the implied loops.

Exercise 38

1. a.   A = IFIX(X)/IFIX(Y)
   b.   C = AMOD(X1,X2)
   c.   K = MOD(N1,N2)
   d.   RR = DSQRT(F/G+B**2)
   e.   S = SQRT(FLOAT(N))
   f.   NUM = 0
          DO 10 N = 1,5000
      10 NUM = MAX1(WRONG(N),FLOAT(NUM))
   g.   KT = MID(1,1)
          DO 10 J = 1,200
          DO 10 K = 1,300
      10 KT = MINO(KT,MID(J,K))

3. a. Function to left of equals sign is illegal.
   b. Argument not in real mode.
   c. This function must have only one argument.
   d. This function must have two or more arguments and they must be in the integer mode.
   e. Nothing.

Exercise 39

1. a. O.K.
   b. Function call has too few arguments.
   c. Function misspelled; should be GIM, not G.
   d. O.K.
   e. O.K. (ABS(A) is another function in actual argument list.)
   f. H(15) is out of the array size, I (integer) in actual argument list cannot be matched with A(real) in dummy argument list.
   g. O.K.
   h. O.K.
   i. O.K.
   j. Except for processors which convert modes automatically, mixed mode among dummy arguments (N,A,B) with actual arguments (2,4,6).

3. a. CALL COMP(A,B,C)—from calling program
   ```
   FUNCTION COMP(A,B,C)  ⎫
   COMP = (A*B+4.7)/C    ⎬  Function Subprogram
   RETURN                ⎪
   END                   ⎭
   ```

   b. CALL DISC(QTY,PRICE)—from calling program
   ```
   FUNCTION DISK(QTY,PRICE)   ⎫
   DISC = (QTY*PRICE-600.00)*.05 ⎬  Function Subprogram
   RETURN                     ⎪
   END                        ⎭
   ```

c. CALL RESLT(N,K,J)—from calling program
FUNCTION RESLT(N,K,J)
A = N ⎫
B = K ⎪
C = J ⎬ These statements could have been written as:
D = A*B/(C−3.4) ⎪ RESLT=SQRT (FLOAT(N)*FLOAT(K)/ (FLOAT(J)-3.4))
RESLT = SQRT(D) ⎭
RETURN
END

d. CALL TOPS(CH2(n),CH4(n),CH5(n)) ←— The actual arguments in CALL
                                        will be single elements (n)
FUNCTION TOPS(CH2,CH4,CH5)   from the three CH arrays.
SUM = CH2+CH4+CH5
HIGH = AMAX1(CH2,CH4,CH5)   The dummy arguments in the
TOPS = HIGH/SUM   FUNCTION have the same names
RETURN   but are not arrays.
END

Exercise 40

1. a. SUBROUTINE ONCE(R,N,S,A). Dummy arguments cannot be numbers.
   b. SUBROUTINE COMPAR(N,P,Q). No subscripts or expressions allowed in
       dummy arguments.
   c. SUBROUTINE NUMBR(J,K,Z,J2) ⎫ Dummy arguments do not have to be
   d. SUBROUTINE TEAM(G,W,C)   ⎬ same name, but must agree in mode,
   e. SUBROUTINE WHEN(M,A)   ⎭ order, size, and number.

3. Error 1, line 1: should be SUBROUTINE, not SUBPROGRAM.
   Error 2, line 1: parentheses missing around (X,Y,Z).
   Error 3, line 2: missing = in DO 10 K = 5,20,3.
   Error 4, line 3: missing = in X = Y*Z+K.
   Error 5, line 5: missing statement number on CONTINUE.
   Error 6, line 8: SUBROUTINE may not call itself.
   ERROR 7, lines 8-9: missing RETURN statement.

Exercise 41

1. a. MP—COMMON A,B,NN(10)
          CALL SUB1

       SR—SUBROUTINE SUB1
          COMMON A,B,NN(10)

   b. MP—REAL JACK,MAN
          COMMON X,JACK,Y,MAN(2,4),Z
          CALL SUB2

       SR—SUBROUTINE SUB2
          COMMON A, B, C, D, C(2,4), E

   c. MP—REAL DP*8   SR—SUBROUTINE SUB3
          INTEGER SM*2   REAL C*8
          COMMON L,K,DP,SM   INTEGER A,B,D*2
          CALL SUB3   COMMON A,B,C,D

3. a.

A	B(1)	B(2)	B(3)	C	D	←— main program
A	B(1)	B(2)	B(3)	C	D	←— subroutine

   b.

J(1)	J(2)	K	X	Y(1)	Y(2)	Y(3)	←main program
L	N(1)	N(2)	F(1)	F(2)	F(3)	A	←subroutine

c.

R	J(1)	J(2)	M(1)	M(2)	M(3)	M(4)	← main program
A	B(1)	B(2)	B(3)	K(1)	K(2)	K(3)	← subroutine

Exercise 42

1. a. COMMON A,B,C/ALPHA/N,NN
   b. COMMON X,Y,Z/BETA/R,S//P,Q
   c. COMMON /GAMMA/K//J,N
   d. COMMON F,G,H/SIGMA/H

3. BLOCK DATA
    REAL NAME(8), HIGH(10), LOW(6)
    COMMON /FIRST/NAME//HIGH, LOW
    DATA NAME/'WASH','INGT','ON, ','GEO.'
    1/HIGH/5*0.0,5*1.0/LOW/3*5.2,3*6.4/
    END

5. EQUIVALENCE (A,MAX(1),SMALL (2,2)),(B,SMALL(3,2)),(BIG(1),SMALL(1,1))

SMALL (1,1) BIG (1)	SMALL (2,1) BIG (2)	SMALL (3,1) BIG (3)	SMALL (1,2) BIG (4)	SMALL (2,2) A MAX (1)	SMALL (3,2) B MAX (2)	SMALL (1,3) MAX (3)	SMALL (2,3) MAX (4)	SMALL (3,3) MAX (5)

b. EQUIVALENCE (MAX(5),SMALL(3,2)), (C,MAX(4),BIG(1))

SMALL (1,1)	SMALL (2,1) MAX (1)	SMALL (3,1) MAX (2)	SMALL (1,2) MAX (3)	SMALL (2,2) MAX (4) C BIG (1)	SMALL (3,2) MAX (5) BIG (2)	SMALL (1,3) BIG (3)	SMALL (2,3) BIG (4)	SMALL (3,3)

c. EQUIVALENCE (D,MAX(3)),(F,G,MAX(2),SMALL(1,3),BIG(2)),(E,SMALL(2,3))

SMALL (1,1)	SMALL (2,1)	SMALL (3,1)	SMALL (1,2)	SMALL (2,2)	SMALL (3,2) MAX (1) BIG (1)	SMALL (1,3) F G MAX (2) BIG (2)	SMALL (2,3) E D MAX (3) BIG (3)	SMALL (3,3) MAX (4) BIG (4)	MAX (5)

d. EQUIVALENCE (MAX(1),SMALL(8)),(K,L,M,MAX(2)),(R,S,SMALL(4)),
    1(BIG(2),SMALL(6))

SMALL (1)	SMALL (2)	SMALL (3)	SMALL (4) R S	SMALL (5) BIG (1)	SMALL (6) BIG (2)	SMALL (7) BIG (3)	SMALL (8) MAX (1) BIG (4)	SMALL (9) MAX (2) K L M	MAX (3)	MAX (4)	MAX (5)

e. EQUIVALENCE (SMALL(1,2),BIG(4),MAX(5))
   This EQUIVALENCE is illegal because it extends memory *prior* to that allocated for the arrays.

	SMALL (1,1) BIG (1) MAX (1)	SMALL (2,1) BIG (2) MAX (2)	SMALL (3,1) BIG (3) MAX (3)	SMALL (1,2) BIG (4) MAX (4)	MAX (5)	. . . .

Exercise 43

1. a. ENTRY SET(K,A,B,N)
   b. ENTRY NIX(K2R,A,ZZ)
   c. ENTRY CLASS(DEBIT,CREDIT,BALNCE)

3.

CALL	A	B	Final
1. SUB1	5.0	0.0	A 9.0 B 400.0
2. PGM1	7.0	0.0	
3. PGM1	9.0	0.0	(The values for A and B are established
4. SUB2	9.0	18.0	in the main program and, though the
5. PGM1	9.0	20.0	subprograms change names,

concentrate on which main program
value is being manipulated.)

5. X = 10.0

7. a. Dummy variables KEEP, SLOW, and Z will be referenced by value, not by location.
   Dummy variable LOW will be referenced by location, not by value.
   b. This is an illustration of the variable DIMENSION feature. Array MATRIX will have its DIMENSIONs sent to the subprogram JUMP through variables J and K (i.e. 50 X 50).
   c. Error: actual arguments may not be written in slashes, only dummy variables when making reference by location.
   d. Variable G will be referenced by value, not by location. Variable H will be referenced by location, not by value.
   e. The variable DIMENSIONs of the array IRAY are sent to SUBROUTINE LEAD with a change in array name to KT. The DIMENSIONs sent result in a 2 X 3 array for use by the SUBROUTINE.

Appendix C
Programming Problems

Problems in this appendix are organized according to chapter groupings. Several problems are interrelated throughout a number of chapter groupings. These problems are identified by listing the associated problems.

Group 1 (Chapters 1-4) 1.1 A program reads the stock prices for three corporations (IBM, AT&T, and General Motors). The prices are punched in one data card, and, after reading the prices, the program is to find the smallest price in this set and print this value.

a. Analyze this problem and prepare a written statement of its desired result, data elements, and processing factors.

b. Flowchart this problem.

1.2 A program calculates and prints the monthly commission earned by each salesman in a firm. The program also calculates the total sales and total commissions for the company. Each salesman's identification number, total monthly sales amount, and commission rate are punched in one card. The firm has no more than 100 salesmen.

a. Analyze this problem and prepare a written statement of its desired result, data elements, and processing factors.

b. Flowchart this problem.

1.3 A firm's engineering department is designing a new product and wishes to analyze some research data related to the product. One thousand test observations have been taken on the product. The research director suggests that you prepare a computer program to take each test value and, based on the value's size, complete one of the following steps. (Assume all values are in the range 0-50 and each observation is punched one to a card.)

If a test value is in the range:

0 through 9.999: multiply the value by 3 and accumulate this result with all other results in this range.

10 through 24.999: divide the value by 2 and accumulate this result with all other results in this range.

35 through 50: add 6.4 to the value and accumulate this result with all other results in this range.

After completing the above steps: (1) write the final result in each range; (2) take the square root of each range's result; (3) sum the square roots from (2) above; and (4) write the sum of the square roots from (3) above.

a. Analyze this problem and prepare a written statement of its desired results, data elements, and processing factors.
b. Flowchart this problem.

1.4 A wholesale firm grants customer discounts which vary according to the size of each sale. The following discount schedule is used by the firm:

Sale Size	Discount
less than $250.00	0%
$250.00 - $499.99	2%
$500.00 - $999.99	5%
$1000.00 and over	8%

The firm asks you to design a computer program for processing customer sales. The program will read customer cards each of which contain: (1) a customer identification number, (2) the number of product units sold, and (3) the sales price per unit for the product sold.

The program is to calculate the gross amount of each sale, the discount allowed (if any), and the net sale amount (gross sale - discount). The program should also compute the total sales, total discounts, and total net sales for the firm. Finally, the program should write:

For Each Customer Sale	Company Totals
customer identification	total gross sales
number of units sold	total discounts allowed
sale price per unit	total net sales
gross sale amount	
discount amount	
net sale amount	

a. Analyze this problem and prepare a written statement of its desired results, data elements, and processing factors.
b. Flowchart this problem.

1.5 The developer of a large business complex is interested in examining his rental income possibilities. He has just completed a large office building which has 400 office spaces. It is estimated that all office space will be leased at a monthly charge of $200 per unit. It is also estimated that for each $10 increase in the monthly lease charge, one less office unit will be rented. For each $10 increase in lease charges above $500 per unit, 2 less units will be rented. Each $10 increase above $600 will result in 4 less units being rented and each $10 increase above $1000 will lose 7 rental units. The developer wishes to know which monthly lease charge will maximize his total revenue and asks you to prepare a computer program to determine that rental charge.
a. Analyze this problem and prepare a written statement of its desired results, data elements, and processing factors.
b. Flowchart this problem.

1.6 The Barocci Company makes a large portion of its sales on credit. Customers using this buying arrangement agree to the credit terms outlined below. The company wants a computer program which will be run once each month. It should maintain customer accounts by reading beginning balances, purchases, payments, and credits on account. The program should accurately compute finance service charges and ending balances.

The following details apply to the company's credit agreement with customers. (1) Customers may pay their entire balance in 30 days from date of billing with no finance charge. (2) If the balance is not paid in 30 days, a finance charge is computed on the basis of an adjusted balance calculated as the previous period's balance less payments and credits made during the current billing period. (3) Finance charges are determined by applying a rate of 1.5% per month to the first $500.00 of adjusted balance. A rate of .75% per month will be applied to any balance in excess of $500.00. (4) When the adjusted balance for a period is $33.00, or less, the finance charge will be 50¢ rather than the computed amount.

   a. Analyze this problem and prepare a written statement of its desired results, data elements, and processing factors.

   b. Flowchart this problem.

1.7   In order to economize in the purchase of material, the Stone Company computes an economic order quantity (EOQ) prior to placing an order. The firm wants to computerize this task and asks you to prepare a program to do this job. The formula for calculating the EOQ is:

$$EOQ = \sqrt{\frac{2 \times A \times O}{U \times C}}$$

where: A is the material's annual demand in units
        O is the cost per order placed
        U is the purchase price per unit of material
        C is the cost of carrying the material in inventory
           and is expressed as a percentage of its purchase price per unit

Each item of material to be purchased will have the values of A, O, U, and C punched into a single card. The EOQ is to be calculated and printed.

   a. Analyze this problem and prepare a written statement of its desired results, data elements, and processing factors.

   b. Flowchart this problem.

1.8   The Gardner Company manufactures three products. The unit cost for material, labor, and overhead are shown in the table below. The selling price for each product is: A = $17.50, B = $16.00, C = $8.00. Management is interested in knowing what the total sales, total manufacturing costs, and gross profit would be from several different combinations of product mix. Gross profit is computed as total sales minus total costs. Product mix relates to the number of units of each product produced and sold in combination with the other products. For instance, one mix might be 10 units of A, 20 of B, and 30 of C, another mix would be 15 of A, 10 of B, and 35 of C, and so forth.

Product	Manufacturing Costs Per Unit		
	Material	Labor	Overhead
A	$4.00	$6.00	$6.00
B	2.50	8.00	$4.00
C	.75	1.20	2.40

The production manager asks you to prepare a computer program which will calculate: (1) total sales for any number of product mixes, (2) total costs for any number of product mixes, and (3) gross profit for any number of product mixes.

   a. Analyze this problem and prepare a written statement of its desired results, data elements, and processing factors.

   b. Flowchart this problem.

1.9   The Evans Company, a marketing research firm, is studying consumer preferences on several different products. Field research has been completed primarily through the preparation of questionnaires. The firm desires a computer program to tabulate the results of these questionnaires. The questionnaires each contain 20 questions to be answered either yes, or no, or no preference. In addition, questions 5, 10, 15, and 20 each have five subquestions answered if the main question is answered "yes." The subquestions also have yes, no and no preference responses possible. The program should tabulate the number and percentages of yes, no, and no preference answers for each question. It is expected that there will be from 1975 to 2000 questionnaires. You are asked to prepare this program. The data from any one questionnaire will be punched into one data card.

    a. Analyze this problem and prepare a written statement of its desired results, data elements, and processing factors.

    b. Flowchart this problem.

1.10 At the end of each monthly interest period, the Keep Safe Savings and Loan Association credits (adds to) depositors' accounts with interest they have earned during the period. The association asks you to prepare a computer program to calculate and update depositors' accounts. The program should read four items for each depositor: (1) a depositor identification number, (2) deposit balance at the beginning of the interest period, (3) deposit balance at the end of the period, and (4) a code which indicates the type of savings account held by the depositor.

    After reading the input values, an average deposit balance is calculated, the appropriate interest rate is applied to each savings account, and the amount of interest computed. A new updated account balance is then calculated and a listing of the depositor's identification, beginning balance, ending balance, account type, interest rate, amount of interest, and updated account balance is printed.

    Assume the following interest rates for each account type:

Account	Type	Rate
Regular	1	5-1/2%
Special	2	6-1/2%
Long-term	3	8%

The general formula for the calculation of interest on an amount is:

$$int = P(1 + i)^n - P$$

where:
  int = the amount of interest
  P   = the principal on which the interest is being computed
  i   = the interest rate
  n   = the period over which the interest is being computed

    a. Analyze this problem and prepare a written statement of its deisred results, data elements, and processing factors.

    b. Flowchart this problem.

Group 2 (Chapters 5-7) 2.1 Prepare a flowchart and program to read two values which are punched into one card. After reading, the first value is to be multiplied by 7 and added to a location named SUM. SUM is then divided by the second value. Values 1 and 2, as well as SUM, are printed with appropriate captions. Use the following values and punch them into a single data card.

Card Columns	Punched Values	Description
1-5	482.5	Value 1
6-7	blank	
8-10	2.4	Value 2

2.2   The computation of debt/equity ratios are commonly made by financial analysts. This ratio is computed by dividing a company's debt by the total of its debt and stockholders equity. Flowchart and write a program to compute the debt/equity ratio for the ABC and XYZ companies. Punch all data into a single data card as shown below:

Card columns	Punched Values	Description
1-7	235000.	ABC - debt
8-14	178000.	XYZ - debt
15-19	blank	
20-26	500000.	ABC -stockholders equity
27-33	856000.	XYZ - stockholders equity

2.3   The Douglas Corporation desires a computer program which will analyze sales data at the end of each ten-day working period. You have been asked to prepare a program to read and analyze ten dollar amounts. Management wants to know what the total dollar amount of sales has been during the period and what the average daily sales have been for the ten days.

The program should accomplish the following: (1) Read a data card which will have ten dollar amounts punched consecutively beginning in column one. (2) Total the ten dollar amounts. (3) Calculate an arithmetic average of the dollar amounts. (4) Write: (a) one line, with caption, showing total sales, (b) one line, with caption, showing average sales, and (c) two lines, the first with sales amounts 1-5 and the second with amounts 6-10.

Prepare a flowchart and FORTRAN program to make these calculations. Punch the following ten values into one data card to test your program.

Columns	Values
1-8	02110.50
9-16	52180.26
17-24	00200.32
25-32	02500.56
33-40	00115.62
41-48	32144.71
49-56	78250.88
57-64	00051.92
65-72	07218.15
73-80	22441.20

2.4   The Joan Rae Company is considering two investment possibilities for some of their idle cash funds. The company has asked you to flowchart and write a program to calculate the total interest which could be earned under each of the following two alternatives. Write the computed values with appropriate captions. Assume the firm has $78,000 of cash to invest.

Option 1.   Invest cash to earn 8.42% interest compounded annually for 12 years.

Option 2.   Invest cash to earn 12.27% interest compounded anually for 8 years.

The basic formula to calculate a compound amount is:

$$A = P (1+i)^n$$

where: A is the compound amount
          P is the principal amount invested
          i is the rate of interest
          n is the period over which compounding is to take place

Punch all of the input values into one data card as follows:

Columns	Values	Description
1-7	078000.	Principal to invest
8-12	.0842	Interest rate - option 1
13-14	12	Compounding period - option 1
15-19	.1227	Interest rate - option 2
20	8	Compounding period - option 2

2.5   The calculation of depreciation expense is a common task of the corporate accountant. Annual depreciation expense under the straight line depreciation method is computed by the following formula:

$$DE = (AC - SV)/L$$

where: DE   is the depreciation expense

AC   is the cost of the asset being depreciated

SV   is the expected salvage value at the end of the asset's service life

L   is the service life of the asset

The Gardner Company desires a computer program to calculate the annual depreciation expense under the straight line method. You are asked to flowchart and prepare a program which: (1) reads in data values for an asset; (2) computes the annual depreciation expense; and (3) writes the cost, salvage value, service life, and depreciation expense on one line using appropriate captions.

The input data values should be punched in one data card and appear as:

Columns	Values	Description
1-7	250000.	Asset Cost
8-9	blank	
10-15	37500.	Salvage Value
16-19	blank	
20-21	17	Years of Service Life

2.6   The Municipal Gas Company bills its customers by measuring the total cubic feet of gas consumed and charges rates which vary with total consumption. The company asks you to prepare a computer program to calculate customer billings. The program is to read customer cards, each of which contains a customer identification number and the total number of cubic feet of gas consumed in the billing period. After reading a card, the customer is to be billed according to the following cumulative schedule: 0-100 cu. ft. @ .04 per foot, 100.1-250 cu. ft. @ .0275 per foot, and usage over 250 cu. ft. @ .015 per foot. Flowchart and prepare a program to compute and print (with appropriate headings and captions) each customer's bill. The program should also accumulate and write the total amount of gas consumed and the total customer billings for the company. Punch three data cards and a trailer card for testing your program. You should create your own input and output FORMATs but use the following customer information with your program.

Customer Number	Gas Consumed
12345	50.2 cu. ft.
23456	200.5 cu. ft.
34567	1000.0 cu. ft.

2.7   (Refer to problem 1.1). Read problem 1.1. Find the most recent stock market price quotations for IBM, AT&T, and General Motors in the local newspaper or the *Wall Street Journal*. Punch these prices in one data card using columns 1-10 for IBM, columns 11-20 for AT&T, and columns 21-30 for General

Motors. All columns will not be used in these fields. Prepare a program to read these values and to select and print the smallest price. Use your own FORMAT specifications for input and output. Use an appropriate caption for your output value. Flowchart the program if you have not done so as a part of problem 1.1.

2.8 (Refer to problem 1.2.) Read problem 1.2. Prepare a program to calculate sales amounts and commissions. The input values are punched in cards with columns 1-6 used for salesmen identification numbers, columns 7-9 blank, columns 10-18 for salesmen monthly sales, column 19 blank, and columns 20-23 for salesmen commission rates. Prepare your own FORMAT specifications for input and output. Use appropriate headings and captions with your output. Flowchart the program if you have not done so as a part of problem 1.2. Use the following data values with your program.

Salesman Identification	Monthly Sales	Commission Rate
123456	48500.00	.025
234567	102645.55	.153
345678	23476.25	.097
456789	258642.00	.036
567890	6755.80	.25
999999	(trailer card)	

2.9 (Refer to problem 1.3.) Read problem 1.3. Prepare a program to calculate the values for each range. Each observation is punched in columns 1-6 of a separate input data card. Prepare your own FORMAT specifications for input and output. Use appropriate headings and captions with your output. Flowchart the program if you have not done so as a part of problem 1.3. Use the following data values with your program.

Observation Values
7.632
12.443
5.110
33.021
50.000
26.368
99.999 (trailer card)

2.10 (Refer to problem 1.4.) Read problem 1.4. Prepare a program to calculate the sales and discount information desired. The customer cards are punched with customer identification in columns 1-5, number of units sold in columns 10-15, and sales price in columns 20-25. Prepare your own FORMAT specifications for input and output. Use appropriate captions and headings with your output. Flowchart the program if you have not done so as a part of problem 1.4. Use the following data values with your program.

Customer Identification	Units Sold	Sales Price
12345	12500.	33.50
23456	02000.	.15
34567	00150.	1.00
45678	01000.	.55
56789	02200.	12.50
99999 (trailer card)		

2.11 (Refer to problem 1.6.) Read problem 1.6. Prepare a program to compute a customer's ending balance including any applicable finance charge. The program should read five items for each customer: (1) an identification number, (2) a prior period ending balance (that is, the current period beginning balance), (3) payments made during the period, (4) purchases made during the period, and (5) any credits (reductions) made to a customer account.

Applicable finance charges and the account ending balance for the current period should be computed. Prepare your own FORMAT specifications for input and output. Use appropriate captions and headings with your output. Flowchart the program if you have not done so as a part of problem 1.6. Use the following data values with your program. Input data card columns are shown with the data values below.

Cols. 1-5 Customer Identification	Cols. 10-16 Previous Balance	Cols. 20-26 Purchases	Cols. 30-36 Payments	Cols. 40-46 Credits
12345	$1041.23	$ 22.35	$1055.00	$ 0.00
23456	25.50	0.00	25.50	0.00
34567	330.00	287.45	0.00	25.00
45678	2500.00	57.23	2000.00	300.00
56789	0.00	97.58	0.00	7.58
99999 (trailer card)				

2.12 (Refer to problem 1.7.) Read problem 1.7. Prepare a program to calculate the economic order quantities for the products shown in the test data below. Data for each product is punched in a single data card. Columns 1-2 are used for product identification, columns 3-9 for annual demand values, columns 10-15 for cost per order placed, columns 20-25 for purchase price per unit, columns 30-35 for cost of carrying material. Prepare your own FORMAT specifications for input and output. Use appropriate headings and captions with your output. Show the values read as well as the EOQ in your output. Flowchart the program if you have not done so as a part of problem 1.7. Use the following data values with your program.

Product	Demand	Cost/Order	Purch/Price	Carry/Cost
10	90000.	$20.00	$ 5.00	.10
20	3500.	16.75	250.00	.225
30	10500.	6.25	300.00	.15
99 (trailer card)				

Note: To find the square root of a value, two options are available: (1) exponentiate the value by .5 or (2) use the square root function. This function is discussed in chapter 15.

2.13 (Refer to problem 1.10.) Read problem 1.10. Prepare a program to compute interest on depositors' accounts and to update the account balances. The average balance should be computed by adding the beginning and ending account balances and dividing the sum by 2. Prepare your own FORMAT specifications for input and output. Use appropriate headings and captions with your output. Data for each account will be punched into a single data card as follows: columns 1-5 account identification number, column 9 account type, columns 20-29 beginning deposit balance, and columns 30-39 ending deposit balance.

Flowchart the program if you have not done so as a part of problem 1.10. Use the following data values with your program.

Account Identification	Account Type	Beginning Balance	Ending Balance
12345	1	$50000.00	$60000.00
23456	2	75000.00	50000.00
34567	3	45000.00	95000.00
99999 (trailer card)			

2.14 The coefficient of correlation, r, may be computed by the following formula:

$$r = \frac{N\Sigma XY - (\Sigma X)(\Sigma Y)}{\sqrt{(N\Sigma X^2 - (\Sigma X)^2)(N\Sigma Y^2 - (\Sigma Y)^2)}}$$

Flowchart and prepare a program which will read a deck of input cards. Each card contains a value for X and a value for Y. Columns 1-10 are used for the X values and columns 11-20 for the Y values. All values have two decimal places. A trailer card containing a value of 9.99, in the X field, will follow the data cards. When the trailer card is encountered, the coefficient is to be written and processing terminated. Also, print each pair of X and Y values. Prepare your own FORMAT specifications for input and output. Use appropriate headings and captions with your output. Use the following data values with your program.

X Values	Y Values
53.25	45.67
36.30	43.76
88.35	89.54
84.40	79.45
64.45	66.99
9.99	

2.15 On September 26, 1972, the Vice-President (finance) of Butter Inc. asks you to age the accounts receivable. He believes that collections are slowing down considerably, and that at least 50 percent of all receivables are more than 30 days past due. Furthermore, he is of the opinion that 65 percent of all accounts more than 60 days past due are uncollectible.

All accounts receivable are punched on individual data cards. Each data card has the following information: columns 1-6 customer number, columns 7-13 dollar value of account receivable, and columns 14-16 date account receivable is due (Julian calendar). The Julian calendar assigns consecutive numbers to the days of the year. September 26, 1972 is the 270th day of 1972. September 25 is the 269th day, September 24 the 268th day, and so forth. A trailer card containing all *blanks* in columns 1-6 will follow the accounts receivable cards.

Flowchart and prepare a program which will compute the total dollar value and percentages of receivables that are (1) 30 or less days past due, (2) more than 30 days, but less than 61 days past due, and (3) more than 60 days past due. Also calculate the number and percentage of accounts in each category. Prepare your own FORMAT specifications for input and output. Use appropriate headings and captions with your output. Use the following data values with your program.

Customer Number	Receivable Amount	Date Due
123456	$1022.37	265
234567	567.22	150
345678	3001.25	022
456789	10.78	230
567890	644.00	225
678901	2493.28	243

2.16 (Refer to problem 2.3.) Alter problem 2.3 in the following respects:
   (1) The program should read 10 (or more) cards. Each card will have one item of data punched into it. Each data field will remain at a maximum size of 99999.99.
   (2) The last card in the data deck will be a trailer card which contains 99999.99.
   (3) Print out *each* sales amount on a separate line. Use captions or headings to indicate that the sales items being printed are individual amounts from separate quarters.

2.17 Flowchart and write a program to take time measurements, expressed in seconds, and convert the seconds into the more conventional measures of hours, minutes, and seconds. Your program should read values which could be five digits in length (there are 86,400 seconds in a 24 hour day). Use your own FORMAT for input. For output, use appropriate captions and print the total seconds read as well as the hours, minutes, and seconds. For example:

SECONDS	= HOURS	+ MINUTES	+ SECONDS
37428	10	23	48
25367	7	2	47

Group 3 (Chapters 8-13) 3.1 (Refer to problem 1.5.) Read problem 1-5. Flowchart and prepare a program to compute the monthly rental charge which will give the maximum total monthly avenue. All values for this program may be initialized in the program. (Consider using the DATA statement.) Prepare your own FORMAT specifications for output. Use appropriate headings and captions with your output. Display the following items related to the maximum revenue: (a) maximum revenue dollar value, (b), monthly rental charge giving the maximum revenue, and (c) number of office units occupied at the monthly rental charge listed in (b).

3.2 The following three problems deal with the creation and manipulation of an array. The descriptive paragraph which is given below applies to all three problems.
   Dimension an array called ITEM. In each of the following problems, flowchart and write a program to read 100, or fewer, data values into the array. Assume that a maximum of three data values are punched in any one data card though a card may have only one or two values. Use a FORMAT of 3I5 for the data cards. The data cards will be followed by a trailer card which has a 9 punched in *column 16*. Assume all data values are positive and non-zero. Use the following data values (on five cards) with your programs.

	Cols. 1-5	Cols. 6-10	Cols. 11-15
	Value 1	Value 2	Value 3
Card 1	00100	00050	01525
Card 2	blank	00006	00010
Card 3	02650	blank	02595
Card 4	blank	03225	blank
Card 5	00060	99999	00734

A. After reading values into the ITEM array, sum the non-zero values and calculate the average of these values. Print the ITEM array, with its original values, the sum of the positive values, and the average. Prepare your own FORMAT specifications for output and use appropriate headings and captions.

B. After reading values into the ITEM array, some values will be zero. Write a program which will create a second array, named KEEP, to store the non-zero elements from the ITEM array in the order of their appearance in ITEM. Print both the ITEM and KEEP arrays. Prepare your own FORMAT specifications for output and use appropriate headings and captions.

C. After reading values into the ITEM array and storing the non-zero elements in the KEEP array, write a program which will *reverse* the values in the KEEP array (that is, the first value becomes the last value and vice versa, the second value becomes the second last value and vice versa, and so forth). Print (1) the ITEM array and (2) the KEEP array both before and after reversing the values in the array. Prepare your own FOR-MAT specifications for output and use appropriate headings and captions.

3.3   In December 1626, Peter Minuit, governor of the Dutch West India Company is reputed to have purchased Manhattan Island from the Indians for $24 in kettles, axes, and cloth. If the Indians had invested their receipts at 5 per cent, compounded annually, what would that investment be worth at the end of the current year?

Flowchart and write a program to compute this compound amount. Initialize all data values in the program (consider using the DATA statement) and declare your answer to be a DOUBLE PRECISION variable data name. See problem 3-5 for the applicable formula. Prepare your own FORMAT for output. Use appropriate captions and headings. Write all of the initial values as well as the computed answer.

3.4   (Refer to problem 1.9.) Read problem 1.9. The Evans Company employs you to prepare a computer program to tabulate the number and percentages of yes, no, and no preference responses to the 20 main questions as well as the five subquestions related to main questions 5, 10, 15, and 20. In completing this program store the questionnaire responses in three one-dimensional arrays or in a 3 by 40 array. The three rows correspond to the responses of yes, no, and no preference. The forty columns correspond to the 20 main questions plus the five subquestions related to each of the main questions, 5, 10, 15, and 20. Prepare your own output FORMAT to present the summarized questionnaire data and percentages. Use approximate headings and captions. The following five input data cards may be used with your program. The data for any one questionnaire is punched in the first 40 columns of a data card. The columns of data correspond to the following questions.

Columns	Description
1-5	Responses to main questions 1-5
6-10	Responses to subquestions of main question 5
11-15	Responses to main questions 6-10
16-20	Responses to subquestions of main question 10
21-25	Responses to main questions 11-15
26-30	Responses to subquestions of main question 15
31-35	Responses to main questions 16-20
36-40	Responses to subquestions of main question 20

Input data is coded as follows: 1 = yes, 2 = no, and 3 = no preference.
The following data values may be used with your program.

Input Data Card Columns

1-5	6-10	11-15	16-20	21-35	26-30	31-35	36-40
11233	blank	21312	blank	13111	12333	12311	12331
22111	11332	22322	blank	12122	blank	22211	11111
31221	22123	11221	11233	33333	blank	32233	blank
11111	33221	22222	blank	12332	blank	12323	blank
21223	blank	33211	32123	11211	11211	12111	22311

9 (trailer card)*

*Use the END= option if available.

3.5   The use of compound interest is frequently made in reaching business decisions. The formula for computing the compound amount of $1 is:

$$c = (1+r)^n$$

where: c   is the compound amount
         r   is the rate of interest
         n   is the compounding period

Flowchart and write a program to print a table of compound amounts of $1 at rates of interest of 1%, 2%, 5%, 8% and 10%. Print the compound amounts for the annual periods 1 through 10, 15, 20, 25, 50, 75, and 100. Store the compound amounts in five arrays (one for each interest rate). Read in the interest rates using your own FORMAT specifications. Display the table with the annual periods down the left side and columns for each interest rate across the page. Use your own output FORMAT specifications including appropriate headings and captions.

3.6   The concept of present value is used extensively in making business decisions. The formula for computing the present value of $1 is:

$$p = \frac{1}{(1+r)^n}$$

where: p   is the present value
         r   is the rate of interest
         n   is the discounting period

Flowchart and write a program to print a table of present values of $1 at rates of interest of 1%, 2%, 5%, 8%, and 10%. Print the present values for the annual periods 1 thorugh 10, 15, 20, 25, 50, 75, and 100. Store the present values in five arrays (one for each interest rate). Read in the interest rates using your own FORMAT specifications. Display the table with the annual periods down the left side and columns for each interest rate across the page. Use your own output FORMAT specifications including appropriate headings and captions.

3.7   Suppose you own a choice piece of land which you wish to sell. On January 1, 1973, you receive the following offer for your property: (a) a payment of $50,000 *now,* or (b) the buyer uses the land with a $15,000 payment on *December 31, 1992.* If you can earn 5 per cent, on the average, with your money, which amount should you accept?

Flowchart and write a program to assist you in making your choice. Use your own FORMAT specifications for input and output. Display all the pertinent information related to this problem with appropriate headings and captions.

3.8 Two important statistical measures are the mean (average) of a group of values and the standard deviation of the values. The standard deviation measures the dispersion of the values around the mean. The two formulas used to calculate these measures are:

$$\text{Mean} = \Sigma X/N$$

$$\text{Standard Deviation} = \sqrt{\frac{\Sigma(X^2) - \frac{(\Sigma X)^2}{N}}{N-1}}$$

where: Σ means "sum of"
      X represents the values being summed
      N is a count of the number of values

Flowchart and write a program which will calculate the mean and standard deviation for a set of values punched three to a card in columns 1-27. The program should read and store these values in an array. After computing and printing the mean and standard deviation, the program should scan the array and print all values which exceed (+ or −) one standard deviation from the mean. Use your own FORMAT specifications for output. Use appropriate headings and captions. The following values may be used with your program.

Cols. 1-7	Cols. 11-17	Cols. 21-27
1832.54	1654.53	1950.32
1954.27	1722.18	2001.21
2632.66	2020.05	3150.66
0950.38	2138.22	0765.05
3211.21	1750.14	9999.99*

*trailer card—use End-option if available

3.9 The Hanson Company produces five products. The unit production costs for material, labor, and overhead expenses are shown in the following table.

| | Cost Per Unit | | |
Product	Material	Labor	Overhead
A	$4.00	$6.00	$6.00
B	2.50	7.00	3.50
C	2.00	7.50	7.00
D	1.75	3.45	3.45
E	.75	7.00	3.50

In planning for pricing their products and for production scheduling, management wants to identify the production mix which has the lowest total cost. The company has three possible options for the production of different product combinations. The following table shows the number of units of each product which can be manufactured under each option.

| | Units Produced | | |
Product	Option 1	Option 2	Option 3
A	1000	2000	3000
B	1000	500	1000
C	2000	1000	500
D	6000	5000	4000
E	8000	8000	9000

Management asks you to flowchart and prepare a computer program to analyze the data. Management would like to know (1) the cost of producing each product under each option, (2) the total cost of each option, and (3) the option (production mix) which gives the least total cost.

Input data consisting of the material, labor, overhead expenses, and the units produced under each option are punched into cards. These values are to be read by the program and stored in six one-dimensional arrays. These arrays are assigned to: (a) material costs, (b) labor costs, (c) overhead costs, (d) option 1 units produced, (e) option 2 units produced, and (f) option 3 units produced.

Prepare your own FORMAT specifications for input, using the data given above, and for output. Use appropriate captions and headings.

3.10 The Brussat Research Company has just completed a survey to find the annual incomes of persons residing in a particular marketing area. The income figures have been punched into data cards and are to be read by a computer program which will construct a frequency distribution. The research director has asked you to flowchart and write this program. The director indicates that the income figures are punched 16 to a data card although the last data card may not have all 16 fields filled. A trailer card will follow the data deck and has −5555 punched in columns 1-5.

To construct a frequency distribution, it will be necessary to have a range associated with each class of data. This program will use 10 ranges. The upper limits of each range will be read in as the first data card. Only nine limits will be punched into the first card because the tenth range will hold anything in excess of the upper limit of the ninth range.

The program output should appear as shown below.

BRUSSAT RESEARCH COMPANY

INCOME SURVEY

INCOME RANGES		INCOME	TOTAL	AVERAGE
LOWER	UPPER	FREQUENCY	INCOMES	INCOME
0	XXXXX	.	.	.
XXXXX	XXXXX	.	.	.
.	.	.	.	.
.	.			
.	.			
XXXXX AND OVER				

TOTAL INCOMES COUNTED . . .   XXXX
TOTAL INCOME - ALL RANGES . . .   XXXXXX

The use of subscripting and DO loops will be necessary to handle this data easily. Consider the following possibilities when writing your program: (1) each lower range will have to be computed; (2) a series of arrays will have to be used (unless you use a large two-dimensional array); and (3) if you use a series of arrays, consider these: LIMIT(9) for the upper limits, IDATA (16) to temporarily hold each input card, IFREQ (10) to hold frequency counts, ITOT (10) to hold total income dollars, and IAVE (10) to hold average incomes (in dollars only).

The following upper range limits should be used with the program: (1) 2999, (2) 5999, (3) 9999, (4) 14999, (5) 19999, (6) 29999, (7) 49999, (8) 69999, and (9) 89999.

The following data values for income should be used and punched with 16 values in the first data card and 14 values in the second. The trailer card will be punched separately.

91500	37250	72000	10000	19999	62800
55300	02000	07500	27850	12000	05198
63500	44300	04000	15300	92999	69999
88300	23350	13250	70000	22500	08000
06000	18500	14000	16750	13200	25000

3.11 The controller of the Evans Company asks you to prepare a program (or programs) to compute depreciation for fixed assets under three methods: (1) straight-line, (2) sum-of-the-years digits, and (3) double-declining-balance. The controller would like to have a schedule of depreciation for each method as illustrated below. The input data values for each asset being depreciated are punched into a single card. All input cards will have the following form: columns 1-4 asset identification number (any trailer card will have -999 in these columns), columns 5-15 asset cost, columns 20-30 expected salvage value, and columns 35-40 expected service life.

The following data values may be used with your program(s).

Asset Number	Cost	Salvage Value	Life
1234	50000.	2000.	10
5678	80000.	3000.	5
−999 (trailer card)*			

*Use the END= option if available.

The output depreciation schedules should have the following form.

DEPRECIATION METHOD: (print straight-line, sum-of-digits, or declining-balance here)

ASSET NUM	COST	SALVAGE VALUE	LIFE
XXXX	XXXXX	XXXXXX	XX

YEAR	ANNUAL DEPRECIATION	ACCUMULATED DEPRECIATION
.	.	.
.	.	.
.	.	.

Note: this problem may be divided and written as either separate programs or written as one large program producing all three depreciation schedules. Each type of depreciation is explained below in a manner suitable for preparing separate problems. Ignore the separation of the explanations when preparing a single program.

Flowchart and prepare a program(s) to produce the depreciation schedule(s).

Accumulated depreciation is simply an amount representing the total depreciation taken up to and including the year being printed.

The straight-line depreciation method subtracts the salvage value from an asset's cost before computing the annual charge for depreciation. The following formula applies:

Annual Depreciation = (Cost − Salvage)/Life

The sum-of-the-years digits depreciation method can be computed by using the following formulas:

year 1 depreciation	=	depreciable cost of asset*	X	useful life (years) / sum-of-the year digits**
year 2 depreciation	=	depreciable cost of asset	X	useful life (years) − 1 / sum-of-the-years digits
year 3 depreciation	=	depreciable cost of asset	X	useful life (years) − 2 / sum-of-the-years digits

.
.
.

The declining-balance depreciation*** method uses a rate which is twice the straight-line rate. Salvage value is ignored in this method. The following formulas apply.

$$\text{year 1 depreciation} = \text{cost} * (2 * \text{straight-line rate})$$

$$\text{year 2 depreciation} = \text{cost} - \frac{\text{accumulated depreciation}}{} * (2 * \text{straight-line rate})$$

.
.
.

3.12 Business data processing frequently involves the handling of dates (day, month, year). Dates are often expressed in numeric terms such as 101572 or are written more formally as October 15, 1972. Conversion of dates from one form to the other is necessary in many processing applications. Flowchart and write a program which will take both of the conditions given below and change the dates as directed.

1. Read a date, punched in written form (that is, October 15, 1972), and display the date in equivalent numeric form (that is, 101572). Assume the following format for the input data card: columns 1-9 month (alphabetic), column 10 blank, columns 11-12 day of the month, column 13 comma, column 14 blank, and columns 15-18 year.

2. Read a date, punched in numeric form (that is, 101572), and display the date in equivalent written form (that is, October 15, 1972). Assume that input dates are punched in columns 1-6.

Use your own format and captions to display both the dates read and the converted dates. Use any set of three dates, in each form, to test your program.

3.13 The Lend Lease Savings and Loan Association has asked you to flowchart and write a computer program to (1) calculate the monthly financial payment a

*(cost less salvage value)

**(sum-of-digits = life*(life+1)/2)

***An option frequently used with declining-balance depreciation is to convert the annual depreciation to the straight-line method when the annual straight-line amount exceeds the double declining-depreciation amount. This option may be included in programming this depreciation method.

borrower is required to make in repaying a mortgage loan and (2) to prepare a monthly payment schedule to be given to the borrower. The monthly payment is calculated by taking the amount of the mortgage and multiplying it by the formula:

$$\left(\frac{i}{1 - \frac{1}{(1+i)^n}} \right)$$

Input data will be punched in cards with the following format (use the example values shown below to test your program): columns 1-5 mortgage number (such as 12345), columns 6-11 mortgage dollar amount (such as 022400), columns 12-16 annual interest rate (such as .0625)—i in the above formula, columns 17-18 mortgage life in years (such as 25)—n in the above formula, columns 19-25 annual property taxes (such as 0785.00), and columns 26-31 annual insurance premium (such as 089.50).

Note: the interest rate, mortgage life, property taxes, and insurance premium are *annual* amounts. You will have to make a conversion of these items to calculate monthly amounts in your program.

Print a mortgage payment schedule for the first twelve months and every twelfth month thereafter until the end of the mortgage. Taxes and insurance should be *added* to the monthly financial payment which you compute. The payment schedule should have the following column headings:

MONTH	BEGINNING MORTGAGE	MONTHLY PAYMENT	INTEREST	TAXES	INSURANCE	ENDING MORTGAGE

The monthly payment is the total of the financial payment, insurance, and taxes. Each month's interest is computed by multiplying the monthly interest rate by the beginning principal balance. The financial payment each month covers both the interest and some portion of the beginning principal balance. The amount which applies to the principal reduces the principal balance carried over to the following month.

Use your own format for printing each line of data values. Be careful of the last payment on a mortgage—it may not come out evenly!

3.14 Assume that the following customer invoices are received in the order indicated. Write a generalized sort routine which would array these invoices in ascending customer account number order. Remember that it is necessary to maintain the identity between the customer number and the associated amount of the balance due. Prepare your own input format. Complete the program by printing the values in their correct order.

Invoice Register Data

Customer No.	Balance Due
1072	$265.70
1012	119.80
1400	22.65
1001	11.60
1302	900.00
1508	100.00
1927	1.22
1111	10.00
1201	441.88
1491	3.05

Group 4 (Chapters 14-17) 4.1 Flowchart and write a program to deal with the following payroll elements. Employee pay rates are read and stored in a table at the beginning of the program. Year-to-date and current pay period information is then read for each employee. The appropriate pay rate is taken from the table and the payroll is claculated and printed. Each type of input is explained below.

Pay rates (PAYTAB array) are stored in any array which is 4 rows by 4 columns. The rows indicate various wage levels and the columns indicate wage classes. Each employee's wage rate is determined by the intersection of the row and column which pertains to his wage level and class. Four cards contain the sixteen pay rates. Each card holds data for one row with the data punched in column order. These cards appear as:

$$\boxed{\text{X.XX} \mid \text{X.XX} \mid \text{X.XX} \mid \text{X.XX}}$$

The year-to-date gross pay (YTD) array is 200 rows by 2 columns. Column 1 holds employee numbers. Column 2 holds the dollar value of the employees' year-to-date gross pay. One input card is used to read the year-to-date gross pay for each employee. These cards appear as:

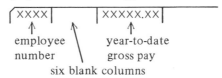

These cards are followed by a trailer card containing a -999.

Each employee has a current pay period card containing the hours worked during the current period and his wage level and class information. This card appears as:

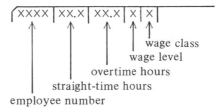

These cards are followed by a trailer card containing a -888.

This program should (1) read and store the PAYTAB data, (2) read and store the YTD data, and (3) compute the current pay information on each employee. To compute the current payroll information, compute the straight-time and overtime gross pay (at time and one-half) by multiplying the appropriate pay rate (from the PAYTAB table) by the number of hours worked. After calculating an employee's current gross pay, add it to his previous year-to-date gross pay. Print a payroll report containing the following headings:

EMPLOYEE NUMBER	STRAIGHT TIME HOURS	OVER- TIME HOURS	PREVIOUS YTD GROSS PAY	CURRENT ST. GROSS	OT. GROSS	NEW YTD GROSS

After printing the final line of employee data, print totals for the previous year-to-date gross pay, current straight-time and overtime gross pay, and the new year-to-date gross pay. Use your own format for the display of computed figures. You may use the following data values to test your program. Pay rate data:

Card 1	3.00	4.50	5.75	6.25
Card 2	4.00	5.15	6.10	7.00
Card 3	5.00	6.30	7.15	8.50
Card 4	6.00	7.50	8.05	9.00

Year-to-date gross pay:

Card 1	2468	1800.00
Card 2	3721	2732.14
Card 3	4497	3450.00
Card 4	5362	1212.12
Card 5	6781	1862.37

Current pay information:

Card 1	2468	40.0	10.0	1	3
Card 2	2525	35.8	0.0	3	4
Card 3	4497	40.0	0.0	2	2
Card 4	4553	24.9	0.0	2	4
Card 5	5362	37.5	10.0	4	1
Card 6	6780	40.0	12.5	1	2

4.2   Flowchart and write a program to solve the following matrix multiplication. Initialize the data values, rather than reading them. Consider use of the DATA statement. Print all three matrices. Prepare your own FORMAT specifications for output and use appropriate headings and captions.

MAT 1				MAT 2			MAT 3	
175	451	323		79	16		1,1	1,2
219	77	445	.	88	41	=	2,1	2,2
222	192	220		27	83		3,1	3,2
110	180	100					4,1	4,2

Note: the following illustration may help in determining how to multiply two matrices.

$$\text{MAT3}(1,1) = \text{MAT1}(1,1)*\text{MAT2}(1,1) + \text{MAT1}(1,2)*\text{MAT2}(2,1) + \text{MAT1}(1,3)*\text{MAT2}(3,1)$$
$$\text{MAT3}(1,2) = \text{MAT1}(1,1)*\text{MAT2}(1,2) + \text{MAT1}(1,2)*\text{MAT2}(2,2) + \text{MAT1}(1,3)*\text{MAT2}(3,2)$$

4.3   The Nash Company has completed a study of production costs and product sales demand. As a result, the firm can reasonably estimate the fixed costs and variable costs that will be incurred. Company management has asked you to prepare a program which will: (1) calculate after-tax income, and (2) calculate breakeven points in both units and dollars. The program is to be used with an unlimited number of potential sales and cost combinations.

Input to this program will use two types of cards. The first card type will carry tax and variable cost information. The format of this type of card will be: column 1 card ID code, columns 2-5 corporate tax rate, columns 6-8 variable marketing costs per unit, and columns 9-13 variable production costs per unit.

1	X.XX	.XX	XX.XX

I1   F4.2   F3.2   F5.2

Note that variable marketing costs are stated as a percentage of the selling price whereas variable production costs are a constant amount per unit produced.

The second card type will carry information about volume, price, and fixed cost. The format of this type of card will be: column 1 card ID code, columns 2-7 estimated sales volume (in units), columns 8-13 sales price per unit, columns 14-19 fixed marketing costs (in even dollars), and columns 20-25 fixed production costs (in even dollars).

2	XXXXXX	XXX.XX	XXXXXX	XXXXXX
I1	F6.0	F6.2	F6.0	F6.0

The program should:

1. Read all data cards. The cards are arranged so that all type 1 cards precede the type 2 cards. All data values should be read into arrays prior to processing. This will require your consideration of trailer cards to separate each type of input card.

2. Compute total sales, total fixed costs, total variable costs, taxes, after-tax income, and breakeven points in dollars and units, *for each combination* of type 1 and type 2 data.

Formulas for calculating unit and dollar breakeven points are as follows:

$$\text{unit breakeven} = \frac{\text{total fixed cost}}{\text{sales price @ unit} - \text{variable cost @ unit}}$$

$$\text{dollar breakeven} = \frac{\text{total fixed cost}}{1 - \dfrac{\text{var. cost @ unit}}{\text{sales price @ unit}}}$$

3. Write out the following items in column form, across the page, for each sales volume: (a) estimated sales volume, (b) unit sales price, (c) total sales dollars, (d) total fixed costs, (e) total variable costs, (f) total taxes, (g) after-tax net income, (h) breakeven point in units, and (i) breakeven point in dollars.

Flowchart and prepare the program using the following data values.

```
10.50.0503.00
10.48.1015.00
10.52.1004.00
2050000025.00250000400000
2125000030.50678500532500
2030000053.25750000600000
```

4.4   The Faith West Hospital has a high turnover of patients. This keeps their accounts receivable process in constant flux. The hospital would like you to flowchart and write a program which could be run daily to *merge* new patients' records with existing patients' accounts receivable records. The process of merging requires the use of two files. One file contains the existing accounts receivable records (called the old master file), and the second file holds the new accounts receivable. When the files are merged, the new accounts receivable are inserted into the existing accounts receivable records so that a new file (called the new master file) is created with all the accounts in ascending order.

The following data values are to be used for input to this program. The first five cards are to be read and stored as the old master file. The second set of five cards are the additions to be merged with the old master records. Note that each set of cards is sorted into ascending order.

Old   Master   Cards

Cols. 1-5	Cols. 10-25	Cols. 30-36
Acct. Number	Patient Name	Acct. Balance
12345	JONES, A.	187.25
23456	MANSON, C.	233.59
34567	WILLIAMS, B.	8.32
45678	ZILLMAN, C.	1274.96
47823	ZONKA, L.	76.34

New Accounts Receivable

Cols. 1-5	Cols. 10-25	Cols. 30-36
Acct. Number	Patient Name	Acct. Balance
11223	ANDERSON, C.	0.00
21238	MAGEE, M.	0.00
25678	SKORONSKI, J.	0.00
30486	THURSTON, M.	0.00
49855	ZWAKI, R.	0.00

Prepare the instructions necessary to merge these two files into a single new file (new master file). Use your own technique to identify the last card in the file. Print the new merged file using appropriate headings and captions. Use your own format specifications for output.

4.5   Use the output from problem 4.4 as input to this problem. The Faith West Hospital asks you to flowchart and write a program to *match* and *update* the patients' accounts receivable records. Each account in the file shown below (called a detail or transaction file) is compared with the accounts in the new master file and, for all matching account numbers, the charge amount is added to the patient's account receivable balance. The charges have been sorted into ascending order. However, there is not necessarily one charge amount for each account receivable account. There may be no charge, one charge or more than one charge. Prepare a program to match and update the accounts receivable and, after completion of the account updating, print an accounts receivable report showing each patient's account number, name, and current balance. Use your own format for the report. Use appropriate headings and captions.

Transaction File

Cols. 1-5	Cols. 10-16
Account Number	Charge Amount
11223	125.40
12345	10.00
12345	6.75
21238	10.80
21238	37.50
25678	16.25
30486	8.05
30486	123.50
34567	13.85
34567	55.15

4.6   The following problem deals with a simple payroll calculation and requires the use of one arithmetic statement function for *each* of the following computations: (1) employee gross pay (overtime at time and one-half), (2) employee income tax withheld, (3) employee FICA tax withheld, and (4) employee total deductions.

Each data card will contain the following information on an employee: columns 1-9 social security number, columns 10-13 straight-time hours worked, columns 14-17 overtime hours worked, columns 18-22 hourly pay rate, columns 23-24 number of personal exemptions, columns 25-31 medical insurance premium, and columns 32-38 union dues.

The program is to read the data for one employee, compute the gross pay, determine the deductions and net pay, and display the employee's payroll information under the following headings:

SS NR GROSS TAX FICA MEDICAL DUES TOT DED NET PAY

The income tax withheld is to be determined by: (1) multiplying the number of exemptions by 13.50, (2) subtracting the result from the gross pay, and (3) withholding $29.00 plus 22 percent of any amount over $169.00 from the remaining gross pay.

FICA tax is to be determined by withholding 4.75 percent from the gross pay.

Flowchart and write a program to compute the payroll. Use your own format specifications for the payroll values to be printed. The following data may be used to test your program.

			Card Columns			
1-9	*10-13*	*14-17*	*18-22*	*23-24*	*25-31*	*32-38*
388320538	40.0	10.0	5.25	04	24.00	5.00
392443892	40.0	30.0	8.00	03	48.00	10.00

4.7 This problem calls for the use of a main program and two subroutines. The program is to read data pertaining to the sales of two separate products. These products are sold through four company sales districts. You are to flowchart and write a program to: (a) accumulate the total number of units sold for each product, by district, (b) accumulate the total dollar value of units sold for each product, by district, and (c) calculate the average selling price for each product, by district.

Input data will be punched in cards with the following format: column 1 district Code (1,2,3,4 for the four districts and 9 for the trailer card), columns 2-5 units of product A sold, columns 6-12 total value of product A sold, columns 13-16 units of product B sold, and columns 17-24 total value of product B sold.

Each data card reflects one set of sales for one district. There may be several data cards for each district, and the data cards will not be in any specific order—they will be in random order.

The main program in this problem should perform the accumulation of units and sales while one subroutine calculates average selling prices and a second subroutine prints the results. The printed output is to be a report displaying the following items for each product, by district: (1) total units sold (2) total dollar value of units sold, and (3) average selling price of units sold.

Use your own format to display the output report. Make use of appropriate headings and captions. The following data may be used in testing your program.

Col. 1	Cols. 2-5	Cols 6-12	Cols. 13-16	Cols. 17-24
1	0500	1250.25	1550	60345.20
2	1000	0800.00	0220	05337.50
3	1800	3255.15	2345	18468.25
4	2500	2500.00	1880	18800.00
3	3250	7525.25	0060	00995.50
4	0050	0100.00	0250	02525.25
2	2100	2200.00	1425	32658.20
4	4750	5000.00	2835	30285.50
1	0875	2738.45	5325	98560.00
3	1250	2500.00	1650	87600.00
9				

4.8   When a corporation issues bonds the accountant records the issue by computing the present value of the bond contract and annually records the payment of interest (including the amortization of any bond premium or discount). The controller of your company asks you to flowchart and prepare a program to complete this task. The program is to be composed of four subparts: (1) a main program to read the basic data, (2) one subroutine to compute the present value of the bond contract, (3) a second subroutine to print headings for a bond amortization table, and (4) a third subroutine to compute and print the bond amortization table. Each of these programs is explained below:

The main program reads all of the basic data on a bond contract. The following items are included in this data (use the sample data to test your program): (1) face value of the bonds (5 million dollars), (2) interest rate stated on the bonds (6%), (3) market rate of interest for money (8%), and (4) life of the bonds (10 years).

Use your own format for reading this information. The main program will call and control the following three subprograms.

The present value subroutine calculates the value of the bond contract. This value is the present value of the promise to repay the $5 million principal in 10 years plus the present value of the promise to pay 6 percent interest annually for the next 10 years (assume annual payments for this program). These two calculations are made as follows:

$$\text{Present value of principal} = \frac{P}{(1+i)^n}$$

where: P = face value of the bonds (principal)
         i = market rate of interest
         n = number of years covered by the bonds

$$\text{Present value of interest payments} = (P \times r) \times \left(\frac{1 - \dfrac{1}{(1+i)^n}}{i} \right)$$

where: P = face value of the bonds (principal)
         i = market rate of interest
         n = number of years covered by the bonds
         r = interest rate stated on the bonds

After computing the present value of the bond contract, determine whether they were issued at either a premium or discount. The principal value of the bonds should be subtracted from the present value of the bonds. If the result is positive, the difference is the premium paid by the bonds' buyers. If the result is negative, the difference is the discount.

When the market rate of interest and the stated rate of interest are not equal, the bonds will be issued at either a premium or a discount. The premium or discount is amortized over the life of the bonds. A schedule or table of this amortization may be prepared using the present value information computed above. The table should have the headings shown below and these headings should be printed by the heading subroutine.

```
      BEGINNING INTEREST NOMINAL PREM/DISC UNAMORT. ENDING
YEAR LIABILITY   CHARGE  INTEREST   AMORT.  PREM/DISC LIABILITY
```

The amortization table subroutine computes the amounts applicable to each year's amortization of the bond premium or discount. These amounts will be displayed under the headings printed by the heading subroutine. The amounts are determined as follows:

1. Beginning liability is the present value of the bond contract computed in the first subroutine.
2. Interest charge is the actual interest expense incurred for the year and is computed by multiplying the beginning liability by the market rate of interest.
3. Nominal interest is the amount of interest paid in cash this year and is computed by multiplying the principal amount of the bonds by the interest rate stated on the bonds.
4. Premium/discount amortized is the difference between the interest charge and the nominal interest.
5. Unamortized premium/discount is the original amount of premium or discount, computed in the first subroutine, which remains after subtracting the amount amortized for the current year.
6. Ending liability is the beginning liability adjusted for the premium or discount amortized. Premium amortization is deducted from the beginning liability and discount amortization is added. The ending liability from one year becomes the beginning liability for the next year.

Use your own format specifications to display the amounts in the amortization table.

4.9   The following RANDU subroutine produces random numbers between 0 and 1. This subroutine is included in the IBM *Scientific Subroutine Package.* The variable IX is used to transmit a "seed" value from the calling program to the RANDU subroutine. The variable IY is used to send a "seed" value back to the calling program so it can be used for a subsequent call for a random number. The variable YFL holds the random number.

```
SUBROUTINE RANDU(IX,IY,YFL)
IY = IX * 65539
IF (IY) 5,6,6
5 IY = IY + 2147483647 + 1
6 YFL = IY
  YFL = YFL * .4656613E-9
  RETURN
  END
```

The calling program must send an *initial* "seed" value to the RANDU subroutine. A recommended value is 49999997. The value is sent by the calling program only with the *first* call to the subroutine. Subsequent "seed" values are generated by RANDU and are made available through variable IY. When the calling program receives the seed (IY), it must move (that is, store) this value in variable IX prior to calling for another random number. The essential statements in a calling program are shown below.

```
      IX = 49999997
      .
      .
      .
  100 CALL RANDU (IX,IY,YFL)
      IX = IY
      .
      .
      .
      GO TO 100  (this instruction may be any type of return to call for
      .                another random number such as a DO loop's CONTINUE,
      .                an IF statement, etc.)
      .
      END
```

Random numbers, by definition, should each have an equal chance of occurring. Therefore, to simulate the flipping of a coin by drawing random numbers, we could divide the values returned by the RANDU subroutine so that values less than .5 were called heads and values .5 or greater were called tails. We would expect that, on a random basis, 50 percent of the numbers would be heads and 50 percent tails. Flowchart and write a program to draw 2000 random numbers, 100 at a time. Each random number called should be tested to determine whether it is a head or tail. A counter of the heads and tails should be kept and, after each group of 100 numbers has been called, a summary of the draws should be displayed under the following headings:

CUMULATIVE NUMBERS GENERATED	- - - - -CURRENT 100- - - - -				CUMULATIVE DRAWS			
	-HEADS-		-TAILS-		-HEADS-		-TAILS-	
	NUM.	%	NUM.	%	NUM.	%	NUM.	%

Use your own format for displaying the values derived by calling for the random numbers.

4.10   Willie Butterfingers was carrying a deck of inventory cards to the data processing center for processing. Unfortunately, he tripped on the stairs and the cards were hopelessly mixed. Willie does not know a thing about these cards but he did know that you were going to process them with a program to update inventory balances for recent issues and receipts of inventory.

Willie brings in the mixed deck of cards to you. There are 3000 cards (which we will scale down to 14 to make the data handling manageable). As the top programmer in your firm, you decide that the best way to handle the situation is to write a main program and subroutine to do the following: (1) the main program will read each data card and store each type of card (there are 3 types) in an array; (2) call a subroutine to sort each array's values into ascending order by inventory item number; (3) update the inventory by taking the beginning balances, adding the receipts, and deducting the issues; and (4) print an inventory status report.

The inventory data cards will have the following format: column 1 (inventory beginning balance cards have a 9, inventory issuance cards have a 3, and inventory receipt cards have a 5); columns 2-6 identification number of the inventory item (all cards have an ID number in these columns); columns 7-9 blank; columns 10-13 a number of inventory units (balance, receipts or issues); column 14 blank; and columns 15-18 inventory unit cost price (in dollars and cents) on beginning balance cards, and month and year on issue and receipt cards (1072 means October 1972.) Assume a beginning balance card exists for any receipt or issue card.

Print the following heading on the inventory status report:

INVENTORY STATUS REPORT

INVENTORY NUMBER	BEGIN.	- - - - - - - - - - - - - UNITS - - - - - - - - - - - - - RECVD	ISSUED	ENDING	UNIT COST	ENDING VALUE

Flowchart and write a program to process the inventory data and prepare the status report. Use the following data, in the order shown, to test your program.

956789	2500	137
345678	400	1072
534567	300	1072
945678	50	27
912345	5000	1025
323456	2250	1072
312345	8000	1072
556789	1500	1072
356789	2750	1072
923456	3000	875
545678	350	1072
334567	1000	1072
512345	4500	1072
934567	1500	200

Appendix D
FORTRAN Reference Guide

FORTRAN Element	Text Reference	Explanation
ARGUMENTS	304, 308, 316 320, 326	See text.
Location versus Value	375	See text.
ARITHMETIC IF See IF statements		
ARITHMETIC STATEMENTS	56-60, 77-80 158, 210, 249, 251, 254	$a = b$ where: a is subscripted or non-subscripted variable. b is an arithmetic expression or logical expression.
ARITHMETIC STATEMENT FUNCTIONS See FUNCTIONS		
ASSIGN–ASSIGNED GO TO	174	ASSIGN i TO m . . . GO TO m, $(x_1, x_2, x_3, \ldots, x_n)$ where: i is an executable statement number. It must be one of the numbers $x_1, x_2, x_3, \ldots, x_n$. $x_1, x_2, x_3, \ldots, x_n$ are executable statement numbers in the program unit containing the GO TO statement. m is a nonsubscripted integer variable which is assigned one of the statement numbers: $x_1, x_2, x_3, \ldots, x_n$.

FORTRAN Element	Text Reference	Explanation
BACKSPACE	394	BACKSPACE *a* where: *a* is an unsigned integer constant or integer variable that represents a data set reference number.
BLOCK DATA SUBPROGRAMS	358	BLOCK DATA · · This subprogram contains · only DATA, COMMON, END DIMENSION, EQUIVA-LENCE, and Type statements.
CALL	331, 366, 374	CALL *name* $(a_1, a_2, a_3, \ldots, a_n)$ where: *name* is the name of a SUBROUTINE subprogram. $a_1, a_2, a_3, \ldots, a_n$ are the actual arguments that are being supplied to the SUBROUTINE subprogram. Each may be of the form &n where *n* is a statement number (See RETURN *i* Statement).
CARRIAGE CONTROL	131	Codes must be enclosed in single quote marks (') or preceded by a 1H code. blank next line 0 (zero) 1 blank line – (minus) 2 blank lines 1 (one) top of next page + (plus) suppress spacing

CHARACTERS	46	Source Program Characters
		 Alphabetic
		   A through Z (also $ in some systems)
		 Numeric
		   0 through 9
		 Special
		     (blank)
		   + (plus)
		   – (minus)
		   / (slash or division)
		   = (equals)
		   . (period)
		   ) (closing parenthesis)
		   * (asterisk or multiply)
		   , (comma)
		   ((opening parenthesis)
		   ' (apostrophe)
		   & (ampersand)

FORTRAN Element	Text Reference	Explanation
CLOSED FUNCTIONS		
See FUNCTIONS		
CODES		See text.
A	134	
D	207	
E	149	
F	49, 144	
G	223	
H	61, 132, 137	
I	50	
L	252	
P	235	
T	237	
X	61, 131	
COMMON		COMMON $/r/a\,(k_1),\,b(k_2),\,\ldots\,/r/c(k_3),$
BLANK COMMON	344-346, 355-358	$d(k_4),\,\ldots$ where: $a,b,\ldots,c,d,\ldots$ are variable names or array names that cannot be dummy arguments. $k_1,k_2,\ldots k_3,k_4 \ldots$ are optional and are each composed of 1 through 7 unsigned integer constants, separated by commas, representing the maximum value of each dimension in an array.
LABELED COMMON	355-358	$/r/\ldots$ represent optional common block names consisting of 1 through 6 alphameric characters, the first of which is alphabetic. These names must always be embedded in slashes.
COMPLEX MODE	249	See text.
COMPLEX TYPE		
See TYPE		
COMPUTED GO TO		
See GO TO		
CONSTANTS		
COMPLEX	249	*Complex Constant:* an ordered pair of signed or unsigned real constants separated by a comma and enclosed in parentheses. The first real constant in a complex constant represents the real part of the complex number; the second represents the imaginary part of the complex number.

FORTRAN Element	Text Reference	Explanation
INTEGER	44, 140	*Integer Constant:* a whole number written without a decimal point.
LITERAL	61, 137, 234	*Literal Constant:* a string of alphameric and/or special characters, delimited as follows: 1) The string can be preceded by *w*H where *w* is the number of characters in the string. 2) The string can be enclosed in apostrophes.
LOGICAL	252	*Logical Constant:* a constant that specifies a logical value. There are two logical values: .TRUE. and .FALSE. The words TRUE and FALSE must be preceded and followed by periods as shown above.
REAL	44, 142, 149, 210	*Real Constant:* has one of three forms: a basic real constant, a basic real constant followed by a decimal exponent, or an integer constant followed by a decimal exponent. A basic real constant is a string of decimal digits with a decimal point. If the string contains fewer than eight digits the basic real constant occupies four storage locations (bytes); if the string contains eight or more digits, the basic real constant occupies eight storage locations (bytes). The storage requirement (length) of a real constant can also be explicitly specified by appending an exponent to a basic real constant or an integer constant. An exponent consists of the letter E or the letter D followed by a signed or unsigned one or two digit integer constant. The letter E specifies a constant of length four; the letter D specifies a constant of length eight.
CONTINUE	104	CONTINUE may be placed anywhere in a program where an executable statement is permitted. Normally used to end a DO loop.

FORTRAN Element	Text Reference	Explanation
DATA	218-222, 250, 252, 358	DATA $k1/d1/, k2/d2/, \ldots, kn/dn/$ where: each k is a list containing variables, subscripted variables (in which case the subscripts must be integer constants), or array names. Dummy arguments may not appear in the list. Each d is a list of constants (integer, real, complex, logical, or literal), any of which may be preceded by $i*$. Each i is an unsigned integer constant. When the form $i*$ appears before a constant, it indicates that the constant is to be repeated i times.
DATA NAMES See SYMBOLIC NAMES		
DEFINE FILE	398	DEFINE FILE $a_1 (m_1, r_1, f_1, v_1)$ where: a represents an integer constant that is the data set reference number. m represents an integer constant that specifies the number of records in the data set associated with a. r represents an integer constant that specifies the maximum size of each record associated with a. f specifies that the data set is to be read or written either with or without format control; f may be one of the following letters: L indicates that the data set is to be read or written either with or without format control. E indicates that the data set is to be read or written under format control (as specified by a format statement). U indicates that the data set is to be read or written without format control. v represents a nonsubscripted integer variable called an *associated variable*. At the conclusion of each read or write operation, v is set to a value that points to the record that immediately follows the last record transmitted. At the conclusion of a find operation, v is set to a value that points to the record found.

FORTRAN Element	Text Reference	Explanation
DIMENSION	100, 271, 293, 345, 376	DIMENSION $a_1(k_1), a_2(k_2), \ldots a_n(k_n)$ where: $a_1, a_2, a_3, \ldots, a_n$ are array names. $k_1, k_2, k_3, \ldots, k_n$ are each composed of one through seven unsigned integer constants, separated by commas, representing the maximum value of each dimension in the array.
DO	102-112, 113-125, 188, 274, 277, 293	*End of DO Initial Test* *Range Variable Value Value Increment* DO x i = m_1, m_2, m_3 where: x is an executable statement number appearing after the DO statement. i is a nonsubscripted integer variable. m_1, m_2, and m_3, are either unsigned integer constants greater than zero or unsigned nonsubscripted integer variables whose value is greater than zero. m_3 is optional; if it is omitted, its value is assumed to be 1. In this case, the preceding comma must also be omitted.
DOUBLE PRECISION	204	DOUBLE PRECISION $a(k_1), b(k_2), \ldots, z(k_n)$ where: $a, b, \ldots, z$ represent variable, array, or function names. $(k_1), (k_2), \ldots, (k_n)$ are optional. Each k is composed of one through seven unsigned integer constants, separated by commas, that represent the maximum value of each subscript in the array.
END	66, 322, 334	END is a nonexecutable statement that defines the end of a main program or subprogram. It must be the last physical statement. It may not have a statement number.
END = See READ statements		
END FILE	394	END File a where: a is an unsigned integer constant or integer variable and represents a data set reference number.
ENTRY	366	ENTRY *name* $(a_1, a_2, a_3, \ldots, a_n)$ where: *name* is the name of an entry point in a subprogram.

FORTRAN Element	Test Reference	Explanation
		$a_1, a_2, a_3, \ldots, a_n$ are the dummy arguments corresponding to an actual argument in a CALL statement or in a function reference.
ERR = See READ statements		
EQUIVALENCE	360	EQUIVALENCE $(a, b, c, \ldots), (d, e, f, \ldots)$ where: $a, b, c, d, e, f, \ldots$ are variables (not dummy arguments) that may be subscripted.
EXPLICIT TYPE See TYPE		
EXPONENTS	59, 78, 184	See text.
EXPRESSIONS See ARITHMETIC STATEMENTS		
EXTERNAL	324	EXTERNAL $a, b, c, \ldots$ where: $a, b, c, \ldots$ are names of subprograms that a calling subprogram passes, as arguments, to other subprograms.
FIND	399	FIND $(a'r)$ where: a is an integer constant or unsigned integer variable and represents a data set reference number; a must be followed by an apostrophe ('). r is an integer expression that represents the relative position of a record within the data set associated with a.
FORMAT	48-51, 60-63, 128, 207, 223, 253, 278	$xxxxx$ FORMAT $(c_1, c_2, \ldots, c_n)$ where: $xxxxx$ is a statement number (1 through 5 digits). $c_1, c_2, \ldots, c_n$ are format codes. The format codes are:

aIw	describes integer data fields
$paDw.d$	describes real data fields
$paEw.d$	describes real data fields
$paFw.d$	describes real data fields
aZw	describes hexadecimal data fields
$paGw.s$	describes integer, real, complex, or logical data fields
aLw	describes logical data fields

FORTRAN Element	Text Reference	Explanation
		aAw describes alphameric data fields
		'Literal' Transmits literal data
		wH transmits literal data
		wX indicates that a field is to be skipped on input or filled with blanks on output
		Tr indicates the position in a FORTRAN record where transfer of data is to start
		a(. . .) indicates a group format specification

where: a is optional and is an unsigned
integer constant used to denote
the number of times the format
code is to be repeated. If a is
omitted, the code is used only once.

w is an unsigned, nonzero, integer
constant that specifies the number
of characters in the field.

d is an unsigned integer constant
specifying the number of decimal
places to the right of the decimal
point; i.e., the fractional portion.

s is an unsigned integer constant
specifying the number of significant digits.

r is an unsigned integer constant
designating a character position
in a record.

p is optional and represents a scale
factor designator of the form nP
where n is an unsigned or negatively
signed integer constant.

(. . .) is a group format specification.
Within the parentheses are format
codes separated by commas or
slashes. Group format specifications can be nested to a level of
two. The a preceding this form is
called a group repeat count.

Notes:

1. Complex data fields in records
   require two successive D, E, F, G,
   or A format codes. These codes
   may be grouped within parentheses.

2. Both commas and slashes can be
   used as separators between format
   codes (see page 128f.).

FORTRAN Element	Text Reference	Explanation
FUNCTIONS		
OPEN FUNCTIONS	303	Listed on page 305.
CLOSED FUNCTIONS	308	Listed on page 306.
ARITHMETIC STATEMENT	313	$name(a_1, a_2, a_3, \ldots, a_n) = expression$ where: *name* is the arithmetic statement function name created by the programmer.
		$a_1, a_2, a_3, \ldots, a_n$, are dummy arguments. They must be unique (within the statement) nonsubscripted variables.
		expression is any arithmetic or logical expression that does not contain subscripted variables. Any statement function appearing in this expression must have been defined previously.
FUNCTION SUBPROGRAMS	321	*Type* FUNCTION *name*$*s$ $(a_1, a_2, a_3, \ldots, a_n)$ where: *Type* is INTEGER, REAL, DOUBLE PRECISION, COMPLEX, or LOGICAL. Its inclusion is optional.
		name is the name of the FUNCTION.
		$*s$ represents one of the permissible length specifications for its associated type. It may be included optionally only when *Type* is specified. It must not be used when DOUBLE PRECISION is specified.
		$a_1, a_2, a_3, \ldots, a_n$ are dummy arguments. They must be non-subscripted variable, array, or dummy names of SUBROUTINE or other FUNCTION subprograms. (There must be at least one argument in the argument list.)
GO TO		
ASSIGNED GO TO		
See ASSIGN statement		
COMPUTED GO TO	165	GO TO $(x_1, x_2, x_3, \ldots, x_n), i$ where $x_1, x_2, x, \ldots, x_n$, are executable statement numbers.
		i is a nonsubscripted integer variable whose current value is in the range: $1 < i < n$.
UNCONDITIONAL GO TO	86	GO TO *xxxxx* where: *xxxxx* is an executable statement number.

FORTRAN Element	Text Reference	Explanation
IF		IF (a) x_1,x_2,x_3
ARITHMETIC IF	83	where: a is any arithmetic expression except complex.
		x_1,x_2,x_3, are executable statement numbers.
		Control is transferred to x_1 when the value of the expression (a) is less than zero, to x_2 when equal to zero, and to x_3 when greater than zero.
LOGICAL IF	156	IF(a) s
		where: a is any logical expression.
		s is any executable statement except a DO statement or another logical IF statement.
IMPLICT	265	IMPLICIT $type*s(a_1,a_2,\ldots),type*s$ $(a_1,a_2,\ldots)$
		where: $type$ is one of the following: INTEGER, REAL, COMPLEX, or LOGICAL.
		$*s$ is optional and represents one of the permissible length specifications for its associated type.
		$a_1,a_2,\ldots$ are single alphabetic characters each separated by commas, or a range of characters (in alphabetic sequence) denoted by the first and last characters of the range separated by a minus sign (i.e., (A-D)). The IMPLICIT specification statement must be the first statement in a main program and the second statement in a subprogram.
INTEGER TYPE See TYPE		
LOGICAL MODE	251	See text.
LOGICAL STATEMENTS See ARITHMETIC STATEMENTS		
LOGICAL IF See IF statements		
NAMELIST	240	NAMELIST$/x/a,b\ldots c/y/d,e,\ldots$ $f/z/g,h,\ldots i$
		where: x,y, and $z,\ldots$ are NAMELIST names.
		$a,b,c,d,\ldots$ are variable or array names.
OPEN FUNCTIONS See FUNCTIONS		

FORTRAN Element	Text Reference	Explanation
OPERATORS		
ARITHMETIC OPERATORS	58	The arithmetic operators are as follows:

Arithmetic Operator	Definition
**	Exponentiation
*	Multiplication
/	Division
+	Addition
−	Subtraction

Order of Computation: Computation is performed from left to right according to the hierarchy of operations shown in the following list. If there are consecutive exponentiation operators, the evaluation is from right to left.

Operation	Hierarchy
Evaluation of functions	1st
Exponentiation (**)	2nd
Multiplication and division (* and /)	3rd
Addition and subtraction (+ and −)	4th

Valid Combinations for Exponentiation (**)

Base	Exponent
Integer (either length) or Real (either length)	**	Integer (either length) or Real (either length)
Complex (either length)	** Integer (either length)

| LOGICAL OPERATORS | 159 | The three logical operators, each of which must be preceded and followed by a period, are as follows (where A and B represent logical constants or variables, or expressions containing relational operators): |

Logical Operator	Example
.NOT.	.NOT.B
.AND.	A.AND.B
.OR.	A.OR.B

FORTRAN Element	Text Reference	Explanation
		Order of Computations in Logical Expressions: The order in which the operations are performed is:

Operation	Hierarchy
Evaluation of functions	1st (highest)
Exponentiation (**)	2nd
Multiplication and division (* and /)	3rd
Addition and subtraction (+ and −)	4th
.LT.,.LE.,.EQ.,.NE., .GT.,.GE.	5th
.NOT.	6th
.AND.	7th
.OR.	8th

FORTRAN Element	Text Reference	Explanation
RELATIONAL OPERATORS	158	The six relational operators, each of which must be preceded and followed by a period, are as follows:

Relational Operator	Definition
.GT.	greater than ($>$)
.GE.	greater than or equal to ($\geqslant$)
.LT.	less than ($<$)
.LE.	less than or equal to ($\leqslant$)
.EQ.	equal to ($=$)
.NE.	not equal to ($\#$)

FORTRAN Element	Text Reference	Explanation
PAUSE	201	PAUSE PAUSE *n* PAUSE *'message'* where: *n* is a string of 1 through 5 decimal digits, none of which can be greater than 7. *'message'* is a literal constant.
READ DIRECT ACCESS READ	399	READ (*a'r, b,* ERR=*d*) *list* where: *a* is an integer constant and represents a data set reference number; *a* must be followed by an apostrophe ('). The data set being read must be defined with a DEFINE FILE statement. *r* is an integer expression that represents the relative position of a record within the data set associated with *a*.

FORTRAN Element	Text Reference	Explanation
		b is optional and, if given, is either the statement number of the FORMAT statement that describes the data being read or the name of an array that contains an object time format.
		ERR=*d* is optional and *d* is the statement number to which control is given when a device error condition is encountered during data transfer from device to storage.
		list is optional and is an I/O list.
FORTRAN IV READ	51-54, 113-122, 170, 173, 279, 295	READ(*a,b*,END=*c*,ERR=*d*) *list* where: *a* is an unsigned integer constant and represents a data set reference number.
		b is optional and is either the statement number or array name of the FORMAT statement describing the record(s) being read, or a NAMELIST NAME.
		END=*c* is optional and *c* is the number of the statement to which transfer is made upon encountering the end of the data set.
		ERR=*d* is optional and *d* is the number of the statement to which transfer is made upon encountering an error condition in data transfer.
		list is optional and is an I/O list.
REAL TYPE See TYPE		
RETURN		
SIMPLE RETURN	322, 334	RETURN
RETURN *i*	373	RETURN *i* where: *i* is an integer constant or variable whose value, say n, denotes the nth statement number in the argument list of a SUBROUTINE statement; *i* may be specified only in a SUBROUTINE subprogram.
REWIND	394	REWIND *a* where: *a* is an unsigned integer constant and represents a data set reference number.
STOP	65	STOP STOP *n* where: *n* is a string of 1 through 5 decimal digits.

FORTRAN Element	Text Reference	Explanation
SUBROUTINE NAME	332, 374	SUBROUTINE *name* $(a_1,a_2,a_3, \ldots ,a_n)$
		.
		.
		.
		RETURN
		.
		.
		END
		where: *name* is the SUBROUTINE name.
		$a_1,a_2,a_3, \ldots ,a_n$ are dummy arguments. (There need not be any.) Each argument used must be a non-subscripted variable or array name, the dummy name of another SUBROUTINE or FUNCTION subprogram, or of the form * where the character "*" denotes a return point specified by a statement number in the calling program. The * is used with the RETURN i statement.
SUBSCRIPTS	98, 182, 269, 291	See text.
SWITCHES	177	SENSE,OVERFLOW,UNDERFLOW, DIVIDE CHECK
SYMBOLIC NAMES	40-46	*Symbolic Name*—from 1 through 6 alphanumeric characters, the first of which must be alphabetic. No special characters are permitted.
TYPE SPECIFICATIONS		
COMPLEX	264	$Type*s\ a*s_1\ (k_1)/x_1/,b*s_2(k_2)/x_2/, \ldots$
INTEGER	264	where: *Type* is INTEGER, REAL,
LOGICAL	264	LOGICAL, or COMPLEX.
REAL	262	$*s,*s_1,*s_2, \ldots$ are optional. Each *s* represents one of the permissible length specifications for its associated *type*.
		$a,b, \ldots$ are variable, array, or function names.
		$(k_1), (k_2), \ldots$ are optional and give dimension information for arrays. Each *k* is composed of one through seven unsigned integer constants, separated by commas, representing the maximum value of each dimension in the array.
		$/x_1/,/x_2/, \ldots$ are optional and represent initial data values.

FORTRAN Element	Text Reference	Explanation
VARIABLE FORMAT	245	See text.
VARIABLE NAMES See SYMBOLIC NAMES		
WRITE DIRECT ACCESS WRITE	399	WRITE $(a'r,b)$ *list* where: a is an integer constant and represents a data set reference number; a must be followed by an apostrophe ('). The data set being written must be defined with a DEFINE FILE statement. r is an integer expression that represents the relative position of a record within the data set associated with a. b is optional and, if given, is either the statement number of the FORMAT statement that describes the data being written or the name of an array that contains an object time format. *list* is optional and is an I/O list.
FORTRAN IV WRITE	64, 113	WRITE(a,b) *list* where: a is an unsigned integer constant and represents a data set reference number. b is optional and is either the statement number or array name of the FORMAT statement describing the record(s) being written, or a NAMELIST name. *list* is optional and is an I/O list.

Index